Frederick Law Olmsted, circa 1890.

Frederick Law
OLMSTED
and the Boston Park System

Cynthia Zaitzevsky

THE BELKNAP PRESS OF HARVARD UNIVERSITY PRESS

Cambridge, Massachusetts, and London, England   1982

Library of Congress Cataloging in Publication Data

Zaitzevsky, Cynthia.
Frederick Law Olmsted and the Boston park system.

Includes bibliographical references and index.
1. Boston (Mass.)—Parks—History.
2. Olmsted, Frederick Law, 1822–1903.
3. Landscape architects—United States—Biography.
I. Title.
SB483.B73Z34   712′.5′0924 [B]   82-6042
ISBN 0-674-31830-7   AACR2

Designed by Gwen Frankfeldt

cc

To the memory of my father

FRANCIS BERTRAND McCARTHY

1905–1982

Preface

"NOTHING ELSE compares in importance to us with the Boston work . . . I would have you decline any business that would stand in the way of doing the best for Boston all the time." So wrote Frederick Law Olmsted to his partners in 1893.

Although Olmsted's evaluation of its importance has been generally accepted, the Boston municipal park system has never been the subject of a detailed study. In the past decade and a half Olmsted has begun to reemerge from almost fifty years of comparative neglect: his early books are being reprinted, comprehensive biographies have appeared, two volumes of a projected twelve-volume series of his personal and professional papers have been published, and numerous exhibition catalogues have been issued. The vast body of Olmsted's work, however, is only beginning to be explored.

This study of the Boston park system is based on three large collections of primary materials: city records, both published and unpublished; Olmsted's correspondence, donated several years ago by his successor firm to the Library of Congress; and the firm's graphic archives, consisting primarily of drawings but also including photographs, lithographs, plant lists, and other records still located at his office in Brookline, Massachusetts, now the property of the National Park Service. Correlation of these three types of documentation has made it possible to reconstruct Olmsted's design process to a degree rarely possible with any designer. While the Olmsted correspondence and public records in various cities have been used extensively by other scholars, this book is perhaps unique in its detailed study of the drawings, more than a thousand of which exist for the Boston park system.

The organization of the book is primarily topical rather than chronological. However, Part One deals with the city's topographical history, the mid-nineteenth-century park movement, and Olmsted's early life and career; all three chapters conclude with the year 1878, the date of Olmsted's first contract with the Boston Park Commission. The five chapters in Part Two cover all aspects of the Boston parks except the process of their design. I have used the same format for each park, although only Franklin Park has a chapter to itself: a description and, in many cases, illustrations of each site before it became a park; the political background and any special circumstances of the commission; an analysis of the adopted plan; a discussion of the design concept for the park or, in the case of Franklin Park, Olmsted's central theory of the restorative value of natural scenery; and a summary of each park's history after Olmsted's retirement and the near completion of the park system in 1895.

Part Three deals with Olmsted's design process, beginning with an account of his firm after he moved from New York to Brookline. A chapter is devoted to each of the four stages of the design process. The Epilogue deals with the Boston system as a whole after 1895, with the various trends in park planning and recreation, and with the widespread sociological changes that have affected historic parks throughout the United States.

This book treats only Boston's municipal system and only those parks that reached the stage of a preliminary plan, or at least well-defined studies, by the time of Olmsted's retirement. Although I discuss briefly the beginnings of the Boston metropolitan park system, this is not a full examination of that system. Similarly, the many small municipal parks and playgrounds designed by the Olmsted firm after 1895 lie outside the scope of this book. Three unexecuted projects are discussed, along with one or two parks, such as Charlestown Playground, which were executed with significant deviations from the Olmsted plan. However, sites acquired by the city before 1895 but not designed until after that date

are excluded. One exception is Franklin Field, which is important less for its design than for its status as an ancillary ground to Franklin Park.

A word is perhaps in order concerning the term "park." Olmsted considered a park to be a public ground that had no purpose other than the enjoyment of natural scenery. By this definition, Franklin Park is Boston's only park. I have tried to conform to his usage wherever possible, but "park" sometimes appears here as a generic term. In a sense, Olmsted did the same thing when he used the phrase "Boston park system" for a chain of public grounds that included only one true park.

Since I am an art historian specializing in the architecture, landscape architecture, and city planning of the nineteenth century, I have put particular emphasis on Olmsted's landscape theories and his design process. However, this project has taken me into the less familiar territory of American social and political history, civil engineering, botany and horticulture, and the technological as well as aesthetic aspects of landscape architecture. I am not an expert in any of these fields, but I have sought the advice of experts to provide the multidisciplinary breadth that a study of Olmsted demands.

Reproducing the drawings and plans for the Boston park system presented special problems because of the very large size of the originals. Since this is not a catalogue, dimensions are not given, but when spread out, most of the drawings cover the surface of a standard-sized drafting table. Ultrarefined photographic techniques have been used to reproduce the lithographs and some of the drawings. However, because of their fragile condition, other drawings could not be rephotographed using these techniques, and still others, such as the planting plans, are too outsized to allow anything but illustration of details.

The Olmsted National Historic Site and other local repositories own exceptionally fine old photographs of the Boston parks. I am pleased to be able to reproduce here a number of previously unpublished images by such important but still relatively unknown Boston photographers as Augustine H. Folsom, Thomas E. Marr, and Leon Abdalian, as well as by members of the Olmsted firm, such as John C. Olmsted and Percy R. Jones, whose views were often of professional quality.

I am happy to acknowledge the assistance I have received in this project from many institutions and individuals. I am most grateful to the Radcliffe Institute, Harvard University, and the American Council of Learned Societies for the grants and fellowships that have supported the research. I should like to thank the following Olmsted scholars, architectural historians, park activists and other friends: William Alex, Charles E. Beveridge, Theresa Cedarholm, Albert Fein, Margaret Henderson Floyd, Sheila Geary, Betsy Shure Gross, Richard Heath, Arthur Krim, Charles C. McLaughlin, James F. O'Gorman, Laura Wood Roper, S. B. Sutton, and Ellen Weiss.

The staffs of the following institutions have helped greatly in the research process: the Boston Athenaeum; the Boston Park Department; the Fine Arts, Government Documents, Microtext, Prints, and Rare Books departments of the Boston Public Library; the Brookline Public Library; the Frances Loeb Library, Graduate School of Design, Harvard University; the Library of Congress, Manuscript Division; the Society for the Preservation of New England Antiquities; and the University of Lowell Library.

My greatest debt in this area is to the past and present owners of the Olmsted archive in Brookline. Exactly ten years ago, Artemas Richardson, then president of Olmsted Associates, allowed me access to these archives over a period of several months. Without the opportunity to study the hundreds of drawings, prints, and photographs for the Boston park system, I would not have been able to write first a dissertation and then this book. Since 1980 the staff of the National Park Service at the Olmsted National Historic Site, especially Shary Page Berg and Elizabeth Banks, has also been most helpful. The assistance of Mary Tynan, staff member under both ownerships, has been invaluable throughout.

For assistance in the specialty of plant materials, I am indebted to Richard E. Weaver, Jr., of the Arnold Arboretum and to Joseph G. Hudak, formerly of Olmsted Associates.

I cannot adequately thank John Coolidge for recognizing at the outset the importance of the project and for making many helpful criticisms. My parents, Catherine and Francis McCarthy, also read the manuscript, which has gone through many metamorphoses. Finally, I owe an immeasurable debt to my husband, Nikita Zaitzevsky, for his enthusiasm and encouragement.

July 1982
Brookline, Massachusetts

Contents

———◆———

ONE

The Background

It is practically certain that the Boston of today is the mere nucleus of the Boston that is to be.

—Public Parks and the Enlargement of Towns, 1870

Bird's-eye view of Boston, July 4, 1870.

I

Topographical Development of Boston 1630–1878

Frederick Law Olmsted's park system, designed for the Boston Park Commission and constructed between 1878 and 1895, was one of the most massive public projects ever undertaken by the city. When complete, it totaled over 2,000 acres of open land reserved from ordinary uses. It stretched from the Common and Public Garden at the foot of the State House to the outer limits of South Boston and West Roxbury, with smaller neighborhood parks and playgrounds in almost every section of the city.

The core of the park system was its five-mile-long, continuous portion, the "emerald necklace," as it has come to be called, consisting of five major parks (Back Bay Fens, Muddy River Improvement, Jamaica Park, Arnold Arboretum, and Franklin Park) and their connecting parkways (Fenway, Riverway, Jamaicaway, and Arborway). Commonwealth Avenue, already laid out as part of the Back Bay residential district, connected the new park system with the existing Common and Public Garden. In 1897 Columbia Road was widened and joined to the Dorchesterway and the Strandway, linking Franklin Park with Marine Park in South Boston. Figure 1 is a plan of the emerald necklace published in 1894; the proposed extension of Charlesbank from the Public Garden to Cottage Farm Bridge shown on the plan was not constructed until after the turn of the century. Figure 2, dated 1887, shows the connections among the parks of the emerald necklace, Marine Park, and the Chestnut Hill circuit in Brookline and Brighton.

More important than either the size or extent of the park system was its role as a prototype. Olmsted's master plan set the stage for later projects of even more ambitious dimensions. His ideal of comprehensive, regional planning of open space has become an established precept of professional landscape architects and city planners, and his fervent belief in the value of natural scenery near densely settled urban centers is increasingly appreciated in today's climate of environmental awareness.

What did Olmsted find when he first arrived in Boston in 1878? What raw topographical materials did he have to work with, and how had the city changed in the hundred years of expansion since the Revolutionary War?

The topographical history of Boston began long before the first Englishman settled on the Shawmut peninsula. Millions of years of violent geological change, climaxed by the advance and retreat of glaciers, had shaped the peninsula, the harbor, the Boston basin, and the irregular contours of the whole region. Whenever Olmsted found an interesting ledge, drumlin, or kettlehole, he carefully incorporated it into his design, just as he often preserved the more ephemeral vegetation of a site. Most of the time, however, Olmsted had to deal not with the remains of geological prehistory but with problems of much more recent origin. In the course of over two hundred years of settlement, most of Boston's hills had been leveled, its coves filled, and its shores dramatically extended—all by the hand of man.

Figure 1 (opposite)
Plan of the park system
from the Common to
Franklin Park, 1894.

Figure 2 (opposite)
The emerald necklace
parks, with links to the
Common, Chestnut Hill
Reservoir, and Marine
Park, 1887. This shows all
of Olmsted's municipal
system except the small
neighborhood parks.

Although the transformation of Boston had accelerated markedly in the years immediately before Olmsted's arrival in the 1870s, it had begun in 1625, when the Reverend William Blaxton, a reclusive Anglican clergyman, settled on what is now called Beacon Hill. He was followed five years later by the Puritans of the Massachusetts Bay Company under Governor John Winthrop. The original settlers were attracted by the sheltered harbor and easily protected peninsula, which was joined to the Roxbury mainland by a narrow strip along the line of what is now Washington Street. There was a source of pure water near Blaxton's farm, and the landscape was dominated by an odd configuration known as the Trimountain, consisting of Pemberton, Beacon, and Mount Vernon hills. All that is left of this early landmark is a truncated remnant of Beacon Hill.[1]

The settlers lost little time in turning their bleak environment into a smaller-scaled, primitive version of the London many of them had come from. Within fifteen years, streets had been laid out, frequently named after their English counterparts; permanent houses had been built; and the shore line was being changed by the construction of wharves, Town Cove, and the Mill Pond. The Puritans settled on that part of the Shawmut peninsula (renamed Boston at the official date of founding in 1630) between the Trimountain and Boston Harbor, in what is now the North End and the central business district. This remained the center of population for well over a century, as is shown in a series of eighteenth-century maps of Boston. The first of these, published by Captain John Bonner in 1722 (Figure 3) reveals a bustling town of a hundred streets, lanes, and alleys, and three thousand houses. Bonner's map went through several editions up to 1769. Although the successive versions show intensive development over the years, there was little expansion beyond the original area of settlement.[2]

The most beautiful eighteenth-century map of the city, and the only one that indicates the topography of what is now "greater" Boston, is Henry Pelham's aquatint engraving, surveyed in 1775 and published in London in 1777 (Figure 4). At the center of the map is the peninsula of Boston proper, with the familiar outline and street patterns of the later Bonner editions. (Figure 5 shows a detail of the Pelham map.) Facing Boston Harbor, Long Wharf juts out among the bristling shapes of many smaller wharves. The Mill Pond is confined by a dam. Although there is an intricate network of streets on the harbor side of Boston, there are only scattered dwellings, gardens, and orchards on the Trimountain to the west. Boston Common, originally part of Blaxton's farm, displays an urbane double row of trees on the Tremont Street side and a single row along Park and Beacon streets (labeled the New Mall), but the part of the Common nearest the water is still wild and marshy. At low tide this end of the Common faced a huge stretch of mud

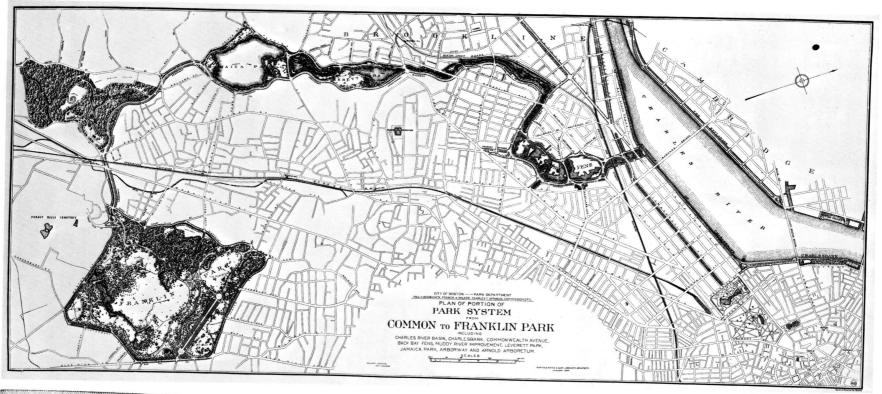

CITY OF BOSTON — PARK DEPARTMENT
PAUL H. KENDRICKEN, FRANCIS A. WALKER, CHARLES F. SPRAGUE, COMMISSIONERS

PLAN OF PORTION OF
PARK SYSTEM
FROM
COMMON TO FRANKLIN PARK
INCLUDING
CHARLES RIVER BASIN, CHARLESBANK, COMMONWEALTH AVENUE,
BACK BAY FENS, MUDDY RIVER IMPROVEMENT, LEVERETT PARK,
JAMAICA PARK, ARBORWAY AND ARNOLD ARBORETUM.

SCALES

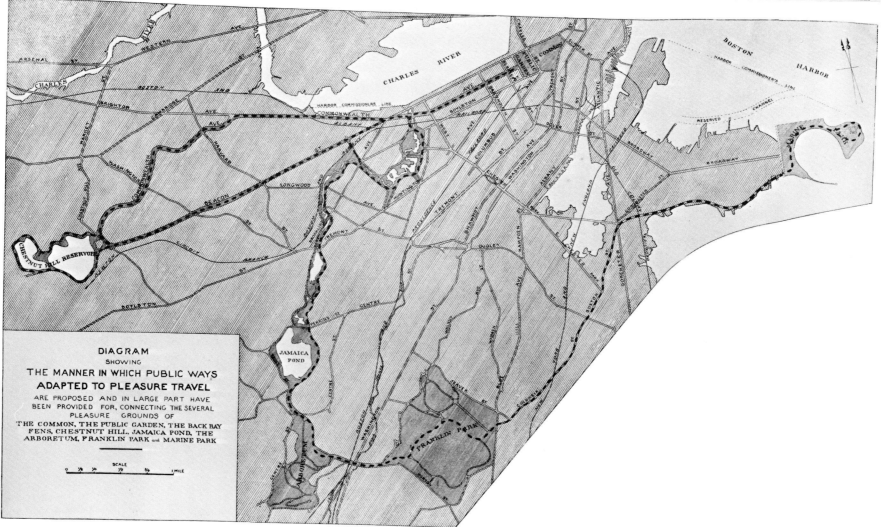

DIAGRAM
SHOWING
THE MANNER IN WHICH PUBLIC WAYS
ADAPTED TO PLEASURE TRAVEL
ARE PROPOSED AND IN LARGE PART HAVE
BEEN PROVIDED FOR, CONNECTING THE SEVERAL
PLEASURE GROUNDS OF
THE COMMON, THE PUBLIC GARDEN, THE BACK BAY
FENS, CHESTNUT HILL, JAMAICA POND, THE
ARBORETUM, FRANKLIN PARK and MARINE PARK

SCALE
0   ⅛   ¼   ½   ¾   1 MILE

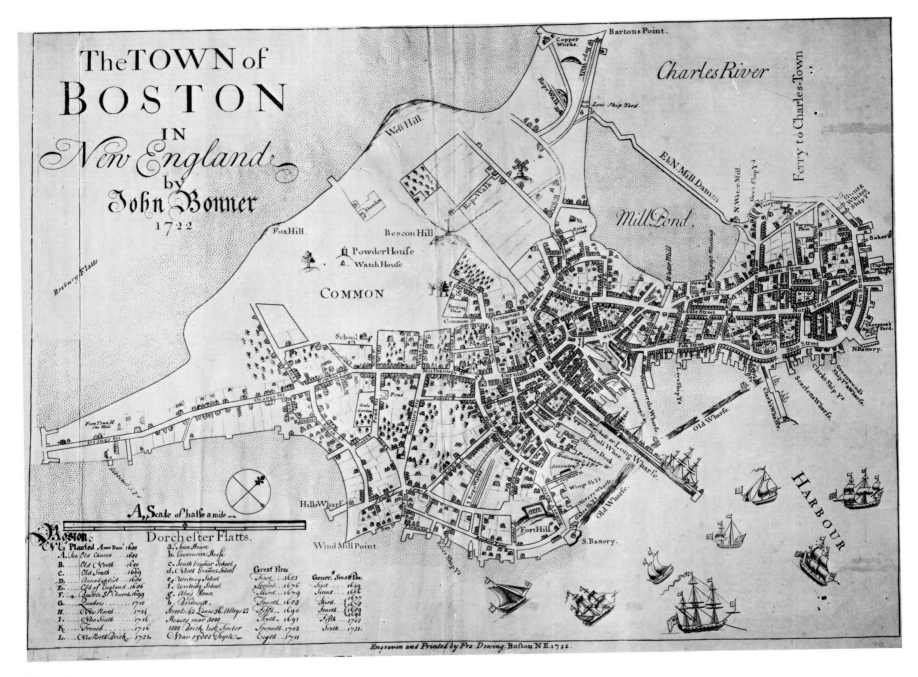

Figure 3
The Bonner map of Boston, 1722.

flats almost as large as the peninsula itself, enclosed by Boston Neck, the great salt meadow at the confluence of Stony Brook and the Muddy River, and the Charles River. This part of the Charles River estuary was first known as the Roxbury Flats and later as the Back Bay. The only access from Boston to the mainland was by the Neck to Roxbury and Brookline or by ferry to Charlestown.

The great surprise of the Pelham map is its revelation of the surrounding countryside. Much of what we now know as Boston, Brookline, and Cambridge was then water, salt meadow, and scant-

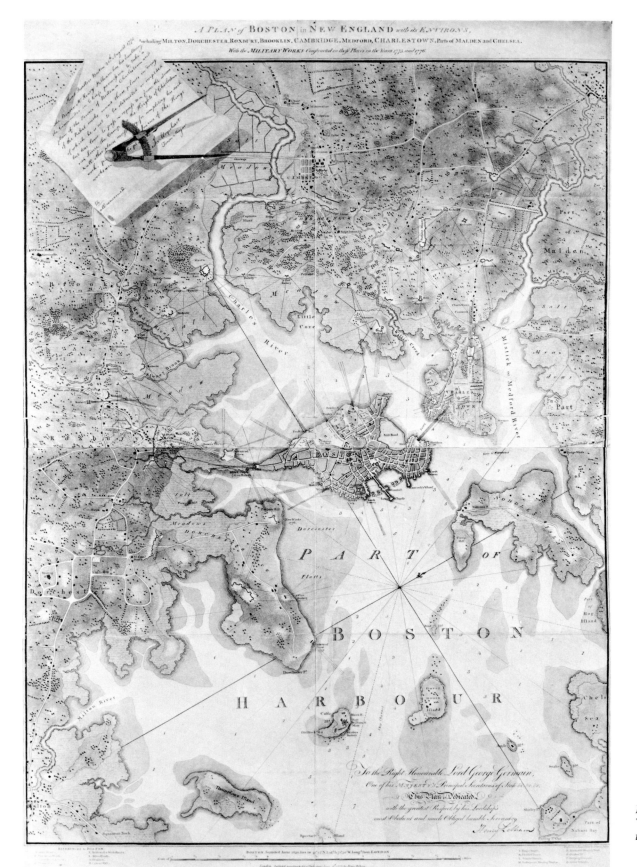

Figure 4
The Pelham map of Boston and environs, 1777.

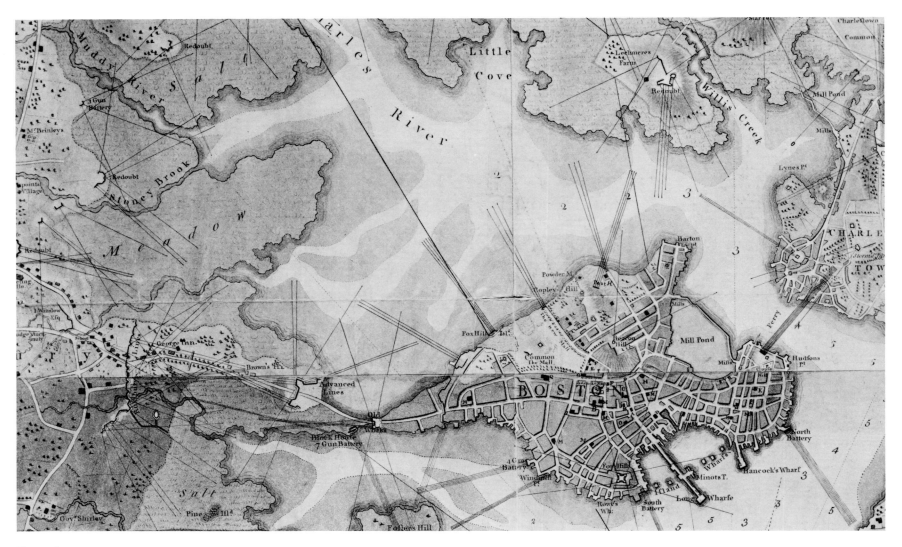

Figure 5
Detail of the Pelham map,
showing the peninsula of
Boston and the Back Bay
salt meadow.

ily populated farmland. East Boston (Noddle's Island) had been incorporated as part of Boston in the 1630s but had scarcely a half-dozen buildings in 1777. Charlestown, confined like Boston to a peninsula and having similar advantages, was rather densely developed. Cambridge, at the top of the map, huddled around Harvard College, although spacious estates lined Brattle Street in the direction of Watertown; its Charles River frontage, which included what is now Brighton on the opposite side of the Charles, was almost entirely salt meadow.

From the first, the colonists had to look beyond Boston proper for their food supplies, for there was

little arable land on the peninsula. Brookline on the Muddy River, Roxbury, and West Roxbury (lying outside the boundaries of the map to the southwest) were for many years the suppliers of Boston's farm produce. Fort Hill and Parker Hill in Roxbury Highlands overlooked the Back Bay salt meadow, and most of the population of that town lived near the Meeting House on Eliot Square. The enormous expanses of Dorchester, which take up almost the entire lower left quadrant of the map, included several hundred acres of salt meadow on and near the neck of land that later became South Boston. By 1777 the marshes on the Boston peninsula had been extensively filled. In fact, as early as 1645, every marsh within the town boundaries had been altered in some way.

For about a decade after the Revolution, Boston kept its colonial aspect. The population in 1790 had stabilized at about 18,000, an increase of less than 2,000 in fifty years. The new buildings being built were largely replacements of the timber structures lost in frequent fires. So devastating were these fires that in 1803 the state legislature passed a bill requiring that all new structures in Boston be built of stone or brick.

Slowly, however, Boston lost its provincial character, as bridges were built connecting it with Charlestown and Cambridge. In 1795 plans were finally adopted for a new State House on Beacon Hill overlooking Boston Common. Within the next twenty-five years, the city took on a new urban elegance, as numerous new churches, public buildings, and houses were erected. Brick in material, Federal in style, and frequently designed by the city's first professional architect, Charles Bulfinch, these buildings set an entirely new tone for Boston.

Topographical changes were also being made, beginning with the development of the Trimountain as a fashionable residential district. In 1795 Harrison Gray Otis, Jonathan Mason, and others formed the Mount Vernon Proprietors and bought John Singleton Copley's twenty-acre property on what is now the south side of Beacon Hill. The syndicate originally intended to have only detached mansion houses with sizable gardens in their spacious new neighborhood, and a few such were built, but a more economical rowhouse scheme was soon adopted. The Trimountain began to lose its bumpy profile when the top fifty feet of Mount Vernon, its western peak, was removed to fill in Charles Street. A less well known venture by Otis was unsuccessful: his 1804 plan to turn the just-annexed South Boston into a residential district similar to Beacon Hill.[3]

Another premature attempt at developing barren land was a modest proposal presented at an 1801 town meeting by the board of Selectmen under Charles Bulfinch's chairmanship. The selectmen's plan, which involved no landfill, was to lay out part of Boston Neck in a rectangular grid, with a central oval green on the site of today's Blackstone and Franklin squares. Some of this land was sold, but it moved very slowly, and the enterprise was hardly a success. Within a few years, however, there was a pressing need for more building space, for the population was increasing geometrically and would more than triple between 1790 and 1825. There were no further attempts at developing outlying areas, as South Boston and Boston Neck still were in the days before railroads and streetcars. Instead, speculators began to eye the coves and crannies indenting the peninsula of Boston proper. The filling of the fifty-acre Mill Pond in the present North Station area, itself created from a salt marsh in the early Colonial period, dragged on for more than a dozen years, as the top sixty feet of Beacon Hill was brought down by cart and dumped into it. One by one, other irregularities in the shoreline disappeared; part of Copp's Hill was taken down to create new land in the North End, and a new waterfront district arose on the site of the former Town Cove.

With the coming of the railroad in the second quarter of the nineteenth century, the transformation of Boston from an isolated provincial town to the "hub" of New England was complete. The same years saw other significant changes. In 1822, after almost two centuries as a town, Boston finally was incorporated as a city. The charter drafted by the city fathers was a rather cautious one that in some respects merely perpetuated the form of town government in a less cumbersome form. The mayor had little more power than his predecessor, the chairman of the Board of Selectmen: he was able only to appoint committees and to exercise a qualified veto over some actions of the City Council, which at that time was a bicameral body, consisting of a Board of Aldermen and a Common Council. It was not until 1885 that the charter was amended to give the mayor significant executive powers.[4]

The impact of the enormous influx of immigrants, mostly Irish, on Boston in this part of the nineteenth century has been well described elsewhere.[5] Between 1825 and 1850 the city's population grew from some 58,000 to 137,000, and immigrants accounted for a large proportion of the increase. The new arrivals concentrated in the North End and Fort Hill sections, driving away more prosperous and settled residents. Many of the older sections of Boston became slums, and the immigrants, for the most part unskilled and destitute, were forced to live under crowded and unhealthy conditions. This dramatic increase in population set the stage for the large-scale landfill operations undertaken in the second half of the century: the new South End and Back Bay.

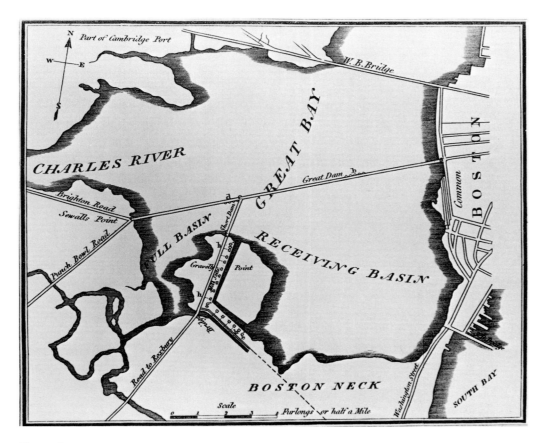

Figure 6
The Mill Dam (Great Dam) and the Back Bay receiving and full basins, 1821.

After the Mill Pond on the site of the present North Station was filled, new dams were built in the Back Bay to provide water power for a greatly enlarged system of new mills of every type, including cotton and woolen factories, proposed by Uriah Cotting and others. That expectation was never fulfilled, however, because Lowell and Lawrence on the Merrimack River became the centers of the Massachusetts textile industry.[6] The Mill Dam, completed in 1821, extended along the line of Bea-

con Street all the way to Brookline, and the Cross Dam divided the Back Bay into a receiving basin and a full basin (Figure 6). With the Back Bay no longer open to free circulation from the ocean, the water tended to stagnate, and the situation was made worse by the construction of long causeways for several railroad lines in the 1830s and 1840s. Although the Back Bay still looked attractive, as is evident in a lithograph of 1850 by John Bachmann (Figure 7), it was no longer refreshing to smell, for a sewer and a city dump emptied into it. This consideration, as well as the pressing need for more space for residential building, prodded the city into massive landfill projects. After the completion of the South End and Back Bay, the city had virtually exhausted the possibilities of expansion through fill, at least on a large scale.

At this point it is necessary to define Back Bay and South End more precisely. In strictly geographical terms, the Back Bay refers to the entire 450-acre area enclosed originally by the Shawmut peninsula, Boston Neck, the great Brookline and Roxbury salt meadow, and the Charles River (see Figure 5), an expanse that was filled by the end of the nineteenth century. As used sociologically, the term Back Bay refers to a cohesive residential district of great importance, both architecturally and as an example of city planning. It comprises only the part of the geographical Back Bay that is bounded by Arlington Street, the Charles River, Charlesgate East and, to the south, Copley Square and Boylston Street, a total of about 200 acres. The nucleus of the South End was the narrow strip of solid land called Boston Neck. It expanded by fill in two directions: to the south into the South Bay and to the north into the geographical Back Bay. Both filling projects were under way at approximately the same time. Although some sporadic filling had already taken place on Boston Neck in the second quarter of the century, the bulk of the South End landfill was begun in 1850; the filling of the Back Bay was started in 1857.[7]

The boundaries of the two areas can be understood more readily by looking at the Colton map of 1855 (Figure 8), in which the South End is well advanced, while the Back Bay is still projected. Both districts were laid out on a grid plan, but the street patterns of the two areas had no relationship to

Figure 7
Bird's-eye view of Boston
by John Bachmann, look-
ing toward the Public
Garden and Common,
1850.

each other, for they were divided by the Providence
and Worcester railroad tracks (the diagonal cross to
the lower left of center on the Colton map). The
principal streets of the Back Bay ran parallel to the
Mill Dam; those of the South End ran parallel to
Washington Street, which earlier was the only
means of access to Boston along the Neck. Thus
separated, the two districts grew according to contrasting planning philosophies, and their histories
are strikingly different.

Both districts were meant exclusively for homes,
interspersed with a few churches and institutions.
Their streets, like those of Beacon Hill, are lined
with rowhouses, although the South End (again like
Beacon Hill) was originally envisioned as a neighborhood of detached houses. Both were projected as
fashionable places to live, although only the Back
Bay lived up to that expectation. As was mentioned
earlier, the development of Boston Neck was anticipated in the Bulfinch plan of 1801. The later,

Figure 8
The Colton map of Bos-
ton, 1855.

greatly expanded South End plan, was designed and constructed in four stages from about 1850 to 1875 and is generally attributed to the engineers E. S. Chesborough and William P. Parrott.[8]

As is often the case with made land, the area has a monotonous flatness, and the long avenues seem to stretch into infinity. In some cases, however, such as Columbus Avenue, which was laid out in the early 1870s as a Parisian-inspired boulevard, the seemingly endless vistas have a focus, generally a church spire. This device also helps to mitigate a rather wearisome architectural uniformity. At first glance the red brick, swell-front facades of the South End houses, with their high stoops and mansard roofs, seem almost identical, although close inspection reveals a variety of detail. Figure 9, "Rainy Day: Boston" by Childe Hassam, shows Columbus Avenue, where Hassam lived, near the intersection of Warren Avenue. The long avenues seen in the Hassam painting contrast sharply with the secluded side streets found elsewhere in the South End—self-contained residential enclaves, often featuring a tiny private park in the London fashion, enclosed by an iron fence. But the South End never caught on as a fashionable neighborhood, and by the end of the nineteenth century, it was a lodging-house district.

The Back Bay, on the other hand, attracted many "proper" Bostonians, and it remained a fashionable residential district until the depression of 1929. Filling, begun in 1857 with gravel brought by railroad from outlying Needham, proceeded in an orderly way from east to west, and building followed only one step behind (see Figure 10). Although interrupted by the panic of 1873, the sale of lots was brisk, and land values rose sharply. The most remarkable feature of the Back Bay is its extraordinary range of architectural styles. Nowhere else in the United States can one see such a variety of late nineteenth-century urban residential architecture.

The plan of the South End, with the exception of Columbus Avenue, reflected the urban ideals of eighteenth-century London, while the Back Bay plan, designed by Boston architect Arthur Gilman, was French in inspiration.[9] Despite its sheer size and the unifying effect of its long avenues, the South End is an aggregate of many little residential units. Perhaps because fill proceeded outward from a nu-

cleus of solid land, no one axis clearly dominates. The boundaries of the district (roughly Dover Street to the east, Lenox Street to the west, Albany Street to the south, and the Providence and Worcester railroad tracks to the north) also seem amorphous. Occasional glimpses of landmarks, such as the spire of the Park Street Church, provide some orientation to the rest of the city, but in general the South End is an easy place in which to get lost.

Figure 9
"Rainy Day: Boston," by Childe Hassam, 1885, showing Columbus Avenue in the South End.

In contrast, the Back Bay is almost relentlessly ordered. Commonwealth Avenue, with its central landscaped mall, is the dominant axis and can be clearly seen from every intersection throughout the district. Most corners are marked by an especially striking church or house, and each block has its own identifiable character. Unlike the South End, where consistency of architectural style helps to define an area that otherwise lacks shape and focus, the variety of styles found in the Back Bay modifies what could have been an almost too rigorous symmetry of plan.

As originally conceived, the Back Bay plan lacked a proper terminus at either end of its east–west axis. However, with the completion of the Public Garden in 1860, Olmsted's Back Bay Fens in the 1890s, and the Charles River Embankment in

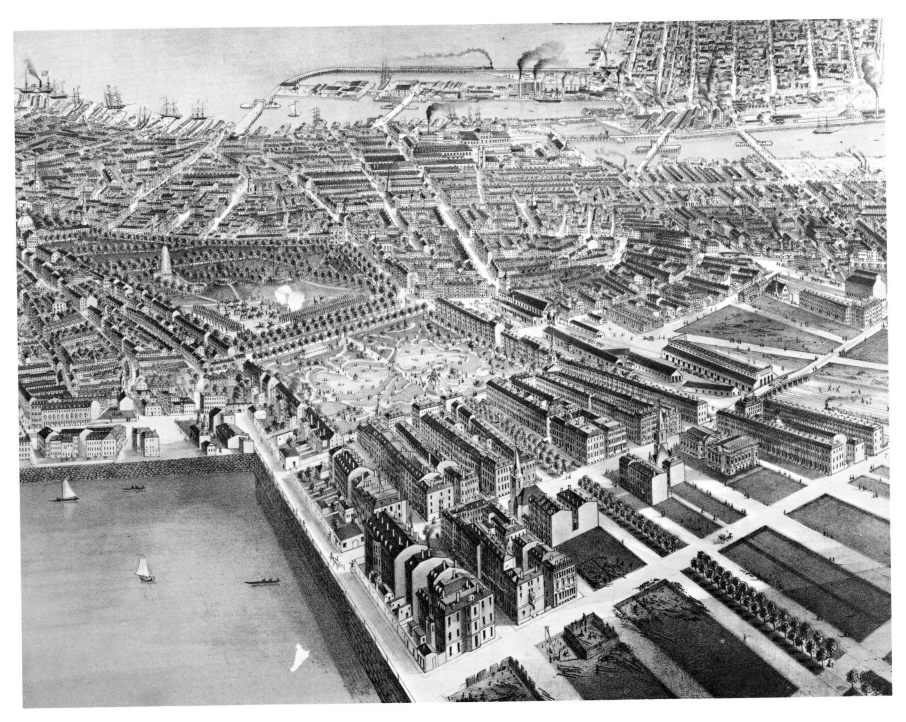

Figure 10
*Bird's-eye view of Boston
by F. Fuchs (detail), July 4,
1870.*

1910, the Back Bay was framed on three sides by parks. Copley Square, although not part of the original plan, helped to define the southern border, and the Providence and Worcester railroad tracks, although hardly an aesthetic amenity, insulated the area from the rapidly declining South End.

In their early history, Bostonians had showed little concern for the preservation of what today would be called "open space." Like every Colonial town, Boston had its common for pasturing cows, a place where boundaries were almost accidental and footpaths simply followed the most direct routes. Formal rows of trees along the borders were the only attempts at landscaping. Later on, its associations with the Revolution gave the Common the character almost of consecrated ground, although cattle continued to graze on its almost treeless meadows until 1830. It was not until the late nineteenth century that Boston's common pasture was gradually transformed into a wooded park.[10]

The Public Garden, now one of the most elegant of Boston's municipal spaces, was not secured as parkland until 1859.[11] Like the Back Bay, it is built entirely on made land. In 1777, as can easily be seen on the Pelham map (Figure 5), nothing existed beyond the Common but marsh and mud flats. In 1794 the Selectmen granted a fringe of flats to the west of what is now Charles Street for use as ropewalks. (The ropewalks are the parallel lines beside the Common in Figure 6.) The site, no longer of negligible value after Charles Street was put through in 1804 and the Mill Dam completed in 1821, was reappropriated by the city in 1824 under Mayor Quincy. Clearly the area was ripe for filling, and its future was a matter of some contention. The citizens of Boston supported Mayor Quincy by denying the City Council the right to sell the property, but developers were persistent in putting forward schemes for residential projects.[12]

The matter was temporarily resolved in 1837 when a group of amateur horticulturists, led by Horace Gray, petitioned the City Council for permission to use the site for a public botanic garden. In 1839 the request was granted, and Gray and his associates engaged an English gardener, John Cadness, to take charge of the project.[13] Although the land was only partially filled and was several feet below street level, the proprietors built a greenhouse and imported rare plants. They also approached A. J. Downing, then at the beginning of his career as a landscape gardener, to prepare a scheme for laying out the grounds as a Public Garden, its boundaries to be defined by a scientifically arranged arboretum.[14]

Gray and his fellow horticulturists apparently underestimated the difficulties of the site, and their plans came to a halt in 1847 when Gray lost his fortune. In 1850 a joint committee of the City Council described the Garden's appearance as dismal and recommended a residential development.[15] But the 1850 Bachmann lithograph (Figure 7) in complete contradiction shows a charming view of the Botanic Garden, with splashing fountain and revolving swings. Not until 1856 did the city acquire

clear legal title to the site—the Commonwealth and private owners also had interests—and in 1859 an act of the legislature finally ensured that it would be kept forever as a Public Garden.[16] In the same year a local architect, George F. Meacham, laid out the grounds substantially as they appear today. The redesign of the Public Garden in 1859–1860 belongs to the history of the Boston park movement and is discussed in Chapter 3.

The Massachusetts Horticultural Society, founded in 1829 by General Henry A. S. Dearborn, Dr. Jacob Bigelow, and other amateur horticulturists, still thrives today. Although the early activities of the society were associated more with the suburbs than with Boston proper, many members of the group were a major force behind the park movement of the late 1860s and 1870s, which was to launch Olmsted's Boston career.

By the early years of the nineteenth century, Boston had become one of the nation's horticultural centers. Many now thoroughly urbanized communities, such as Roxbury, Dorchester, Brighton, Cambridge, and Watertown, were noted for their large estates and famous plant nurseries.[17] Although they were, strictly speaking, amateurs, the owners of many of these estates spent much of their time introducing and cultivating new varieties of fruits, flowers, and vegetables—pears and camellias being favorite specialties. Their passion for horticulture led many of these men to an allied interest in landscape gardening.

The Massachusetts Horticultural Society, one of the first such groups in the nation, was patterned after the Horticultural Society of London, founded in 1804. Its purposes were to hold meetings, form a library, distribute seeds and stocks, and set standards and sponsor competitions in various plant categories. But shortly after the group was formed, its members became deeply involved in a more unusual project: the establishment of the first rural cemetery in the United States. A few years earlier Jacob Bigelow had met with friends to discuss the urgent need for such a cemetery. As a physician, he had long been concerned about the dangers to health from Boston's overcrowded, intown burial grounds, which contaminated the public water sup-

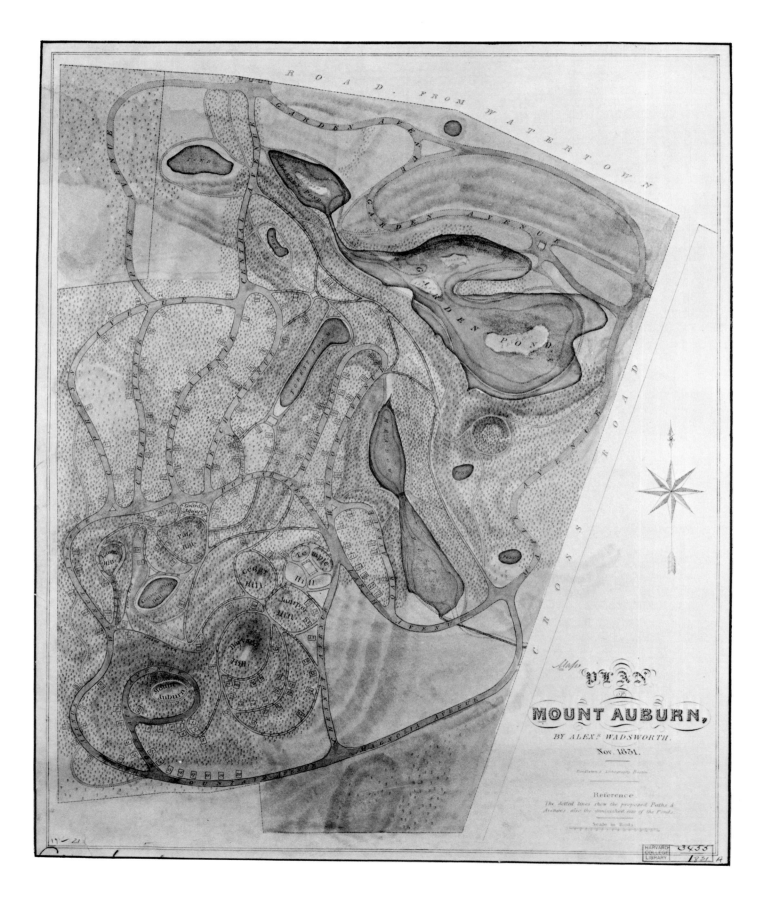

Figure 11
Plan of Mount Auburn
Cemetery, Cambridge and
Watertown, 1831.

ply. Although there were then no extramural cemeteries in the United States, European precedents existed, the most famous being the cemetery of Père Lachaise outside of Paris, established in 1804.

When Bigelow presented his idea to the Horticultural Society, it was well received. Dearborn, the society's first president, took up the cause with particular enterprise. The society needed an experimental garden, and it was decided to include space for this at one end of the rural cemetery. Several sites were considered, and the one called "Sweet Auburn" on the Cambridge-Watertown line was selected. In September 1831, Mount Auburn Cemetery was consecrated.[18]

Shortly after the consecretion, Dearborn, Bigelow, and George W. Brimmer set about getting an accurate topographical survey and deciding on a plan. Although the extramural cemetery prototype was Père Lachaise, the terrain of the French cemetery is flat and its design more formal than that of its Cambridge counterpart. The design appears to have been a collaboration by Dearborn, Bigelow, and Alexander Wadsworth, the civil engineer, with Dearborn probably taking the leading role.[19] Their application of the English eighteenth-century Picturesque landscape style to cemetery design was a strikingly new concept with no precedents in either Europe or the United States (Figure 11). Mount Auburn's winding avenues and paths accentuated the irregular terrain and at the same time provided easy access to every burial lot.

This combination of the picturesque and the practical proved irresistible, and within a few years most major American cities featured a rural cemetery patterned after Mount Auburn. Among the best known are Laurel Hill in Philadelphia (1836) and Greenwood in Brooklyn (1838). From the beginning, the rural cemeteries were favorite spots for evening strolls and Sunday outings (Figure 12). Mount Auburn and its offspring served the living quite as much as the dead. In short, they functioned as country parks well before Olmsted's first example, Central Park, and even before the English parks that were his inspiration, such as Sir Joseph Paxton's Birkenhead Park in Liverpool.

After the first two years, it became apparent that the soil at Mount Auburn was not suited for an experimental garden, and it was discontinued. (The portion of the cemetery set aside for the experimental garden was later used for graves.) In 1835 the cemetery was sold to a newly formed private corporation, the Mount Auburn Proprietors. The Horticultural Society continued to receive a quarter of the proceeds from the sale of lots, and General Dearborn lost none of his enthusiasm for rural cemeteries. In 1848, as mayor of Roxbury, he persuaded that community, still an independent city, to set up Forest Hills Cemetery.[20]

Figure 12
View from Mount Auburn,
1847.

Roxbury did not remain independent for long. With the exception of East Boston, which had been part of the city since the seventeenth century, and South Boston, annexed in 1804, Boston in the mid-nineteenth century was still confined to the fill-expanded boundaries of its original peninsula. Several factors contributed to the movement to annex adjoining towns. As railway and streetcar lines were built, it became increasingly common for people to work in Boston but live at some distance from the city. Many suburban commuters, however, wanted to live and work in the same political entity. Between 1850 and 1873 the pros and cons of annexation were debated in almost every nearby city and town. The pro-annexationists wished to benefit from Boston's increasingly modern water and sewage services, while the opponents cherished their independence and semirural way of life. In 1851 the anti-annexation sentiment was strong enough in West Roxbury for that village to set itself off from the city of Roxbury.[21]

In 1868 Roxbury voted for annexation to Boston. Dorchester followed in 1870, and Charlestown, Brighton, and West Roxbury (reversing its earlier position) in 1873. Brookline, however, resisted the pressures of its pro-annexationists and in 1873 decisively voted to remain independent. After that year the annexation movement lost momentum, and only one more community, Hyde Park in 1912, was added to Boston. By the early 1890s metropolitan commissions had been established to administer water, sewage, and parks, thus removing much of the incentive for annexation.

The immediate result of the expansion of Boston's boundaries was positive. New development in the annexed towns, in contrast to that in the Back Bay and South End, was limited almost entirely to detached, wooden, one-, two- and three-family dwellings for the middle-class. As an unprecedented number of new houses was built—28,000 in Roxbury, Dorchester, and West Roxbury alone between 1872 and 1901—space, fresh air, and healthy surroundings became available to thousands.

On the other hand, it soon became apparent that the boom in development was producing a rather sterile visual environment. There was no overall plan for the subdivision of large parcels of property. Most developers, operating on a small scale, broke up small parcels of land as they appeared on the market. With little capital for extensive preparation of lots, they chose the least expensive type of layout: a standard grid system with frontage lots, which cut down the cost of laying utility lines.[22] The grid system had, of course, been used in the Back Bay and South End, but Brighton, Roxbury, Dorchester, and West Roxbury originally had had a varied and picturesque topography that was quite unlike the uniform flatness of filled land.

Yielding to the pressures of development, ancient farms, with few exceptions, disappeared, and many of the large landowners, including some of the amateur horticulturists, moved to Brookline, Dedham, and other still-pastoral towns. Most important, since the city had no Park Commission until 1875, there was no institutional way to preserve the natural landscape. Much of the impetus for the park movement came from citizens who watched field and forest disappear under regimental rows of houses. Expressing the sense of loss felt by many, a native of Roxbury described the transformation of that neighborhood only five years after annexation:

Parker's Hill with its gray ledges, seamed by the frost of ages, but painted with the soft and parti-colored lichens, and decorated with ferns and nodding grasses, has yielded to the ravages of the drill and sledge hammer, to the pick and shovel . . . The Highlands have submitted their picturesque ledges and forests to the same destructive power, May's woods have fled from Warren Street . . . The dog-tooth violets, the cowslips, the columbines, the anemones, the gentians have fled; the sturdy golden rods and asters yet remain; the rudbeckia and the bur-marigold still make the ditch banks and the low grounds yellow in October; but all but the rugged and resistant plants are gone . . . and blank, unadorned highways have taken their places, fringed no longer with beauty of any kind, but presenting rows and blocks of very inferior houses, too many of them tenantless.[23]

II

The Making
of a Landscape Architect

◆

WHEN Frederick Law Olmsted was born at Hartford, Connecticut, in 1822, his future profession did not exist. What we now call "landscape architecture" was practiced by landscape gardeners or horticulturists, civil engineers, and occasionally architects. Olmsted's education was fragmented and informal. His young manhood was seemingly directionless and marked by a series of false starts, yet by 1858 he had gained sufficient experience and insight to synthesize many disciplines and to create a new profession and a new art.

Olmsted was the first child of John Olmsted, a prosperous dry goods merchant, and Charlotte Hull Olmsted, who died when her son was not quite four.[1] At the age of seven, he was sent to board with a series of country clergymen, most of whom were strict disciplinarians and unimaginative teachers. Yet his childhood held many positive experiences that appear to have balanced what was ostensibly his education. During stays at home he developed a close relationship with his younger brother, John Hull Olmsted. The family, which now included a stepmother and several younger half-brothers and sisters, took frequent vacations, visiting scenic spots in New England and New York. Enjoyment of scenery as an end in itself was a value he grew up with and wholly accepted.[2]

Olmsted had intended to go to Yale, but at the age of fifteen he developed a severe case of sumac poisoning that threatened his eyesight. Instead of attending college, he boarded and studied with Frederick A. Barton, a civil engineer who was also a clergyman, first at Andover, Massachusetts, where Barton taught at Phillips Academy, and then in Collinsville, Connecticut. In the course of three years of leisurely but professionally supervised instruction in civil engineering, Olmsted acquired a sound basis in one discipline that was necessary for his later career.[3]

In 1844, after clerking in a dry goods store in New York City, then serving as an apprentice seaman on a bark bound for China,[4] Olmsted decided that he was best fitted for life as a farmer. To him, scientific agriculture, practiced according to the most modern methods, was as valuable to society and as much a "profession" as the more usual ones of medicine and law. For the next few years he apprenticed at several farms and, although not a regularly enrolled student at Yale, attended courses in chemistry and scientific farming taught by Benjamin Silliman.[5] His first farm, bought for him by his father at Sachem's Head, Connecticut, proved to have poor soil. In 1848 his father bought him a larger and better property on Staten Island, which he farmed at irregular intervals for almost a decade.

For a few years Olmsted seemed to have found his métier. He threw himself into his new life with an energy that surprised his family and friends, although it was characteristic of him for the rest of his life. He efficiently applied Silliman's theories to his own property and was soon winning prizes for his wheat and turnips.[6] He was also putting into practice much that he had learned from Barton about civil engineering; he moved his barns to a better location, changed the line of his driveway, and turned a mudhole behind his house into an attractive and uncontaminated pond. Olmsted earned even more of a reputation from these activities than from his crops and was asked to do similar work on other people's properties.[7]

Soon he felt a pull in a new direction, however. His brother, who had become ill with incipient tuberculosis, hoped to improve his health by taking a walking trip through England and the continent with his college friend, Charles Loring Brace. Viewing the trip as an opportunity to broaden his knowledge of foreign agricultural methods, Olmsted decided to go along.[8] The journal of his travels, begun in the spring of 1850, was published in expanded form in 1852 as *Walks and Talks of An American Farmer in England*.[9] In it, Olmsted demonstrated his ability to observe both the social scene and landscape scenery.

From the point of view of his future as a landscape architect, the most important experience for Olmsted in England was his trip to Birkenhead, a new and rapidly growing suburb of Liverpool. It had been planned by the Scots architect Gillespie Graham with wide, well-paved streets and public squares. While at Birkenhead, Olmsted and his companions were escorted by the local baker to the town's new park. Completed only five years earlier from plans by Joseph Paxton, the 125-acre Birkenhead Park (Figure 13) was a revelation to Olmsted, who admitted that "in democratic America there was nothing to be thought of as comparable with this People's Garden."[10] He praised the winding paths, the varying surface of the land, the variety of shrubs and flowers, and he inspected the construction of bridges, carriage roads, and the drainage system. However, the democratic use of the park impressed him even more than its design: "All this magnificent pleasure-ground is entirely, unreservedly, and for ever the people's own. The poorest British peasant is as free to enjoy it in all its parts as the British queen. More than that, the baker of Birkenhead has the pride of an *owner* in it. Is it not a grand good thing?"[11]

In the course of his British tour, Olmsted visited several country estates. Eaton Park, one of the seats of the Marquis of Westminster and possibly designed by the eighteenth-century landscape gardener Lancelot "Capability" Brown (1716–1783), prompted a prophetic comment from the future landscape architect: "What artist, so noble, has often been my thought, as he, who with far-reaching conception of beauty and designing power, sketches the outline, writes the colours, and directs the shadows of a picture so great that Nature shall be employed upon it for generations, before the work he has arranged for her shall realize his intentions."[12]

Although planned parks, suburbs, and gardens impressed Olmsted, even more important was the impact of ordinary English scenery. More than once he had the feeling that he was seeing a landscape he

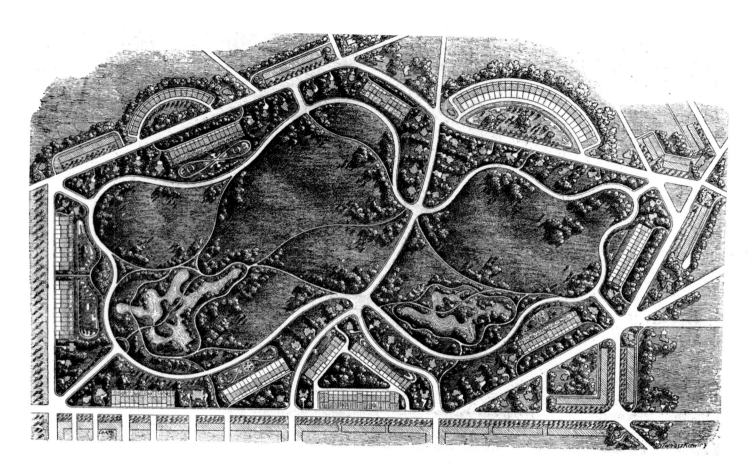

Figure 13
Plan of Birkenhead Park,
Liverpool, England, de-
signed by Joseph Paxton,
1843–1844.

had always known: "Such a scene I had never looked upon before, and yet it was in all its parts as familiar to me as my native valley. Land of our poets! Home of our fathers! Dear old mother England! It would be strange if I were not affected at meeting thee at last face to face."[13]

Olmsted's art was to have many sources. In England he eventually saw grounds by Humphrey Repton and John Nash as well as Paxton and Brown. Within weeks he visited the Rhine and admired its majestic views. The parks of Jean Alphand and Edouard André in France and the redesigning of Paris under Napoleon III were later influences. Nevertheless, the landscape that moved him most throughout his life was the rural England of broad green fields, hedgerows, ponds, and gentle mists. It

remained his aesthetic ideal, although he recognized the futility of trying to reproduce it in an unsuitable climate.

When he returned home, Olmsted cared for his Staten Island farm with something less than his earlier dedication. He was increasingly occupied with writing, turning his English journals into a book. Within the next few years, he also published several articles, including an account for the *New York Daily Tribune* of his visit in 1852 to the North American Phalanx, a Fourierist community in Red Bank, New Jersey, then in its last successful year.[14]

In 1852 Olmsted was asked to go south as a reporter for the newly established *New York Daily Times*. On his first trip, which lasted four months and took him through the eastern slave states,

Olmsted set out with an open mind but found life in the South appallingly backward. His observations, written in the same journalistic style as *Walks and Talks,* appeared first in the *Times* and were later published in book form as *A Journey in the Seaboard Slave States.* On a second trip Olmsted was accomplished by his brother on an itinerary that probably did the latter's health no good. John Hull Olmsted wrote the resulting book—*A Journey through Texas; or, a Saddle-Trip on the South-western Frontier*—from his brother's notes. On the whole, they found conditions in this part of the South no better than in the seaboard states, with the exception of the small German community of Neu-Braunfels near San Antonio. To Olmsted this was clear proof of the superiority of free labor over slavery. For several years he followed and supported the activities of the Texas Free-Soilers. After John's return home, Olmsted continued through the mountains of Mississippi, Alabama, Georgia, Tennessee, and North Carolina. His account of this last trip was published, after considerable delay, as *A Journey in the Back Country.* The southern books were immediately successful and confirmed Olmsted's reputation as a writer.[15]

In 1855 Olmsted became part owner of a publishing firm, Dix and Edwards, and editor of its periodical, *Putnam's Monthly Magazine.* Leaving the Staten Island farm in the hands of his brother and a hired manager, he moved to an apartment in New York City. For close to two years he was engrossed in soliciting articles from such authors as Ralph Waldo Emerson, Henry Wadsworth Longfellow, and Harriet Beecher Stowe. In 1856 he made a second trip to England, this time as an agent of Dix and Edwards. On his return to New York, Olmsted found the firm on the verge of bankruptcy, which finally came in August of 1857. Olmsted was bitterly discouraged by the collapse of a life he had found so satisfying.[16]

Within a few months, Olmsted was to take the step that would determine the rest of his life: applying to be superintendent of the new Central Park. However, it is important to realize that his decision was not a break with the first half of his life but a logical outgrowth of it. Although the episodes as a dry goods clerk and a seaman were in fact false starts, Olmsted's activities as a student of civil engineering and as a farmer, writer, and publisher were all useful in his later career.

Meanwhile, Olmsted was a man in his middle thirties adrift in New York. Reluctant to return to his Staten Island farm, he searched for something to do and, by chance, heard of an opportunity. For years there had been a campaign to build a great park in New York City; now 770 acres of barren land in the middle of Manhattan had been secured and surveyed by Egbert Viele, a topographical engineer. Political conflict between the city and state had held up progress, but by the summer of 1857 the New York State Legislature had appointed nine commissioners to oversee the project. A superintendent was needed to take charge of clearing the land and constructing the park and to manage the park police. One of the commissioners, Charles Wyllys Elliott, suggested to Olmsted that he apply. Although the pay was small ($1,500 a year), the job appealed to him. For his petition to the commissioners, he was able to secure the signatures of William Cullen Bryant, the botanist Asa Gray, and Washington Irving. Olmsted won the appointment over several other influential contenders.[17]

Characteristically, he became totally absorbed in his work, although there were many unpleasant surprises, such as the dismal character of the land itself, which consisted mostly of ledges, swamps, and "the overflow . . . of pigsties, slaughter houses, and bone-boiling works." The only signs of life were squatters' huts and herds of marauding wild goats. And Olmsted, the "unpractical," unpolitical man, as he was later to describe himself, found himself in a political tug of war between the commissioners and the Democratic holdovers, of whom Viele was one, from earlier city appointments. He was sneered at by his subordinates and deliberately led through the mud on his first visit to the site. Following the panic of 1857, there was massive unemployment in New York City, and the new superintendent was under intense pressure to hire as many laborers as possible. He took on 900, as many as he could use productively, and refused to hire more.[18]

After his brother John's death in November 1857, Olmsted threw himself even more deeply into the affairs of Central Park, setting a pattern of overwork that persisted for the rest of his life. Although

Viele had made a plan at his own expense, which was formally adopted in 1856, the commissioners were apparently not satisfied with it. They announced a competition for a new plan, and the English-born architect Calvert Vaux asked Olmsted to collaborate with him. Courteous as always, Olmsted did not want to offend Viele (who by this time had been appointed engineer in chief) by entering, but his superior apparently didn't regard Olmsted as a serious competitor and told him to go ahead. Olmsted and Vaux worked evenings and Sundays on the plan, and when the entries were judged in April 1858, their joint effort, "Greensward," won.[19]

Although later modified in some details, principally by the addition of about seventy acres between 106th and 110th streets, Greensward (Figures 14 and 15) was executed essentially as planned. The designers were stuck with a rigidly rectangular site five times longer than it was wide, with few topographical assets other than a number of steep ledges. Two reservoirs, totaling 143 acres, divided the park virtually in two. Since the parkland had been taken out of the rectangular grid of Manhattan's street system, Olmsted and Vaux had to provide four transverse roads to carry ordinary city traffic across the park. By using some ingenious devices, the designers were able to keep the cross-traffic out of sight, reduce the intrusion of the reservoirs, and achieve variety and a seemingly natural irregularity of terrain.

The separation of different types of traffic has been one of the most widely praised features of Central Park. In addition to letting the city traffic through at four points, Olmsted and Vaux had to provide for carriages, horseback riders, and pedestrians within the park proper. Accordingly, they designed paths, carriageways, and bridle paths in three distinct circulation patterns that rarely intersected at grade. The park was dotted with archways, allowing the three types of traffic to move at different levels with no danger of collision. Finally, the transverse roads for city traffic were sunk well below the park level, crossed by still more arches. "Coal carts and butchers' carts, dust carts and dung carts" were thus able to get from one side to the other without being seen by visitors to the park.[20]

Olmsted and Vaux conceived of the park as a place where the city dweller could find refreshment from the sights and sound of urban life and enjoy scenery that would seem both limitless and natural. To this end, the park boundaries were thickly planted and until the twentieth century, the border plantations screened out surrounding buildings. The reservoirs were also masked by trees, and drives led away from them. The winding system of roads and paths, which has sometimes been criticized as over-contrived, forced the carriages to drive more slowly and, by allowing the visitor to pass back and forth between ever-changing views, made the park seem larger than it was. The southern part of the park was pastoral; the northern part, where most of the ledges were, was more heavily wooded. But there was constant variety of scenic effect in both halves, and broad views of meadow and water alternated

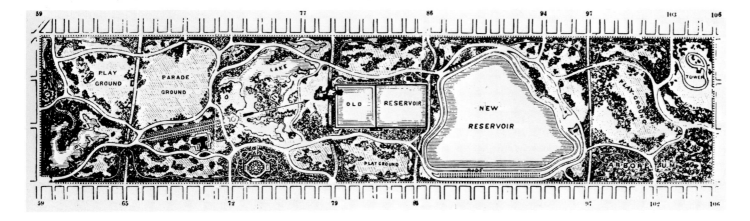

Figure 14
The "Greensward" plan for Central Park, 1858, by Olmsted and Vaux. The park was later enlarged by the addition of four blocks to the north (right of plan).

CENTRAL PARK.

with secluded, sheltered spots. The only formal element in the park was the Mall, planned for fashionable "promenading" and sociability, and it was deliberately placed off-axis.[21]

How were a farmer turned writer and an architect able to achieve, on their first try, such a bril-

liant landscape design? The question has often been asked and can be answered only in part. In the early years of the nineteenth century, as noted at the beginning of this chapter, what we now call "landscape architecture" was practiced by horticulturists, civil engineers, or architects. It was rare for any of these specialists to have a broad understanding of landscape design. Horticulturists knew little of engineering and tended toward fussy effects and the overuse of exotic plants. Engineers were often deficient in aesthetic judgment and botanical knowledge. Architects were inclined to consider the grounds merely as adornments to their buildings. None of the three was likely to view a landscape as a setting that could profoundly influence human beings and their behavior.

Steps toward a synthesis of these three disciplines and toward a comprehensive philosophy of landscape design had already been taken in both England and the United States. Joseph Paxton, the designer of Birkenhead Park, was a horticulturist whose career was almost as varied as Olmsted's. His experiments in the use of iron and glass construction for conservatories led him to the extraordinary engineering tour de force of the Crystal Palace in 1851. He also designed conventional buildings, frequently in an Italianate style. Near Chatsworth, where he was employed by the Duke of Devonshire, he laid out a plan for the village of Edensor, although the houses were designed by a Derby architect, John Robertson. Later in his life he produced a remarkable transportation plan for London, the Great Victorian Way, which was never executed.[22]

In the United States the first rural cemeteries, such as Mount Auburn, and the writings and designs of A. J. Downing (1815–1852) were critical in preparing the way for the work of Olmsted and Vaux. Downing came from the horticultural or landscape gardening tradition, but his interests were far broader than those of most of his fellows. He was intensely concerned with both architectural design and the social implications of landscape planning. He collaborated with many of the best American architects of the period, and on a trip to England in 1850, he met Calvert Vaux and persuaded him to come to the United States as his architectural partner.[23]

The stylistic sources of Central Park are readily apparent. As with Mount Auburn Cemetery, Birkenhead Park, and the estates on the Hudson River and elsewhere designed by Downing, the primary influence was eighteenth-century English landscape gardening. Although the most direct aesthetic source for Central Park and for Olmsted's later park designs was the "pastoral" type of landscaping prac-

ticed by Capability Brown, the writers of the Picturesque movement of the late eighteenth century were also important in molding his thought. The principal theorist of the movement was Sir Uvedale Price, whose *Essay on the Picturesque* Olmsted had read as a boy.[24]

Price and the Reverend William Gilpin, author of *Forest Scenery,* another of Olmsted's boyhood favorites, were reacting against the landscape forms used by Brown, which were themselves a reaction against the French- and Dutch-inspired formal gardens of seventeenth-century England. The aesthetic terms "Sublime" and "Beautiful" had been defined by Edmund Burke in 1757 in his *Philosophical Enquiry into the Origins of Our Ideas of the Sublime and the Beautiful.* According to Burke, the Sublime was characterized by vastness, solitude, and obscurity; objects or scenes embodying it frequently produced fear and awe in the beholder. Beauty, on the other hand, was associated with delicacy, smoothness, gradual variation, and flowing lines. Price accepted these categories but felt that a third, the Picturesque, should be added. Picturesque landscapes were those that could be represented in painting, and they displayed variety, intricacy, irregularity, contrast, and surprise, as well as, at times, the more negative qualities of irritation and accident. As Price noted, only the categories of the Beautiful and the Picturesque were "subject to the improver; to *create* the sublime is above our . . . powers."[25]

Although Price did not publish his essay until 1794, the term "Picturesque" had been in common use for some time. Retrospectively, the term is generally used to describe the entire development of irregular and naturalistic landscape gardening in eighteenth-century England. In this modern sense the word usually includes the Beautiful (pastoral) landscapes of Capability Brown, as well as those of his successors. The Picturesque movement is often divided into three stages. The first, from about 1710 to 1730, was dominated by philosophers and writers, such as Alexander Pope, rather than by practitioners. The actual gardens of the period, including Pope's own at Twickenham, are best described as Rococo, combining typically Baroque formal axes with wriggling paths and watercourses. The second period, from about 1730 to 1770, was dominated by the work of William Kent and Capability Brown and featured the Beautiful qualities of smoothness and finish, as shown in closely mown lawns, artificial streams with bare banks, and trees planted in clumps and in a dense belt encircling the property. The third period, circa 1770 to 1818, culminated in the writings of Price, Gilpin, and Richard Payne Knight and the work of Humphrey Repton.[26]

Unlike Price and Gilpin, Repton was a professional landscape gardener. (He is said to have invented the term.) His practice, like Brown's was limited almost exclusively to large country estates, although toward the end of his career he designed the much smaller grounds of several suburban villas and also branched into urban design with the plans for Bloomsbury, Cadogan, and Russell squares in London. Many of Repton's designs have survived, and almost all are documented in the beautifully illustrated "Red Books" he presented to his clients. Repton preferred a modified form of the Picturesque that included some elements of the Beautiful. He regarded himself as Brown's successor and was indignant to find his master's work attacked by Price and by Richard Payne Knight in a long poem, "The Landscape." Repton lived into the first decades of the nineteenth century, and his work anticipates the Victorian period in both a positive and a negative sense. He was eminently practical in his approach to landscape gardening and repeatedly stressed the importance of "utility." He was also moving toward a synthesis of disciplines. Fully aware that gardening skill alone was insufficient, he stressed that a landscape designer must also "possess a competent knowledge of *surveying, mechanics, hydraulics, agriculture, botany* and the general principles of *architecture*."[27]

In his own work, Repton moved progressively away from Brown's landscape ideals. The shift involved a change of emphasis from parks to gardens, from rusticity to comfort and convenience, from large-scale to small-scale effects, and from unified to compartmentalized spaces. In his last years, Repton was the master of the trellis, the bower, the enclosed garden of horticultural rarities, and the formal terrace, all trends of nineteenth-century landscape gardening that Olmsted later deplored in public parks, although he did not necessarily criticize their use in private gardens.[28]

Although from reading and traveling Olmsted was knowledgeable about stylistic trends in planned landscapes, his ideal was to create "natural" scenery—something of a contradiction in terms. Imitating "nature" had, of course, been the aim of all naturalistic landscaping since the eighteenth century. The problem is that nature was perceived differently by different theorists and practitioners. To Brown, nature was pastoral; to Price, it was rugged and unkempt. Olmsted showed particular sensitivity and subtlety in balancing the pastoral (Beautiful) and Picturesque ideals and in interpreting both in terms of the particular geological terrain and native plant materials of whatever site he was asked to treat.

We know little about the exact nature of the collaboration between Olmsted and Vaux on the design of Central Park, but it is clear that their backgrounds were complementary. As his partner, Vaux made up for Olmsted's most serious deficiency: inexperience in architectural design. With the exception of a few rustic stone bridges in the northern section, which were designed by Olmsted, the bridges and arches in Central Park (Figure 16) were designed by Vaux and are among its most charming features. He also must have brought coherence and discipline to the landscape design per se. He had, after all, been in partnership with Downing for two years and had spent much of the past five years completing Downing's unfinished works. Olmsted's background in agriculture and engineering were surely useful to Vaux, but it was undoubtedly because of his practical experience on the park site that Vaux asked him to collaborate. On the other hand, Olmsted cherished his role as superintendent of Central Park, quite independently of his part in its design, with a vehemence that Vaux could not comprehend. (His appointment had, of course, preceded their collaboration.) Later Olmsted went so far as to say that if participating in the design of Central Park had jeopardized his position as superintendent, he never would have agreed to do it.[29]

Such devotion to an arduous, unappreciated, and poorly paid job is a little hard to understand. It is worth quoting one or two sections from a long letter Olmsted wrote to Vaux a few years later, when a temporary misunderstanding had arisen between them. The position as superintendent suited him exactly, he wrote.

If a fairy had shaped it for me, it could nt have fitted me better. It was normal, ordinary and naturally outgrowing from my previous life and history . . . The advantages offered in the office of the Superintendence for spending a good deal of my life in the park, being with the people in it, watching over it and cherishing it in every way—living in it being a part of it . . . were valued by me at a valuation which you thought nonsensical childish and unworthy of me . . . that this was something deeper than a whim you know, for . . . it existed . . . years before it attached itself to the Central Park, as was shown by the fact that while others gravitated to pictures, architecture, Alps, libraries, high life and low life when travelling I had gravitated to parks— spent all my spare time in them, when living in London for instance.[30]

Olmsted then discussed his and Vaux's respective roles:

There are several properties in the park held or properly belonging to us. 1st the General design, in which our property is mutually equal and indivisible. 2d Detail of General design, from which can not be separated something of "superintendence" and in which also there is equality of property between us. 3d Architectural design & superintendence in which I have no appreciable property—which is wholly yours. 4th Organization & management of construction force in which you have very little property, though more than I have in the last. 5th Administration & management of the public introduction to and use of the park, in which you have very little property and which I hold to be my most valuable property in it. The relation of the last to the first is vague but intimate.[31]

This last statement, interesting as it is, does not clarify the two partners' collaboration on landscape *design*, for Olmsted says that he and Vaux have "a mutually equal and indivisible property" in both the general design and the details. However, it emphatically proves that Olmsted's concept of a park, its proper use, and, by implication, its design was much broader than Vaux's.

In May 1858 the Central Park commissioners changed Olmsted's title to architect in chief and

Figure 16
The Trefoil Arch, Central Park. Stereograph, circa 1875.

raised his salary to $2,500 a year. In his new position Olmsted continued his duties as superintendent and also assumed Viele's. The office of chief engineer was abolished, and although Viele was no longer formally connected with Central Park, he later sued the commissioners, claiming that they had never paid him for his plan and that it had been "copied" by Olmsted and Vaux.[32] As construction began on the park, Olmsted's already taxing duties increased; at times he was supervising as many as 4,000 men. In 1859 Olmsted also took on heavy family responsibilities when he married his brother's widow, Mary Perkins, and became stepfather to her three children.

By the end of that summer, Olmsted had become ill and was granted a leave of absence to study park design and management abroad. He spent the fall in England and on the Continent revisiting some parks he had seen before, such as Birkenhead, but viewing them this time as a professional. Perhaps the most important aspect of this trip was the time he spent in Paris, where he saw a city in the process of being reshaped. In 1854 Napoleon III and his prefect of the Seine, Georges

Haussmann, had embarked on a massive building program involving boulevards, public architecture, parks and squares, and new sewage and water systems. Little was completed in 1859, but Olmsted must have seen huge construction projects at almost every turn. In Paris he also met Jean Alphand, the designer of the Bois de Boulogne and the Bois de Vincennes.[33]

Although this was a working holiday, as most of his European trips were to be, Olmsted came home refreshed to resume work on Central Park and on new collaborations with Vaux. Of these the most important was a design, unfortunately never executed, for the layout of upper Manhattan north of 155th Street. He and Vaux advised a departure from the city grid, feeling that a suburban character would be more appropriate for the rough land. With this plan, Olmsted inaugurated a long series of imaginative and farsighted city and suburban designs. Whether the plan was for an entire town such as Riverside, Illinois, shown in Figure 17, or for the subdivision of a single estate, these community designs always had the same objectives. First, Olmsted urged a "comprehensive" approach: that is the plan should always be seen as part of a larger whole, taking into consideration the entire surrounding city, town, or metropolitan district and its probable future growth. Second, he always advised laying out streets in accordance with natural topography. Last, Olmsted was intensely concerned with providing a comfortable environment for residents, recommending that lots be of ample size and have adequate setback and that heavy through traffic be excluded. These last two considerations generally led, as in the unexecuted Manhattan plan, to a curvilinear street pattern, with direct cross streets only on the outskirts of the district.[34]

The Civil War interrupted Olmsted's career in landscape design. In 1861 he was appointed executive secretary of the United States Sanitary Commission, the direct forerunner of the American Red Cross, by the unanimous decision of the commissioners, and for the next two years, he directed hospital transports and coordinated the activities of great numbers of people.[35] To fulfill the duties of his appointment, he took a leave of absence from Central Park, and Vaux and Ignaz Pilat, an Austrian landscape gardener, carried on in his stead.

Political pressure, a recurring problem in the history of Central Park, forced Olmsted and Vaux to resign their positions in the spring of 1863.

Increasingly, Olmsted found that his authority was being undermined as executive head of the Sanitary Commission, and he was still in debt from the failure of Dix, Edwards and Company. When he heard about a lucrative opening as resident manager of the Mariposa Mining Company in the Sierra Nevada foothills, he took the job, traveling to California (by boat for most of the route and by train across the Isthmus of Panama) in the fall of 1863, his family following several months later. But there turned out to be unforeseen financial problems with the Mariposa estate, and two years after he took charge, the company went under, through no fault of his. Fortunately, he had taken on a few independent landscaping jobs: Mountain View Cemetery in Oakland and a preliminary plan for the College of California.[36]

The most permanent result of Olmsted's California sojourn was the success of his struggle to have the Yosemite Valley and the adjoining Mariposa Big Tree Grove set aside as public reservations. Appointed to the eight-man board of the Yosemite Commission by the governor of California, he also wrote a preliminary report on Yosemite, but the report was suppressed. The state of California muddled its management of Yosemite so badly that in 1906 it was returned to the federal government. Still, the land was secured and the precedent set for later, more effectively organized conservation campaigns, such as that for Niagara Falls in 1887, in which Olmsted also played an important role.[37]

Meanwhile, the Central Park commissioners had offered Olmsted and Vaux reappointment as landscape architects of Central Park. Vaux had been asked to design a large park for Brooklyn, which was then a separate city, and had already done a sketch plan, but he did not want to undertake the project by himself. Despite the success of Central Park and his prospects for independent work in California, Olmsted had serious doubts about both his health and his abilities, and his former partner had to woo him back to the new profession over a period of several months. As Vaux looked back on their collaboration on Central Park: "If . . . you had been disheartened, there very likely might have

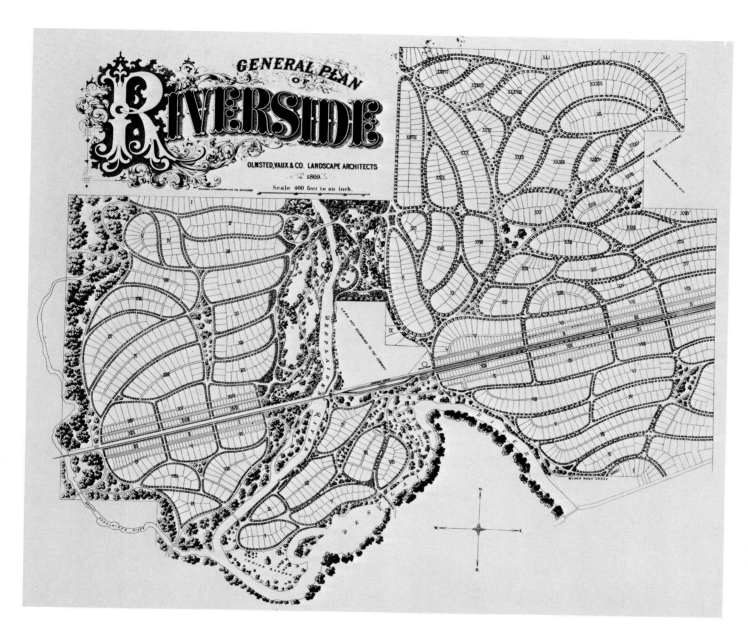

Figure 17
Plan for Riverside, Illinois,
by Olmsted and Vaux,
1869.

been no park to chatter about today for I alone was wholly incompetent to take it up . . . I feel it no less . . . now, and enter on Brooklyn alone with hesitation and distrust."[38] He urged Olmsted: "We may have some fun together yet. I wish you could have seen your destiny in our art. God meant you should I really believe at times, although he may have something different for you to do yet he cannot have anything nobler in store for you."[39]

Olmsted answered with a curiously ambivalent appraisal of his own abilities:

I am sorry to say that I do not feel myself capable of being a landscape gardener—properly speaking—but I have a better and more cultivated taste in that department of art than any other, very much—having none in any other—and if I had the necessary quality of memory, or if my memory had been educated in botany and gardening when I was young, I might have been. But I can do anything with proper assistants, or money enough—anything that any man can do. I can combine means to ends better than most, and I love beautiful landscapes and rural recreations and people in rural recreations—better than any body else I know. But I dont feel strong on the art side. I dont feel myself an artist, I feel rather as if it was sacrilegious in me to post myself in the portals of art.[40]

Fortunately, Vaux was able to coax Olmsted back to New York to codesign Prospect Park and resume supervision of Central Park. Olmsted and

Vaux persuaded the Prospect Park Board to make a major change in the park's boundaries, and combined with the site's excellent soil, the changes made their job much easier than it had been in Central Park. Prospect Park (Figure 18) is customarily placed, along with Central and Franklin parks, in the "great triad of Olmsted's works," and many consider it his best.[41] While Central Park was a triumph of ingenuity over difficult design conditions and an almost miraculous achievement as the prototypical "country park," Prospect Park is a more satisfying aesthetic whole. Freed from the constricting demands of a narrow rectangular site, the designers

Figure 18
Design for Prospect Park, Brooklyn, by Olmsted and Vaux, 1866–1867.

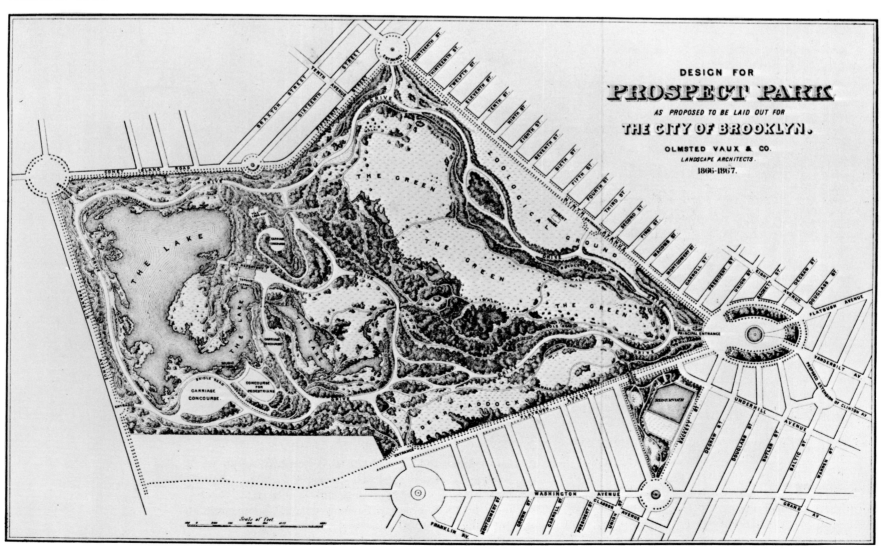

Figure 19
The Long Meadow, Pros-
pect Park (marked "The
Green" on the 1866–1867
plan).

were able to employ broad curving spaces (Figure 19) with constantly varying sight lines. Although it is only about half the size of Central Park, Prospect Park conveys more of a sense of spaciousness. Olmsted and Vaux kept footpaths, bridle paths, and carriageways separate, as they had in Central Park, even though it was not necessary to provide transverse roads for ordinary city traffic. Vaux again designed numerous bridges, arches, and other park structures (Figure 20). Finally, the rich soil at the Brooklyn site produced large vigorous trees and a general luxuriance of vegetation that had not been possible in the thin, rocky covering of Central Park.

Almost from the beginning, Olmsted and Vaux conceived of Prospect Park as the central focus of a system of parks for Brooklyn. As early as 1868, they coined the term "parkway" in a report urging the Brooklyn commissioners to connect Prospect Park to the ocean by one scenic drive and to Central Park by another over the East River. They also designed three smaller parks for Brooklyn: the Parade Ground (1867), Fort Greene Park (1867), and Tompkins Park (1871). In 1873 the partners were commissioned to design Morningside Park in Manhattan, although the plan was shelved for fourteen years, after which they made substantial changes; and in 1875 Olmsted prepared a plan for Riverside Drive and Park.[42]

Other important joint commissions by Olmsted and Vaux include a campus plan for Berkeley, Cali-

Figure 20
The Nethermead Arches,
Prospect Park.

fornia (1866–1867); the community design for Riverside, Illinois, previously mentioned (1868–1869); and a plan for South Park, Chicago (1871). In 1872 Olmsted and Vaux dissolved their partnership "for reasons of mutual convenience," although they did occasionally collaborate again on individual projects, such as the revised plan for Morningside Park (1887).[43]

Shortly after the partnership was terminated,

Olmsted bought a row house at 209 West Forty-Sixth Street and converted its large first-floor dining room into an office. He continued to do business from this address until 1883, when he moved to Brookline permanently. Even without Vaux, and in spite of the depression that began in 1873, Olmsted received many new commissions. He also continued his responsibility for the New York and Brooklyn parks. In 1874 Olmsted made a formal working arrangement, although not a partnership, with Jacob Weidenmann, a Swiss architect who, like Vaux, had turned to landscape design after his arrival in the United States. Whether this "arrangement" involved true collaboration on designs, as it had with Vaux, or whether both men merely drew on the same pool of assistants and draftsmen is not entirely clear.[44]

Olmsted's health began to fail again in 1877, and he was also under increasing harassment from the politicians who controlled the New York Park Department. At the end of the year he asked for and received a leave of absence from his duties at Central Park for the first three months of 1878 to visit Europe and regain his strength. Before he left, however, the park commissioners decided that New York no longer needed a landscape architect (Central Park, in their eyes, being complete and in no further need of creative oversight) and abolished Olmsted's position. The dismissal and all that led up to it left wounds from which Olmsted never fully recovered.[45] Increasingly, his working life became centered on Boston rather than New York, but the story of the Olmsted firm in the second half of its founder's career belongs to a later chapter.

III

The Boston Park Movement

———◆———

BOSTON responded with surprising promptness to the example set by Central Park. Unfortunately, there was little scope for large public grounds within the municipal boundaries as they existed in the late 1850s, for with the exception of East Boston and South Boston (both too remote for "central" parks), the city was still confined to its original peninsula. However, the documents of the period clearly indicate that the improvements made to the Public Garden in 1859–1860 were intended as Boston's answer to Central Park.

After the Proprietors of the Public Garden lost their financial backing in 1847, the ground was used only sporadically for horticultural purposes, and its future remained uncertain for many years. Downing's plan was apparently never executed, and

the Bachmann lithograph of 1850 (Figure 7) and photographs taken slightly later in the decade show a simple landscape treatment. More grandiose schemes were proposed frequently in the press.[1] The land was finally secured forever for park purposes in 1859, and a Special Committee appointed by the Boston City Council was directed to report on a plan for improving it. Following the example of New York, the committee held an anonymous competition. In their report they described the work in progress on Central Park, referring also to Birkenhead and other European parks, and added:

While other cities are expending fabulous amounts in the improvements of parks, squares, gardens, and promenades, what should we do? To be behind in these matters would not only be discreditable to our city, but positively injurious to our commercial prosperity, and in direct opposition to the wishes of a vast majority of the citizens . . . The area of our city is too small to allow the laying out of large tracts of land for Public Parks, and it behooves us to improve the small portions that are left to us for such purposes.[2]

"Arlington," the plan selected by the committee and approved by the City Council, was by a Boston architect, George F. Meacham.[3] His design (Figure 21) combined formal and picturesque elements. A strong central axis from Charles Street to Arlington Street focused on Commonwealth Avenue, then under construction. There were also geometrical flower beds, but the outlines of both the pond and the pathway system were highly irregular. Space was also set aside for a city hall, a playground, and a greenhouse. The original Meacham plan displays a certain *horror vacui;* is is so overloaded with "features" that there is minimal space for trees, shrubs, and grass.

The city engineer, James Slade, who had apparently made an earlier plan himself, modified Meacham's plan, adding contours so that the land

Figure 21
Plan for the Boston Public Garden by George F. Meacham, 1859.

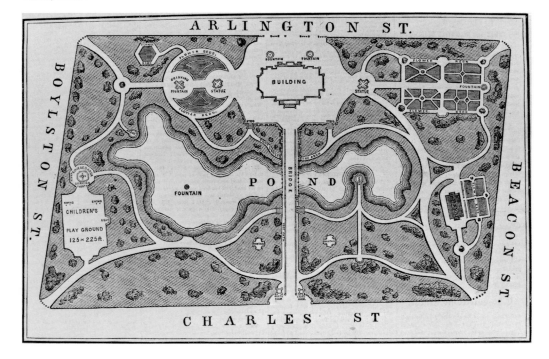

would not appear obviously man-made.[4] He also subdued the formal elements of Meacham's plan somewhat, eliminating most of the geometrical flower beds, although the paths that were to have outlined them remained. (Later on, formal beds were introduced along the central axis and remain to this day.) A greenhouse was built on Charles Street. The space allocated to a city hall ("Building" on the plan) was instead devoted to an equestrian statue of George Washington by Thomas Ball. Meacham's pond and his pathway system were retained and are still largely as he planned them. Construction proceeded rapidly, and by the early 1860s, the Public Garden was complete (Figure 22).

The Public Garden is best considered as a preamble to the much more ambitious plans for parks and park systems that were proposed for Boston in the late 1860s. Although the Civil War interrupted the impetus of the movement throughout the country, public park efforts resumed with vigor in 1865.[5] As we have seen, Brooklyn immediately proceeded with Prospect Park, and both Philadelphia and Baltimore set aside large parcels of land for ultimate use as parks. After the success of Central Park, Olmsted was much in demand, not only to provide plans but to lecture, contribute articles, and support park movements in various cities.[6] In Boston, however, a combination of political and economic circumstances kept the park movement from yielding immediate results.

In October 1869 a group of citizens presented to the City Council a petition for a public park, signed by approximately forty individuals and corporations, including Marshall P. Wilder, a prominent horticulturist, and Jordan Marsh and Company. Responding to this petition, the Common Council established a Joint Special Committee, consisting of the president and four members of the Common Council and an unspecified number of aldermen, to report on what action the city government should take. This committee held two public hearings in November 1869 and, as a result of the testimony at these two hearings, passed an order requesting Mayor Nathaniel B. Shurtleff to petition the Massachusetts General Court to pass an act authorizing the city of Boston to purchase land for one large park or several small parks.[7]

In the month before the hearings, the Boston

Figure 22
View of the Public Garden
from Arlington Street, by
Edwin Whitefield, 1866.

papers were full of editorials and letters on the subject of parks. An unsigned editorial in the *Boston Advertiser* printed a few days before the first hearing was referred to several times in the testimony. The editorial quoted a section on "What Boston May Do" from *The Public Grounds of Chicago* by the landscape designer H. W. S. Cleveland.[8] Cleveland had stated that Boston did not need a central park but should instead have a system of improvements over the surrounding country, making use of natural features and existing attractive homes and farms. Road improvements and drainage, Cleveland felt, were of the first importance. He advised building parks outside of Boston, in Roxbury perhaps, although the site he recommended most strongly was the Middlesex Fells area in Malden, Medford, and Stoneham. In some respects, Cleveland's pro-

posal contained the germ of the metropolitan park system concept, although he appeared to feel that the desired results could be accomplished with a minimum of public ownership of land. One part of Cleveland's article, quoted out of context, caused a good deal of controversy: Cleveland imagined a visitor to Boston saying "What do you Bostonians want of a park, with such wealth of natural beauty all around you, and almost every foot of it so tastefully improved by private hands?"[9]

The testimony at the two hearings, led by Wilder, was recorded verbatim and also reported in the press. With one exception, the speakers strongly supported the establishment of parks, although the sites and types of parks suggested varied widely. Although a few of those offering testimony felt that only small "breathing spaces" within the city were needed, some advocated parks in Cambridge, Quincy, and Medford. Most of the speakers seemed well aware that the communities around Boston would not remain rural much longer and that steps should be taken quickly to secure open land for the public before the population grew much more.[10]

George B. Emerson, an authority on trees, favored building two small, accessible parks, but he concurred with Cleveland's belief that the roads within a fifteen-mile radius of Boston should be improved and ornamented with a variety of trees. In general, the testimony split between those who favored small parks close to the center of the city so that working people might walk to them, and those who believed that improved means of transportation, such as the steam railroad, could inexpensively take people much farther out into the country for recreation. In the latter category, the most impressive testimony was that of Elizur Wright, who presented the first of his many arguments for preserving the Middlesex Fells.[11] Many people favored filling and improving the Back Bay full basin and building a park on Parker Hill.

Some advocates did not appear before the committee in person. Uriel H. Crocker, a conveyance lawyer, wrote a letter, first to the *Boston Advertiser* and then to the Joint Special Committee, describing a system of parks and accompanied by a plan (Figure 23).[12] Crocker's plan included embankments on both the Cambridge and Boston sides of the Charles River, but its main feature was a continuous wind-ing parkway leading from the Charles River to Chestnut Hill Reservoir. The greater part of the land lay in Brighton, as yet unannexed, with portions in Boston, Brookline, and Cambridge. Rather than imitating Central Park by providing a site where "a drive of considerable length might be made to wind so ingeniously that those who passed over it should not be made unpleasantly aware of the fact that they were riding round and round within narrow and confined limits," Crocker proposed an extended linear park in which people could ride or drive directly into the open country.[13] The advantages of his plan, Crocker felt, were that it made use of three natural features, the Charles River, Corey Hill in Brookline, and the Chestnut Hill Reservoir in Brighton, and that it was a more truly central plan than most of those suggested, being accessible by foot as well as by carriage and horse from a number of different points.

Although Crocker's plan was never executed *in toto*, portions of it were realized in some of the projects of the eighties and nineties. It was received quite well in the press and elsewhere, although this was probably the plan that Elizur Wright, whose vision was of large metropolitan reservations rather than an urban park system, described as a "straggling concatenation of little parklets leading from the Back Bay out to the Chestnut Hill reservoir."[14]

At the end of 1869 and the beginning of 1870, Olmsted received a number of letters about the growing park movement in Boston, most asking him to participate in various ways. James T. Fields and Edward Everett Hale asked him to contribute articles for the *Atlantic Monthly* and the *New Examiner;* Crocker sent Olmsted a copy of his plan and offered to drive him over the site; Charles G. Loring, a connoisseur of Egyptian art, who was later to become director of the Museum of Fine Arts, wrote to him in favor of the Crocker plan; Robert Morris Copeland, a landscape gardener and former partner of H. W. S. Cleveland, sent him an editorial he had written for the *Boston Advertiser* and asked Olmsted to comment on the subject in the New York press; and James Haughton asked Olmsted to testify in favor of public parks for Boston before the House Judiciary Committee of the Massachusetts Legislature, where the bill filed by Mayor Shurtleff was under review.[15]

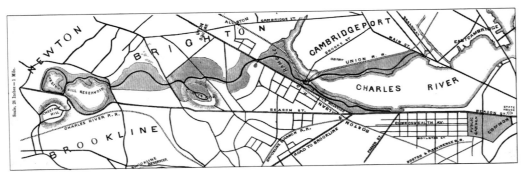

Figure 23
Metropolitan park system proposed by Uriel H. Crocker, 1869.

Olmsted's replies to this influx of correspondence about Boston parks have been lost. However, his attitude can be deduced from his actions or, rather, his lack of action. He was clearly reluctant to take sides, or to give the slightest appearance of doing so, at this early and sensitive stage of the park movement. He did not write articles for the *Atlantic Monthly* and the *New Examiner,* and he did not testify before the House Judiciary Committee. He did, however, agree to give a lecture on public parks at the Lowell Institute under the auspices of the American Social Science Association. Those active in the park movement appear to have considered Olmsted's lecture a substitute for his appearance before the Judiciary Committee. The bill was pending at the time of the lecture (February 25, 1870), and members of the General Court were issued special invitations.[16]

The newspaper accounts show that the lecture, "Public Parks and the Enlargement of Towns," was presented to a large and enthusiastic audience.[17] Nevertheless, the proponents of individual park schemes must have been somewhat disappointed, for the lecture was general, with few references to Boston and none at all to specific projects or sites. Instead, Olmsted presented a persuasive and practical argument for the establishment of parks. In his view, parks had a beneficial effect on the health, disposition, and morals of city inhabitants, particularly the poor and sickly. Central Park, for example, provided not only fresh air and healthy exercise but brought together people of all classes in a friendly and noncompetitive way. In one of his few references to Boston, Olmsted described its inevitable rapid growth: "It is practically certain that the Boston of today is the mere nucleus of the Boston that is to be. It is practically certain that it is to extend over many miles of country now thoroughly rural in character."[18]

It is impossible to say whether the legislators were influenced by Olmsted's lecture, but the Park Act of 1870 was passed on May 27, subject to acceptance by two-thirds of the legal voters of Boston. The act, drafted by Uriel Crocker, would have created a metropolitan rather than a municipal commission, consisting of the mayor of Boston, four commissioners appointed by the governor, and four by the Boston City Council, empowered to take

lands and lay out parks near the city as well as within its limits.[19]

On the eve of the election, opponents of the legislation distributed a handbill claiming that it would authorize the establishment of parks in the unannexed suburbs at the expense of Boston taxpayers. This was not strictly true, for the act provided that a special commission appointed periodically by the Supreme Judicial Court would determine the amount to be refunded to Boston by the other cities and towns; but in all fairness, the bill was confusingly worded. In spite of the last-minute sabotage, the required two-thirds vote was very nearly reached (9,233 to 5,916). Of Boston's sixteen wards at the time, only three (East Boston, Dorchester, and part of South Boston) rejected the bill. The newspapers attributed its failure to the Dorchester voters, maintaining that a special effort had been made to convince them that parks would be laid out elsewhere at their expense. Nevertheless, in December 1870, a new petition was made to the City Council, and the entire process was begun again. A special commission was appointed to redraft the bill, but this bill came to an impasse in the City Council and never reached the legislature. No further efforts were made to initiate park legislation until the end of 1873.[20]

But the subject of parks was not forgotten. In an editorial in the *Boston Advertiser* of December 2, 1869, Robert Morris Copeland had outlined a municipal and metropolitan park system of awesome proportions.[21] Within the city proper, he advocated taking one of two sites, the first including the Back Bay basin and Parker Hill, and the second, Fort Hill and the Stony Brook valley in Roxbury. It was the metropolitan features of his plan, however, that were most striking. (Unfortunately, the plan itself was apparently never drawn; so far as is known, it exists only in descriptive form.) He proposed several large parks extending from Squantum on the south to Newton Corner on the west and Medford on the north and including many sites, such as Spot Pond and the Waverley Oaks, that were later incorporated into the metropolitan park system of the 1890s. Copeland advised linking the parks by a "boulevard" or circumferential parkway one hundred feet wide. On the east the boulevard was to continue to Chelsea (now Revere) Beach, then turn south to Point Shirley in Winthrop. From there, bridges and ferries could complete the circle to the islands of Boston Harbor and back to Squantum. Copeland urged that a metropolitan park commission be empowered to take the lands needed for public use—the boulevards and parks—as well as some adjacent lands that could be resold for development. The affected communities would bear the cost of land acquisition, while Boston would pay the cost of construction.

In 1872 Copeland published a book entitled *The Most Beautiful City in America: Essay and Plan for the Improvement of the City of Boston.*[22] Unlike his suggestions of 1869, the essay and plan were limited to Boston's municipal boundaries at the time. (Perhaps the failure of the 1870 park bill had con-

vinced him that Boston was not ready for a metropolitan plan.) Copeland advised meeting the future needs of the city for more and wider streets, increased commercial space, and ample grounds through a comprehensive "city plan." The first half of the essay dealt with Boston's economic requirements; the second half described the city's topographical features in some detail and gave the reasons for the choice of park sites.

The plan (Figure 24) includes a few of the features Copeland had recommended in 1869. He felt that because of Boston's varied topography, many small parks were more desirable than one large park of several hundred acres. Even so, Copeland's 1872 plan includes the large Back Bay–Parker Hill park mentioned in 1869, which would certainly have totaled close to 300 acres. Fort Hill in Roxbury was also on the 1872 plan, as was Williams Park near the West Roxbury border and the Stony Brook Valley. Most of the other sites were in Dorchester and were chosen to preserve attractive topographical features. All the parks, large and small, were to be linked by a network of widened streets. An improved sewage system was a vital part of Copeland's plan, especially for the Back Bay, which he intended to dam and turn into a freshwater lake, and Stony Brook.

If his essay were not available to explain them, portions of Copeland's plan would be puzzling, for since his time Boston has grown in ways other than he anticipated. He was convinced that all level ground and all river valleys would be needed for industry and that shipping would monopolize the waterfront. This explains why he planned only three waterfront parks and why East Boston, which is an island, was allotted only a handful of tiny interior squares. Copeland anticipated that residential development would have to be clustered on hillsides and that the city's existing residential districts would be taken over by commerce. This presumably explains the two wedge-shaped parks in the South End, which Copeland expected would become a business center, and the obliteration of the north side of Beacon Street for a broad avenue. Through hindsight we can see the defects of Copeland's plan, but it had many excellent features, and parts of the city, notably Parker Hill and Dorchester, would have benefited if it had been executed.

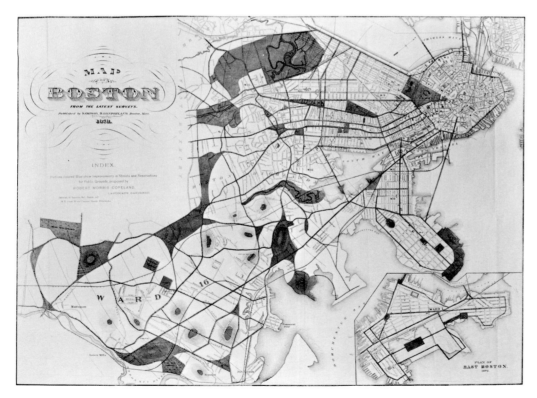

Figure 24
Map of Boston, showing improvements in streets and reservations for public grounds proposed by Robert Morris Copeland, 1872.

When Charlestown, Brighton, and West Roxbury voted for annexation in October 1873, two editorials appeared in the *Boston Advertiser,* which, though unsigned, must have been written by Copeland.[23] In the first, called "The Suburbs of Boston," part of which was quoted at the end of Chapter I, he vividly described the adverse changes that had overtaken Roxbury and Dorchester in the few years since annexation and urged that the natural beauty of the newly annexed towns be protected. The second editorial offered a remedy in the form of a system of parks

in different parts of the future or present city, and to be connected with a broad and well-made avenue 100 to 200 feet wide, which should, like the circumference of the circle, give boundary and form to the whole city, and be so connected by radial lines that from all parts to all parts there would be direct and easy avenues of communication, and the main avenue or boulevard would thread as it were all the parks and public grounds and bring them into a common system, and give a beautiful and convenient drive for the citizens in the different parts of the environs.[24]

This is the same plan Copeland had outlined in 1869, although here he does not specify exact locations.

The annexations also stimulated an abortive attempt late in 1873 to reintroduce the park question into the City Council. Early in 1874 Mayor Samuel Cobb took office, and in his inaugural address he urged the prompt establishment of public parks. Shortly afterward a special commission was set up, consisting of the mayor, two aldermen, three members of the Common Council, and three citizens at large, to study the matter.

The opinions expressed at the commission's hearings, held in June 1874, were not markedly different from those of the 1869 hearings, and some of the participants were the same.[25] There was little discussion of parks outside the city limits, but by now these limits had been considerably expanded. Uriel Crocker presented a variant of his earlier plan with the addition of a link from Chestnut Hill reservoir across Bussey Farm (now the Arnold Arboretum) in West Roxbury to the thickly settled part of Roxbury. Since most of Crocker's plan lay in Brighton, his park system was no longer as metro-

politan in scope as it had been in 1869, although it probably still included an embankment on the Cambridge side of the Charles, and his parkway would have had to cross Brookline to get from Chestnut Hill reservoir to West Roxbury. Most of the people testifying were in favor of a "water park" on either the Back Bay or the Charles River, and a petition of 1,500 signatures was presented for such a park on the Back Bay.[26]

The most imaginative and ambitious proposal to emerge from the 1874 hearings was that of Ernest W. Bowditch, a young engineer who had been informally associated with Robert Morris Copeland from about 1871 until Copeland's death in March 1874.[27] Bowditch testified twice and then published his plan, with an accompanying letter, in the *Boston Advertiser.*[28] As presented then and in expanded form the following year, his plan had much in common with Copeland's metropolitan park system. The sites in the 1874 version lay to the west and south of Boston within the six-mile circle of the State House. Bowditch interpreted Copeland's "boulevard" as an extension of Commonwealth Avenue from the Back Bay to the intersection of Tremont Street (now Huntington Avenue) with the Muddy River. From there the avenue would continue to Ward's and Jamaica ponds, where it would divide into two parts, one running from the west side of Jamaica Pond to Chestnut Hill reservoir and ultimately to Fresh Pond in Cambridge, and the other going past the Bussey Farm to a large park on the West Roxbury/Dorchester border, and to a smaller park on the Dorchester bank of the Neponset River. A portion of the Back Bay near the South End was to be turned into a water park of about a hundred acres.

Bowditch maintained that by including much land that was already publicly owned (such as several reservoirs and rural cemeteries), this system of five large parks connected by a parkway could be acquired at a reasonable cost. The purity of the metropolitan water supply would also be assured by keeping the land around the reservoirs open. With the exception of the Cambridge unit, which, like the small parks in South and East Boston, was to be constructed later, most of the lands included in Bowditch's 1874 plan lay within Boston's boundaries. However, it is impossible to have a continuous

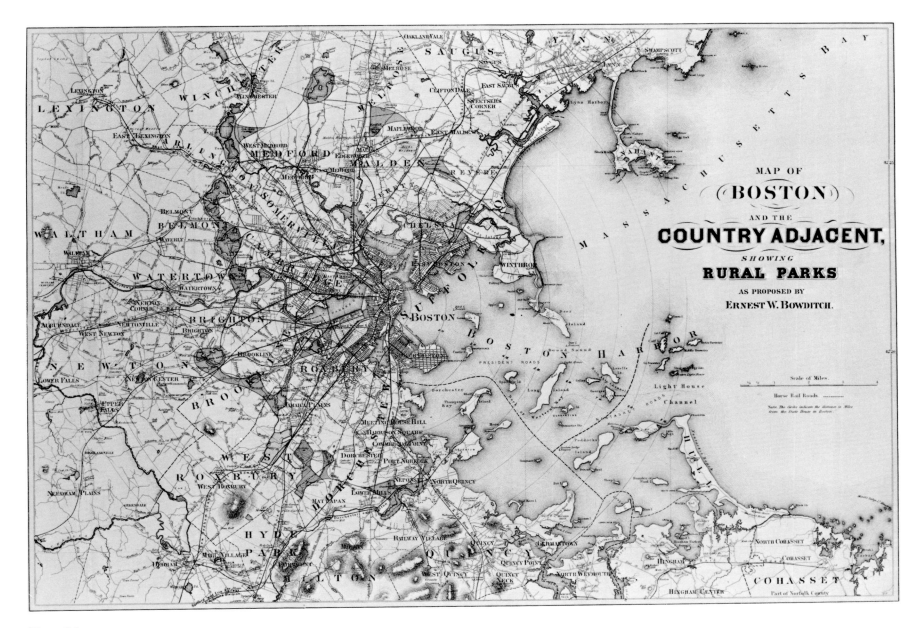

Figure 25
Map of metropolitan Boston, showing the rural parks proposed by Ernest W. Bowditch, 1875.

park system from Brighton to West Roxbury without passing through Brookline, and Bowditch's plan included, as Crocker's must also have done, a sizable piece of that town.

Early in 1875 Bowditch published a two-page pamphlet, "Rural Parks for Boston," and a plan.[29] As Figure 25 shows, the plan was an expansion of the park system he had proposed a few months earlier and was also derived from Copeland's proposal.

It shows a full circle of parks from Chelsea to Squantum, although the harbor islands are not included. The southern and western sectors are almost identical to the 1874 plan. To the north and northwest he added parks around Spy, Mystic, and Spot ponds, around Woodlawn Cemetery and Prospect Hill (now Waites Mount) in Malden, and at Chelsea Beach. As in 1874, one of his principal concerns was protecting the metropolitan water supply.

Bowditch proposed to include an area of 5,356 acres in his 1875 park system, about 60 percent of which was already publicly owned, and he recommended that the expense be divided proportionally between Boston and the towns that would be affected.

There is no question that Copeland should be given credit for the concept behind Bowditch's plan. It is possible, in fact, that Copeland had made a drawing, now lost, of his metropolitan park plan, which Bowditch used as the basis for his own. Bowditch was then only twenty-four and had been educated as an engineer, not as a landscape gardener or "planner." Nevertheless, he made significant changes in park sites, and his plan seems more compact and coherent than Copeland's. By using the upper valley of the Muddy River as a link between the Back Bay and Jamaica Pond, Bowditch also worked out the connections between the inner city parks more successfully; in this respect his plan anticipates Olmsted's. It is impossible, however, to make a just comparison between a visual plan and a verbal description, and the question of the precise contribution of each should probably be put aside until much more is known about both Copeland and Bowditch. The plan published in 1875 under Bowditch's name is a most impressive achievement and one that was not equaled—in metropolitan planning, at least—until 1893.

It is tempting to speculate on the sources of the Copeland/Bowditch plan, for several historical parallels come immediately to mind. It shows a striking resemblance, for example, to the planning of Paris, Vienna, and other originally walled European cities that were undergoing radical transformations, including the construction of grand boulevards on the site of former fortifications, during the same years that Boston was planning parks.[30] A more obscure source but one closer to home was a small book on Boston published in 1844 by the self-styled "city builder," Robert Fleming Gourlay.[31] Copeland obviously knew Cleveland's book, *The Public Grounds of Chicago*, in which he proposed surrounding that city with a boulevard three hundred feet wide and fourteen miles long.[32] Geology, however, seems by far the most likely reason for Copeland's circumferential scheme for, as has often been noted, the most scenic sites in the vicinity of

Boston follow a horseshoe-shaped fault line around the city.[33] In all probability, Copeland was inspired less by European plans based on medieval bulwarks than by the far more ancient conformation of the Boston basin.

Still another metropolitan plan presented to the city in the 1870s was one promoted by Charles Davenport, a Cambridge manufacturer; this project exploited the banks of the Charles River in a manner clearly reminiscent of the Alster Basin in Hamburg. Davenport pushed his scheme for elaborate, planted embankments over a period of many years, altering it slightly according to changing circumstances. One version (Figure 26) seems to date from about 1875, for he has incorporated certain elements of Crocker's plan and also, almost as an afterthought, some of Bowditch's sites (on inset, not shown). He ignored the most important feature of the Copeland/Bowditch plan, however, by leaving out the connecting boulevards.[34]

The members of the 1874 commission apparently listened to Bowditch and Crocker as well as to the far more numerous advocates of "water parks," for the commission's report recommended not only that a park should be laid out "in some part of the territory between Arlington Street and Parker's Hill" but that "a series of parks of moderate size, connected by proper roads, be laid out between the third and fourth mile circles; and that the land for a second series of larger size, beyond the first, be secured at once; these outer parks need not be improved until the growth of the city makes it necessary."[35] The sanitary benefits of parks were also stressed in the report, as they had been in the testimony of Bowditch and many others.

As a result of the commission's report, an order was presented to the City Council early in 1875 requesting that the mayor again petition the legislature to pass a park bill. Surprisingly, there was considerable opposition to the order, and it was approved only after long debate in both branches of the City Council. The order was saved largely through the vigorous support of George A. Shaw, a member of the Common Council, and Hugh O'Brien, then an alderman, who was to become mayor in the late eighties. The original order presented to the City Council had asked for a bill authorizing the taking of lands for parks only

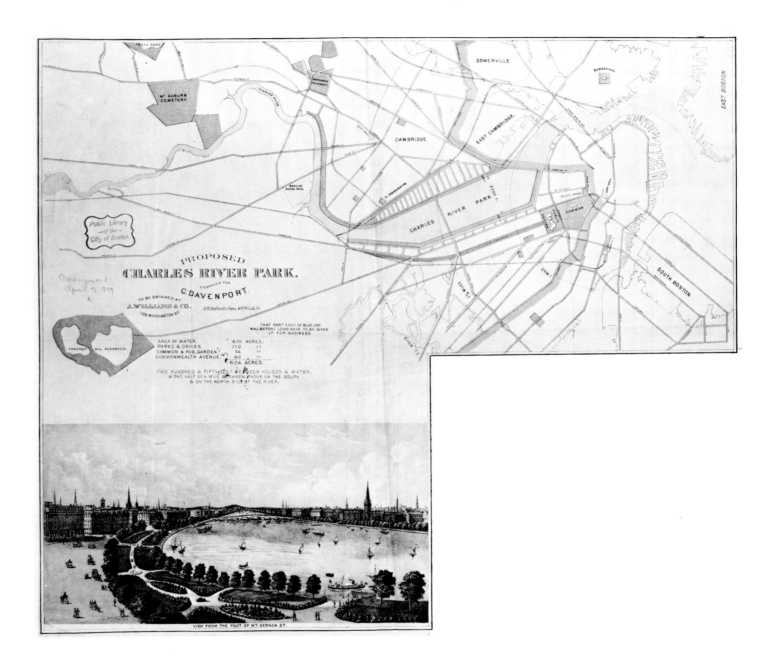

Figure 26
Charles River Park proposed by C. Davenport circa 1875, one of his many schemes for the Charles River basin.

within the city limits. When it was finally approved, the order had been extensively amended. Through the efforts of Uriel Crocker, who had been a member of the Common Council since 1873, the amended order included a provision that enabled adjoining cities and towns to take lands for parks.[36]

The Park Act, which was passed in May 1875, followed the amended order very closely. It required the approval of a simple majority rather than a two-thirds plurality of the legal voters of Boston, and this approval was obtained at a special election held June 9, 1875.[37] Unlike the unsuccessful act of 1870, it established a municipal rather than a metropolitan commission, consisting of three commissioners, appointed by the mayor of Boston and approved by the City Council, who were empowered to take lands only within the city limits. The six-year struggle to create a truly metropolitan park commission had therefore failed and would not be revived until the early nineties. The new law did enable the cities and towns adjoining Boston to elect park commissioners and lay out parks, with the approval of a majority of the legal voters. However, Brookline proved to be the only town to take advantage of this provision, although it would have allowed parks in much of the metropolitan area. All of Bowditch's park system plan, for example, could have been carried out, with the exception of the parks in Medford and Malden.

The financing of the proposed park system was outlined far more precisely than it had been in the earlier bill. All appropriations for acquisition and improvement of land in Boston had to be approved by a two-thirds vote of both branches of the City Council, which effectively tied the hands of the park commissioners on several occasions, as will be seen later.

In July 1875, Mayor Cobb appointed three prominent businessmen, Charles H. Dalton, William Gray, Jr., and T. Jefferson Coolidge, as park commissioners. Coolidge resigned at the end of 1876, but Dalton and Gray remained on the commission until 1885, when an entirely new board was appointed by Mayor O'Brien. Dalton proved to be the leading figure during the Park Commission's first decade and was chairman for most of this period. He came from a family of distinguished physicians, and during the Civil War he had been an agent of the Commonwealth at Washington and an active worker in the United States Sanitary Commission. When the war was over, he turned his attention to Massachusetts General Hospital, where he was a member of the committee that chose the site for McLean Hospital in Belmont, Massachusetts, and later the chairman of McLean's building committee. At the time of his appointment to the Park Commission, Dalton was treasurer of the Manchester Print Works. He was later appointed a member of Boston's first Subway Commission in 1894.[38]

In addition to his duties as treasurer of the Atlantic Cotton Mills, Gray was a prominent member of the Massachusetts Horticultural Society, becoming its president in 1878. He had also been one of the three citizens at large on the 1874 park commis-

sion.[39] Coolidge was treasurer of the Lawrence and Amoskeag Manufacturing Companies. In 1889 he was appointed minister to France by President Harrison and remained in that position until Cleveland was reelected in 1893.[40]

The park commissioners' first action was to insert a notice in the Boston papers asking that "civil and landscape engineers" and other citizens with special information on lands suitable for public parks present their views at a public hearing. After the first large hearing, the commissioners followed the practice of holding daily open office hours. Throughout the fall and winter of 1875–1876 at least eighty people visited the office, and many submitted plans or read prepared papers. A few, such as Bowditch, who presented a variant of his earlier plan, were professional engineers or landscape gardeners, but the majority appeared to be simply private citizens with ideas for parks. Representatives of civic groups in East and South Boston and elsewhere petitioned for parks in their particular localities, and owners of land offered to sell it to the city. As might be expected, in the course of six months of hearings, almost every location within the city that was remotely suitable for a park was suggested, from the Charles to the Neponset, as well as many new sites in West Roxbury.[41]

The commissioners appear to have studied all these suggestions very carefully and to have personally examined all the sites. They sought Olmsted's advice, apparently in a rather casual manner, on at least two occasions during this period. Dalton and Olmsted had been acquainted since at least 1872, for Olmsted had prepared plans first for the site and then for the grounds of McLean Hospital. But in spite of Olmsted's national reputation and his professional relationship with Dalton concerning McLean, the Boston Park Commission did not officially retain him at this time in even an advisory capacity.[42]

Late in October 1875 Olmsted drove over the proposed Boston park sites with the commissioners, but there is no record either of the exact sites visited or of Olmsted's response. In any case, the commissioners' plans must still have been very tentative. By April 1876, however, when they were about to make their final decisions, they again asked Olmsted to drive over the ground. Olmsted's response to the proposed sites is recorded in a letter that exists only in the form of a very rough draft. From a few remarks at the beginning of this draft, it is clear that Olmsted felt handicapped and embarrassed because the commission had not given him a definite professional responsibility, and he had not been able to master the whole situation. Most of the letter is devoted to a discussion of four sites, two of which he recommended without reservation: the Charles River Embankment and Jamaica Pond. Olmsted was also enthusiastic about the land to be used for the "main" park (West Roxbury, now Franklin, Park), although he advised some adjustments in boundaries. He also suggested changes in the boundaries of the Back Bay and Parker Hill parks, which appear to have been projected then as a single park. (Interestingly enough, he made no reference to the engineering problems posed by the Back Bay, problems that would become one of his main concerns a few years later.) Olmsted also criticized the narrowness and inconvenience of the approaches to the parks and advised "greater liberality in the new parkways and bolder and more sweeping improvements of existing streets leading toward the park than you seem to contemplate."[43]

Only a few weeks after consulting with Olmsted, the park commissioners published their first comprehensive report, written by Dalton. One of the most important documents ever produced by the commission, the report is far more than an outline of recommended sites. The commissioners projected a long-range scheme for a connected park system, which they justified on many grounds, including population density, economics, and sanitation. They gave as their very first consideration in selecting park locations, "accessibility for all classes of citizens by walking, driving, riding, or by means of horse or steam cars."[44] Although the parkways were designed for pleasure traffic and provided only for the first three categories of transportation, all of the parks were easily reached by railroad or horse-drawn streetcars. (After the electrification of Boston's street railway system in the late 1880s, additional electrified lines were laid out on nonparkway routes to many parts of the system.)

The general plan included a series of inner-city parks, a series of "suburban" parks in the newly annexed areas, several connecting parkways, and

widenings and extensions of existing streets (Figure 27). The sites in the inner city were selected primarily because they were located near densely populated sections where, in most cases, parks would alleviate actual or potential sanitary nuisances. Four waterfront parks were included: at City Point, South Boston; West Wood Island, East Boston; Savin Hill, Dorchester; and on the Charles River from Leverett Street to the Cottage Farm Bridge. Parks were also planned on the South Bay and the Back Bay, the latter connected with another park on Parker Hill. Locations for the outer parks were at Jamaica Pond, in West Roxbury, and in Brighton adjacent to the Chestnut Hill Reservoir; these sites were selected because of their rural character and natural scenic beauty.

The parkways connected the Back Bay Park with Parker Hill, Parker Hill with Jamaica Pond, and Jamaica Pond with West Roxbury (Franklin) Park. A fourth, the Harrison Square Parkway, was to go from West Roxbury Park to Dorchester Lower Mills. The commissioners strongly advised that a parkway extend from the end of the Charles River Embankment at Cottage Farm Bridge to the park in Brighton, but they were unable to recommend a route, because it would have to run through Brookline. Similarly, although they also advised taking action as soon as possible to secure lands for a second series of suburban parks between the six- and eight-mile circles (the metropolitan plan again), they were unable to do this themselves, since it required the cooperation of the adjoining cities and towns.

Between 1878 and 1895 the plan of the Boston park system as a whole was gradually altered and elaborated until it showed only a general resemblance to the park commissioners' 1876 plan (see Figure 27). Some elements of that plan were kept; others were dropped. New parks were added, often because of pressure from local residents. Still other sites were suggested, considered for a while, and then rejected, generally on Olmsted's advice. The connections between the parks were worked out with particular care.

The South Boston, East Boston, Back Bay, West Roxbury, and Jamaica Pond parks were all constructed, although with some alterations in boundaries, as were most of the parkways and street im-

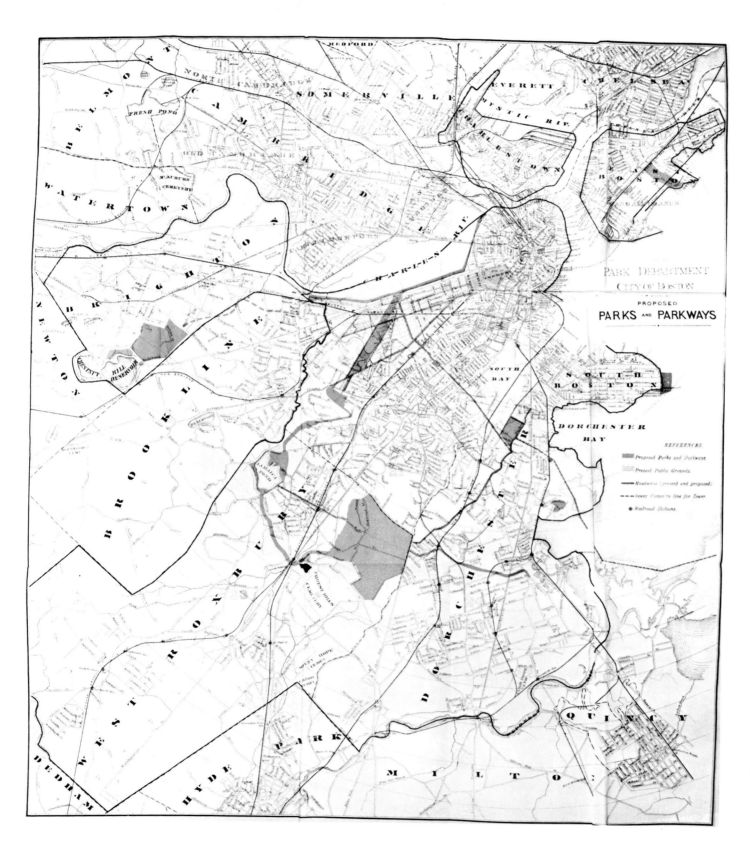

Figure 27
Parks and parkways pro-
posed by the Boston park
commissioners in 1876.

provements. A park was built on the Charles River between Leverett and Combridge streets, but the embankment was not extended to the Cottage Farm Bridge until after Olmsted's death. The Brighton park was not carried out, nor was the South Bay park. At Olmsted's suggestion, the Muddy River Improvement was substituted for the Parker Hill Park. Negotiations had already begun with Harvard to include the Arnold Arboretum in the park system, but those plans were still indefinite, so the site was not shown on the 1876 plan. Charlestown was so densely populated that the commissioners were unable to find a suitable park site there; later two sites were found for a small park and a playground.

The commissioners' report was widely read, and their recommendations were resoundingly endorsed at a public meeting held at Faneuil Hall in June 1876. (One speaker suggested that if the report were given to children to read, they would put aside their novels, "even those with yellow covers.")[45] The Joint Committee of the City Council on Common and Public Grounds, to which the report was referred, also gave it their unqualified approval.[46] Nevertheless, the report languished in the City Council for over a year.

The sticking point was the commissioners' request for an appropriation of almost $5 million for land, with the city raising the funds by issuing bonds, as provided in the Park Act. The appropriation was debated vigorously in both branches of the council. Like the country as a whole, the city had been in a depressed financial condition since the crash of 1873, and in Boston the situation was aggravated by the economic repercussions of the Great Fire of November 1872. Some councillors felt that this made a large park loan unwise, while others felt it imperative to take advantage of the low cost of land and labor and the low interest rates. Many expressed doubt that the assessed value of the land, $5 million, would come close to covering its actual cost. Furthermore, the City Council was considering another large loan for a new sewage system. The two projects appeared to be competitive, and the sewage system the more urgent. The chief supporters of the commissioners' scheme in this round of debates were Uriel Crocker of the Common Council and Hugh O'Brien of the Board of Aldermen. George Shaw, although still in favor

of parks, aligned himself with the more financially conservative members of the council. Olmsted was kept informed of the progress of the discussion by his friend and frequent collaborator, the architect Henry Hobson Richardson, and presumably also by Dalton. Early in 1877 the park commissioners, awaiting some sort of action by the City Council, closed their offices and discharged their clerk.[47]

In July of that year the City Council finally voted an appropriation of $450,000 to be used for the purchase of no less than one hundred acres of land for a park in the Back Bay. The appropriation was very meager for a park of this size, and many people felt that the council had deliberately made it insufficient, hoping to kill the whole park scheme. The commissioners, however, immediately reopened their offices, engaged a surveyor, and began negotiations with landowners. The surveying was a complicated task, since most of the land was under water most of the time. The strict limitations on price forced the commissioners to buy land where the deepest channels of water intersected the mud flats and marshes. They were also asked to provide as much frontage for house lots as possible. For these reasons they ended up with an area in approximately the same location as that projected in their report, but with very different proportions.[48]

By March 1878 the commissioners had purchased the necessary land, made a boundary map with soundings, and begun making arrangements for dredging and filling. Rather than commissioning a plan from Olmsted or anyone else, they decided to hold an open competition, just as the Public Garden committee had done almost twenty years earlier. Both groups apparently felt it would be politically unwise to give such important jobs to outside firms without first opening the field to local talent. Olmsted did not enter this competition, and when asked to judge it, he wrote describing his mistrust of competitions. Although architectural competitions were common, he explained, many architects disliked and refused to enter them. Furthermore,

the difficulties to which I have referred in the case of architectural competitions are greatly increased when the choice of a plan for dealing with *grounds* is in question. The plans and sections of designs for this purpose are extremely deceptive to all but the most practised eyes, *while no such aid to the imagination as is afforded by the elevations* of an architect is possible. Even perspective views from particular points are delusive.[49]

Besides the conceptual problem of determining how suitable a competition plan would be if actually executed, Olmsted cited the potential danger from unsuccessful competitors, who would take the rejection of their plans as

a snub to cherished ambitions if not as a rankling injustice. You are thus likely to have established many prejudiced centres for the propagation against you of more or less bitter criticism, misunderstanding and misrepresentation.

There have been many difficulties attending the administration of the New York Parks which I am able to trace to causes having their root in the jalousies, disappointments and animosities bred in a competition in which Mr. Vaux and I were successful 20 years ago.

No aid I could give in the selection of a plan to receive your premium would materially lessen either class of objections to the competition, which I have indicated. Advising your choice I should place myself in a leaky boat with you. Keeping out of it I retain a professional position in which it is possible I may yet be of service to you.[50]

There were twenty-three entries in the Back Bay park competition. The plans, which were presumably kept by the park commissioners, as was the usual practice then, have all been lost, but the names of about half a dozen of the contestants are known from articles in the Boston papers. The commissioners obviously shared the press's lack of enthusiasm for the competition plans. The $500 prize was awarded to Hermann Grundel, listed in the City Directory as a florist. However, they did not want to use his plan, which the *American Architect and Building News* described as "childish." It included a narrow and wriggling pond of about nineteen acres, artificial hills, rustic summer houses, and other picturesque features. The entries of the landscape gardening firms of Lee and Curtis and of Bowditch and Copeland received the most favorable comment. Just as Olmsted had predicted, the commissioners found themselves in a "leaky boat," and within a few months they would ask him to prepare a plan for the Back Bay.[51]

TWO

The Parks

Jamaica Pond—a natural sheet of water, with quiet graceful shores . . . shaded by a fine natural forest-growth to be brought out overhangingly, darkening the water's edge and favoring great beauty in reflections and flickering half-lights.

—Report of the Landscape Architect, 1881

Jamaica Pond, 1900.

IV

Pioneering Projects:
The Fens and the Arboretum

———————◆———————

BEFORE examining in detail Olmsted's first two Boston projects, it is useful to look briefly at his earlier park system schemes. Olmsted consistently viewed every park design as part of a comprehensive city plan. For him a park was never an ornamental addition to a city but an integral part of its fabric and a force for future growth on several levels: geographic, economic, social, and cultural. He felt that ideally every large city should have a variety of public grounds, including, but not limited to, a large "country park." The first time he explicitly formulated this concept was in his 1868 report to the Brooklyn park commissioners, when he proposed linking Prospect Park to other scenic and recreational areas by parkways. In Manhattan Olmsted was frustrated by the city's dogged commitment to

the grid plan and its consequent tendency to set aside for parks only land that was completely unsuited for building. Although he was less than enthusiastic about the site of Morningside Park, he did his best to design it as a neighboring but contrasting ground to Central Park.[1]

In other communities the aims of the citizenry were more in keeping with Olmsted's own philosophy. In Chicago his former associates in the Sanitary Commission generated a park movement of major proportions. By February 1869 bills had been passed for three park systems on the north, west, and south sides of the city. Unfortunately, each system was governed by a separate board, and bureaucratic problems prevented a unified design solution for all three. In 1870 Olmsted and Vaux were commissioned to design the South Park system, which consisted of two connected parks totaling more than 1,000 acres. The execution of this grand scheme was stalled by the Chicago fire of 1871, which destroyed all the records, contracts, and plans for the South Park, although it did not touch the site. Nevertheless, Olmsted and Vaux's plan for the Upper Division, later Washington Park, was carried out in part (with some alterations by H. W. S. Cleveland at the request of the park commissioners), and four Parisian-style boulevards were also constructed. In 1893 Jackson Park (originally the South Park, Lower Division) was chosen for the World's Columbian Exposition, and the Olmsted firm redesigned the still bleak and largely unimproved lakeside site.[2]

In Buffalo a like-minded group of citizens led by William Dorsheimer worked for and achieved what was certainly the most complete park system prior to Boston's (Figure 28). They first sought Olmsted's advice in 1868; by 1881 the city had secured 600 acres, and the design was taking shape. The core of the system was a 350-acre country park, buffered on three sides by a large rural cemetery, a privately developed picturesque suburb, and the grounds of the state hospital for the mentally ill (the last a Richardson/Olmsted collaboration). Branching off from the central complex were several parkways leading to smaller public grounds, of which the most important was the Front, on a bluff overlooking Lake Erie.[3]

In Boston in 1878, the stage was set for what would be the country's most comprehensive park system of the era. Bostonians of the time were as progressive as their counterparts in Brooklyn, Chicago, and Buffalo, but as we have seen, they were characteristically cautious in making decisions. The topography of the city forced them to think in terms of a system rather than a single large park. Charles Dalton, with the support of the other park commissioners and the general public, had come up with a workable schematic plan for a series of parks and parkways. Although Olmsted, the nation's most eminent landscape architect and designer of park systems, had social and professional ties with Boston, a combination of conservatism and local pride kept the city from hiring him at the outset.

In 1878, when he wrote his "leaky boat" letter to the Boston park commissioners, Olmsted had been home only a few weeks from his fourth trip to Europe. Accompanied by his stepson John Charles, he had sailed in January 1878 in poor physical health and deeply distressed by his final rupture with Central Park. Nevertheless, he and John followed a strenuous itinerary through England, the Low Countries, Germany, Italy, and France. Ill and demoralized as he was, Olmsted took copious notes of all he saw: the zoos at Regent's Park in London and at Frankfurt am Main, Munich's English Garden, and the botanic gardens at Venice and Pisa. He also revisited Birkenhead.[4]

He returned home still feeling unwell and with little to occupy him in New York. The firm had jobs in progress elsewhere in the country, but Olmsted decided to spend the summer sharing a house on Kirkland Street in Cambridge with the E. L. Godkins. His relationship with the Boston Park Commission was still informal, but following the Back Bay park competition fiasco, he had been asked to make studies for the park. Charles Sprague Sargent, director of the Arnold Arboretum, had asked him to do similar studies for their grounds. Sargent hoped to include the Arboretum in the Boston park system, although that was not achieved until almost five years later.[5]

Olmsted's first challenge was to resolve the difficult topographical and engineering problems posed by the Back Bay park site, which had consisted almost entirely of salt marsh during the Colonial period (see Figure 5).[6] As we saw in Chapter I, the Back Bay residential district was built entirely on fill on the old receiving basin, created after the Mill and Cross dams were constructed in 1820 (Figure 6). The hundred acres that Olmsted was asked to turn into a park was the much smaller full basin to the west of the Cross Dam.

As the population of Boston and Brookline increased after 1820, the full basin became progressively more foul. The Muddy River and Stony Brook, which together drained several thousand acres in Roxbury, Dorchester, and Brookline, emptied directly into it. Being estuaries of the Charles, both streams were tidal for a considerable distance upstream, and both tended to back up and overflow at unusually full tides. Flooding was a particularly serious problem along Stony Brook in Roxbury,

Figure 28
Sketch map of Buffalo,
showing Olmsted's park
system plan for the city.

where its valley was shallow and the surrounding land low. Both streams received raw sewage, which was carried downstream and deposited in the Back Bay full basin. As the tide fell, some of this was carried off to sea, but the residue lay on the mud flats, baking odoriferously in the sun. Eventually it became incorporated into the mud. Under these conditions, the last vestiges of the salt marsh could not remain healthy for long. When the park commissioners surveyed the area in 1877, animal life was no longer able to survive in the waters of the Back Bay.[7]

While the 1850 Bachmann lithograph (Figure 7) and many other prints and photographs show the appearance of the receiving basin before the land was filled, similar views of the full basin are very rare. Figure 29 is a photograph taken in the late 1860s by Augustine H. Folsom, a Roxbury photographer, showing the Samuel Dudley House on Tremont Street near Francis Street in Roxbury (the approximate site of the present Peter Bent Brigham Hospital).[8] In the background is a panoramic view of the full basin with Boston in the distance. The

railway lines and most of the receiving basin are hidden behind Gravelly Point, the peninsula projecting into the Back Bay on the right. (See Figure 6.)

The park proposed by the commissioners in 1876 was in the form of a narrow parallelogram, connected by one arm to the Charles River and by another to the proposed park on Parker Hill (Figure 30). When the commissioners were finally able to begin surveying and negotiations in 1877, their severely limited appropriation forced them to buy land in the least promising parts of this extremely unpromising site, and they ended up with a park that curved in the direction of Brookline rather than leading directly to Parker Hill and Roxbury.

As far as it can be reconstructed, the early chronology of the Back Bay park (now the Fens) is as follows.[9] On June 3, 1878, the commissioners decided to award Hermann Grundel the competition prize of $500 but not to use his ineffectual design.[10] Instead they approached Olmsted, who agreed to become their professional advisor and to prepare studies for a plan that would satisfy them, although it was not until December than Olmsted signed a contract on these terms.

The summer of 1878, still a time of semi-convalescence for Olmsted, turned out to be extraordinarily productive. In the files at the Olmsted National Historic Site in Brookline are sheaves of drawings on tracing paper, all dating from these months: the first studies for the Boston park system by Olmsted and his stepson John Charles, who had joined the firm in 1875. By midsummer John, under Olmsted's direction, was working on the first studies for the Fens. Both men now had ample opportunity to examine the site and gain a deeper understanding of its difficulties than Olmsted had been able to grasp in his hurried visits in 1875 and 1876, when the commissioners had driven him over the proposed sites for the whole park system. The first precisely dated study of the Fens by the firm is the third, and successful, study of October 24, 1878.

Although the park commissioners were satisfied with this plan, Olmsted had serious reservations about it. He asked to meet with the city engineer, Joseph P. Davis, before the plan was formally adopted. A four-hour conference among Olmsted, the park commissioners, Davis, and the superinten-

Figure 29
View of the Back Bay full basin from Parker Hill, Roxbury, in 1866.

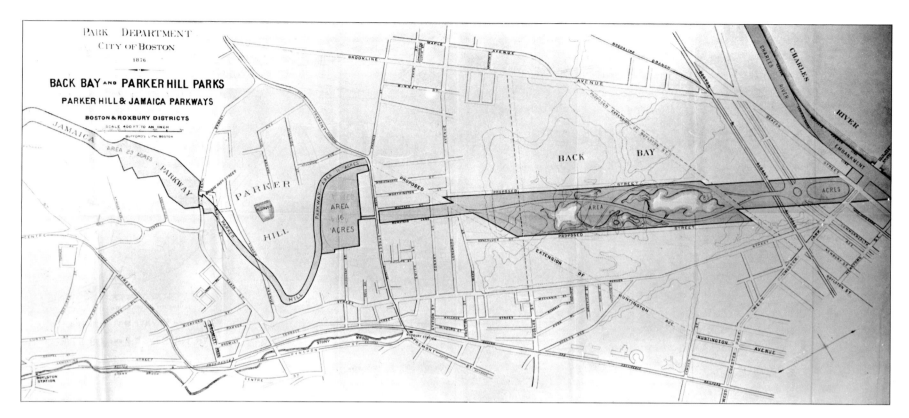

Figure 30
Back Bay and Parker Hill
parks with connecting
parkways as proposed by
the Boston park commis-
sioners, 1876.

dent of sewers, held probably in November 1878, proved helpful, and Olmsted continued to consult with Davis over the next several weeks.[11]

Davis's department had already made tentative plans for a conventional masonry storage basin to hold the overflow of waters from the Muddy River and Stony Brook. Such a basin would be both unattractive and costly, and Olmsted sought to modify the basic concept into an acceptable landscape design. The immediate result was that the October 24 plan had to be completely recast, particularly in the Beacon Entrance section (from Boylston to Beacon streets), which had to be the outlet area for Stony Brook.

Much of the following year was spent in working out solutions to the technical and design problems that had been revealed in the meetings with the city engineer. The commissioners' annual report for 1879, published in January 1880, included Olmsted's first report as landscape architect advisory and his first published plan for Boston—the

"Proposed Improvement of Back Bay" (Figure 31).[12] The lithographed plan shows a wiggling watercourse, typical of the streams that meander through natural salt marshes. The marshland itself is also indicated (short dashed lines) and distinguished from the borders of the park, which were to be planted more conventionally with trees and shrubs. The Charles River water gate, which would regulate the ebb and flow of the tide, is plainly labeled. The Muddy River gatehouse can also be seen just below Brookline Avenue (top of plan), and the Stony Brook gatehouse is located to the right of Huntington Entrance (intersection of Huntington Avenue and Parker Street, bottom of plan).

The rationale behind the plan was very far from what was commonly understood as a park, as Olmsted painstakingly explained; the design was primarily a sanitary improvement, the main feature of which was a storage basin for the storm waters of Stony Brook. A second aim was to restore the salt marsh to its original condition. Intercepting

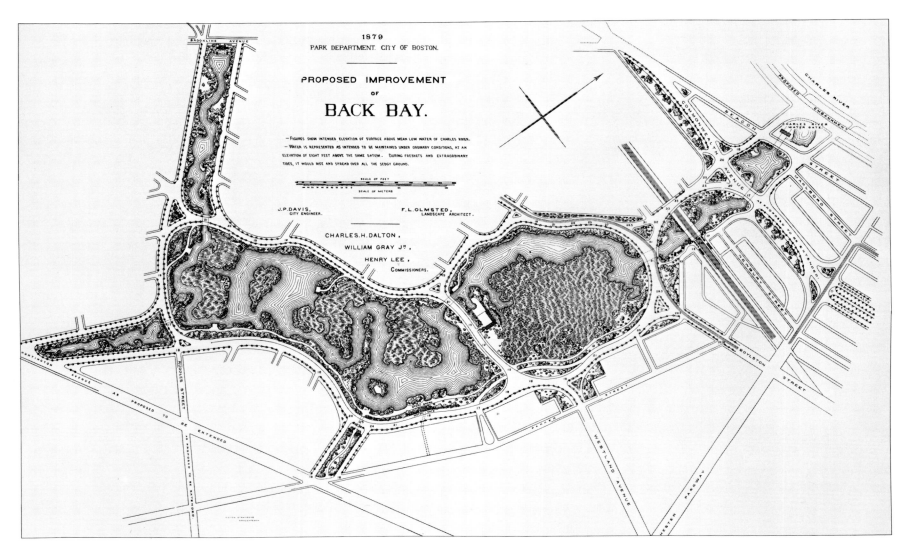

Figure 31
Olmsted's first published
plan for the Back Bay
Fens, 1879.

sewers were to be constructed, Muddy River would be diverted to the Charles by a conduit, and the ordinary flow of Stony Brook carried out by a similar conduit. The flow of salt water in and out of the thirty-acre basin was to be carefully regulated. During times of flood, approximately twenty additional acres could be covered with water.[13]

Olmsted thus could use only about half the total acreage of the park for recreational purposes. The major parkway of the system (now the Fenway), paralleled by a bridle path, ran along the eastern border, with a second road (now Park Drive) on the other side. Footpaths ran along the borders but not into the interior of the park. Several city streets had to traverse the park, necessitating the construction of several bridges.

Except for the trees that lined the roadways, Olmsted had to use marsh grass and shrubs that could tolerate salt spray and occasional total immersion in sea water during storms and high tides. He therefore designed the area so that it would appear to be a natural salt marsh around which a city had happened to grow. The effect of such a marsh in the city, he explained,

would be novel, certainly, in labored urban grounds, and there may be a momentary question of its dignity and appropriateness . . . but [it] is a direct development of the original conditions of the locality in adaptation to the needs of a dense community. So regarded, it will be found to be, in the artistic sense of the word, natural, and possibly to suggest a modest poetic sentiment more grateful to town-weary minds than an elaborate and elegant garden-like work would have yielded.[14]

Eventually Olmsted prevailed upon the park commissioners to change the name from Back Bay to Back Bay Fens, in keeping with the character of the scenery.

Given the difficult nature of the site, construction proceeded fairly rapidly. Nevertheless, it was many years before the effect Olmsted wanted was achieved, and in later reports he reiterated the sanitary aims of the design and the "unparklike" nature of the whole work.[15] Minor changes were later made to the 1879 plan. By the late 1880s, Longwood Entrance (between Brookline Avenue and the intersection at Fen Bridge above Tremont Entrance)

had been widened to correspond to the width of the Muddy River Improvement. In 1891 and 1892 the Olmsted firm made a series of revised studies for Tremont Entrance, and this entrance, actually a vestigial parkway that was to have led to the never-executed Parker Hill Park, became a small, neighborhood square adjacent to the Isabella Stewart Gardner Museum.

The Fens was complete at the time of Olmsted's retirement in 1895, but the salt marsh design survived for only another fifteen years. Figure 32 is a rare early view, about 1898, showing the Fens as it was intended to appear. There had been problems almost from the beginning, for the tide- and flood-control system so carefully worked out by Olmsted and the city engineer had been misused and overloaded. When the Charles River dam was completed in 1910, the water flowing into the Fens from the Charles was fresh instead of salt, thus rendering the entire design obsolete. Although John C. Olmsted, Frederick Law Olmsted, Jr. (who joined the firm in 1895), and Arthur Shurtleff (a former student of Olmsted's, who later changed his name to Shurcliff) made detailed recommendations to the park commissioners for a redesign of the Fens in that year, no action was taken. Instead the Fens was used as a kind of dumping ground for fill taken from other projects, such as the excavation of the subway.[16]

In 1921 Shurtleff, again with Olmsted Brothers as consulting landscape architects, prepared plans and a report for a comprehensive redesign of the Fens that would violate as little as possible the visual character of the original design, while adapting to changed conditions. But again no action was taken. Shurtleff prepared plans for alterations in the southern basin (between Agassiz and Fen roads) in 1925, which appear to have been carried out. The most damaging alteration in recent years has been the building of the Charlesgate interchange in the mid-1960s. This network of overpasses from the Charles River at Storrow Drive to Boylston Street has virtually destroyed Beacon Entrance.[17]

Of Olmsted's design for the Fens, little is left today, other than the general boundaries, two major bridges, the Stony Brook gatehouse, and some of the original trees. The marshes are, of course, gone, and most of the waterways have been altered. It is futile to regret the original salt marshes and salt-

Figure 32
Bird's-eye photograph of
the Back Bay Fens, looking
toward the Boylston Street
Bridge, circa 1898.

water vegetation, since the damming of the Charles was necessary and inevitable. On the other hand, the failure to carry out a comprehensive new design for the Fens after the dam was built was a serious error of judgment. Since World War II, maintenance efforts have been spasmodic, and much of the northern basin has been taken over by a common reed (*Phragmites communis*), which, although not unattractive in itself, grows as high as thirteen feet and forms a dense physical and visual barrier. Rose gardens, victory gardens, and memorials have been added over the years to the northern and southern basins with no regard for the original design. Today the Fens is a rather peculiar collection of spaces that appear to be connected entirely by accident.[18]

By contrast, the Arnold Arboretum retains more of the character and landscape effect of Olmsted's design than any other part of the Boston park system. Additions have been made to the grounds and especially to the plantings, but they have been generally sympathetic with the original scheme.

The design of the Arboretum should probably be regarded as a collaboration between Olmsted and Charles Sprague Sargent (Figure 33), its first director. Sargent's tenure extended from 1872 until his death in 1927, and his benevolent dictatorship

of more than a half century over the institution he helped to form has been a major reason for its continued success.

Sargent was born in Boston in 1841, the son of Henrietta Gray Sargent and Ignatius Sargent, who was an enthusiastic amateur horticulturist as well as a successful merchant and banker. By 1852 the family was living year round at Holm Lea, their Brookline property, near the shores of Jamaica Pond. Ignatius eventually expanded his estate to 130 acres. The Sargents were frequent visitors to at least two other horticultural showplaces: the Wellesley estate, famous for its gardens, of Horatio Hollis Hunnewell; and Wodenethe, the Hudson River property of Ignatius's cousin Henry Winthrop Sargent. Wodenethe had been laid out with the assistance of A. J. Downing, Henry Sargent's neighbor and close friend.[19]

Other than his early exposure to large-scale horticultural improvements, there was little in Sargent's early life to indicate his later eminence in botany. His career at Harvard was anything but splendid: out of a class of ninety, he managed to place eighty-eighth. After graduating from college, he served in the Union Army, then spent three years traveling in Europe. When he returned home in 1868, he took up the management of Holm Lea as a full-time occupation.[20]

The land that eventually became the Arnold Arboretum was located only a short distance from Holm Lea: the Benjamin Bussey farm of about 210 acres between Centre and South streets in Jamaica Plain. Like Ignatius Sargent, Bussey had consolidated his property by buying several smaller farms in the early years of the nineteenth century. In 1842 he willed his estate to Harvard for use as an agricultural school. Since the will allowed for lifelong tenancy by Bussey's heirs, the entire property did not become available to Harvard until 1873, although Bussey's granddaughter released about seven acres for the agricultural school in 1869.[21]

In later years Sargent described the Bussey homestead as a "worn-out farm." By Holm Lea standards, it was undoubtedly neglected, but the spot still had many beautiful features in the 1870s, including a natural stand of hemlocks on a steep slope (Hemlock Hill), overlooking a winding stream, and Bussey Hill, which had a view over all of Boston. Bussey allowed the public to stroll through his grounds, even providing bridges and rustic seats. His woods were a favorite haunt of Margaret Fuller during the years (1839–1842) that she lived in Jamaica Plain, and she often brought her literary friends to enjoy the views from Hemlock Hill. Thus, years before it became the Arboretum, Bussey Farm served as an informal park.[22]

In 1868 James Arnold of New Bedford, another tree-loving amateur horticulturist, died and willed a relatively small sum (approximately $100,000) to three friends, George B. Emerson, John J. Dixwell, and Francis E. Parker, as trustees. Emerson was primarily an educator, but he was also a respected authority on trees and was the author of *Trees and Shrubs Growing Naturally in the Forests of Massachusetts*, first published in 1846. As mentioned in Chapter III, he testified in favor of "breathing spaces" and improved roads at the 1869 park hearings.[23]

It was Emerson who first proposed that the Arnold bequest be used to establish an arboretum, in accordance with Arnold's apparent wish. Although the will read that the money was to be used "for the promotion of Agricultural or Horticultural improvements, or other Philosophical or Philanthropic purposes at their discretion," this rather vague directive was intended to give the trustees some lee-

way in case the arboretum project did not work out. Emerson wisely felt that the fund should be used for the arboretum itself and not for the acquisition of land at current real estate prices. The logical solution was to give it to an institution such as Harvard, which already had some land. He and the other two trustees met with Asa Gray of the Harvard Botanic Garden, who favored the idea but wanted the arboretum on Observatory Hill in Cambridge, next to the Garden. This proved to be impractical, and after considering other alternatives the Arnold trustees settled on Bussey Farm as the best site. An indenture to this effect was signed by the trustees and Harvard President Charles W. Eliot on March 29, 1872.[24]

Gray, who was nearing retirement at about this time, began to feel overwhelmed by teaching and other responsibilities. Between 1872 and 1874 he requested and was granted four assistants; Sargent, who became director of the Botanic Garden, was the only one who was not a botanist. In fact, he

Figure 33
Charles Sprague Sargent in the library at the Arnold Arboretum Administration Building.

seemed to have no credentials for the job beyond his social position and a modest reputation as a gentleman landscape gardener. Once appointed to the new position, however, he slipped into his slot in life as if it had been preordained. As an undergraduate, he had not even taken Gray's course in elementary botany, and now he had to be tutored personally by the great man. Gray at first found that Sargent had "a vast deal to learn," but he was soon praising his dogged perseverance. Sargent's immediate duties were to reorganize the seven-acre Botanic Garden, which had been founded in 1805 and which emphasized herbaceous plants arranged in symmetrical display beds and greenhouses. Sargent made many dramatic improvements in the seven years that he was in charge of the Botanic Garden, but it did not offer him enough scope for his energy and ambitions.[25]

He was also director of the Arnold Arboretum, an operation with great possibilities but little money to realize them. The Arboretum fund, small to begin with, was strictly curtailed by the terms of the indenture: only one-third of the income could be used each year until the accumulated capital amounted to $150,000. Sargent took seriously the mandate of the indenture, to grow "all the trees, shrubs, and herbaceous plants, either indigenous or exotic, which can be raised in the open air at the said West Roxbury."[26] (Jamaica Plain is part of the former town of West Roxbury, both annexed to Boston in 1873.) Although there was ample room on the Bussey land for a considerable collection of trees, there were not sufficient funds available to build roads, well-designed walls and gates, or anything more than the simplest possible arrangement of the tree collections. But Sargent, the landscape gardener only newly turned botanist, had ambitions that were as much aesthetic as scientific. He wanted the Arboretum to be as outstanding in landscape design as it would be inclusive in its collections.

In June 1874, when Boston was holding its hearings on public parks, Sargent wrote to Olmsted:

In the general agitation into which the popular mind has now fallen in regard to a public Park or Parks I think I can see some hope for our Arboretum. It has occurred to me that an arrangement could be made by which the

ground (130 acres) could be handed over to the City of Boston on the condition that the City should spend a certain sum of money in laying out the grounds and should agree to leave the planting in my hands in order that the scientific objects of the trust could be carried out.[27]

In order to persuade the city authorities to take action, Sargent needed a plan and rough estimate.

Olmsted's initial reaction to Sargent's idea was decidedly cool; he doubted that a park and an arboretum could be combined successfully. His response also sheds some light on the manner in which he and Sargent worked together on this plan, although it predates the actual collaboration by four years.

I should not like to undertake to form a plan until I had seen the ground and discussed the general propositions with you. It might turn out that I differed with you radically about it or that I should advise a course and that you would adopt it which made it unnecessary for you to employ me on a plan. Indeed a park and an arboretum seem to me to be so far unlike in purpose that I do not feel sure that I could combine them satisfactorily. I certainly would not undertake to do so in this case without your cooperation and I think it would be better and more proper that the plan should be made by you with my aid rather than by me with yours.[28]

Eventually, however, Olmsted became so enthusiastic about the Arboretum project and championed it so vigorously that in later life Sargent forgot that the idea had originated with him and not with Olmsted. Olmsted spent a good part of the summer of 1878 working on the preliminary plan for the Arboretum, for which he asked no fee. Sargent, with characteristic efficiency, was able to raise almost overnight, from friends and relatives, the $2,000 needed for a topographical survey and other expenses.[29]

While Sargent began preliminary negotiations with the city and Harvard, Olmsted started on the plan, shown in Figure 34. After the land had been thoroughly surveyed, he saw a number of problems, the first of which was the irregular shape of the property. Later the city brought two additional parcels of land to the north at his recommendation. A marshy meadow near what was to be the main en-

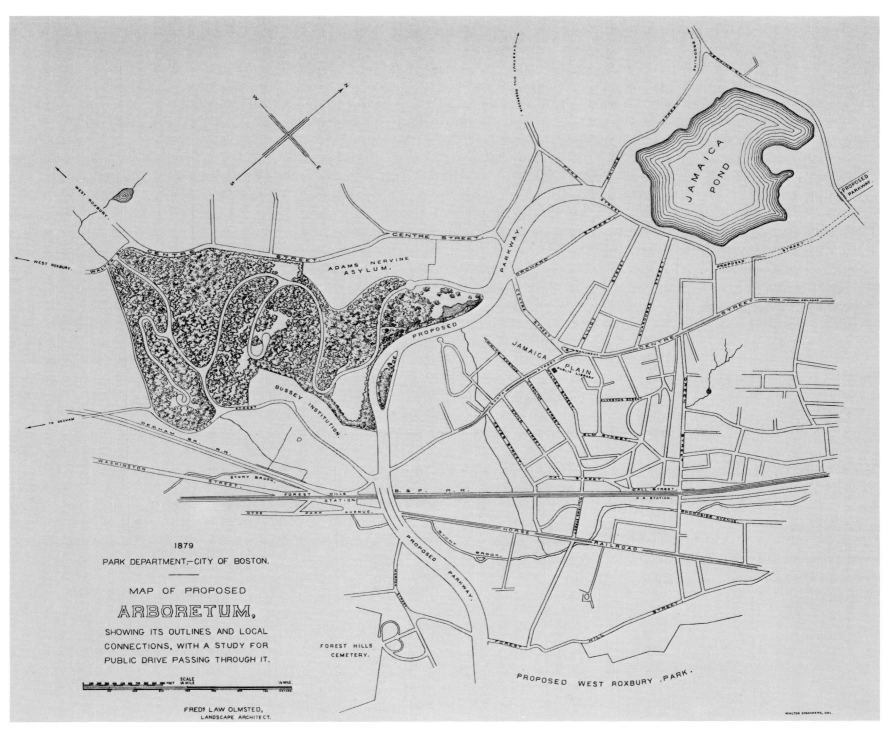

Figure 34
Olmsted's plan for the Ar-
nold Arboretum, 1879.

trance to the Arboretum also had to be drained in order to be usable for planting. The natural woods of the Bussey farm were incorporated into the plan, and as can be seen on a modern map (Figure 35), there are still substantial groves of natural woods in the Arboretum.

The final plan for the roads and tree collections was preceded by an extraordinarily long series of studies. The trees had to be grouped by family and genus according to the natural order, and the main road had to pass through them in such a way that they could be seen in logical sequence. The problem was not unlike that of designing a museum in which the galleries must be arranged in strictly chronological order, with the difference that the Ar-

boretum collections, once installed, could not be moved.

Despite the didactic purpose, both Sargent and Olmsted wanted a naturalistic effect that fitted in with the topography and the existing stands of trees. Sargent proposed to place each group of trees on the main avenue, so that

a visitor driving through the Arboretum will be able to obtain a general idea of the arborescent vegetation of the north temperate zone without even leaving his carriage. It is hoped that such an arrangement, while avoiding the stiff and formal lines of the conventional botanic garden, will facilitate the comprehensive study of the collections, both in their scientific and picturesque aspects.[30]

Figure 35
Map of the collections in the Arnold Arboretum, 1975.

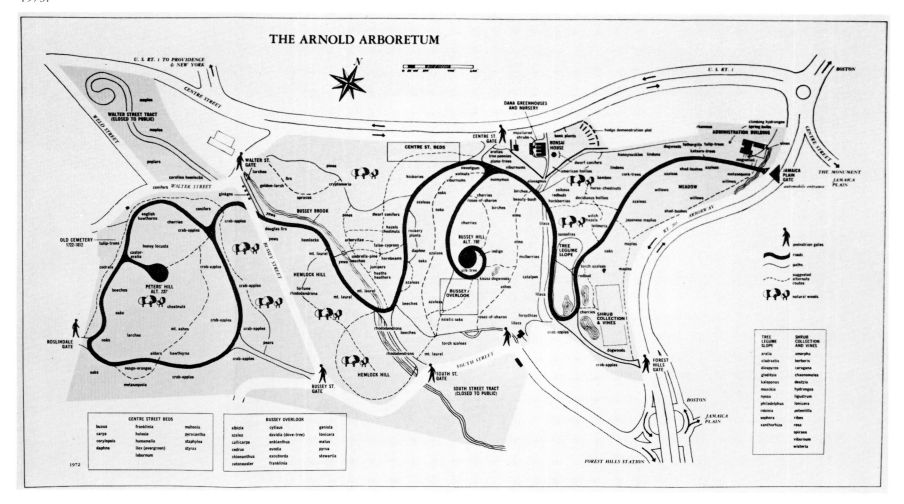

In blending the scientific and the picturesque, Sargent and Olmsted were brilliantly successful. The modern map shows the tree collections, which exist today almost exactly as they were planned.

The negotiations to make the Arboretum a part of the Boston park system took more than four years. President Eliot resisted the idea but eventually gave in, as did the Boston City Council. In December 1882 the agreement between Harvard and the city was finally signed. In all important respects it was identical to that outlined by Sargent eight years earlier: the city purchased the Arboretum grounds from Harvard, bought several acres of adjacent land, and leased it all back to Harvard for a thousand years, while retaining responsibility for building and maintaining roads and policing the grounds. Harvard gained a professionally designed arboretum, and Boston gained a park. All in all, $100,000 had been made to go a very long way.[31]

The four-year delay gave Sargent plenty of opportunity to exercise his innate perfectionism. In the early stages of planning, Olmsted prepared studies for every conceivable alternative for the road system, including one for "the longest possible road." He and John also began a lengthy series of studies for the distribution of the tree collections. Even after approval of the agreement, two Olmsted apprentices—Charles Eliot, who was President Eliot's son, and Henry Sargent Codman, Sargent's nephew—labored under Sargent's vigilant eye to refine the tree collection plan still further. It was not until 1885 that this plan, completed by Codman, was accepted and blueprinted.[32]

The almost inescapable conclusion that Sargent was as much codesigner as client is supported by several other circumstances. For most other parts of the park system, Olmsted wrote at least one detailed report carefully explaining the rationale behind his plan. No such document exists for the Arboretum. Instead, a report by Sargent, in his characteristically terse and understated style, accompanied the first Arboretum plan.[33] Another persuasive argument is that there are many visual parallels between the Arboretum and Holm Lea, which Sargent designed himself. Contemporary accounts and views (Figure 36) and what remains of the estate today show many groupings of trees and shrubs, treatments of vistas, and other landscape effects that

Figure 36
Holm Lea, the Charles
Sprague Sargent estate,
Brookline, circa 1908.

are strikingly similar to those in the Arboretum.[34] Sargent came from the amateur landscape gardening tradition. Accustomed to working on a large scale, he, like Henry A. S. Dearborn at Mount Auburn, was capable of translating his personal aesthetic vision into a broader medium than the gentleman's country estate.[35]

By all accounts, Sargent was an unpredictable, difficult, and not very lovable man, and no one has ever claimed he was a genius. Yet he founded a remarkable institution, and he won the friendship and respect of many giants of his day, including Olmsted and Richardson.[36] Furthermore, his achievements at Holm Lea and his coauthorship of the Arboretum design were explicitly recognized by Mariana G. Van Rensselaer, a perceptive critic of landscape architecture. Of the Arboretum, she wrote,

Of course Professor Sargent has not worked alone. With his acquiescence Olmsted laid out the walks and drives,

Figure 37
The Syringa (*lilac*) *collection at the Arnold Arboretum, 1908.*

Figure 38
The Kalmia (*mountain laurel*) *collection at the Arnold Arboretum, 1908.*

and at every subsequent step men of knowledge and skill have assisted him. But they have always been controlled and sometimes have been trained by him. Everything has been done according to his decisions and under his eye. In the truest sense the Arboretum is his creation, and in the truest sense it is a great work of art.[37]

Grading began on the main drive in the spring of 1883. Road building, the major construction work in the Arboretum, took about ten years to complete. Installation of the permanent tree collections began in 1886 with beeches, ashes, elms, and hickories. As soon as each section of road was completed, Sargent proceeded to plant it. In 1894 the Peters Hill section of the Bussey farm was added, to be used mostly as reserve space. For a long time it featured Sargent's huge collection of hawthorns. The South Street and Walter Street tracts shown on the modern map were added in the present century. Figure 37, showing the *Syringa* (lilac) collection, and Figure 38, the *Kalmia* (mountain laurel) collection, are two of many magnificent views of the Arboretum taken around the turn of the century by Thomas E. Marr, a Boston photographer.

Its dual function as a museum and a park has preserved the integrity of the Arboretum's design. The road system carefully planned by Olmsted has not been tampered with. The tree collections, the arrangement of which Sargent fussed over for so many years, have reached their full growth. New plants capable of growing "in the open air at the said West Roxbury" have been added. More than one hundred years after its founding, the Arboretum still fulfills the intentions of its codesigners.

V

"Franklin Park and Related Matters"

———————◆———————

OLMSTED took endless pains with Franklin Park, which he clearly felt to be the most critical part of the whole park system. The result was a plan that many people believe ranks with Central Park and Prospect Park as one of Olmsted's three masterpieces of park design. Franklin Park is significant not only as an artistic achievement but as a visual statement of one of Olmsted's most important ideas. Central to Olmsted's thought was the conviction that modern city dwellers need contact with the natural world in order to preserve not only their physical health but also their mental tranquillity.

To meet these needs, a space must be provided large enough to screen out surrounding buildings and to give the illusion of unlimited space. Public gardens and squares, recreation grounds and "sanitary improvements," however important and necessary, cannot fill this function, nor can any ground that is used to show off elaborate displays of horticulture, architecture, or sculpture. The scenery in such a park, according to Olmsted, need not be spectacular but should have a "pleasingly simple, rural aspect." The planting should be similarly natural in effect, using predominently native materials, and any necessary buildings should be as inconspicuous as possible. Such a public ground fills Olmsted's definition of a park. He expressed these ideas repeatedly, but perhaps nowhere as eloquently as in *Notes on the Plan of Franklin Park and Related Matters*, the report that accompanied the park plan.[1]

A large park in the West Roxbury district had

been the central feature of the park commissioners' plans since their first deliberations in the mid-1870s. The 500-acre site they selected was approved enthusiastically by Olmsted when he visited the city in 1876, and a plan of the location (Figure 39) and a description were included in their first major report.[2] Not until 1881, however, was an appropriation for the park approved. In 1883 the public was admitted to the still unlandscaped grounds, and the following year, the topographical survey was completed. Anticipating that funds from Benjamin Franklin's bequest to the city of Boston, due to mature in 1891, would be available to pay for con-

struction costs, the commissioners changed the name from West Roxbury Park to Franklin Park.

At the time of land taking, the site consisted of about a dozen small farms, each with a house, barns, and other outbuildings. Some land had been purchased by speculators with an eye to eventual development, but the depression of 1873–1879 had prevented them from having any success.[3] None of the natural topographical features had been seriously disturbed by such minimal construction efforts as had taken place by 1884. The scenery, typical of most of rural Massachusetts, was peaceful and pastoral but not particularly dramatic. Figure 40 shows a view across the parkland before it was laid out. As Olmsted described the character of the land:

The all-important feature of the West Roxbury site is a gentle valley nearly a mile in length and of an average breadth between the steeper slopes of the bordering hills of less than a quarter of a mile. Relieved of a few houses, causeways and fences, left with an unbroken surface of turf and secluded by woods on the hillsides, this would at once supply a singularly complete and perfect though limited example of a type of scenery which is perhaps the most soothing in its influence on mankind of any presented by nature.[4]

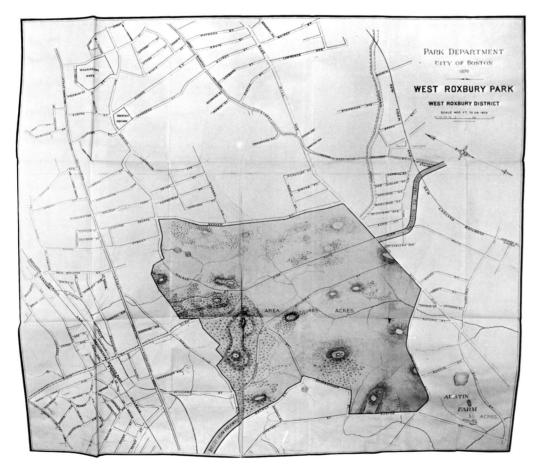

Figure 39
West Roxbury (Franklin)
Park as proposed by the
Boston park commissioners
in 1876.

Although intensive residential development had not yet reached this part of West Roxbury, the site was easily accessible by the New York and New England railway on the east and the Boston and Providence line on the west. (See Figure 39.) It was also approached on all sides by major streets, of which the most important was Blue Hill Avenue on the east side, which would eventually connect Franklin Park with Boston by the electrified street railway system and with the metropolitan park system at the Blue Hills in Milton. The roads on the west side and on the site were narrow and crooked.

Olmsted's plan for Franklin Park was developed in 1884 and 1885. These were highly critical years in Boston politics, and for a time execution of the plan seemed to be in jeopardy. As mentioned in Chapter I, Boston had been governed as a city only since 1822. Moreover, the charters of 1822 and 1854 gave little real power to the mayor, who had only a limited veto power and the right to appoint committees. In 1885, however, amendments to the city charter transferred all the executive powers of the city government to the mayor, while the City Council retained the legislative powers. The mayor could veto any order passed by the council, although the council could override his veto by a two-thirds vote.[5]

Under the Park Act of 1875, the three park commissioners were appointed by the mayor, subject to the approval of the City Council. It is not surprising that the commissioners generally shared the political party and the views of the mayors who appointed them, although they served without pay and were in this sense "out of politics." Charles Dalton and William Gray were appointed by Mayor Samuel Cobb, and their appointments were renewed by successive administrations for ten years.

In 1884 there was a major upheaval in Boston politics, reflecting a similar upheaval on the state and national levels. In that year many Republicans left their party to defeat the presidential candidacy of James G. Blaine and to elect Democrat Grover Cleveland. In Massachusetts this movement involved a de facto coalition between the former Republicans (who called themselves Mugwumps), the Irish-American Democrats, and the Yankee Democrats. A month after the presidential election, Boston elected Hugh O'Brien, the first Irish Catholic mayor in its history, who served four successive one-year terms from 1885 through 1888. O'Brien, whose stand, as an alderman, in favor of parks was discussed in Chapter III, was also the first mayor to take office under the amended charter of 1885. He appointed a new Board of Park Commissioners that exactly paralleled the coalition: Patrick Maguire, the editor of the weekly *Republic* and a powerful political boss; John F. Andrew, a prominent Mugwump and the son of Massachusetts' Civil War governor; and Benjamin Dean, a Yankee Democrat.[6]

The transfer of political power to the Boston Irish Democrats was greeted with consternation by the city's Brahmins. Much to their surprise, O'Brien's administration proved to be intelligent, honest, economical, and reform-oriented. By the end of his first term, he had won the praise and approval of both Republicans and Mugwumps.[7]

A similar phenomenon occurred on the level of the Park Commission. Early in 1885 Charles Eliot

Figure 40
Franklin Park before construction in 1883.

Norton, professor of fine arts at Harvard and a friend of Olmsted's, wrote to him that "the Irish dynasty has fairly settled itself upon the throne in Boston."[8] Mayor O'Brien's board did not take office until May 1, and Olmsted's initial reaction to the new commissioners, as shown by his letters to Norton and others, was negative.[9] He felt that the three new men were uninterested in parks, and he was skeptical about whether they would comply with the new Civil Service regulations. His feelings were undoubtedly confirmed when the new board immediately rescinded the resolution under which he had been employed.[10] At stake was Franklin Park: Olmsted had just completed the preliminary plan, and his renewed contract was to have included payment for this and for a three-year period of supervision. The new commissioners apparently felt that the outgoing, "lame duck" board should not have passed such an important resolution, but a few weeks later they approved a new contract with Olmsted, having substantially the same terms.[11] He gradually established a comfortable working relationship with the new commissioners, and by 1889, in an address given before the New England Club, he was able to look back positively on a decade of association with the Boston Park Commission.[12]

The execution of the Franklin Park plan was

also delayed and impeded by the city's method of taking land. Under the 1875 Park Act the commissioners could take land by eminent domain, determine the damages for such land takings, and assess betterments on real estate directly benefited by an adjacent park. Funds for the acquisition of land came from bonds issued by the city under the Public Park Loan, and, although not specified by the act, funds for construction came initially from appropriations made by the City Council from money raised by taxation.[13] Although this method of financing the park system worked in the long run, it did not work very smoothly, and significant modifications were necessary. Some of the land, including parts of Franklin Park, was given up very reluctantly and only after long litigation and the payment of excessive damages. It also proved difficult to raise as much money through betterments as had been hoped. The city had a fixed debt limit, which could not be exceeded without special legislation. Such legislation was filed by Mayor O'Brien on the advice of his Park Commission, and a bill was passed in 1886, authorizing a loan of $2.5 million beyond the city debt limit. This money, issued in yearly installments of $500,000, was used primarily for Franklin Park.[14]

On January 30, 1886, Commissioners Dean, Andrew, and Maguire held a board meeting at the Olmsted firm's field office in Franklin Park, to which they invited Mayor O'Brien. This occasion was the first formal unveiling of the Franklin Park plan (Figure 41). As part of his presentation, Olmsted read a paper, presumably a draft version of *Notes on the Plan of Franklin Park and Related Matters*. At their February 10 meeting the commissioners officially adopted the plan and asked Olmsted to prepare his statement for publication.[15]

As can be seen from the plan and as described in his *Notes,* Olmsted divided Franklin Park into two distinct but unequal sections, a practice he is not known to have used in any of his other major parks. Approximately two-thirds of the acreage, at the southern end of the park (left side of the plan), was reserved for the Country Park. This was the park proper, to be used solely for the enjoyment of natural scenery, and it included both the "gentle valley nearly a mile in length" and the nearby rocky wooded hills. Olmsted felt that Glen Road was

needed for through traffic from Blue Hill Avenue to Forest Hills Street, and it was therefore kept, although rebuilt and slightly rerouted. Glen Road also formed a logical topographical division between the Country Park and what Olmsted called the "forecourt" or Ante-Park.[16]

The Ante-Park (right side of the plan) was subdivided into several secondary areas, with rather extensive provisions for sports and other activities that Olmsted considered unsuitable for the park proper. The most important space was the Playstead, a thirty-acre field reserved for schoolboy sports. This was the first part of the park to be constructed and formally opened to the public (Figures 42 and 43). The field, a natural meadow, was graded and made suitable for sports but otherwise little changed. Rather than providing bleachers, Olmsted planned an extraordinary boulder terrace 800 feet long, which was planted with vines and shrubs and served as a natural platform. He also designed a building on the terrace where spectators could buy food and take cover from the rain. An arch in the boulder terrace led directly from the playing field into the basement or locker room area of the shelter.[17]

The Ante-Park also included a grand mall, called the Greeting, which, like the Mall in Central Park, was planned for promenading on foot, horseback, and carriage. Other subdivisions included an amphitheater for concerts, a deer park, Long Crouch Woods to be used for a zoo of native animals, a playground for very small children (what today would be called a "tot lot," Olmsted labeled the "Little Folks' Fair"), and Sargent's Field, a small area for active sports. The Steading was set aside for the Boston Park Commission offices, although the commissioners never occupied the "rocky, sterile knoll" that Olmsted reserved for them.[18]

Except for the Nursery and Refectory Hill, both on the periphery of the plan, the Country Park had no subdivisions unrelated to its primary purpose: the enjoyment of natural scenery. Olmsted was emphatic that within this area, a mile long and three-quarters of a mile wide, there should be no decorative features, no scientific or horticultural displays, and no provision for any sport or activity that would attract large throngs of people. He especially cautioned against elegant gardening effects; native

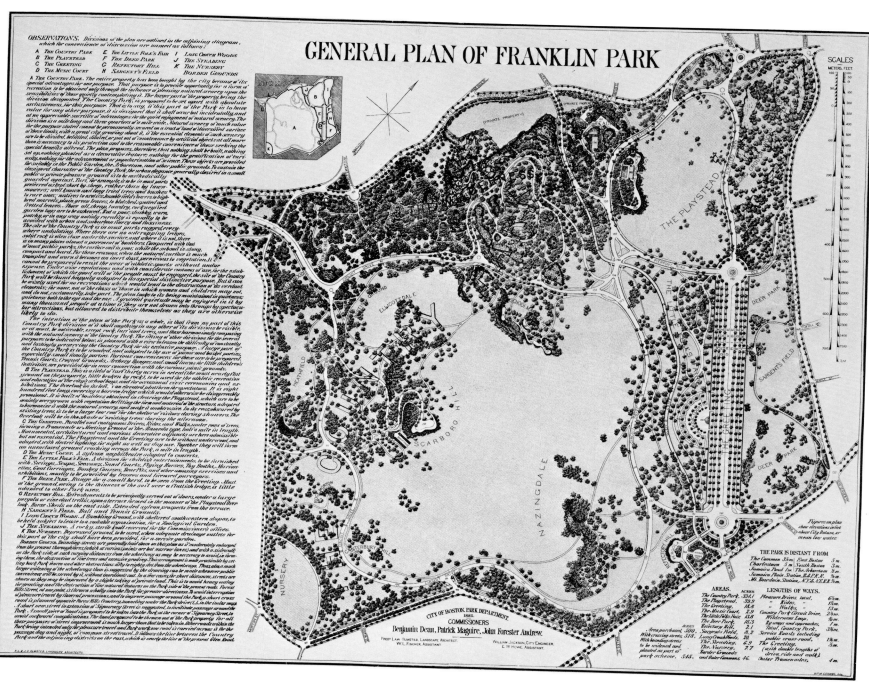

Figure 41
General plan of Franklin Park by F. L. Olmsted, 1885.

trees, shrubs, and wildflowers were to be used rather than exotics, and the turf was to be cropped by sheep rather than by lawn mowers. Within the Country Park, the main space was the great valley (Figure 44); to the northwest was a smaller curving space called Ellicottdale, which was sometimes used for croquet or for lawn tennis, a sport with portable nets (Figure 45). These central spaces were framed by the rocky, wooded Wilderness (Figure 46) and by Schoolmaster and Scarboro hills, all provided with systems of paths and/or roads, picnicking facilities, and in some cases, small rustic shelters.[19]

Throughout Franklin Park, topographical features were given names that recalled earlier owners, such as Ellicottdale, Heathfield, and Abbotsford. Nazingdale, part of the valley in the Country Park, was named after a part of Essex County, England, from which many of the early Roxbury settlers had come. Schoolmaster Hill was named after Ralph Waldo Emerson, who as a young man had taught school in Roxbury. (Emerson had died only a few years earlier, in 1882.)[20]

Figure 42
View southwest across the Playstead at Franklin Park, showing the Overlook and Shelter.

Figure 43
Entrance to the Playstead from School Street.

Figure 44
The Country Park: view
across Nazingdale looking
northwest toward School-
master Hill, 1904.

Figure 45
Lawn tennis in Ellicott-
dale, 1903.

Figure 46
Woodland path in Franklin Park, 1895.

Country Park the main road was Circuit Drive; the Playstead was also surrounded by a loop road (Pierpont and Playstead roads). The riding pad that began in the Back Bay Fens entered Franklin Park at Forest Hills Entrance and continued within the Wilderness, and there was to have been a double riding course in the Greeting. The circulation systems of the two park divisions were almost entirely separate, converging only near the Blue Hill Avenue entrance and at the Valley Gate. Carriage roads, footpaths, and the bridle path came together at the Valley Gate, but pedestrians and carriages could pass from the Ante-Park to the Country Park only during the day when the gate was open.[21]

The spatial organization of Franklin Park was worked out as carefully as the circulation system, and here the distinction between the two divisions was less clear-cut. Essentially, Franklin Park consists of one large and several smaller central open spaces framed by densely wooded hills and ledges. Olmsted thought in terms of two broad sight lines: one extending almost due south from the Playstead across the Country Park and Forest Hills Cemetery to the Blue Hills of Milton, the other from Refectory Hill looking west toward the Arnold Arboretum. As he explained:

The centre lines of the two broad fields of extended vision . . . cross nearly at right angles, the point of their crossing being where the Ellicott and Nazing dales run together, nearly midway between the two hanging woods of Schoolmaster Hill and Abbotswood crags. This locality, being at the centre of the property, may be considered the pivot of the general landscape design. Looking in the general direction of the lines . . . crossing it from either of the four quarters of the Park, a moderately broad, open view will be had between simple bodies of forest, the foliage growing upon ground higher than that on and near the centre lines. From wherever these larger prospects open, the middle distances will be quiet, slightly hollowed surfaces of turf or buskets, bracken, sweet-fern, or mosses, the backgrounds formed by woodsides of a soft, even subdued tone, with long, graceful, undulating sky lines.[22]

Although the two divisions of the park were spatially connected, the activities in the Ante-Park were concealed by low plantings in buffer strips along Glen Road. Similar strips were formed by

Olmsted intended the Country Park to be entirely enclosed by a boulder wall, but only a portion of this wall along Glen Road appears to have been constructed. The Country Park was to be closed at night, while the Ante-Park could remain open and lit for concerts and other activities. Within the wooded areas near the boundaries of the park. One such strip between Glen Road and the Circuit Drive is unmarked on the early plans but is known today as the "Sausage." The Greeting, although much bigger in relation to the total size of the park than the Mall in Central Park, had only minimal spatial significance, since it was pushed off to one side near Seaver Street and was well insulated by buffer strips (the Sausage, the Deer Park, Sargent's Field, and Long Crouch Woods). Thus this very large and strongly architectonic element did not dominate the park. In Central Park, Olmsted and Vaux had achieved the same end by placing the Mall off-axis to the park as a whole.

The plan of Franklin Park, especially its road and pathway system, has a more than casual resemblance to that of Birkenhead Park (see Figure 13) near Liverpool, which Olmsted had first visited in 1850.[23] Like Franklin Park, Birkenhead was bisected by a cross drive (Ashville Road), which was used for ordinary traffic, while the main park drive was meant only for pleasure traffic. Birkenhead originally had gates, like the Valley Gate at Franklin Park, closing off the park drive from the cross drive. The arrangement of the circuit and loop drives and footpaths and the disposition of open spaces in Franklin Park is also somewhat reminiscent of the English park. Although Paxton's drives and walks are more sinuous and obviously artificial than Olmsted's, they serve the same purpose of providing fresh views of a central open space from a multitude of points within a fairly limited area. But the two parks are quite dissimilar in several respects, most notably the use of the land between the main drive and the park boundaries. In Franklin Park, these areas contain several natural hills and ledges, the Wilderness, and dense boundary plantations, all of which tend to enclose the park and sequester it from the surrounding city. Olmsted extended the illusion of unbroken countryside by allowing distant views only in the directions of the Blue Hills and Arnold Arboretum, both of which would always remain open. By contrast, the comparable spaces in Birkenhead Park were especially set aside for row houses and detached "villas," although not all of these were constructed.[24] Despite this important distinction, the similarities in circulation and spatial organization between Franklin and

Birkenhead parks strongly suggest that Olmsted was consciously reworking at least some elements of the plan that had so impressed him as a young man.

Franklin Park, unquestionably the most important part of the Boston system, is also frequently described as one of Olmsted's three greatest parks, along with Central and Prospect. Opinion has varied as to just what place in this "great triad" Franklin Park should occupy. Central Park has historical priority and is justly famous, although its rigidly rectangular site and topographical limitations led to a generally less satisfactory overall plan than the two later parks allowed. Franklin and Prospect parks are more closely comparable: both are about the same size and shape, and in both the designers had considerable freedom, first in determining precise boundaries and then in arranging the internal spaces and functions. John C. Olmsted considered Franklin Park to be "probably the best piece of work . . . done by its designer."[25] On the other hand, the eminent historian of landscape architecture, Norman T. Newton, feels that Franklin Park falls somewhat short of Prospect Park, largely because, to him, its central open space is not as impressive as the great curving sweep of the Long Meadow.[26] However, it seems clear from the portion of the *Notes* just quoted that Olmsted planned the space very carefully to make the best use of existing topography. (The Long Meadow was manmade.) The central space was meant to be framed by existing hills and "hanging woods," with the "pivot" of the design where Ellicottdale and Nazingdale come together.[27] (See Figures 41 and 44.)

All three parks, as well as the approximately fifteen other country parks designed by Olmsted, were planned primarily to provide city dwellers with the physical and psychological benefits that he felt could be gained only from contemplation of scenery. Despite today's climate of environmental awareness and enthusiasm for all things "natural," Olmsted's views on the restorative value of rural scenery are still poorly understood. To some critics, who see his ideas either as a quaint relic of nineteenth-century romanticism or as a reaction to urban ills that no longer exist, such as coal smoke and bacterial epidemics, or who view city parks as irrelevant now that people have cars and can get to the "real" country, these views now seem out of touch with the times.[28]

Olmsted's wholehearted and poetic response to nature is amply evidenced in his *Walks and Talks* of 1852, which also gives intimations of his later views on the restorative value of such scenery to city-dwelling men and women. The roots of his thought obviously go back still further: to his youth in Connecticut, to the vacations with his family in New England and New York, and to his rather precocious explorations of Price, Gilpin, and other authors in the Hartford Public Library. A large proportion of his later professional reports and much of his correspondence deal with the same issue. Of this substantial literature, three major pieces stand out.

The earliest, the address on "Public Parks and the Enlargement of Towns," delivered to the American Social Science Association at the Lowell Institute in Boston in 1870, deals with the subject in a broad sociological context.[29] Here Olmsted discussed the inevitable growth of towns, as their easier and more civilized way of life drew people away from the country. However, the crowding of city life, he felt, made people high strung and wary of one another and susceptible to disease. Because of the purifying effect of sunlight and foliage on the air, parks could reduce disease. (He also recommended tree-lined streets.) Similarly, the nervous and antisocial effects of town congestion could be eased by bringing people together in a noncompetitive way in the large spaces of a country park.

The second paper, a pamphlet on Mount Royal published in 1881, consists primarily of Olmsted's plea to his Canadian clients to follow through with his plan and not spoil their mountain by mistaken improvements; from this develops what is probably his fullest statement about landscape architecture as an art.[30] In the final pages he describes, as an example of the ultimate aim of such art, the "restful, soothing and refreshing influence" of mountain scenery on a hypothetical invalid being brought by carriage to the top of Mount Royal.[31] The prospects that open up before her, level by level and sequence by sequence, are almost magically evoked in these lines—perhaps the most vivid descriptive passage Olmsted ever wrote.

Notes on the Plan of Franklin Park and Related Matters, a compact book of 115 pages, must, however, be considered Olmsted's great work on the subject. Although only a relatively small part deals directly with the restorative value of rural scenery, the pages that focus on this concept are the heart of the book and the *raison d'être* for the rest. The key portion is in Section II of Part Second: "The Purpose of the Plan." Here Olmsted again describes the harmful effect on the mental and nervous system of exclusive association with artificial things or with "natural things seen under obviously artificial conditions."[32] He concedes that several types of recreation may mitigate the harm, but the only effective antidote is the enjoyment of rural scenery.

Olmsted also distinguished between urban beauty and the beauty of rural scenery. The former is found primarily in gardens and, while pleasing, is too obviously artificial to act as an antidote to city life: "A little violet or a great magnolia blossom, the frond of a fern, a carpet of fine turf of the form and size of a prayer rug, a block of carved and polished marble, a vase or a jet of water,—in the beauty of all these things unalloyed pleasure may be taken in the heart of a city."[33] By contrast: "there is a pleasure-bringing beauty in the same class of objects—foliage, flowers, verdure, rocks and water—not to be enjoyed under the same circumstances . . . a beauty which appeals to *a different class of human sensibilities* . . . the beauty of rural scenery."[34]

One important characteristic of pleasing rural scenery, in Olmsted's mind, is its unity of visual effect. Details are subordinate to the overall impression: "Scenery is more than an object or a series of objects; more than a spectacle, more than a scene or a series of scenes, more than a landscape, and other than a series of landscapes."[35]

Rural scenery, in Olmsted's view, gives the mind an emotional impulse different from that produced by the beauty of a garden or courtyard, "within which vision is obviously confined by walls or other surrounding artificial constructions."[36] Franklin Park offered just such scenery:

Given sufficient space, scenery of much simpler elements than are found in the site of Franklin Park may possess the soothing charm which lies in the qualities of breadth, distance, depth, intricacy, atmospheric perspective, and mystery. It may have picturesque passages (that is to say, more than picturesque objects or picturesque "bits"). It may have passages, indeed, of an aspect approaching grandeur and sublimity.[37]

The type of scenery Olmsted preferred for a country park obviously derived from his emphasis on its restorative value. In Chapter II we saw that Olmsted's style had its roots in eighteenth-century English landscape gardening. The term "Picturesque," it was observed, is often used broadly to describe the entire development of irregular and naturalistic landscaping in that period, and in this sense Olmsted's landscaping is Picturesque. However, he used the "Picturesque" style in its narrower sense—that is, the Picturesque as opposed to the Sublime or the Beautiful—very selectively. His choice for country parks was invariably the Beautiful or Pastoral, as it is more conveniently called: a mode of landscaping in the direct tradition of Capability Brown, featuring broad open meadows or greenswards, set off by low hills, lakes, and groups of trees. As he states explicitly in the above quote, Picturesque, or even Sublime, passages might be used as foils to the predominantly Pastoral mood.

Why did Olmsted prefer the Pastoral to the Picturesque? Clearly because such scenery was more likely to produce the desired tranquilizing and restorative effect on city dwellers. Again, he states this plainly.

The park should, as far as possible, complement the town. Openness is the one thing you cannot get in buildings. Picturesqueness you can get. Let your buildings be as picturesque as your artists can make them. This is the beauty of a town. Consequently, the beauty of the park should be the other. It should be the beauty of the fields, the meadow, the prairie, of the green pastures, and the still waters. What we want to gain is tranquillity and rest to the mind.[38]

Like his landscape style, Olmsted's theory had many sources. *Notes,* for example, contains quotations from Wordsworth, Emerson, Lowell, Ruskin, and Mrs. Gaskell, to list only a few. From boyhood on, Olmsted read widely in works by standard eighteenth- and nineteenth-century authors as well as by a good many rather obscure ones. It has been well

established that at a very young age he was strongly impressed by the writings of Horace Bushnell and Johann Georg von Zimmerman.[39] Bushnell, a prominent Congregational theologian and the Olmsted family minister in Hartford, developed the theory of "unconscious influence," a concept he used to describe human relationships but which Olmsted appears to have transposed to explain the effect of nature on man. By the time he was twenty-two, Olmsted had read Zimmerman's *Uber Die Einsamkeit (Solitude Considered)* at least twice; the eighteenth-century Swiss physician's discussion of the curative influence of natural scenery on troubled minds became another permanent strand of his thought.

Olmsted's fully matured theory of the restorative value of rural scenery has much in common with the writings of the major literary figures of his time, including Wordsworth and Emerson. Many of Olmsted's passages on the value of natural scenery, such as the ones quoted here, seem to parallel the writings of the English romantic poet and the American transcendentalist, although close examination reveals minor but significant discrepancies. In the celebrated poem "Tintern Abbey," Wordsworth tells how scenery produces in him:

> —that serene and blessed mood,
> In which the affections gently lead us on,—
> Until, the breath of this corporeal frame,
> And even the motion of our human blood
> almost suspended, we are laid asleep
> In body, and become a living soul:
> While with an eye made quiet by the power
> Of harmony, and the deep power of joy,
> We see into the life of things.[40]

He describes how the memory of such scenery brings him "tranquil restoration . . . mid the din of towns and cities."[41] (Remembered scenery seemed in his case to be a more powerful antidote than the actual experience.) But Wordsworth's excursions were nearly always solitary, or accompanied only by his sister, and they lacked the communality that to Olmsted was all-important. Furthermore, Wordsworth had a decided taste for grandeur and sublimity: his affinity was with "the sounding cataract . . . the tall rock, the mountain, and the deep and gloomy wood" rather than with the "green pastoral landscape."[42]

Emerson's long essay "Nature" also offers points of comparison with Olmsted. Of the restorative value of scenery he says: "To the body and mind which have been cramped by noxious work or company, nature is medicinal and restores their tone. The tradesman, the attorney comes out of the din and craft of the street, and sees the sky and the woods, and is a man again. In their eternal calm, he finds himself."[43] Emerson also gives some attention to rural or pastoral scenery, as opposed to the more dramatic manifestations of nature favored by Wordsworth. His comments on the visual unity of scenery make an interesting comparison with an earlier-quoted passage by Olmsted ("Scenery is more than an object or a series of objects . . ."). By nature, Emerson says, "we mean the integrity of impression made by manifold natural objects . . . The charming landscape which I saw this morning is indubitably made up of some twenty or thirty farms. Miller owns this field, Locke that, and Manning the woodland beyond. But none of them owns the landscape. There is a property in the horizon which no man has but he whose eye can integrate all the parts, that is, the poet."[44]

Who could better be described as such a poet than Olmsted? Moreover, not only did he integrate all the parts of a landscape visually, he integrated them literally as well. In Franklin Park (and in others with similar topographical advantages), Miller's, Locke's and Manning's farms were brought into the public domain, the boundary lines eliminated, discordant elements removed, and the underlying unity of the scenery revealed through his design.

Olmsted shared with the romantics and transcendentalists the intensity of their personal response to nature, and like them, he ascribed a central importance and universality to this response, but he added another dimension that they either ignored or merely suggested. His social philosophy, beautifully summed up by Laura Wood Roper, Olmsted's biographer, was as important as his landscape aesthetic:

The peculiar ideal that motivated his work was not a catchy one . . . He called it "communicativeness," and

by it he distinguished the civilized man from the barbarian. Communicativeness involved recognizing, and acting consistently on the recognition, that one had an essential community of interest with other human beings, regardless of regional, class, economic, color, religious or whatever differences . . . Communicativeness had no room for narrowly selfish interests, whether of individuals or groups or classes.[45]

Olmsted's social ideal was not something apart from or unrelated to his landscape work. Instead he viewed pastoral landscapes, and country parks in particular, as settings where people of all classes could come together "communicatively," without the veiled hostility and wariness that mark most business and social encounters:

Consider that the New York Park and the Brooklyn Park are the only places in those associated cities where, in this eighteen hundred and seventieth year after Christ, you will find a body of Christians coming together, and with an evident glee in the prospect of coming together, all classes largely represented, with a common purpose, not at all intellectual, competitive with none, disposing to jealousy and spiritual or intellectual pride toward none, each individual adding by his mere presence to the pleasure of all others, all helping to the greater happiness of each. You may thus often see vast numbers of persons brought closely together, poor and rich, young and old, Jew and Gentile.[46]

How could rural scenery so transform people's behavior, and how exactly did it improve their physical and psychological well-being? Modern urban life, in Olmsted's view, requires an unrelenting vigilance and alertness, the use of intellectual as opposed to intuitive qualities of mind, and a continual self-protectiveness—the constant weighing of one's own interests against those of others.[47] In order to "unbend" the overtaxed faculties one must occupy the imagination with "objects and reflections of a quite different character from those which are associated with their bent condition."[48] Thus the surroundings must offer the greatest possible physical and visual contrast with the city, allowing mental relaxation and the awakening of the intuitive, nonanalytical, nonverbal side of the mind, and giving people enough space so that they feel unthreatened, physically and otherwise, by each other. Rural scenery, according to Olmsted, was able to accomplish this by producing a gradual, involuntary response in the viewer: "The chief end of a large park is an effect on the human organism by an action of what it presents to view, which action, like that of music, is of a kind that goes back of thought, and cannot be fully given the form of words."[49]

Given Olmsted's convictions on the restorative value of rural scenery, his insistence on proscribing unsuitable activities from the Country Park makes

perfect sense. The sad fact is, however, that Franklin Park served the purpose intended by its designer only briefly and only in part. Changes in the actual plan were minor and, in some cases, positive: Scarboro Pond (Figure 47) for example, was constructed in 1891 from a revised plan by the Olmsted firm. However, the Park Commission never received the funds anticipated from Benjamin Franklin's will, and the depression of 1893–1897 created still more financial problems, even though Mayor Nathan Matthews initiated legislation for further loans beyond the city debt limit. As a result, the Greeting, the Music Court, and the Little Folks' Fair were

Figure 47
Sheep bound for home near Scarboro Pond, circa 1916.

never completed according to plan. The large axial space intended for the Greeting was set aside but never laid out; it has long since been annexed for zoo purposes.[50]

Hardly had Franklin Park been built than it became a battleground for competing interests. Since it was the only really large public space in the city, pressure was put on the commissioners to allow it to be used for everything from prayer meetings to labor rallies. The undesirable activities that Olmsted had feared began to encroach almost immediately. The turf Playstead was overused; the Boston Natural History Society wanted more space for a zoo than Olmsted had provided; the mayor wanted more bridle paths; and golfers began to use the Country Park "experimentally" in the nineties (Figure 48).[51] In the present century the Lemuel Shattuck Hospital has been constructed on Morton Street near Forest Hills Entrance, and the White Schoolboy Stadium has preempted a large part of the Playstead. Increased automobile traffic and declining maintenance since World War II have also been serious problems.

Figure 48
Golf in the Country Park,
1903.

Olmsted had attempted to prevent misuse of the park by providing areas such as the Playstead and Greeting within it. He also urged repeatedly that the city acquire a level piece of land adjacent or close to the park that could be used for active sports. Not only was this kind of activity inappropriate to Franklin Park, but the rugged and undulating surface was unsuited to large gatherings of people. Olmsted recommended acquiring land for such purposes to successive boards in 1876, 1886, and—finally with positive results—in 1892. Located on Blue Hill Avenue a short distance from Franklin Park, the Muster Ground as Franklin Field was initially called, had the same relationship to the park as the Parade Ground had to Prospect Park. It consisted of a flat field that could be flooded in winter for safe ice skating and could be used in summer as a parade ground, a playing field, or a place "for the display of fireworks and balloon ascensions."[52] But Franklin Field proved to be only partially successful in diverting undesirable uses from the park.

In plain fact, Franklin Park has not functioned as Olmsted intended. Why not? The question cannot be answered simply, but certain issues may be explored.

First, some problems seem to be generic to large city parks. August Heckscher has made a comparative study of various kinds of open spaces in American cities, including large urban parks. He describes "every city's central park" as follows: it dates from the last half of the nineteenth century; it is conveniently accessible to the downtown area; it is large, generally covering several hundred acres; and it includes major cultural institutions either within or near its borders. Examples are Fairmount Park in Philadelphia, Piedmont Park in Atlanta, and Balboa Park in San Diego, as well as Central, Prospect, and Franklin parks. People feel intensely about these parks, which have tended to become stages for major events in the city's history and the scenes of public protests, demonstrations, and outdoor oratory. Over time certain problems have developed in all of the parks. Contrary to the original plans, large-scale, specialized recreational facilities have been built in most and, especially in recent years, all have become difficult to maintain and police. As they become shabbier and more dangerous, they become less and less popular with the general public, and the city is even less willing to invest money in them.[53]

Franklin Park has had more than its share of all these problems. As we have seen, the Country Park was used for golf even before the turn of the century. Although it was not the use Olmsted intended, the golf course has at least ensured that no buildings are constructed in the valley. More serious has been the growth of the zoo beyond the boundaries Olmsted allotted to it and the erection of the stadium and hospital. Most damaging of all has been a dramatic decline in maintenance in recent decades, which has left most of the Olmsted structures in ruins and has destroyed all but the hardiest of the original plantings. Furthermore, Franklin Park has not had some of the advantages of most large urban parks. The symbolic significance attached to most of them has belonged since the Revolution to Boston Common. Instead, Franklin Park has developed a negative image: it is perceived as being particularly remote and dangerous. It is also seen by whites as belonging exclusively to Boston's black community rather than to the city as a whole. In fact, although it lacks the central location of large parks in most other cities, it is no farther away from downtown than a number of popular local recreation spots, and its crime rate is lower than in many of the city's other parks.[54] In terms of racial and social balance, Franklin Park is bordered on two sides by parts of Roxbury and Dorchester, now predominantly black; on the third side by a largely white, middle-class neighborhood in Jamaica Plain; and on the fourth side by Forest Hills Cemetery, its inhabitants classless, at least in death. While the park has been the scene of tensions, it has the potential of being not only a citywide but an interracial resource.

What about Olmsted's views on the restorative value of rural scenery? The fact that people are often afraid to walk in the large city parks is a sad contrast to his vision of a pastoral landscape where people could meet "communicatively." It is important to remember, however, that he never expected the beneficial effects of rural parks to happen automatically. To him, the success of a large country park was contingent on its adequate management.

In fact, it was the chance of supervising Central Park that drew Olmsted there, long before he had any thought of designing it.[55] There is ample evidence that during their early history Olmsted's country parks functioned as he intended much of the time and that failures were due to mismanagement rather than to weaknesses in his concept. City after city would hardly have followed the example of New York and Brooklyn had the parks not fulfilled people's expectations.

The seeds of later problems were present from the beginning, however, as elements not in the original plans were introduced, and as the parks were inadequately supervised and their original purpose forgotten. For much of the twentieth century, mismanagement has been the rule rather than the exception, and the nineteenth-century parks have gone rapidly downhill, as Heckscher convincingly demonstrates. Although Franklin Park was certainly enjoyed and appreciated for a time as Olmsted intended (and still is, to a certain extent), its problems came early and were particularly acute because of its relative distance from downtown and the fact that it had so much competition from other parts of the park system. Paradoxically, Franklin Park was overused for purposes, such as active sports, it was not designed for and was underused for the passive recreation and quiet enjoyment of scenery Olmsted had intended. The city's response to the park's problems has been to increase the number of "attractions:" golf course, zoo, rose garden, stadium, and so on—a policy that has only aggravated the situation.

Two Olmsted-designed landscapes in greater Boston, although planned for altogether different purposes, have come to function as country parks. People seek them out for just that quiet enjoyment of scenery Olmsted meant them to find at Franklin Park. These are World's End in Hingham, designed, although never developed, as a subdivision, and the great tree museum of the Boston system, the Arnold Arboretum. World's End, an oddly shaped peninsula formed by two drumlins that thrust out into Boston Harbor, is now owned by the Trustees of Reservations, a private, nonprofit land trust.[56] The Arboretum, as we have seen, is owned by Boston but managed by Harvard University. What do these two places have in common? First, both sites are well maintained and supervised. Second, there are no buildings at all in World's End and only two, both well designed and sensitively sited, in the Arboretum. Third, cars are allowed in the Arboretum only on weekdays and by special permit, and they are completely prohibited at World's End. Finally, there are no recreational facilities whatever—not so much as a picnic table—at either place. By chance, the Arboretum and World's End have fulfilled the chief condition Olmsted required of Franklin Park: they offer the greatest possible contrast to the city. Consequently, they "work" as country parks in a sense that Franklin Park no longer does.

Yet World's End and the Arboretum are far too small to serve this purpose indefinitely by themselves. It should also be emphasized that the failure of Franklin Park is only relative; many who come to play golf or visit the zoo also enjoy the scenery. However, the park must be restored more completely to its original function as well as be restored and maintained physically, and there are signs that this may happen. Unfortunately, Boston, like most other American cities, is in a state of fiscal crisis that does not allow it to provide adequate policing and maintenance for any of its parks. Damage to parkland by automobiles and motorcycles also remains a problem, and Franklin Park's bad "image" has proved hard to shake.

More positively, there is now greater appreciation—at least among a segment of the public—of Olmsted and of nineteenth-century parks than has been the case for many years. The environmental movement and the even more recent historic preservation movement, the national Bicentennial, recent publications on Olmsted and his career, and several major Olmsted exhibitions have all contributed to a greater awareness of historic landscape architecture. Franklin Park has benefited from this national trend and also from energetic local efforts. In 1975 a group of organizations and individuals dedicated to improving the park formed the Franklin Park Coalition.[57] Their accomplishments have already been im-

pressive: publicity for the park has improved, and the city has been stimulated into doing more actual work on the grounds.

In fact, there is currently substantial public and private investment in Franklin Park. When Heckscher wrote about city parks in 1977, Buffalo was the only American city to have prepared a master plan for its nineteenth-century park. Boston has now commissioned one for the Fens and one for Franklin Park. (Funds are available for such capital improvements for city parks but not for routine maintenance, which is still the major problem.) The Boston Zoological Society is beginning construction on an addition to the zoo, at a cost of $21 million from a combination of public and private sources. While a zoo on this scale was hardly Olmsted's intention, the space it occupies, the Greeting, was never constructed according to plan, and the buffer strips that insulated the Greeting now serve to screen the zoo from the rest of the park. The new zoo plan has been under continuous and strict review by the Department of the Interior because Franklin Park is listed on the National Register of Historic Places. In working out details of design and construction, the Boston Zoological Society has been sensitive both to Olmsted's plan and to the desires of the community.

The brightest hope for the future of Franklin Park is the fact that it is needed now more than at any time in its history. The flight from the city characteristic of the 1950s and 1960s is now being countered by a back-to-the-city movement, and the excellent and inexpensive housing stock in nearby Dorchester and Jamaica Plain is being rapidly bought up by middle-class families. With the current energy crisis and the high cost of gasoline unlikely to be relieved in the near future, city parks will be used more heavily than ever before. (This trend can already be observed in Franklin Park and other parks in Boston.) As he stated repeatedly in *Notes,* Olmsted designed not only for his generation of Bostonians but for their "heirs." Franklin Park belongs as much to 1985 as to 1885.

VI

The Emerald Necklace Completed

———————◆———————

Bᴜ ᴛʜᴇ late 1880s the Back Bay Fens was almost completely constructed, and the Arnold Arboretum and Franklin Park were well under way. Nevertheless, ten years after Olmsted signed his first contract with the Boston Park Commission, two major elements in the continuous portion of the park system, the "emerald necklace," as it has come to be called, had not yet been started: the Muddy River Improvement and Jamaica Park. Preliminary work was in progress on Marine Park in South Boston. Portions of the parkway that was to thread through and connect these parks from the Fens to South Boston were then being built, although this massive project took many years to accomplish. By 1895, however, when Olmsted retired, the emerald necklace was essentially complete.

The Muddy River Improvement had not been part of the commissioners' 1876 plan. Instead, they had recommended a site on Parker Hill in Roxbury, to be connected by parkways to the Fens and Jamaica Pond. The suggestion for improving the banks of the Muddy River in both Boston and Brookline came from Olmsted, although there was strong support from the town of Brookline. Ernest Bowditch had included the upper valley of the Muddy River in his 1875 metropolitan park plan, so the concept was not entirely new.

Like the Fens, the Muddy River Improvement is largely man-made. Unlike the Fens, Olmsted's plan is still apparent, although there have been numerous changes, some subtle and others less so. His naturalistic landscaping was so successful that people today generally regard the Muddy River Improvement as a piece of wild land "left over" after development. Although no good photographs of the Muddy River area in its pre-Olmsted state seem to have survived, maps, surveys and descriptions by Olmsted and others clearly show that it was reshaped almost as completely as the Fens.[1]

The land that is now included in the Muddy River Improvement falls into two topographical units: from the end of the Fens at Brookline Avenue to Tremont Street (now Huntington Avenue), and from this point to Perkins Street above Ward's Pond. The differences between these two sections, although still noticeable, were more marked before the land was transformed into a park. To simplify discussion, the first part will be called Muddy River, and the second Leverett Park, the name it was eventually given.

The Muddy River proper was originally a part of the great Back Bay salt marsh, as can be seen in Figure 5. Before Olmsted's plan was executed, the river was a narrow, winding tidal creek that formed the boundary between Boston and Brookline and gave Brookline its first name, Muddy River. Leverett Park began with a large marsh beyond Tremont Street. Above this point the land rose sharply, forming a series of wooded knolls similar to those surrounding Jamaica Pond directly to the south. The part of the Muddy River Improvement around Ward's Pond, the largest of three glacial, kettlehole ponds, was retained in Olmsted's plan with little change.[2]

By 1880 the pressures of increasing population were changing the Muddy River from an inoffensive little stream into a source of disease, and its surroundings from a pleasant valley into a potential slum. The filling of the Back Bay reduced the tidal flow, making the waters increasingly brackish and turning them into an ideal breeding ground for mosquitoes. South of Tremont Street the tide rarely reached the salt marsh, which gradually turned into a stagnant cattail swamp. Although Muddy River drained a much smaller area than Stony Brook, it became overloaded with sewage. Floods, although less severe than those of Stony Brook, were also a problem.[3]

Neither in Boston nor Brookline was there any effort either to preserve the natural features of the Muddy River valley or to develop it according to a comprehensive plan. Streets were laid out block by block as individual speculators subdivided small pieces of land for immediate profit. The Muddy River skirted the Longwood section of Brookline (roughly from St. Mary's Street to Longwood Avenue), one of the town's most attractive residential neighborhoods, but its appearance at this point was seriously marred by the tracks of the Brookline branch of the Boston and Albany Railroad. On the Brookline side the largest landholders in this section were the Sears and Lawrence families, and the Sears property extended across the river into Boston, near the present New England Deaconess Hospital. Near Brookline Village at Tremont Street in both Boston and Brookline was a cluster of dilapidated, unpainted houses, about forty of which had been condemned. Beyond the cattail swamp there was little development on the Brookline side. Most of this land was owned by the Brookline Land Company. Its development was imminent, and the town had already planned a new street, Pond Avenue, from Tremont Street to Perkins Street. Along the full length of the Boston side ran a wooded bank with suburban residences overlooking the valley.[4]

The idea of improving and landscaping the Muddy River was apparently discussed in Brookline as early as March 1880, when the voters at town meeting approved forming a park commission, which according to the enabling legislation of 1875 could act in cooperation with Boston to take land and plan a park that would be located in both municipalities. Late in 1880, Olmsted prepared his first plan, "Suggestion for the Improvement of Muddy River and for Completing a Continuous Promenade from the Common to Jamaica Pond," which was published in the annual reports of both the Boston and Brookline Park Commissions.[5]

Brookline had a long tradition of enlightened town planning. Local government was almost entirely in the hands of an elite group of wealthy and educated citizens, under whose close supervision growth had been for the most part gradual and controlled. The haphazard and unattractive development along the Muddy River was atypical and a matter of considerable concern.

In contrast to Brighton and West Roxbury, Brookline had successfully resisted the pressure to become a part of Boston. Although in 1870 it granted to Boston an area of marshland that later became part of the Back Bay Fens, the town voted overwhelmingly against annexation in a series of elections held during that decade. To this day Brookline has remained a town, governed by an elected board of selectmen. In the early 1870s Brookline's population was about 7,000, and it was still predominantly rural. Much of the land was owned by prominent Bostonians, who came first as summer and later as year-round residents. The beauty of Brookline, with its hilly topography, secluded country lanes, and attractive homes, was noted by A. J. Downing and other nineteenth-century writers.[6]

The Brookline park commissioners were elected by direct vote; in March 1880 the first commissioners elected were Charles Sargent, Theodore Lyman, and Francis W. Lawrence. Sargent served until his death in 1927 at the age of eighty-five, while Lyman and Lawrence were eventually replaced by Henry M. Whitney and William H. Lincoln. Although Lawrence and Whitney were chairmen for much of this period and were not shy or unassertive men, there is no question that Sargent's word was law on park matters. The other members deferred to him to such an extent that the commission effectively stopped functioning when Sargent was out of town. His dictatorship was not quite as benevolent as in the case of the Arnold Arboretum, and on at least two occasions he clashed with the Olmsted firm on matters of design.[7]

The Muddy River was the chief concern of the Brookline commission during its first fifteen years. Although the 1875 enabling act gave it the power of eminent domain, the commissioners appeared reluctant to use that power except as a last resort. In any case, many of the larger takings had to be made jointly with Boston because the owners held land on both sides of the river. Part of the nine-year delay was caused by the fact that the owners of some of the Brookline properties asked prices well over the initial assessed valuations, which then almost doubled over the period of negotiations. Furthermore, Boston could not complete its land takings until the early nineties, when more money became available from loans beyond the city debt limit. Even after all the land had been acquired,

Boston was still unable to start construction immediately. Brookline eventually became impatient and began construction on its side of the river a year ahead of Boston.[8]

Olmsted's first design for the Muddy River, which he modestly titled a "Suggestion," was a simple schematic plan prepared without benefit of a topographical survey. Although his accompanying report was characteristically long and thoughtful, he apparently had only a few days to draw up a plan for inclusion in the annual reports of both the Boston and the Brookline Park Commissions. In his "Suggestion" a gently winding stream replaced the erratic wigglings of the existing tidal river, and the cattail swamp south of Tremont Street was converted to a large pond, connected by a little brook to Ward's Pond. The first Muddy River plan was well received, and together Boston and Brookline authorized a survey and detailed plans. The "General Plan for the Sanitary Improvement of Muddy River" (Figure 49), drawn by John C. Olmsted and published in a special report in October 1881, was an elaboration of the earlier plan, with the parkways, paths, and bridle paths indicated in detail. Interestingly, a secondary parkway (never executed), similar to Audubon Road in the Fens, ran along the entire length of the Brookline side. When the details of the waterway were worked out, it became apparent that the Muddy River would have to follow the existing Boston/Brookline line, which made for some odd quirks in the line of the stream.[9]

The general plan was promptly approved by both the city and the town, but the appropriations made by both were unrealistically small. In Brookline Olmsted's plan was favored by the large landowners, but the commissioners ran into difficulties with many holders of smaller properties. In Boston the route of the parkway proved to be a bone of contention. Olmsted urged the Boston commissioners to choose the route with the most topographic advantages, but the owners of houses abutting the parkway wanted to sacrifice as little of their land as possible. These negotiations took a good deal of time and resulted in some compromises.[10]

Matters dragged on in this fashion for several years, while Boston awaited funds for land and construction. In 1890 Olmsted published a substantially altered plan, "Outline of Revised Plan for the Park-

*Figure 49 (top)
General plan for the sanitary improvement of Muddy River by F. L. Olmsted, 1881.*

*Figure 50 (bottom)
Olmsted's revised plan for the Muddy River Improvement, as published in 1892.*

way and Sanitary Improvement of Muddy River," in the annual reports of both the Boston and Brookline park commissioners. The firm also submitted a report to Brookline but not to Boston.[11] In the revised plan, illustrated here as it was published in 1892 (Figure 50), the Olmsted firm recommended a change in the boundary between Boston and Brookline to follow their proposed new line for Muddy River; this change was passed by the legislature later in 1890. Other than the change in the waterway, the most important modifications were in

the Leverett Park section, where land was added to allow the parkway to follow the most picturesque route, to provide for a large meadow near Leverett Pond and to make room for a series of "natural history pools" between Willow and Ward's ponds. Pond Avenue, the access road running along the Brookline side from Brookline Village at Tremont Street to Perkins Street, was supplemented by an inner drive for pleasure traffic only. Tentative plans were made for an electric car line to run between the two roads. Most of these changes were decided improvements, giving the river a more natural course in the Muddy River section and giving Leverett Park less cramped dimensions.

In the reports accompanying his published plans, Olmsted explained the rationale behind the design. As with the Back Bay Fens, sanitary considerations were most pressing: the increasingly stagnant and brackish condition of the river and swamp had to be alleviated to protect the health of nearby residents. Economic considerations were also important: the improvement of the river banks would encourage the development of attractive neighborhoods and thereby increase the tax base.[12] As he had at the Fens, Olmsted resolved practical problems with a sensitive landscape treatment. The manmade portion of the park, which extends from the end of the Fens at Brookline Avenue to the south-

ern end of Leverett Pond, blends imperceptibly with the natural glacial terrain above Leverett Pond. Olmsted described the Muddy River as the "sequence upon slightly higher ground to the [Fens] in following up a fresh-water course bordered by passages of rushy meadow and varied slopes from the adjoining upland; trees in groups, diversified by thickets and open glades," and its upper valley (Leverett Park) as "a chain of . . . fresh-water ponds, alternating with attractive natural groves and meads."[13] In the lower valley an existing structure just outside the borders of the park—Christ's Church, Longwood, designed for David Sears by Arthur Gilman in 1860—became a picturesque element in the landscape design (Figure 51).[14]

The Boston Society of Natural History was never able to raise funds to use the natural history

Figure 51
The lower valley of the Muddy River and Christ's Church, Longwood.

Figure 52
Ward's Pond looking west
toward Brookline, 1904.

Figure 53
Skating on Jamaica Pond
near Boston. Wood en-
graving by Winslow
Homer, 1859.

pools in Leverett Park as originally planned, for a zoological garden with aquatic birds and animals, and in 1899 they were filled. At the same time numerous changes were made in the planting on the Boston side. While some of these were contrary to the original plan, as will be seen in Chapter XIII, a splendid display of mountain laurel and hybrid rhododendrons was added around Ward's Pond (Figure 52). More recently there have been some mutilating changes, although fewer than in many parts of the park system: the building of an overpass along the Jamaicaway at the intersection of South Huntington Avenue, the sale of the first link of the Muddy River to Sears Roebuck for a parking lot, and the leveling of the rolling meadow near Leverett Pond for a ball field.

Today the major problems in the Muddy River Improvement are water pollution, lack of maintenance, and the threat, thus far not carried out, of widening and straightening out the Jamaicaway. The "chain of pleasant waters" envisioned by Olmsted has become clogged with silt and contaminated by overflow from sewer lines. Except for the oaks, beeches, and a few other long-lived trees, little remains of the original planting. Major intrusions, however, have been few, and this park has much potential for restoration.

As may easily be seen from the plan in Figure 1, Jamaica Park is the last of the three contiguous parks of the emerald necklace. The Fens, Muddy River, and Jamaica Park are in effect one elongated strip of land with a parkway running along the side. By contrast, although the Arboretum and Franklin Park are connected to each other and the rest of the system by parkways, the parks themselves do not touch. Marine Park (see Figure 2) has an even more tenuous connection with its closest neighbor, Franklin Park, by an extended route through Dorchester and South Boston along the widened Columbia Road, the Dorchesterway, and the Strandway.

In his informal consultation with the Boston park commissioners in 1876, Olmsted had endorsed the Jamaica Park part of the scheme without reservation. A few years later, in his report on the park system as a whole, he described Jamaica Pond as a natural sheet of water, with quiet, graceful shores, rear banks of varied elevation and contour, for the most part shaded by a fine natural forest-growth to be brought out overhangingly, darkening the water's edge and favoring great beauty in reflections and flickering half-lights. At conspicuous points numerous well-grown pines, happily massed, and picturesquely disposed.[15]

Jamaica Pond, the only large fresh-water pond in the city, was a logical choice for a park. Until 1848 it had been an important source of water for Boston.[16] Ice making then became its only economic function; by the 1870s, two large icehouses had been built, one on the western side and one at the southeastern corner. The icehouses obviously detracted from the pond's scenic appeal and were also contaminating the water, reasons given by the com-missioners and Olmsted for including the pond in the park system.[17]

Throughout the nineteenth century Jamaica Pond was a favorite recreation spot for people from surrounding communities. Skating was especially popular, as evidenced by the many wood engravings and lithographs published in periodicals such as *Ballou's*. One such view, a wood engraving of 1859 by Winslow Homer, is shown in Figure 53. (An ice-house can be made out just behind the couple in the center.) Before it became a park, only a small strip of land along Pond Street at the southeast end of the pond was open to the public. This served as a mooring for sailboats, as can be seen in Figure 54, which shows this part of the pond as it appeared just before park construction in 1894. Since the late eighteenth century, Jamaica Plain had been a popu-

Figure 54
Jamaica Pond at Pond Street before construction of the park, circa 1892.

and the Muddy River, for relatively little was done to the site. It could almost be considered a conservation project in today's sense of the word. The aim was to preserve its natural character and to make it accessible to the public. A detailed topographical survey was made, showing all the contours and identifying every tree. Some filling was done on the edges of the pond so that a walk could be constructed all the way around. The Jamaicaway defined the eastern edge of the park (at the bottom of Figure 56), and considerable filling and a retaining wall were necessary between Pond and Eliot streets. Other than this and the removal of all but two of the houses, little was altered.

The typically glacial knob-and-kettle terrain to the north and south of Jamaica Pond was left just as it was, although the roller-coaster effect is unlike the gentler contours Olmsted usually preferred. Heavy grading was done only where absolutely necessary on and near the Jamaicaway and other new construction. New planting was generally restricted to these areas also. The shores of Jamaica Pond were already covered with fine specimen trees and groves of pine and beech, some of which still survive. The bathing beach and bath houses originally planned (on the left in Figure 56) were not built because of neighborhood objection.[19]

The two houses retained in the Olmsted plan were the Robert Morse house (upper left in Figure 56) and Pinebank, the Edward Newton Perkins house (on the point to the right in the figure). Both houses were to be used as "refectories," where meals and light refreshment could be purchased, but the Morse house was used as such only briefly and was eventually torn down. Pinebank served first as a refectory, then as quarters for the Children's Museum, and more recently as a Park Department arts center.

The last of three houses by that name built on the same site by the Perkins family, Pinebank has an interesting history that can only be summarized here.[20] The first Pinebank (Figure 57) was built as a summer home in 1806 by James Perkins, senior partner in the China trade shipping firm of James and Thomas Handasyd Perkins. In 1848 his grandson Edward Newton Perkins tore it down and built a new house for year-round use. We do not know who designed the first Pinebank, but the second

Figure 55
Francis Parkman house
and garden at Jamaica
Pond, circa 1892.

lar location for the summer homes of wealthy Bostonians, including Governor John Hancock. Increasingly, these handsome estates were used year-round, or for at least a good part of the year, and as in Brookline, horticulture flourished. A portion of Holm Lea, the Sargent estate, touched on Jamaica Pond. The neighboring property, only a few acres in size, of historian Francis Parkman was famous for its rose garden and for the rare plants he introduced (Figure 55).[18]

The high cost of the expensively "improved" land prevented the park commissioners from purchasing more than about sixty acres around the perimeter of the seventy-acre pond. Except on the north, the park boundaries are rather skimpy. Francis Parkman was given life tenancy of his estate, although construction appears to have begun on the opposite (eastern) side of the pond before his death in November 1893.

As designed by the Olmsted firm (Figure 56) Jamaica Park is an interesting contrast to the Fens

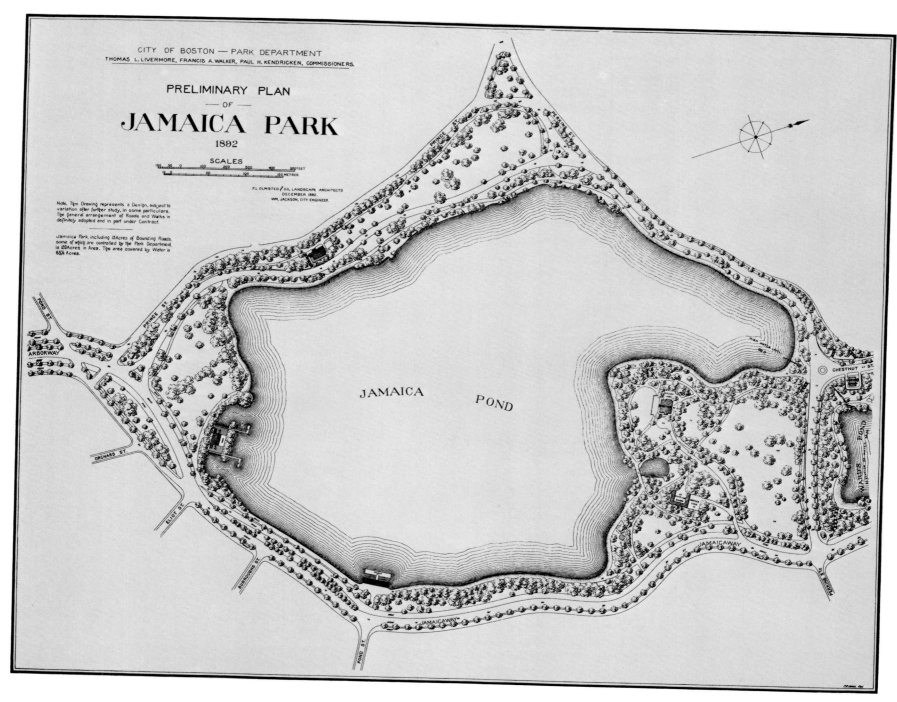

CITY OF BOSTON — PARK DEPARTMENT
THOMAS L. LIVERMORE, FRANCIS A. WALKER, PAUL H. KENDRICKEN, COMMISSIONERS.

PRELIMINARY PLAN
— OF —
JAMAICA PARK
1892

SCALES

F.L. OLMSTED & CO. LANDSCAPE ARCHITECTS
DECEMBER 1892.
WM. JACKSON, CITY ENGINEER.

JAMAICA   POND

Figure 56
Preliminary plan of
Jamaica Park by F. L.
Olmsted and Co., 1892.

Figure 57
The first Pinebank, the James Perkins house, built in 1806, at Jamaica Pond. Daguerreotype, circa 1845.

(Figure 58) was built from the plans of Jean Le-moulnier, a French architect who worked briefly in Boston in the late 1840s and is known to have designed only three buildings, all now demolished.[21] After this elegant mansard-roofed structure burned in 1868, Edward Newton Perkins decided to build a new "English" house on the still sound foundation. John Sturgis, an architect who spent much of his time in England, and his Boston-based partner, Charles Brigham, designed the third Pinebank (Figure 59) in the Queen Anne style just then coming into fashion in England, using ornamental brick and terracotta, materials they employed even more extensively in their next commission, the Boston Museum of Fine Arts in Copley Square.[22] Pinebank still stands, although it is currently in precarious condition, having been gutted by fire in the fall of 1978.

As can be seen at the bottom of Figure 56, the 1892 Olmsted plan included a boat house directly opposite the spot where Pond Street entered the Jamaicaway. (Figure 54 shows this site before construction of the park.) In 1894 Edmund M. Wheelwright, then city architect, prepared plans for a

boat house from the preliminary drawings of the Olmsted firm, but these were never carried out. The present boat house was built in 1913 from plans by William D. Austin.[23] Many local residents had hoped to preserve the gardens of Francis Parkman as a memorial to him, which proved unfeasible, but in 1906 a monument designed by Daniel Chester French was erected on the site of Parkman's house.[24]

Jamaica Park, which with Leverett Park was retitled Olmsted Park in 1900, has changed relatively little since Olmsted's day. After the turn of the century, many of the carefully preserved older trees began to die and were gradually replaced. The hawthorns, cherries, and dogwoods around Jamaica Pond today date from 1910 to 1940, not from Olmsted's time as is sometimes assumed. Skating on the pond has not been safe for many years, but it is still used for boating and fishing. Jogging on the circumferential path is also popular.

The major threat to this part of the park system (along with the still uncertain future of Pinebank) has been inappropriate use of adjacent land. Because the park boundaries are so narrow, the visual impact of nearby buildings is correspondingly increased. Unlike most other parts of the park system, there are no screening plantations, for the pond is meant to be seen from the Jamaicaway and the roads on the western side. Fortunately, to the east of the pond is a pleasant neighborhood of nineteenth- and early twentieth-century detached houses, and to the west, partly in Boston and partly in Brookline, are two large parcels of land that until recently were undeveloped. Seen from the Jamaicaway, these two tracts form a hilly, wooded backdrop to the pond. High-rise development in this district seemed a remote possibility until 1962, when a thirty-story apartment building (Jamaicaway Towers) was built on the corner of Perkins Street and the Jamaicaway, directly across from Ward's Pond. In 1969 a similar high-rise development of three towers was planned for the parcel to the northwest of Jamaica Pond (the Cabot estate).[25] A few years later, a low-rise but high-density development of terraced town houses was discussed for the southwestern parcel (the Hellenic College site). Community action averted the proposed towers on the Cabot estate, which has since been partially developed as low-rise cluster condominiums, with much of the land preserved. The Hellenic College site is as yet undeveloped.

Marine Park was also part of the commissioners' 1876 plan, but they envisioned it as a twenty-seven-acre park, built mostly on fill (see Figure 27.) Olmsted's plan was considerably more ambitious, as can be seen in Figure 60, which shows the first and probably the best of the many plans the firm prepared for this park. He proposed enlarging Dorchester, or City, Point—a narrow fringe of land just beyond the South Boston street grid—and linking it with Castle Island by a causeway, thus forming a protected bay for pleasure boating and swimming. The necessary fill would be obtained by dredging the bay, which was shallow and often exposed at low tide. A pier for promenading and a playground for schoolchildren were also to be provided.[26]

There turned out to be many obstacles to the achievement of this relatively simple plan. Although Boston owned City Point, Castle Island and historic Fort Independence belonged to the United States government. An act of Congress was necessary to grant the city the use of Castle Island, and this was not passed until 1890. (The first plan had been published in 1883.) Meanwhile the Boston Society of Natural History requested space for an "aquarial garden." Site plans for this facility were prepared in 1889 and 1891, but it apparently was not built until after the turn of the century. The federal government reappropriated Castle Island during World War I, and it was only in the 1920s that it was connected to South Boston by fill. (A temporary bridge had previously connected Castle Island and Marine Park.) As with all parks built on made land, the cost of Marine Park was disproportionate to its size; in 1896 it was still incomplete and had cost over $1.25 million out of Boston's total expenditure for parks of approximately $13 million.

The name that was finally adopted was not Olmsted's choice; in his mind the term "park" described only a country park: hence such names as Back Bay Fens and Muddy River Improvement. According to Olmsted, Commissioners Dalton and Gray changed the name from Pleasure Bay to Ma-

Figure 58
The second Pinebank, the Edward Newton Perkins house, built in 1848, Jean Lemoulnier, architect. Photograph, 1866.

Figure 59
The third Pinebank, the Edward Newton Perkins house, built in 1870, Sturgis and Brigham, architects. Photograph, 1893.

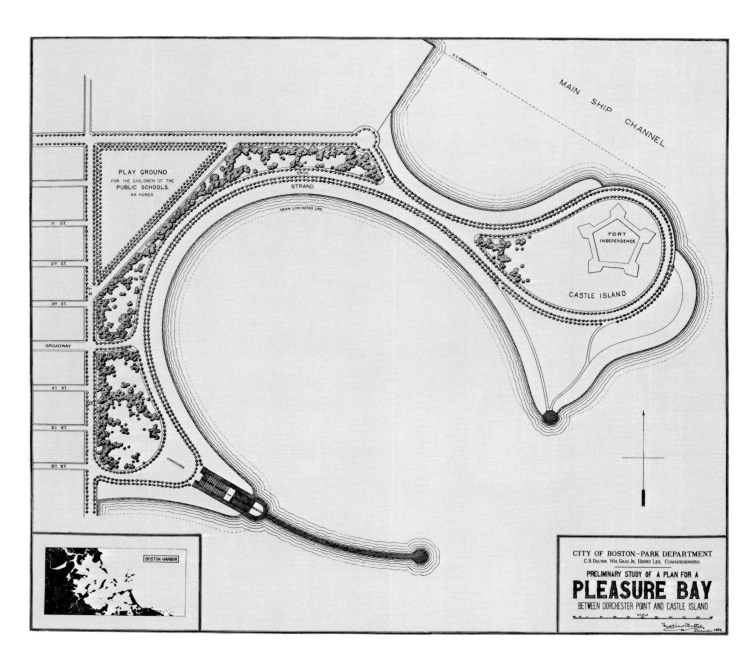

CITY OF BOSTON—PARK DEPARTMENT
C. H. DALTON, WM. GRAY, JR., HENRY LEE, COMMISSIONERS.

PRELIMINARY STUDY OF A PLAN FOR A

PLEASURE BAY

BETWEEN DORCHESTER POINT AND CASTLE ISLAND

Figure 60
Olmsted's preliminary plan
for a Pleasure Bay between
Dorchester Point and Cas-
tle Island, 1883.

rine Park in his absence, and it became established by custom. On one occasion, he referred to it, somewhat resignedly, as "the South Boston affair." As soon as a temporary wooden pier was built at Marine Park, it was flocked by Sunday "prome-naders" (Figure 61). Despite the protracted period of construction, Marine Park was the most popular part of the system in Olmsted's day, and it is still heavily used, although little is left of the original plan.[27]

The parkway (illustrated in Figure 1 with the four segments clearly identified) that connects the emerald necklace parks was conceived as a unit and should be understood as such, despite its varying names. Olmsted proposed several elaborate systems of nomenclature, but the one adopted was relatively simple. The portion running along the outer edge of the Back Bay Fens was called the Fenway; that on the eastern border of the Muddy River Improve-ment and Jamaica Park was called the Riverway from Brookline Avenue to Tremont Street (now Huntington Avenue) and the Jamaicaway from that point to the end of Jamaica Pond; that from Jamaica Pond along the Arboretum to Franklin Park was called the Arborway. The Fenway was built in the eighties, and the rest of the parkway during the early nineties.[28]

In contrast to the main parkway, which was executed as a unit and according to plan, the link from Franklin Park to Marine Park presents a confusing picture. (This section is shown in Figure 2.) The Olmsted firm prepared plans for the final two segments, the Dorchesterway and the Strandway, and construction began in the nineties, although the Strandway was not completed until after the turn of the century. (These two segments have been renamed the William J. Day Boulevard.) Figure 62 shows the Strandway and Marine Park as they appeared from the air in 1930. As suggested in the

commissioners' 1876 report, Columbia Road was the logical connecting route between Franklin Park and the Dorchesterway, but it was an existing street with a number of buildings along it, and it was needed for commercial traffic. It proved impossible to take enough land to make it into a proper parkway. Instead it was laid out like Huntington and Blue Hill avenues, with a street railway in the center and roadways on either side, one for pleasure and the other for commercial traffic. Both the roadways and the central grass strip containing the railway were too narrow to allow for more than token planting. Construction began on Columbia Road in 1897.[29]

Although the first Board of Park Commissioners had emphatically endorsed the concept of connecting parkways in their 1876 report, the superior refinement of Olmsted's design can easily be seen by comparing it (see Figures 1 and 2) to the pinched

Figure 61
Promenading on the temporary pier at Marine Park circa 1892.

Figure 62
The Strandway, Marine
Park, and Castle Island,
1930.

dimensions and awkward junctures of the commissioners' plan (Figure 27). In all fairness, the commissioners were not "designing" parkways but only indicating suggested routes. With characteristic sensitivity, Olmsted adapted the design of the parkway to the varying natural and architectural surround-

ings along the route. Formal and relatively flat as it passes the Fens, intimate and sylvan as it skirts the Muddy River and Jamaica Pond, and majestically ample in width as it approaches the Arboretum, the Boston parkway is one of Olmsted's grandest conceptions.[30]

VII

Small Parks, Playgrounds, and Unexecuted Projects

———◆———

THE fame of the emerald necklace has obscured the fact that the Boston park system also included a number of small local parks and playgrounds, most now destroyed or derelict, in the older and more congested parts of the city. In contrast to the emerald necklace, which was intended to serve the entire city, the local parks were planned as neighborhood "breathing places" and were designed specifically to provide fresh air and healthy exercise for the people living in the tenement districts. An attempt was made to meet the recreational needs of both sexes and all ages; bath houses, playing fields, and gymnastic equipment were provided, as well as walks and benches for what today would be called passive recreation. Charlesbank, the earliest of these parks, became the prototype for the rest. All five of the local parks (Charlesbank, Wood Island Park, Charlestown Heights, Charlestown Playground, and North End Park) fronted on the Charles River, the Mystic River, or Boston Harbor. Most were built largely on made land and thus required little land taking, but construction costs were high.

The Roxbury High Fort project was not strictly a part of the park system, since it was designed for the Department of Common and Public Grounds (which until 1912 had jurisdiction over the Common, the Public Garden, and other small grounds in the city) rather than for the Park Commission, but it is appropriate to discuss it in this context, for it had much in common with the five local parks and playgrounds.

It is generally assumed that all of Olmsted's plans for the Boston park system were executed. In the late 1880s and early 1890s, however, the firm prepared preliminary studies for the treatment of Copley Square, a report and preliminary plan for a park on Parker Hill, and a report recommending the reforestation of the islands of Boston Harbor. None of these projects was ever realized, but all have considerable historical interest.

Charlesbank was originally planned as a major link in the emerald necklace rather than a local park. In 1844 the Scots "city builder" Robert F. Gourlay proposed a visionary, but wholly unrealistic plan for improving the Charles River basin as part of his metropolitan park scheme, and embankments on both sides of the river were an important feature of the plans of both Uriel Crocker (Figure 23) and Charles Davenport (Figure 26).[1] The park commissioners in their 1876 report proposed a plan very like Davenport's: an embankment all the way to the Cottage Farm Bridge with walks, formal rows of trees, a bridle path, and a carriageway beyond Beacon Street, but without the additional row of houses fronting on the river suggested by Davenport.[2] That plan met with opposition from the residents of the water side of Beacon Street, and although the project was revived in the nineties, its realization had to wait until after the turn of the century, when the Charles River dam was built.[3]

By 1880 the commissioners had decided to take a much smaller strip of Charles River frontage between the West Boston and Leverett Street bridges and across Charles Street from the Suffolk County Jail and Massachusetts General Hospital. Rather than providing an unwanted amenity for wealthy Back Bay residents (most of whom were out of town during the summer), they planned instead to offer a variety of recreational facilities for the poor in the crowded tenement district of Boston's West End.[4] At that time no parks were planned for Charlestown, so the Charlesbank site was chosen also because of its accessibility by bridge to this

Figure 63
Charlesbank before construction, 1886.

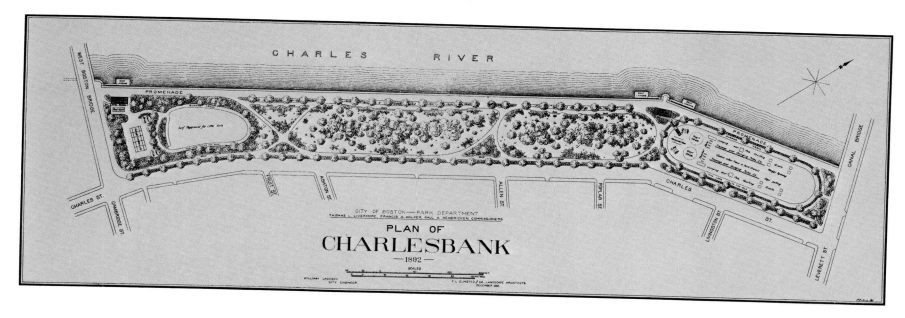

part of the city. Although the park was only ten acres, land taking was protracted, since it required an act of the legislature and lengthy negotiations with the State Board of Harbor and Land Commissioners to obtain permission to build a new sea wall farther out into the river.[5] Occupied mostly by cheaply built warehouses, this stretch of riverside was bleak indeed (Figure 63).

Olmsted presented a preliminary plan of Charlesbank in 1887 and a revised version in 1892 (Figure 64). In the report accompanying the first plan he listed, among the park's main purposes, lowering the midsummer death rate from *cholera infantum* of young children in the West End and providing open-air exercise facilities for people whose occupations were sedentary. Its main use otherwise would be as a refreshing change of scene and air to people visiting it at nightfall after having worked all day "in close and heated buildings." He therefore proposed a level promenade along the entire half-mile length of the river, a gymnastic ground for men, a playground and running track for women and children (revised in 1892 to include gymnastic facilities), and between the two an expanse of raised ground to be planted as a natural grove. Two boat landings and men's and women's athletic buildings were also suggested.[6]

When the park was completed, the promenade (Figure 65) was a much used and festive feature, its railing and long row of lamps forming "a beautiful

glittering line of light along the margin of the river at night."[7] But it was the two outdoor gymnasiums, which opened in 1889 for men and 1891 for women, that brought Charlesbank national fame. Gymnasiums as such were not new. They were a German importation, introduced in 1826 by Profes-

Figure 64
Plan of Charlesbank by F. L. Olmsted and Co., 1892.

Figure 65
The promenade at Charlesbank.

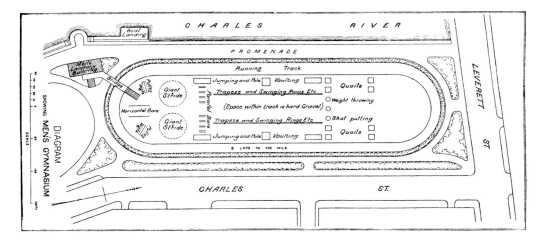

Figure 66
Plan of the men's gymnasium, 1891.

Figure 67
Sand courts in the women's and children's section of Charlesbank, 1892.

sor Charles Follen of Harvard, who set up his own apparatus on the "Delta" in Cambridge, where Memorial Hall now stands.[8] Over the next decades the vogue for gymnastic exercise grew. Charlesbank, however, had the first scientifically designed and administered open-air gymnasiums to be operated free of charge in a public park. The men's gymnasium included areas equipped with horizontal bars, trapezes, and flying rings, surrounded by a cinder running track. The equipment was designed, supplied, and installed by Professor Dudley Sargent of Harvard, but the actual layout was planned by the Olmsted firm (Figure 66). Instruction was given by Superintendent John Graham. In winter the apparatus was taken down, and the ground was flooded for skating.[9]

The gymnasium for women and children was similar but much smaller and without provision for some of the more strenuous activities, such as jumping and shot-putting. For many years it was administered by a staff of trained instructors under the direction of Mrs. Kate Gannett Wells of the Massachusetts Emergency and Hygiene Association.[10] Individual therapeutic programs were provided for women and girls who were referred to Charlesbank by doctors for complaints as various as curvature of the spine and Saint Vitus' dance. A few years before the establishment of Charlesbank, at the suggestion of a friend who had seen them in the public parks of Berlin, Mrs. Wells introduced the first sandboxes in this country at several improvised playgrounds in Boston.[11] The children's part of Charlesbank included several such "sand courts" (Figure 67), as well as a turf playground (Figure 68). A matron or *Kindergartner* taught sewing, crafts, and games to preschoolers, who could be left there during the day while their mothers went to work.[12] (The free gymnastic instruction and child care were supported by private donations for the first two years and then were taken over by the city.)

Both the men's and women's facilities were great successes. In 1893 daily attendance at the women's and children's gymnasium alone averaged 840 during the season, and Sundays, with an average of 665, were considered quiet days.[13] The design of this gymnasium was slightly different from that of the men's; instead of occupying the center of the running track, the equipment was in an enclosed yard of its own, but the apparatus was essentially the same (Figures 69 and 70). While the men's gymnasium was surrounded by an open fence that permitted onlookers to gaze at the "interesting and animated spectacle" (Figure 71), the women's running track and gymnasium were discreetly screened by shrubbery to provide "the seclusion desirable for the sex that uses them."[14]

Between the two gymnasiums was a wide lawn (Figure 72), used mainly by children for exercise of a less organized sort. One observer recalled

the shaded grassy mounds along the middle part of Charlesbank, where the children play informal games, give tea parties and generally disport themselves. I remember one day watching five small boys playing with an infant in a baby wagon. First they ran rapidly about the grass, pushing the wagon with its occupant in front of them as a sort of carroccio or armed chariot. Then they put the baby on the grass and ran and turned somersaults over him, thereby securing much healthful exercise and incidentally giving the baby the time of his life, judging by his comments.[15]

Although Charlesbank has a rather inglorious modern descendant (a Metropolitan District Commission swimming pool and athletic field) located in front of Massachusetts General Hospital and the jail, the park as Olmsted designed it no longer exists. The success of Charlesbank, especially its gymnastic facilities, continued for many years, and similar gymnasiums were set up at Marine Park and two other local parks. However, extensive filling on the Boston side of the Charles River Basin in the 1930s and the widening of Charles Street and construction of automobile overpasses in the 1950s eradicated this pioneering neighborhood park. The site of the present MDC ground was water in Olmsted's time.

The other isolated parks within the system were also designed for densely populated parts of the city at some distance from the emerald necklace. Wood Island Park in East Boston, one of the sites proposed in 1876, was first planned as a very small park with one playground and a few walks, but by 1891 more land was added and the plan was totally

Figure 68
View of Charlesbank with the children's turf playground, 1892.

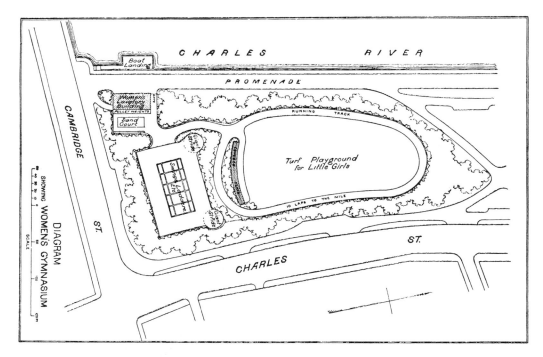

Figure 69
Plan of the women's and children's section. The gymnasium, with giant strides, swings, and ladders, is to the left, 1891.

Figure 70
View of the women's gym-
nasium, 1891.

revised (Figure 73). With forty-six acres, this was by far the largest neighborhood park. It was located directly on Boston Harbor and was reached by Neptune Road, a parkway also designed by the Olmsted firm. Originally a bare and windswept piece of marsh and upland, the site was enlarged by fill and planted with hardy native trees. In function, Wood Island Park was somewhat similar to Charlesbank. The revised plan included outdoor gymnasiums for men and women, a beach, and playgrounds. There were attractive walks as well as grounds for active recreation.[16] As at Charlesbank, the men's gymnastic equipment was removed during the winter, and the ground was flooded for skating (Figure 74).

Wood Island Park served a community that was more homogeneous and self-contained than the West End. In 1880 the population of Wards 1 and 2 (East Boston and the Harbor Islands) was just

Figure 71
View of the men's gymna-
sium, 1889.

Figure 72
Children at play, Charles-
bank, 1901.

under 30,000, many of whom were of Irish birth or descent. By 1925 the population of East Boston had reached 64,069 and was predominantly Italian. Increasingly, Wood Island Park became a focus for neighborhood activities. Renamed World War Memorial Park, it was known familiarly to residents as La Montagnella or the Little Hill. It was the scene of large family picnics and parties, sea bathing, clam digging, and general conviviality. The tradition of organized outdoor exercise was continued by Pauline Bromberg, physical education instructor at East Boston High School, who held yearly demonstrations at Wood Island during the 1920s. City and state authorities, however, seemed unaware of the value to the community of this park, and they gradually phased out its recreational uses. Ironically, Italian prisoners of war were kept there during World War II. In 1949 an act was passed authorizing Logan Airport to seize both Wood Island and the neighboring William Amerina Park for additional runways; in exchange, East Bostonians were

to get a new beach at Orient Heights. The park deteriorated greatly over the next two decades, but its final destruction and that of Neptune Road did not take place until the late 1960s.[17]

The first Board of Park Commissioners had been unable to find any spot for a park in densely built-up Charlestown, but the citizens of that community repeatedly petitioned for recreation areas of some sort. In the early 1890s sites were finally chosen for two small parks in the part of Charlestown nearest Somerville. One, Charlestown Heights (Figure 75), was a lookout area on the slope of Bunker Hill (the real Bunker Hill, not Breed's Hill, where the monument is located) with a view over the Mystic River and beyond. In a park of only four acres, much of it on very steep land, extensive facilities for sports or gymnastics were clearly impossible. Sand courts and a grassy play area were provided for small children. On Bunker Hill Street the sidewalk was widened and planted with trees to allow a generous space for "promenading." At the opposite end of the park, where the ground dropped off sharply toward the river, winding walks and steps were constructed of rough boulderwork similar to that used in Franklin Park and elsewhere in the system. Olmsted's plan was executed as shown, except that the bridge over Medford Street was apparently omitted and replaced by one over Saint Martin

Street (Quincy Street on the plan).[18] Charlestown Heights still exists under the name of Doherty Playground. The promenade near the street is in good condition. The boulder-lined walks and steps are more or less intact, but the lawn between has been converted to basketball courts and swimming pools.

A second park, adjacent to Sullivan Square and the Mystic River, was built for the activities that could not be accommodated at Charlestown

Figure 73
Revised preliminary plan of Wood Island Park by F. L. Olmsted and Co., 1891.

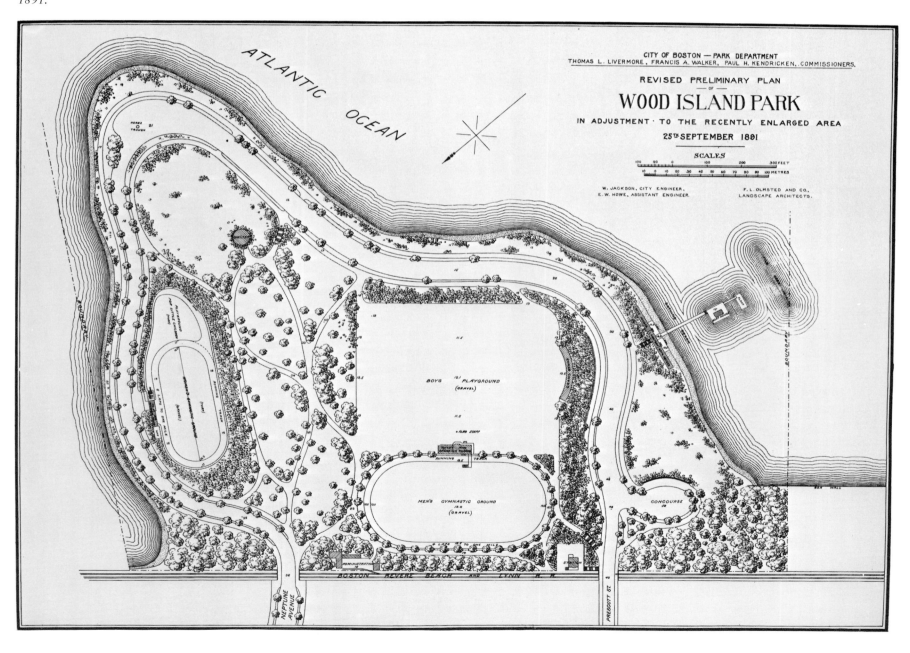

Figure 74
Skating at Wood Island
Park, 1895.

Heights. The site, most of which was water, was chosen in 1891, and the Olmsted firm prepared a plan in the same year, but more than a decade passed before Charlestown Playground was ready for use. Filling dragged on for an interminable time, although the city engineer optimistically reported each year that progress was being made. The Olmsted plan was a simple one: the fourteen-acre triangular site was to be used primarily for ball playing. At the short end of the triangle, near Sullivan Square, were men's and women's gymnasiums. Around the perimeter was a promenade, and bath houses were to be provided. Perhaps because of the long delay, Charlestown Playground as constructed differed markedly from the Olmsted plan. Only one open-air gymnasium and running track was built, and the tree-lined promenades and bath houses were eliminated. Possibly as a substitute, Dewey Beach was constructed on the Mystic River at the foot of Charlestown Heights.[19] Today Ryan Play-ground, as it is called, is a cheerless stretch of land entirely devoted to ball fields.

The North End, the oldest part of Boston, was not provided for in the 1876 park plan. In the early nineties a park was finally secured there, largely through the efforts of John F. "Honey Fitz" Fitzgerald, in his capacity first as city councillor and then as state senator.[20] The North End Park, or Copps Hill Terraces, was designed by Charles Eliot, then a partner in the Olmsted firm. The North End Park was the only part of the municipal system for which Eliot had chief responsibility, although as an apprentice, he had worked on the Arboretum, Franklin, and Marine park plans. Eliot took great satisfaction in designing this small neighborhood park, as is clear from a letter written to his wife one hot July day in 1896:

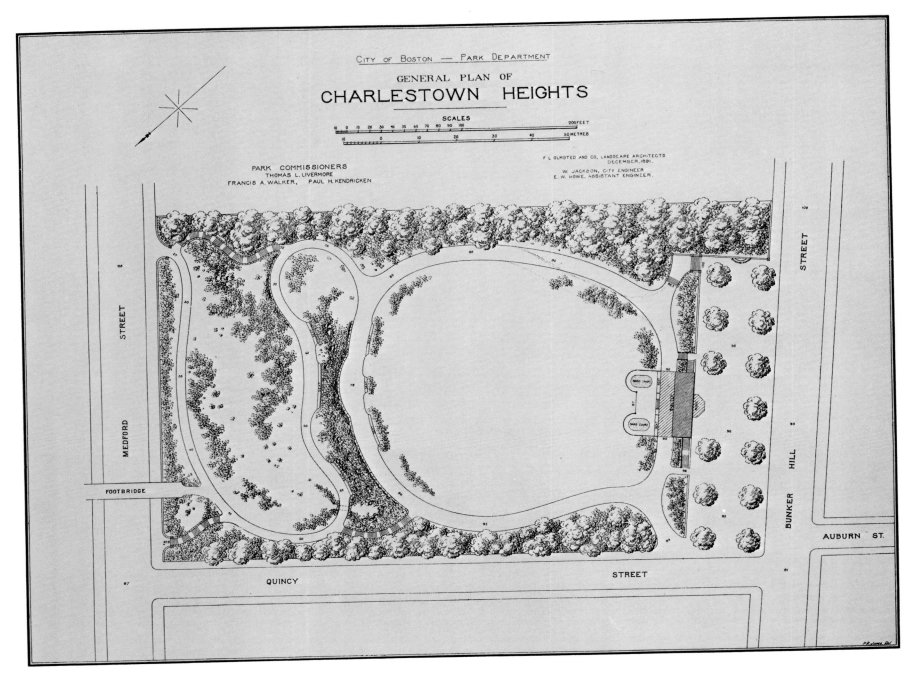

Figure 75
General plan of Charles-
town Heights by F. L.
Olmsted and Co., 1891.

Just through with the Boston Board Park Commission. A long and complicated meeting, yet hardly up to the Metropolitan article. Our plans for the North End Terrace at Copps Hill were at last approved . . . I am smitten with pity for the slum people . . . My walk from Cambridge Field (in construction) through East Cambridge to Charlesbank! Doorsteps crowded with unclean beings, children pushing everywhere, and swarming in every street and alley. What a relief when Charlesbank is reached! The quiet open of the river, the long, long row of twinkling lights on the river wall, the rows upon rows of seats all filled with people resting in the quiet air, and watching the fading of the golden light behind the Cambridge towers. The new terrace at the North End is to be another such evening resting-place. It is good to be able to do something, even a little, for this battered and soiled humanity.[21]

The 1894 plan for North End Park (Figure 76) shows a remarkably ingenious treatment of a difficult site. Eliot designed a multipurpose recreational area adjoining Copps Hill Burial Ground, the only existing open space of any kind in the neighborhood. "Resting places" were to be provided by terracing the side of Copps Hill between Charter and Commercial streets and by making a small lawn with paths and more seating. Access from one part of the park to the other was by a bridge over Commercial Street to the upper level of a double-decked promenade pier. Still further protection for the small beach was offered by a covered pier connected with the women's bath house. All of this was on a site that included only a little more than three acres of dry land.[22] The park appears to have been built according to plan, except for the bridge over Commercial Street, which was eliminated because of the elevated railway under construction at about the same time as the park. Similarly, the little lawn was soon incorporated into the beach.[23] Today only the stone terraces on the slope of Copps Hill survive, in good condition but covered with graffiti. Boston Harbor, like the Mystic River, is no longer fit for swimming. There is now a swimming pool and a large ball field on the site of the beach, and remnants of the promenade pier foundation jut out into the water.

Although the Roxbury High Fort, on the top of Fort Hill, came under the jurisdiction of the Depart-

ment of Common and Public Grounds, its function, dimensions, and landscape treatment were quite similar to those of some of the neighborhood parks done for the Park Commission. The Olmsted firm began studies for this project in September 1895, just when Olmsted retired from practice, so it is unlikely that he had a significant role in elaborating the design. However, a report appeared under his name that was quoted at some length in the *Boston Evening Transcript*.[24]

The remains of the revolutionary fort had been destroyed when a water standpipe was built on Fort Hill in 1869–1870. The standpipe became functionally obsolete when a new reservoir was built on Parker Hill in 1880, but it remained an attractive architectural feature of the hill. In 1888 the standpipe and surrounding grounds (known as Highland Park) were turned over to the Department of Public Grounds in poor condition. The plan prepared by the Olmsted firm, which was executed, called for both the restoration of the standpipe and the reconstruction of the revolutionary earthworks. In addition, the grounds were landscaped for a sitting and observation area, somewhat in the manner of Charlestown Heights, with walks, seats, pudding-stone retaining walls, and extensive use of low-growing, prickly vines and shrubs, such as memorial rose (*Rosa wichuraiana*) and Japanese barberry (*Berberis thunbergii*), which acted as barriers and ground cover on the sloping ground. The site was unsuited for any kind of active recreation. Olmsted objected to the name Highland Park and insisted on the historically accurate and more descriptive Roxbury High Fort. In 1912 and 1913 the Olmsted firm was again retained to landscape grounds that had been added to the site.[25] Recently, the standpipe has been renovated under a grant from the United States Department of the Interior, but except for shrubs planted by a neighborhood group, little has been done to the grounds.

Olmsted's retirement coincided with a shift in the city's park policy. Josiah Quincy, the third mayor of Boston by that name, took office in 1896. He fully recognized the value of the city's large parks and smaller neighborhood breathing spaces, and he urged the completion of all unfinished work, especially on the Strandway, but Quincy also felt

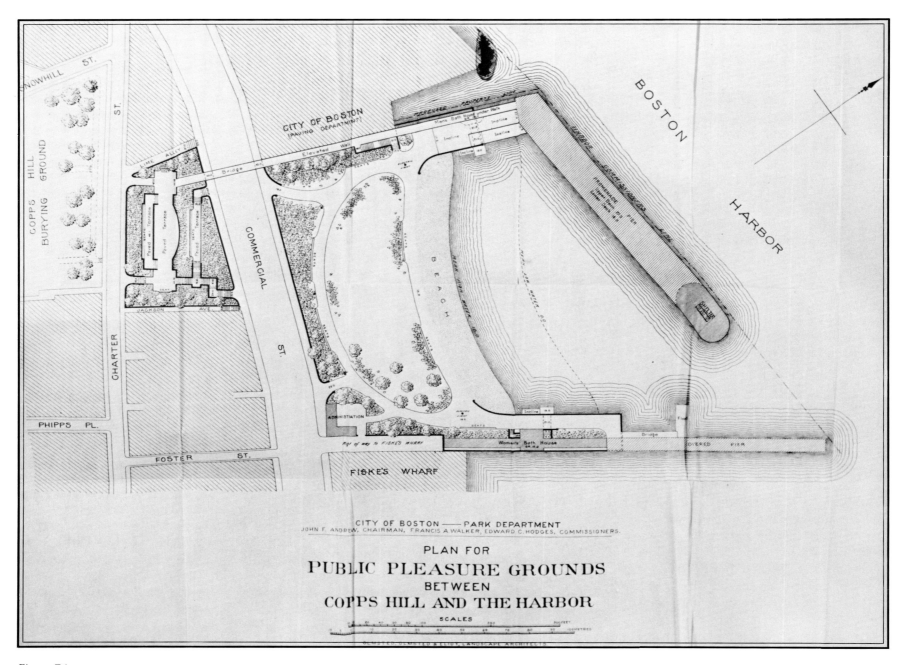

Figure 76
Plan for North End Park
and Copps Hill Terraces
by Olmsted, Olmsted and
Eliot, 1894.

that a new type of recreation ground was a pressing necessity. The small parks of the Olmsted era, with the exception of Wood Island Park and Charlestown Playground, generally did not allow space for ball playing and other competitive sports. Provision for such games had been made at the Playstead in Franklin Park and at Franklin Field, but most ball playing was done in vacant lots. Mayor Quincy urged that space be set aside for playgrounds, which he defined as ball fields for boys over ten. In 1898 he initiated legislation for a system of playgrounds, with at least one in every ward of the city. Half a million dollars was appropriated for the park commissioners to establish twenty-two such grounds; by 1932 there were forty-one.[26] At sites unconnected with parks, the Massachusetts Emergency and Hygiene Association's "tot lot" playgrounds, with sand courts and play equipment, such as seesaws, suitable for little children, continued to flourish and were eventually taken over by the school committee. The playground movement was of national and even international dimensions. From the 1890s through the first decades of this century, cities throughout the country became dotted with such grounds, some strictly utilitarian in appearance but others attractively designed.

The three unexecuted projects designed for Boston by the Olmsted firm did not include any playgrounds or neighborhood parks. All, however, would have been valuable additions to the park system.

Many observers have noted that Copley Square was only recently laid out as an urban square and that it developed more or less by accident out of two small triangles of land left over at the intersection of Boylston Street and Huntington Avenue. Since 1885, when the land was purchased by the city, many treatments, most of them overelaborate and fussy, have been suggested for Copley Square. In 1891 the Olmsted firm contributed a series of alternate solutions simpler than most that have been proposed before or since. (Figure 77 shows a sketch for Copley Square, possibly in Olmsted's hand.) The exact circumstances of these studies is something of a puzzle. The Department of Public Grounds had jurisdiction over the square at the time, but there is

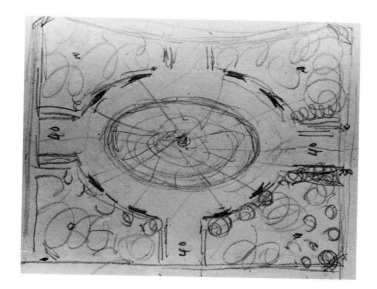

Figure 77
Study for Copley Square (unexecuted project), circa 1891.

no mention in their annual reports of plans or any sort of special appropriation for Copley Square. The roll of drawings at the Olmsted National Historic Site, Brookline, that contains the Copley Square studies also includes studies by the Olmsted firm for the Boston Public Library courtyard and architects' elevations of the courtyard arcade, which was under construction at the time. This makes it seem likely that the trustees of the library were the client for the whole series of studies, but there is no mention of any plans for Copley Square in their annual reports either. Some of the Olmsted studies for Copley Square include seats and small planting areas, and others show a symmetrical treatment using ornamental paving.

Most of the park system proposals of the late 1860s and early 1870s had included a park on the top of Parker Hill in Roxbury. The first Board of Park Commissioners in their 1876 report planned Parker Hill Park as the second link in the system, to be reached by a parkway from Tremont Entrance in the Fens near the present Isabella Stewart Gardner Museum, but at Olmsted's suggestion this was supplanted by the Muddy River Improvement. In 1892, however, the park commissioners asked the Olmsted firm to prepare preliminary plans and a report for a small park on top of the hill.

They suggested two alternate solutions. In the first, a small area would be taken to allow both for future expansion of the reservoir and for an observation tower. The second solution allowed for considerably more space in order to preserve the groves of trees on the slopes of the hill and for branch parkways to connect it with the Fenway and Riverway. A tower was considered necessary in both plans, since it was anticipated that apartment houses would be built up closely around the hill. The second plan featured winding paths, a concourse, and wriggling parkways, designed to avoid a too-steep grade. Although the park commissioners endorsed this plan, the City Council apparently considered it an extravagance and did not appropriate the funds. In 1911 the Metropolitan Park Commission was asked to consider acquiring land on this site but concluded that Parker Hill should be the object of local rather than metropolitan effort. In 1917 the Olmsted firm designed a playground for Parker Hill.[27]

The third unexecuted project was the Harbor Islands reforestation program. In 1886 Olmsted wrote an open letter to *Century Magazine* that included the following observations:

We have another fine city, a city of some repute for its poets, its architecture, sculpture, music, gardening, its galleries and its schools of art. Liberal, provident, thrifty, clean, it sits at the head of a harbor giving directly on the sea. The harbor has made the city. Various islands and headlands make the harbor . . . Once the islands were bodies of foliage. Seen one against another and grouping with woody headlands, they formed scenery of grace and amenity, cheerful, genial, hospitable. But long ago they were despoiled for petty private gains, and the harbor made artificially bald, raw, bleak, prosaic, inhospitable . . . Several of them are the property of the city and are in use for excellent purposes. It would not lessen but enhance their value for these purposes to dress them again with the graces of naturally disposed foliage . . . but the opportunity remains not only unused, but . . . unconsidered,—a matter of no account.[28]

Olmsted's appeal was not made directly to the Boston park commissioners, but a local group, the Boston Memorial Association, heeded his comments and wrote a letter to the commissioners, asking them to undertake the replanting. After consulting with reforestation experts and making several steam-yacht trips to the islands with the commissioners, Olmsted submitted a formal report with recommendations strikingly different from those made for any previous Boston project. No land was to be purchased, since only a few of the smallest islands were privately owned. They were not to be turned into "parks," and therefore Olmsted submitted no plan.[29]

About 400 acres were to be planted with native trees, such as pine, birch, and oak—presumably the original growth. Robert Douglas, who had had success with reforesting similar barren areas in the Middle West, agreed to supervise the entire program on a contract basis, payment to be contingent on the satisfactory progress of the work. Although Douglas was confident of success, the venture was chancy enough that he was unwilling to take the entire responsibility. The commission was therefore to appoint two competent "dictators" (Sargent was one obvious candidate) to choose the types of trees and spacing.[30]

Since land taking and construction were not required, the cost was modest: an annual appropriation of $5,000 for a six-year period was requested, but the appropriation failed to pass. In 1893 Olmsted's Harbor Islands report was reprinted as an appendix to the first Metropolitan Park Commission report. When the proposal was brought before the Boston Park Commission again in 1895, they were unwilling to spend $250 for a new report with plans.[31]

VIII

Plans for Greater Boston

———————◆———————

In the late 1890s, as the Boston Park Commission turned its attention to playgrounds, large-scale planning for parks became the function of the newly formed Metropolitan Park Commission. While an adequate study of the Boston metropolitan park system would require a book of almost the dimensions of the present one, a brief discussion of its early years is appropriate here. The initial planning and land acquisition phase of the metropolitan system overlapped the final construction stages of the municipal system, and conceptually the metropolitan park plan was the almost inevitable outgrowth of Olmsted's achievements in Boston.

Well before 1893, however, the Olmsted firm had designed or given advice on many projects in and near Boston, which, although not part of the municipal system, were closely related to it and the later metropolitan system. Among these are the Chestnut Hill circuit (Commonwealth Avenue in Brighton, and Beacon Street, in Brookline), several subdivisions and street improvements in Brookline, World's End in Hingham, and the Lynn Woods.

Although "metropolitan" here refers strictly to communities close to but politically independent of Boston, at different times the term has included different towns. Many communities that were part of metropolitan Boston in 1869—Dorchester, Brighton, Charlestown, and West Roxbury, for example—were part of municipal Boston in 1875. Distance from the center of Boston is not necessarily a reliable guideline. Brookline is literally embedded in Boston, as a glance at any map will show, but it has remained politically independent and thus metropolitan.

Rivers in many cases form part of the boundaries between cities and towns, and for this reason, comprehensive planning of rivers and their surroundings generally demands a metropolitan effort, as was demonstrated on a small scale by the history of the Muddy River Improvement. Boston Harbor is surrounded by many towns besides Boston, and World's End, although located in suburban Hingham, is an important element in the topography of the harbor. In fact, every community within a twelve-mile radius of Boston is bound closely to the city by geographical, social, and economic ties.

Of all the Olmsted firm's metropolitan projects, excluding the metropolitan park system itself, the one most closely connected with the Boston park system is the Chestnut Hill circuit: the loop around Chestnut Hill Reservoir formed by Beacon Street and Commonwealth Avenue (see Figure 2). Beacon Street, an existing route, was widened and redesigned. Commonwealth Avenue was for the most part a new plan and was designed and constructed in several stages. Neither street was a parkway in Olmsted's sense, since commercial traffic was permitted along with pleasure vehicles. Both were carefully thought out in relation to the park system and touched it at one or more points.

Commonwealth Avenue is divided, both visually and in terms of its construction history, into four segments: (1) from the Public Garden to Massachusetts Avenue (originally West Chester Park), (2) from there through the Fens to what is now Kenmore Square, (3) from the square to the junction with Brighton Avenue, and (4) from there to the Chestnut Hill reservoir. (The fourth segment was originally called "Massachusetts Avenue.") The Olmsted firm designed the second and fourth segments and advised on the first.

The first segment of Commonwealth Avenue was laid out in the 1860s as part of Arthur Gilman's plan for the residential Back Bay. The tree planting of this segment is often attributed to Olmsted, but there is no evidence to support such a claim. It is true that in 1880 Charles Dalton asked Olmsted and Sargent for advice on the planting of the avenue's central green, but the Department of Common and Public Grounds, which then had jurisdiction of that part of Commonwealth Avenue, did not take their advice. Dalton must have expected that the Park Commission would assume management of the avenue, and when that did occur in 1894, the Olmsted firm gave more advice, mostly on new surfacing and such matters.[1] (No plan was made at either time.)

When Olmsted began designing the Back Bay Fens, Commonwealth Avenue stopped at West Chester Park. To avoid having the avenue cross the railroad at an awkward angle, the engineer in charge deflected its line so that it intersected Beacon Street and connected with what was then the beginning of Brighton Avenue. Since a mall on this part of Commonwealth Avenue would have been inconsistent with the informal nature of the adjacent Fens, Olmsted designed it as a curvilinear avenue. (Olmsted's original design for this portion of Commonwealth Avenue may be seen on the right in Figure 31, the plan of the Back Bay Fens). According to John C. Olmsted, this plan was executed, but the half west of the Fens was later torn up because of complaints by the owners of adjacent house lots.[2]

In 1884 the Olmsted firm began studies for the Boston Street Department for a new avenue in Brighton. (The Olmsted plan seems not to have been published as a separate lithograph; the avenue appears at the top of Figure 78 and also in Figure 2). Originally called "Massachusetts Avenue," it began at Brighton Avenue near the Brookline line and extended to the Chestnut Hill Reservoir. Winding through rough and hilly terrain, this fourth segment of Commonwealth Avenue is a complete contrast with the formal, urban treatment of the first segment in the Back Bay. Charles Eliot, then an apprentice in the Olmsted office, described it in his diary: "Yesterday [I followed] JCO over the line of the crazy Mass. Ave. . . . A problem in grades—country very rough—6 in 100—the steepest allowable—and to get this cuts of from 10 to 25 feet are frequent with fills to correspond."[3]

"Massachusetts Avenue" was 200 feet wide and in its first stretch was divided into a central drive with an access road on either side. No provision was made originally for a street railway. There seems to be more than a lingering memory of Uriel

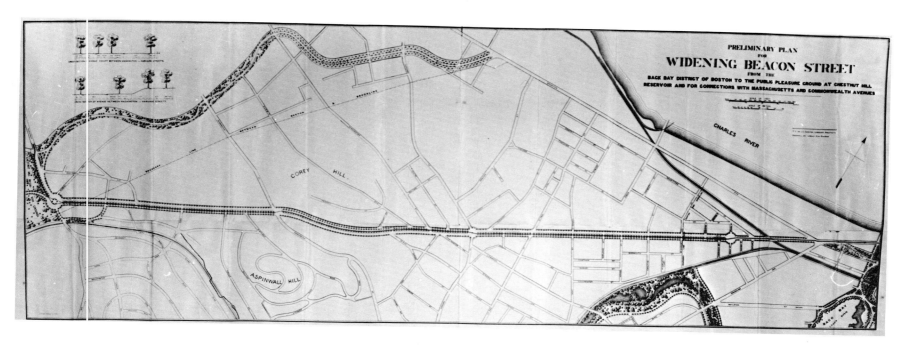

PRELIMINARY PLAN
FOR
WIDENING BEACON STREET
FROM THE
BACK BAY DISTRICT OF BOSTON TO THE PUBLIC PLEASURE GROUND AT CHESTNUT HILL
RESERVOIR AND FOR CONNECTIONS WITH MASSACHUSETTS AND COMMONWEALTH AVENUES

Figure 78
Preliminary plan for widening Beacon Street, Brookline, by F. L. and J. C. Olmsted, November 29, 1886. Beacon Street is the straight street in the lower half; Massachusetts (later Commonwealth) Avenue is the winding one, upper left.

Crocker's proposed park system (Figure 23) in the Olmsted's "Massachusetts Avenue" plan, although the route in the later plan is somewhat different, since it could not cross the border into Brookline. In the stretch between Winchester Street and the reservoir, a dramatic departure was made from the symmetrical plan of the first half between Brighton Avenue and Winchester Street: the same 200-foot strip of land was taken, but instead of being divided into three parallel drives, a single roadway wound informally past steep ledges and around groups of trees (Figure 79). Unfortunately, this informal half was apparently never constructed according to Olmsted's design.

By 1909 the plan had been adapted to include a streetcar line, necessitating a uniform plan for the whole fourth segment, with two roadways and a central green strip containing the streetcar tracks. Construction proceeded very slowly, and the planting of street trees was delayed until well after the turn of the century. Consequently, real estate development was diverted to Brookline, where Beacon Street was being constructed with much more dispatch.[4] By 1887 "Massachusetts Avenue" had been renamed Commonwealth Avenue, as had the first part of Brighton Avenue, which was widened to

form the connection with Kenmore Square. By the mid-1890s an extension of Commonwealth Avenue, originally called Newton Boulevard, had been built from the reservoir to the Charles River in Auburndale.

The circuit around Chestnut Hill Reservoir is completed by Beacon Street in Brookline. As early as 1866 Henry M. Whitney, an executive in the Metropolitan Steamship Company, saw the possibilities of Beacon Street, which had been laid out only fifteen years before as a fifty-foot-wide county way (Figure 80). He began buying up farms in the vicinity as an investment, and later he formed a syndicate, the West End Land Company, and bought on an even larger scale. In 1886 Whitney, who was a Brookline park commissioner and a member of the Tree Planting Committee, asked Olmsted to draw plans for widening Beacon Street to a 200-foot avenue. Whitney presented the first Olmsted plan (then called "Extension of Commonwealth Avenue along the line of Beacon Street, Brookline") to the town, offering to give the necessary land for widening and to pay half of the cost of construction.[5]

The plan was approved in spite of some objections, but the width of the street was reduced to 160 feet. An act of the legislature was necessary to

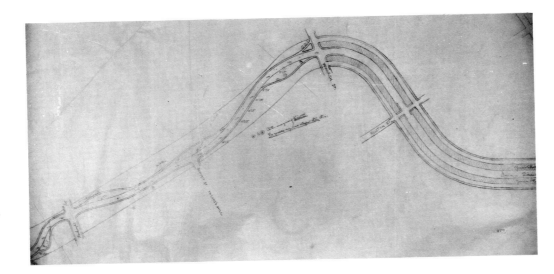

Figure 79
Detail of study for Massa-
chusetts (Commonwealth)
Avenue, Brighton, June 11,
1884.

Figure 80
Beacon Street before wid-
ening, looking east toward
Corey Hill, 1887.

carry out the plan, since Beacon Street was a county, not a town, way. The West End Street Railway Company, of which Whitney was president, put an electrified line along Beacon Street, and the value of the West End Land Company's adjacent holdings increased proportionately. The improved Beacon Street proved immensely profitable for Brookline through increased tax revenues, as well as for Whitney, and it was generally regarded as a triumph.

In the report that accompanied his plan, Olmsted predicted that the widening and improvement of Beacon Street would encourage the growth of a fine residential neighborhood—a logical continuation of the Back Bay district in Boston—on either side of the street. Beacon Street would then be both the principal trunk line of the district and an avenue for pleasure driving, riding, cycling, and walking. Substantial setbacks would be required for all buildings along it, and intersections with cross streets would be spaced as widely as possible.[6] In the section shown with the first plan for "Commonwealth Avenue" (Figure 81), the arrangement was symmetrical, with the street railway in the center and a cycleway, bridle path, roadway, and walk on either side. Rows of trees separated the cycleways and bridle paths and the roadways and walks. When the street was narrowed from 200 to 160 feet, the cycleways and one of the bridle paths were eliminated, although the roadway reserved for pleasure traffic was widened (Figure 82). The Beacon Street plan, in particular the first one, is remarkable for the way in which it combines ample arrangements for all kinds of pleasure traffic with provision for commercial traffic, which was always excluded from parkways. As such, it is an instructive contrast with Columbia Road in Dorchester, also a dual-purpose public way, which was too narrow to serve either kind of traffic comfortably.

In his design for Beacon Street and in the first half of the plan for Commonwealth Avenue in Brighton, Olmsted was influenced by the newly completed avenues of Paris, planned and constructed during the Second Empire under the direction of Baron Georges Haussmann. Olmsted particularly admired the Avenue de l'Impératrice (now Avenue Foch), which is one of the major approaches to the Bois de Boulogne (Figure 83). At

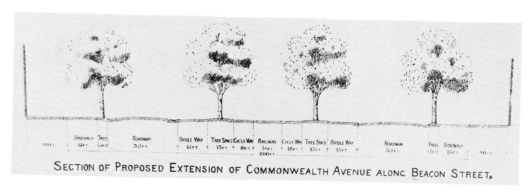

SECTION OF PROPOSED EXTENSION OF COMMONWEALTH AVENUE ALONG BEACON STREET.

Figure 81
Section of the first plan for Beacon Street, October 11, 1886, showing a width of 200 feet and a symmetrical layout.

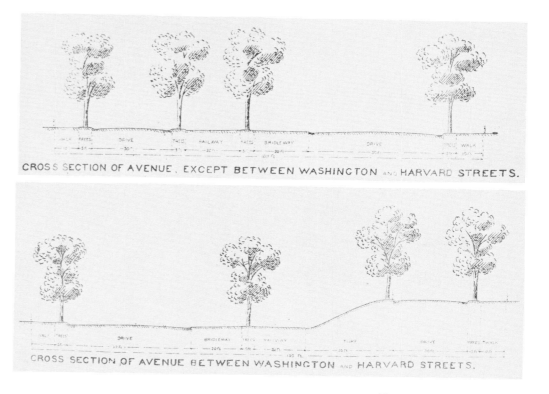

CROSS SECTION OF AVENUE, EXCEPT BETWEEN WASHINGTON and HARVARD STREETS.

CROSS SECTION OF AVENUE BETWEEN WASHINGTON and HARVARD STREETS.

Figure 82
Detail of Figure 78, the plan for Beacon Street as executed. These sections show an asymmetrical arrangement of drives, one bridle path, and a width of 160 feet, except between Washington and Harvard streets.

120 meters, or just under 400 feet, this avenue is almost twice as wide as Commonwealth Avenue in Brighton. The Avenue de l'Impératrice had a wide central drive and a narrow access road on either side, with broad planting strips in between. Although there were no streetcar tracks, the central drive was bordered on one side by a bridle path and on the other by a promenade.[7] The only place in Boston where Olmsted was able to use a comparable scheme was the Arborway, but the Avenue de l'Impératrice was clearly an influence on his plan for Beacon Street.[8]

Another European parallel, of which Olmsted was probably not aware, was the *ciudad lineal*, a new urban concept just being formulated in Spain by Arturo Soria y Mata. In 1882 Soria wrote in the Madrid daily *El Progreso* that the "almost perfect" type of city would be "a single street unit 500

meters broad, extending if necessary from Cadiz to St. Petersburg, from Peking to Brussels."[9] He considered the old compact city obsolete and proposed as an alternative a linear city only a few blocks wide, strung out along train and trolley tracks and enabling the city dweller to enjoy urban amenities while having the countryside literally at his back door. Although a section of the principal street of the Ciudad Lineal (Figure 84) shows a superficial similarity to Beacon Street, it seems unlikely that Olmsted would have had access to *El Progreso*, and Soria's ideas were not disseminated on an international scale until some years later.

Construction of Beacon Street proceeded rapidly (Figure 85), and in its wake arose the elegant residential neighborhood Olmsted had predicted. However, the type of residence built here was neither the detached, single-family house in its own garden recommended by Soria nor the connected town house of Boston's Back Bay, but a relatively new type of multifamily dwelling: luxurious apartment buildings or "French flats," offering at least as much space and greater convenience than the typical row house.[10]

Commonwealth Avenue in Brighton and Beacon Street in Brookline have both survived, although neither in pristine condition. Dutch elm disease has killed most of the street trees, although the town of Brookline has planted replacements of other varieties along Beacon Street. Around the turn of the century, this street's wide drive was used occasionally for sleighing (Figure 86), but the segregation of pleasure and commercial traffic probably did not outlast the widespread use of the automobile. Since at least 1930, the bridle path has been appropriated for parking space (Figure 87). There is little recreational use of Beacon Street today, except on one day each April, when the narrow drive is closed to all but runners in the Boston Marathon, and spectators crowd the sidewalks.

In 1887 Olmsted submitted a plan to the Boston park commissioners for an extension of Audubon Road (now Park Drive) to Burlington (now Audubon) Circle. His recommendation was carried out, and thus Beacon Street was connected with the main park system near the beginning of the Muddy River. Most of the land required was donated by the owners.[11]

*Figure 83 (top)
Section and plan of Avenue de l'Impératrice (later Foch), Paris, showing a symmetrical plan and a width of almost 400 feet.*

*Figure 84 (bottom)
Section of the principal street of Ciudad Lineal, Madrid. Although it allows for two drives, pedestrian walkways, and a trolley, this street is relatively narrow (about 130 feet).*

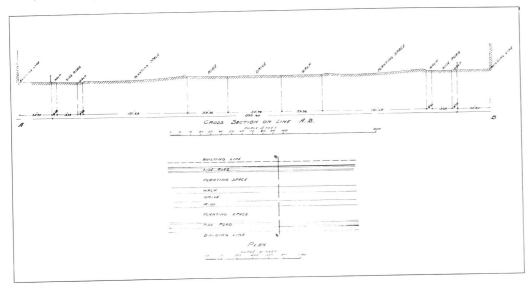

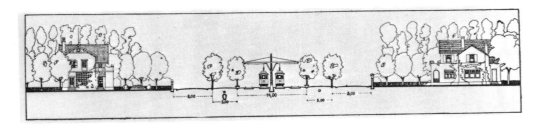

Between 1880 and 1895, the firm prepared plans for at least six housing subdivisions and four street improvements in Brookline, in addition to the widening of Beacon Street.[12] For reasons that are not entirely clear, only two of the Brookline subdivisions were carried out according to plan. The executed and projected subdivisions are: Fisher Hill (1884, executed); the Philbrick estate on the top of Pill Hill (1889, executed); Aspinwall Hill (1880, redesigned 1883–1885 by Ernest W. Bowditch); Corey Hill (1889, unexecuted, laid out in the early 1890s by the engineering firm of Aspinwall and Lincoln); Chestnut Hill or Reservoir Lane Lands (1888, unexecuted, laid out after the turn of the century);

Figure 85
Beacon Street under construction, circa 1888.

Figure 86
Sleighing on Beacon Street, 1901.

Figure 87
Beacon Street, looking east
at intersection with Saint
Paul Street, 1930.

and a plan for the Brookline Land Company (1894, unexecuted, land later used for a playing field). All but one abutted the park system, Beacon Street, or one of the other Olmsted street improvements.

In his plans for small parks and playgrounds, Olmsted designed for an already dense population. Beacon Street, Commonwealth Avenue, and most of the emerald necklace, on the other hand, were designed for communities that had remained sparsely populated but were on the brink of intensive development. The new parks and streets themselves stimulated such development. Brookline, as we have seen, had a history of gradual and controlled growth; the Olmsted subdivisions were planned to provide for the anticipated spurt in population while preserving the town's distinctive hilly topography and rural ambience. Brookline is wedge-shaped, with the narrow end close to the center of Boston and the main roads radiating roughly northeast to southwest: Boylston Street (originally the Worcester Turnpike and now Route 9), Beacon Street, and just over the border in Brighton, Commonwealth Ave-

nue. In contrast to Soria's linear city, where development was limited to a band a few blocks wide along an infinitely extended street, Brookline's residential neighborhoods are the interstices between major traffic arteries, all of which were either designed or modified by Olmsted.

Of the two executed subdivisions, the largest and most important was for Brookline Hill, or Fisher Hill as it is called today (Figure 88).[13] The plan was commissioned in 1884 by George A. Goddard and five other land owners. Like most of the other subdivision projects, it was designed for a hilly site, and Olmsted used the same curvilinear street pattern that had been a hallmark of his plan for Riverside, Illinois, and many later such designs. Besides preserving the topography, curvilinear streets tend to keep through traffic out of residential neighborhoods. Although Fisher Hill lies between Boylston and Beacon streets, the only direct routes between the two are on the borders of the subdivision. It was laid out virtually as planned and is still one of Brookline's most attractive neighborhoods.

Olmsted's street improvements for the town included an unexecuted plan for the rationalization of streets near Brookline Village (1885), widening of Boylston Street and Chestnut Hill Avenue (designed in the early 1890s and executed about a decade later with modifications), and an unexecuted project for "Proposed Brookside Roads in Upper Brookline" (Figure 89), designed in 1894 by Charles Eliot when he was a partner in the Olmsted firm.[14] Had it been carried out, the Brookside Roads plan would have provided an important link between the main park system at Jamaica Pond and the Brookline Reservoir. (This same connection had been part of Ernest W. Bowditch's metropolitan park proposal of 1875.) In 1901–1902 the Olmsted firm did a series of studies for Chestnut Hill Parkway, still another elaboration of the Bowditch/Eliot Plan, with a connection to Chestnut Hill Reservoir. Since this parkway would have included some land in Boston, the town petitioned the Metropolitan Park Commission to carry it out. The plan was rejected on the basis that Brookline was already amply provided with parks.[15]

Another Olmsted subdivision plan, for World's End in Hingham, belongs in a discussion of metro-

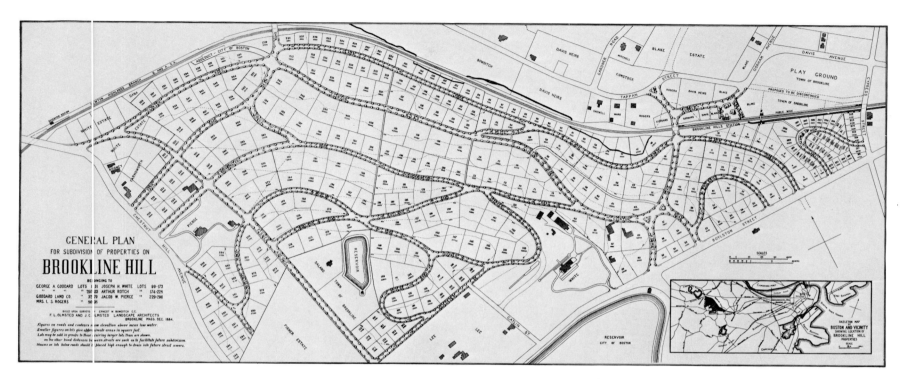

Figure 88
General plan for subdividing Brookline (now Fisher) Hill, F. L. and J. C. Olmsted, 1884.

politan projects because of its location on Boston Harbor and also because of its much more recent role as a public reservation. What is now called World's End consists of two islands formed of drumlins (like most of the islands in Boston Harbor), and artificially connected to each other and to the mainland.[16] Figure 90, an aerial photograph taken in 1927, shows Cushing's Neck, part of mainland Hingham, in the foreground, the larger of the two islands, Planter's Hill, just beyond, and the smaller island, World's End proper, attached to Planter's Hill by a causeway. The narrow bar of Nantasket Beach is at the upper right. The land on this man-made peninsula was used for hunting, pasture, and hay meadow. In 1855 John R. Brewer, a Boston businessman, purchased ten acres of land on Cushing's Neck for a summer residence. By 1882 his holdings consisted of all of Planter's Hill and World's End, with the exception of one twenty-acre lot, as well as two smaller islands in Hingham Harbor and most of Cushing's Neck, where the house and farm buildings were located. From the 1850s until the mid-1930s, the Brewers farmed and raised

livestock on their estate, which at its largest was almost 400 acres.[17]

In 1886 Brewer asked Olmsted to make a subdivision plan for Planter's Hill and World's End. He apparently had no immediate intention of developing the land but wanted to have a plan in case it became financially necessary to sell part of his property.[18] The Olmsted plan, lithographed in 1890 (Figure 91), divided the land into 163 lots of varying sizes. The roads were laid out in a curvilinear pattern similar to that used on Fisher Hill in Brookline. To plan a rather compact residential district in this remote part of Hingham in 1890 was not as odd an idea as it first appears. Brewer probably intended a suburban development rather than a summer colony, for the Plymouth-to-Boston railroad was within walking distance of the proposed subdivision. In 1890 World's End was more accessible to Boston than it is today.

Brewer and his heirs never subdivided the property, but over a period of about fifteen years his heirs laid out the streets with only minor deviations from Olmsted's plan. The result was a subdivision without lots and without houses—an elaborate system of roads leading nowhere. However, this seems not to have been an abandoned subdivision project but one that was adapted to new ends, specifically, tree planting. One of Brewer's greatest interests had been the reforestation of the Boston Harbor islands, including those he owned. In 1880 there were apparently only three trees on World's End, all elms. By 1888 Brewer was successfully planting many more on "the barren, dry, clay banks of his hills."[19] Since they wished to keep the pasture and meadow land open, the Brewers did not attempt to develop a natural, dense forest of native trees. Instead, many trees of foreign origin, such as Norway maples and English oaks were used along the roads, and because of the exposed site, they were planted in double rows and more closely spaced than was usual in street plantings. Except for selected spots such as the top of Planter's Hill, where groves were planted, the fields on either side of the roads were kept open. The tree planting program on World's End also extended to Sarah and Langley islands in Hingham Harbor, which the Brewer family donated to the town in 1947.[20]

In 1936 John Brewer's last surviving child died, and shortly thereafter most of the buildings, including the Brewer mansion, were torn down. The land lapsed into relative disuse, especially after World War II, although the fields were always mown. In 1945 World's End was considered as a site for the United Nations. In 1967 the site was acquired by the Trustees of Reservations, which has maintained World's End essentially as the Brewers left it. Olmsted's tree-lined roads, the open fields, and the views of water in every direction are unencumbered by buildings, automobiles, or ball fields. Although a distant view of the roller coaster at Paragon Park on Nantasket Beach lends a slightly surrealistic touch, this sea-locked point of land does indeed feel like the end of the world.

In 1893 the metropolitan park system dreamed of by Copeland, Bowditch, and Crocker finally was realized, thanks to the efforts of Charles Eliot and the writer Sylvester Baxter. The groundwork for their achievement was laid in 1882, when the state legislature passed an act enabling any city or town

in the Commonwealth to set up a park commission and acquire lands within its own borders. (The park legislation of 1875 had applied only to Boston and communities directly bordering it.) In 1889 the city of Lynn, twelve miles north of Boston, acquired a 2,000-acre tract of natural forest, one-third of the total area of the city. Most of this land had been held in common until the early eighteenth century and thus was reentering the public domain. The ponds in the reservation, part of Lynn's water supply, had been created by damming several swampy valleys between the hills. Olmsted was consulted at the start of the project and gave his unqualified approval to the acquisition of the land and its use as a forest reserve and a place of recreation, but he apparently did not provide a plan.[21] The city raised $35,000 for the Lynn Woods, and that amount was matched by gifts from private citizens. "Thus," as Charles Eliot expressed it, "for the small sum of seventy thousand dollars the 'city of shoes' has obtained a permanent and increasingly beautiful possession which is already bringing to her a new and precious renown."[22]

The first step toward the establishment of the metropolitan park system came in 1890 when Eliot formed the Trustees of Public Reservations (now the Trustees of Reservations). During his boyhood summers on Mount Desert Island in Maine, Eliot had developed a profound love of wild nature, and as a man he channeled this love into remarkably progressive efforts on behalf of what today would be called conservation. He first proposed such an organization in an article for *Garden and Forest* on the Waverley Oaks—a venerable stand of trees in Belmont and Waltham. In the article, which attracted national attention, he suggested, in addition to a metropolitan park commission that would acquire large reservations, an incorporated association of private citizens whose appropriate role would be to hold free of taxes smaller tracts or "surviving fragments of the primitive wilderness of New England . . . as the Public Library holds books and the Art Museum pictures—for the use and enjoyment of the public."[23] Using his colleagues in the Appalachian Mountain Club as a core of enthusiasts, Eliot wrote letters to several influential people, including Olmsted and Sargent, asking their assistance. He also received a good deal of unsolicited

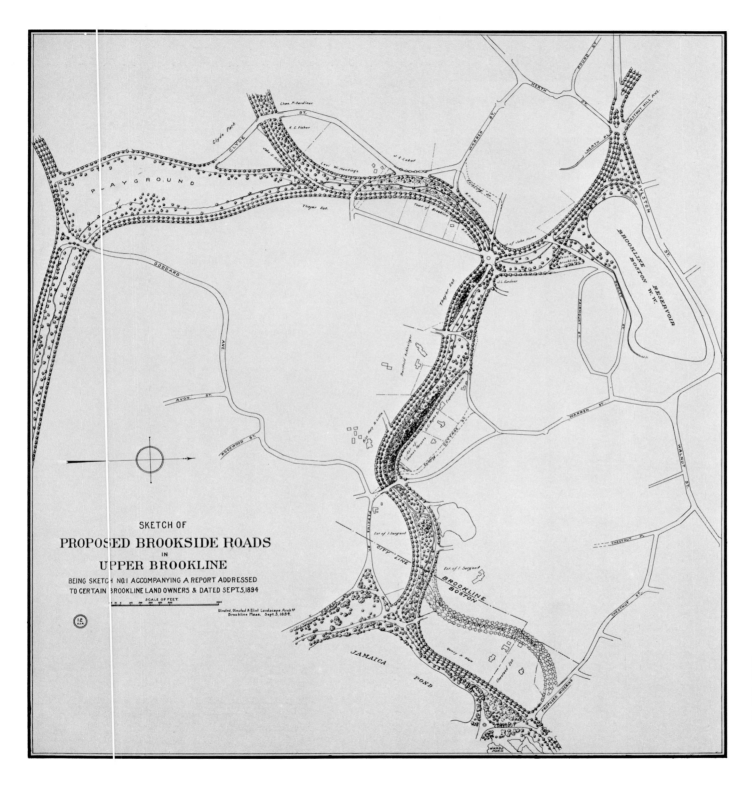

Figure 89
Proposed Brookside roads
in upper Brookline by
Olmsted, Olmsted and
Eliot, 1894.

Figure 90
Cushing's Neck, World's
End, and Nantasket. Aerial
photograph, 1927.

support, including a letter from H. W. S. Cleveland, who suggested including the Middlesex Fells. (Both the Fells and the Waverley Oaks became part of the metropolitan park system rather than of the holdings of the Trustees of Reservations.) Only fifteen months after the appearance of Eliot's article, the new organization was approved by the legislature. It soon became known internationally and was the inspiration for the British National Trust, formed a

few years later.[24] The Trustees of Reservations now owns more than fifty properties, including World's End.

In its first two years the Trustees surveyed the available open-space resources of the Commonwealth and also investigated the possibility of establishing a metropolitan park commission. In June 1892 Governor Billy Russell, a boyhood friend of Eliot's, signed a bill establishing a temporary Met-

Figure 91
General plan for subdividing Planter's Hill and World's End, F. L. Olmsted and Co., 1890.

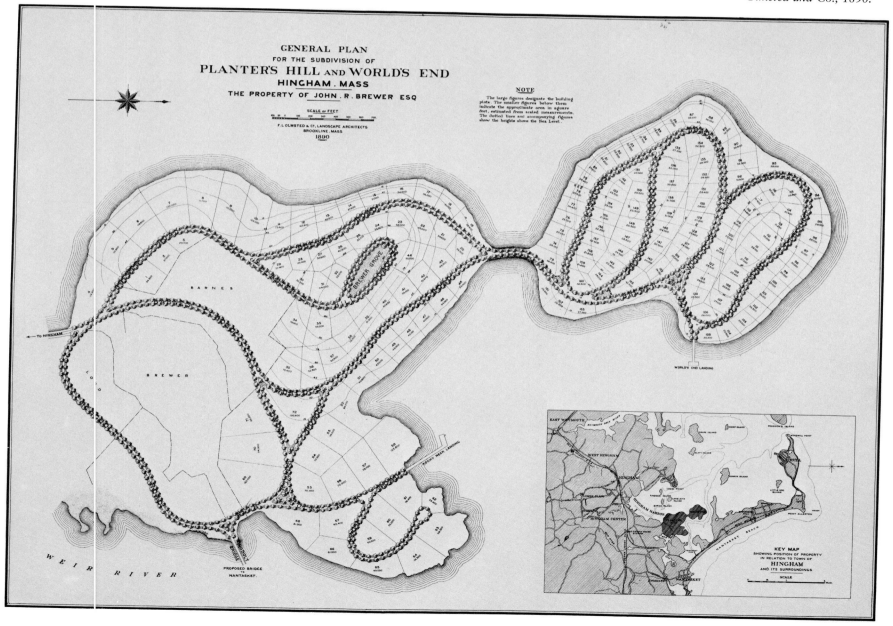

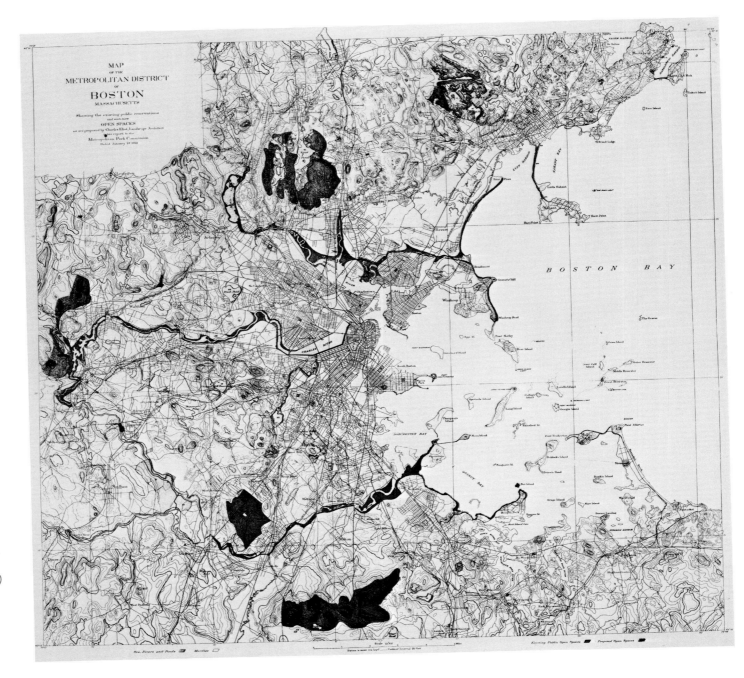

Figure 92
Metropolitan Boston in
1893, showing the reserva-
tions and other new open
spaces (dark areas on map)
proposed by Charles Eliot
to the Metropolitan Park
Commission.

ropolitan Park Commission and appointed Charles Francis Adams, Philip A. Chase, and William B. de las Casas as commissioners. They engaged Eliot as landscape architect and Sylvester Baxter as secretary to prepare a comprehensive study with recommendations to submit to the 1893 session of the General Court.[25]

Baxter, a cosmopolitan and many-talented individual, whose interests included poetry, city planning, and Mexican architecture, was a journalist and a disciple of the Utopian novelist, Edward Bellamy. He was an organizer of Bellamy's Nationalist movement in Boston, and he saw in park planning an application of the movement's principles. Baxter was perhaps Olmsted's most loyal champion in Boston, publishing influential articles in the *Boston Herald* and *Garden and Forest.* He believed in a comprehensive, metropolitan approach to all urban problems, and in 1891 he published a remarkable book, actually a distillation of his *Herald* articles, entitled *Greater Boston: A Study for a Federalized Metropolis Comprising the City of Boston and the Surrounding Cities and Towns.* From 1871 to 1875, before he went to Europe to study at Leipzig and Berlin, Baxter wrote for the *Boston Advertiser.* He must have known R. M. Copeland and his scheme for metropolitan parks, published in the *Advertiser* in 1869 and 1874. As a resident of Malden, he was active in the movement begun by Elizur Wright to preserve the Middlesex Fells, and he wrote to Olmsted about the Fells as early as 1880. Baxter gave much time and energy to promoting first the Trustees of Public Reservations and then the Metropolitan Park Commission. In later life he served on the Malden Park Commission, the Metropolitan Improvements Commission, and the Metropolitan Improvement League.[26]

In January 1893 the temporary commission published a report that included detailed contributions by Eliot and Baxter. The metropolitan sites proposed included forest reservations (Middlesex Fells, Stony Brook Reservation, and Blue Hills Reservation), river reservations on the Charles, Neponset, and Mystic rivers, and ocean reservations such as Revere Beach. (Figure 92 shows the sites proposed by Eliot as well as existing public open spaces within the metropolitan area, such as the Boston park system and the Lynn Woods.) Within days after this report was published, the junior partner of the Olmsted firm, Henry Sargent Codman, died suddenly of appendicitis in Chicago, and Eliot was offered a partnership in the firm, which he accepted only on the condition that he could continue his work for the Metropolitan Park Commission and for the Cambridge Park Commission, which had just employed him to make recommendations for parks in that city. Although after March 1893 Eliot did this work as a partner in the Olmsted firm, it was always made clear that he was the designer and partner in charge of the Metropolitan and Cambridge projects.

Land was rapidly acquired for the metropolitan system, but Eliot was frequently disturbed by the commission's sluggishness in adopting general plans and providing adequate forestry procedures. Another complication was the passage of the Boulevard Act in 1894, a measure designed to ease unemployment. The original metropolitan park report had recommended connecting parkways and boulevards, but not to the extent mandated by the new law. Some of the new boulevards, however, such as Blue Hill Avenue, proved useful in connecting the municipal and metropolitan park systems and thus supplemented the West Roxbury Parkway, already planned jointly by the metropolitan and Boston park commissions to connect the Arnold Arboretum and Stony Brook Reservation. During the next four years Eliot carried a very heavy load of work for the Olmsted firm, which undoubtedly contributed to his contracting meningitis, of which he died in 1897. After his death the Olmsted firm continued to be responsible for the metropolitan park system.[27]

Although this book is primarily concerned with the municipal park system and its principal designer, Frederick Law Olmsted, the metropolitan park system is a fitting conclusion to a survey of Olmsted's greater Boston projects. First, it represents the achievement, after long delay, of some of the ideas and plans presented at the first Boston park hearings between 1869 and 1875. Olmsted fully appreciated the significance of the metropolitan system as the logical continuation of the municipal system. Most important, he considered it a key work and a landmark from which a new era of landscape architecture would date. As he exhorted his partners in 1893:

with regard to the protection of the good will capital, nothing else compares in importance to us with the Boston work, meaning the Metropolitan quite equally with the city work. The two together will be the most important work of our profession now in hand anywhere in the world . . . In your probable life-time, Muddy River, Blue Hills, the Fells, Waverley Oaks, Charles River, the Beaches, *will be points to date from* in the history of American Landscape Architecture, as much as Central Park. They will be the openings of new chapters of the art.[28]

THREE

The Design Process

*What artist, so noble . . . as he, who with far-reaching
conception of beauty and designing power, sketches
the outline, writes the colours, and directs the
shadows of a picture so great that Nature
shall be employed upon it for
generations.*

—Walks and Talks of an American Farmer in England, 1852

Muddy River Valley from Brookline, Back Bay Fens in middle distance, 1925.

IX

The Olmsted Firm
in Brookline

———————◆———————

Aᴠᴛᴇʀ the dissolution of the partnership with Vaux in 1872, Olmsted ran an essentially one-man office, based in the dining room of his New York home. For five years after beginning work on the Fens and Arboretum plans, he retained the 209 West Forty-sixth Street address, but as his work for the Boston Park Commission grew and as he took on more jobs in New England, he spent less and less time in New York. Beginning in the early eighties, during the design and construction of the Boston park system, Olmsted established a full-scale professional firm, operating from an addition to his new home in Brookline. There he developed a system of education and apprenticeship that was unique among practitioners of landscape design.

Brookline's beauty and civic consciousness and the opportunity to live near his long-time friend and collaborator H. H. Richardson were undoubtedly major reasons for Olmsted's decision first to rent quarters and finally, in 1883, to buy a house in Brookline.[1] Richardson, with characteristic expansiveness, offered him a lot on Cottage Street and wrote urging him "to wait til my return before deciding about moving or building—what do you say to building on my lot (or Hooper's). I think I may own the place in a year and have arranged with Hooper or can (he is with me) to have you build at once . . . It may be advantageous to both of us."[2] On the same sheet of letter paper, Richardson drew a sketch site plan (Figure 93), showing a rearrangement of drives and "your house—a beautiful thing in shingles?"

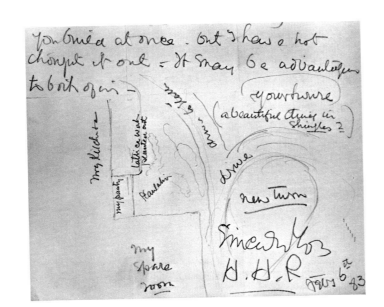

Figure 93
Sketch site plan by H. H.
Richardson for a proposed
house for Olmsted next to
the Perkins-Hooper-Rich-
ardson house, Brookline,
February 6, 1883.

The "beautiful thing in shingles" never material-
ized, for Olmsted finally selected the Boylston-Clark
house of 1809 at 99 Warren Street (Figure 94) a
short walk away from Richardson's home/office en-
clave and just down the road from Sargent's Holm
Lea.[3] Following his own precedent in New York
and Richardson's example in Brookline, Olmsted
used his home as the headquarters of his firm; his
office was the original "north parlor" (Figure 95) of
the Boylston-Clark house, extended to allow room
for a drafting table. Eventually a sun porch was enclosed to make a separate drafting room, and this
became the nucleus of a large rambling office wing.[4]

An unusual number of prominent Boston architects lived in Brookline, although Richardson appears to have been the only one to have his office
there. Richardson rented a spacious house on Cottage Street from his Harvard classmate Edward
Hooper, to which he added a series of flat-roofed,
one-story sheds for drafting and office space,

Figure 94
The Olmsted house,
Brookline, circa 1904.

Figure 95
*The north parlor/office in
the Olmsted house, De-
cember 1886.*

known as "the Coops."[5] The office he established
there in 1878 was apparently the first synthesis of
the French *atelier* method, practiced in Paris in con-
junction with study at the Ecole des Beaux-Arts,
and the Anglo-American apprenticeship tradition
under which most American architects received their
professional training. Olmsted followed Richardson's example and adapted this synthesis to his
own firm and the emerging profession of landscape
architecture.

Richard Morris Hunt—later the designer of Biltmore, the George W. Vanderbilt house in Asheville,
North Carolina, a collaborative enterprise with
Olmsted—was the first American architect to be
trained (1846–1852) at the Ecole des Beaux Arts.[6]
Richardson was the second (1860–1865). They
were followed by many others from this country
who chose the rigorous methods of the French institution. Most of the student's education took place
in the atelier of the professional architect (*patron*)
with whom he had chosen to study and who prepared him for the entrance examinations and the
later competitive student examinations, or *concours*.

Attendance at Ecole lectures was optional and secondary to the main goal of establishing credits by
passing the concours and thus eventually acquiring
enough points to graduate from the second to the
first class. In Richardson's time the Ecole did not
offer a diploma or degree; the only final goal was
the Grand Prix de Rome, awarded to one student (a
French citizen) each year.[7]

Unlike the apprenticeship system practiced in
England and the United States, the atelier was quite
apart from the patron's professional office. Students
never worked on the patron's commissions, but
only on the concours set by the Ecole.[8] In the
United States, by contrast, until architectural
schools were established, architects learned by
working as apprentices on actual projects. The quality of the apprentice's education was thus largely a
matter of chance, depending entirely on the ability
of the head of the firm and the variety and importance of his commissions. Rarely was any systematic
instruction or assigned reading part of the apprentice's experience.

When Richard Morris Hunt returned to New

York in the late 1850s, he set up an atelier which, following the Parisian custom, was entirely separate from his professional office.[9] Hunt trained a generation of architects and educators, including William R. Ware, who founded the first architectural school in this country at Massachusetts Institute of Technology in 1867 and another at Columbia College in 1881. Richardson moved to Brookline in 1874, but he kept his New York office for four more years,

Figure 96
John Charles Olmsted.

sending his sketch designs there to be developed by assistants. At the Coops in Brookline from 1878 until his death in 1886, he combined the French atelier with the apprenticeship system. However, most of the young men in his firm were recent graduates of M.I.T.'s School of Architecture, and what Richardson offered was essentially a postgraduate course.[10]

Olmsted lacked this advantage. Not only was formal education in landscape architecture unavailable in this country until 1900, when Harvard established a Department of Landscape Architecture within its School of Design, but the profession itself had no acknowledged status, still being confused by the general public with both engineering and horticulture. Olmsted, in effect, had to function in at least three roles: as Ecole, as patron, and as head of an ongoing firm. His first apprentice in New York

had been John Charles Olmsted, his nephew and stepson, but John's apprenticeship was an informal one. After the move to Brookline, however, Olmsted instituted a more systematic type of office training that was clearly based on the combination of instruction, assigned reading, and practical experience that Richardson provided at the Coops. His apprentices read under his direction, accompanied him to meetings with clients, and worked on drafting and design problems of graduated difficulty. As his career was nearing its close in 1895, Olmsted wrote that he was preparing a "grand professional post-graduate school" at his office.[11]

The contribution of John Charles Olmsted (Figure 96) to the design of the Boston park system, and his importance in the Olmsted firm, are difficult to overestimate. He was a shy and quiet man, and his reputation has been somewhat overshadowed by the fame of his father and of his half-brother, Frederick Law Olmsted, Jr. When Olmsted had married Mary Cleveland Perkins Olmsted, his brother's widow, in 1859, John was seven years old, the eldest of his three new stepchildren. Educated as a boy at schools in Eagleswood, New Jersey, and Plymouth, Massachusetts, John graduated in 1875 from the Sheffield Scientific School of Yale University. Immediately after graduation he entered Olmsted's New York office. From his youth, John apparently had an easy command of the various technical aspects of his profession, which his father had had to learn relatively late in life. In 1878 he was given an interest in the firm and in 1885 became a full partner. He was the senior member of the firm from 1895 until his death in 1920.[12] At the time of his death, John's abilities as a planner and his sensitive use of plant materials were especially praised. He was also gifted as an architectural designer and was responsible for the preliminary plans for the bridges and other structures in the Boston park system. John's role in the management of the Olmsted office was critically important, especially during the late eighties and early nineties, when the volume of work increased greatly. During this period he supervised a large staff of draftsmen and apprentices. The other partners in the firm, Henry Codman and Charles Eliot, both died in the nineties, so John was largely responsible for the continuity of the firm's work after his father's retirement.

While little is known about the first few years of John's career, the apprenticeship of Charles Eliot (Figure 97), the next member of the firm, is well documented; Eliot kept diaries during this period (1883–1885), and further information is found in the biography written a few years after his death by his father.[13] After graduating from Harvard College in 1882, Eliot spent several months at the Bussey Institution, Harvard's School of Agriculture. He was introduced to Olmsted by his uncle, the architect Robert S. Peabody.

Eliot started his apprenticeship just after the move to 99 Warren Street during the busy spring season, and his first diary entries recount many trips with Olmsted to inspect work at North Easton, Massachusetts; Newport and Providence, Rhode Island; and elsewhere. Toward the end of 1883 and throughout the next year Eliot drafted plans for several of the Boston parks. At first he appeared to spend a good deal of time under Olmsted's direct tutelage, but Olmsted was away on business more and more, and when home was preoccupied with writing reports. Oddly enough, on a few occasions Eliot reported to the office but spent his time reading, because there was not enough work to keep both himself and John busy. At other times he found activity at the office "now dull, now lively."[14] By the end of 1884, however, the load of work had become heavy enough that Henry Sargent Codman was also taken on as an apprentice. In December Olmsted was trying to complete the Arboretum plan (probably the final studies for the distribution of the tree collections) and to prepare the preliminary studies for West Roxbury (Franklin) Park. He urged John to "throw more upon Eliot and let him throw more on Codman," so that John would be free to do what he alone could do.[15]

Like Eliot, Codman was a nephew of an architect with whom Olmsted had frequently worked—in this case, John Sturgis, designer of Pinebank on Jamaica Pond and the Museum of Fine Arts in Copley Square. It is likely, however, that Codman was introduced by another uncle, Charles Sprague Sargent. Codman did not keep a diary, but it can be assumed that his duties were similar to Eliot's, although the office was now much busier. After their apprenticeships, both Eliot and Codman traveled for a year or two in Europe, visiting parks and

Figure 97
Charles Eliot.

other examples of landscape architecture, principally in England, France, Germany, and Italy, although Eliot went as far as Russia. Both men regularly reported to Olmsted their impressions and opinions of European landscape architecture, and both appear to have considered him their mentor while abroad.[16]

From the earliest days of Eliot's apprenticeship, Olmsted had thought highly of his abilities, and he offered him a position in the firm after Eliot's return from Europe in 1887. But Eliot preferred to start his own practice, and for the next six years, he took on a wide variety of independent commissions. Codman returned to the Olmsted office directly upon his return from Europe, becoming a partner in 1889. His chief responsibility became the Chicago World's Fair, and like Eliot later, he did much of the designing of grounds for private houses, a task

Olmsted found increasingly frustrating and wearisome. After Eliot came in as a partner in 1893, he carried a full share of the office work, as well as continuing his responsibilities for the Metropolitan and Cambridge park systems.

In 1890 Olmsted was sixty-eight years old, and he began increasingly to think of the time when he would withdraw from the firm. A day at the Olmsted office was now much more likely to be lively than dull. As Olmsted wrote to his boyhood friend, Charles Brace, in January 1890: "I never had more before me or less inclination to lay off than now, though my arrangements are such that nobody need be dissatisfied if I drop out tomorrow, John and Codman being ready to take up all my work and on an average better qualified for it than

Figure 98
Mariana Griswold Van Rensselaer.

I am. My office is much better equipped and has more momentum than ever before."[17]

Later that year the pace became even more hectic. In September Olmsted wrote to his son Frederick (whom he called Rick) that the business was increasing faster than he could enlarge the organization and adjust methods to meet it. Most clients insisted on dealing only with Olmsted himself, although John and Codman were taking over more and more. Olmsted anticipated that the business would fall off when he was no longer personally associated with it, but he hoped that his reputation, based particularly on his later works, would provide a solid basis for a new era of the firm. To "lead the van" of both profession and firm, Olmsted looked to Rick, then only twenty years old. (Rick did not become a partner until after his father's retirement). Although he regretted that Rick's professional education would not coincide with his own work, as had been the case with John and the other apprentices, he urged Rick to continue to elevate the profession of landscape architecture. Olmsted felt that he had been successful, but only in holding the fort. Continuing his military analogy, he described Rick, John, Eliot, and Codman as "reinforcements," together with Charles Sargent, William A Stiles, and Mariana Griswold Van Rensselaer.[18]

Olmsted's inclusion of these three illustrates the importance he placed on the press as an educator of public opinion. Sargent was undoubtedly included because of his role as co-founder and "conductor" of the periodical *Garden and Forest,* which began publication in 1888. Stiles was the editor and Mariana G. Van Rensselaer a principal contributor. Ostensibly a horticultural magazine, *Garden and Forest* in its ten years of publication dealt with much broader issues than similar publications. Olmsted, John C. Olmsted, Eliot, and Codman were all occasional contributors. Mrs. Van Rensselaer (Figure 98) had begun her distinguished career as an art critic by writing articles on painting and architecture. In 1888 she published an authoritative biography of H. H. Richardson. Perhaps because of her friendship with Olmsted and Sargent, she began increasingly to write on landscape architecture, or "landscape gardening," as she persisted in calling it. Her perceptive and succinctly written articles in

Garden and Forest, Century Magazine, and the *American Architect and Building News,* along with Olmsted's established, and Eliot's emerging, reputation, encouraged a growing interest in landscape architecture as a career. In early 1888 no fewer than five young men, all of whom referred to Mrs. Van Rensselaer's writings as their source of interest, wrote to Olmsted for advice on entering the profession.[19]

Olmsted's answers to these requests for guidance reveal much about his criteria for the profession. In 1891 he responded to such a letter: "If a young man has an unquestionable bent toward my calling, I have every dispostion to encourage him," but he tended to discourage candidates who professed a love of flowers and gardens, which he considered "a direction of artistic inclination rather unfitting a man for our work. At least it suggests that he will care more for beautiful objects and scenes than for scenery in composition, which is the true landscape inclination." He then outlined the course Eliot and Codman had followed, which he recommended for suitable candidates:

Our advice to those whom we can encourage usually is that, (after a college course), they should take special courses in Architecture, Engineering and Drawing, free-hand and mechanical, at the Technological Institute, (or, if Harvard men, partly as post graduate students at Cambridge), and courses in Botany and Horticulture at the Bussey and Arnold Arboretum schools; at the same time visiting the Art Museum, and otherwise making themselves familiar with good pictures and good architecture. After that we put them to such work as they can do in our office, if we can find room for them, and they travel with us (at their own expense) and read under our advice for two or three years. After that they generally make a tour of foreign study.[20]

By 1891 several young men had joined the Olmsted office as apprentices, but not all of them stuck out the full course. Codman's death early in 1893 saddened Olmsted deeply and made him anxious about the future of the firm. His own health had become increasingly feeble. Eliot, in spite of his love of the outdoors, had never had a robust constitution, and Olmsted was reluctant to overburden John with work. He wrote to John seriously advising "throwing up a lot of our business . . . You

should above all things aim to keep up and advance the reputation of the House. Better make little money and live low for a while than fail in that."[21]

The question of the precise contributions of Olmsted and his various partners, from Vaux onward—both to specific projects and to the general operations of the firm—is difficult to resolve. Much of what is called collaboration is merely teamwork or even more frequently a simple division of labor. In many late nineteenth-century architectural firms, the roles of the designing principal, administrative principal, engineering principal, and so on are quite easy to distinguish. Olmsted was fully aware of the more subtle nature of creative design collaboration. In 1893, when Mrs. Van Rensselaer was asked to write an article on Olmsted for *Century Magazine,* he discouraged the suggested *catalogue raisonné* approach, partly because it could not do justice to his partners. As always, he was concerned that Vaux receive due credit for Central and Prospect parks ("But for his invitation I should not have been a landscape architect. I should have been a farmer . . . I do not like to be given credit for the design of these works when he is not given equal credit"), and he eloquently described his working relationship with his more recent partners:

To quite half my works my son John has contributed in an important degree. It is impossible to apportion credit, so much to one, so much to another, for the general result that may come from the striking together of two or more minds in prolonged, practical discussions . . . Not one of us has done anything that the others have not helped him to do. In every one of our works there has been a merging of thought into thought, so that to differentiate individual originations is quite out of the question.[22]

Up to this point, we have looked only at the roles of Olmsted's partners and apprentices, colleagues on an equal or potentially equal basis with Olmsted. But the Boston park system and the firm's other major projects from this period could never have been satisfactorily accomplished without other employees. Although the apprentices did much of the routine drafting, they could not have carried all of it during the busy years of the early nineties. In addition, they did not yet have the experience for the more technical aspects of the work, including supervision of construction. The other employees, about whom there is scant biographical information, carried most of the drafting load, and the more experienced carried many other responsibilities. While some were undoubtedly recruited from engineering offices, much of their training must have taken place at the Olmsted office. As Olmsted noted, it was extremely difficult to find men for these positions:

There is a want of competent men for subordinate positions—much greater than in Architecture, for instance. That is to say, in architectural works, there are always competent builders to take off many cares of business that, in our case, must be assumed by the designing heads. There is much in our affairs for which specifications cannot be drawn, upon which a contractor can be held to do satisfactory work. What the profession wants is competent foremen, undertakers and office assistants to whom the details of design can be delegated as by a chief Architect to his office assistant, and details of field work to resident superintendents, clerks of work and foremen. Such men possessing adequate knowledge in Horticulture, and who would be good second mates at sea, are practically not to be had, while men of corresponding fitness in Architecture or in Engineering are to be had in troops.[23]

Nevertheless, Olmsted found several "good second mates at sea," although he probably had to train them himself. By the early nineties, his staff included several draftsmen and design assistants, a supervisor of construction, and a supervisor of planting. For a time the supervisor of construction was Edward D. Bolton, who had formerly been in Ernest Bowditch's office. Warren H. Manning, whose father owned a large nursery in Reading, Massachusetts, was the supervisor of planting. Manning joined the Olmsted firm in 1888 as a horticulturist and later served as an assistant in design until 1896, when he left the firm to open his own office. The staff of draftsmen and design assistants included Percy R. Jones and James G. Langdon, who between them drew at least three-quarters of the plans for the Boston park system. Jones and Langdon entered the firm some time in the late eighties, and

both retired about 1915. With the exception of Warren Manning, all of these men remained in subordinate positions throughout their working lives.[24]

As outlined originally by Olmsted and Vaux, the firm's procedure in dealing with clients, preparing plans, and seeing that the plans were properly executed remained substantially the same throughout Olmsted's later practice and is described in a memorandum the firm prepared for prospective clients in 1890. Although the memorandum was intended primarily for the owners of private grounds of less than five acres, the basic procedure was the same for much larger projects. The first step was always a preliminary visit to the site for a thorough examination and discussion of the client's needs. At this stage a topographical surveyor was selected, and if the grounds were for a new house, the architect was also brought into consultation. After the topographical survey had been made, the firm then prepared a preliminary or study plan, "intended to be discussed and criticized, and to serve as a provocation . . . to an improved and final solution of the problem."[25] In many cases supplementary plans were prepared before the general plan was settled on.

The general plan showed "with approximate accuracy the outlines of the principal constructive features, such as buildings, yards, terraces, drives, walks, gardens, watercourses, etc. and, probably, the general disposition of plantations and isolated trees. A few explanatory figures of elevation are usually given."[26] Small grounds, where the work was to be done "by the day," required few working drawings. For larger projects and in cases where the work was done by contract, the firm prepared complete working drawings. These included detailed grading plans, profiles, cross sections, and diagrams showing the exact positions, shapes, and sizes of all features to be constructed.

After construction was complete, the firm supplied planting plans and plant lists. They always advised that planting be done by the day rather than by contract. Although the Olmsted firm ordered the plants, they assumed no responsibility for, and received no profit on, them. The firm also insisted on annual supervisory visits for several years to evaluate and modify the original planting. For small grounds close to Boston and requiring relatively few visits, the charge for this entire service was modest:

$300, plus a fee of $50 a year for subsequent supervision. Traveling expenses and the cost of the topographical survey were paid by the client.

For a project on the scale of the Boston park system, the procedure was somewhat different, but the differences were mainly of degree. Olmsted's fee was proportionately larger, and the whole design process was infinitely more complex. For the grounds of a private home the firm prepared an average of about a dozen drawings, while the drawings for the Boston park system total more than 1,200. The preliminary plan for each park was preceded by scores of tentative studies, and the general plan was almost always revised, some plans several times. The revisions sometimes involved major alterations in boundaries and basic changes in the design concept, as was the case with the Muddy River. More frequently, an element was added to or removed from the original general plan; for example, a pond was added to Franklin Park and a swimming beach was removed from Jamaica Park. In these cases the entire plan had to be redrawn and submitted as a revised plan. Most important, almost half of the total number of drawings for the Boston park system were working drawings, and they were extraordinarily detailed and precise.

Unlike most of the previous generation of landscape "gardeners" and some (but not all) of his contemporary landscape designers, Olmsted never provided plans for a client unless the client agreed to have the firm supervise construction and follow the job through with periodic visits after construction and planting. This unvarying rule held for the Boston park system as well. Olmsted felt that his primary responsibility was to assure that the results he and his clients had agreed upon were actually realized. From this point of view, the drawings were merely a means to an end: "We do not sell our drawings. They are our instruments for providing what we do sell . . . We provide drawings as one means among other means of instructing those who are . . . to direct the work."[27]

Consequently, when Olmsted signed articles of agreement with the Boston Park Commission in December 1878, his contract explicitly stated that he should provide a design and preliminary plan for the Back Bay Fens and that he should continue to advise the commission on "elaborating, perfecting and carrying out [the] design" over a three-year period.[28] The Olmsted firm was to provide complete working drawings, and Olmsted himself was to visit the ground at frequent intervals. He was also to be open to consultation (by letter) at any time concerning the details and requirements of the design. An important provision of the 1878 contract was its assurance that the Park Commission would hire competent men of the best professional standing as engineers, architects, and gardeners, who would report directly to Olmsted. This first contract applied only to the Back Bay Fens but was renewed and revised over the years as the scope of Olmsted's responsibilities to the Park Commission expanded.

X

"Getting the Plan"

———————◆———————

In 1884 Olmsted asked John for assistance in "getting the plan" of West Roxbury (Franklin) Park.[1] At the same time he wrote to Charles Dalton, chairman of the Boston Park Commission, about the necessity of incubating a design over a long period of time: "I want to bring your judgement and mine together; to do so may prove to require study upon study, essay upon essay."[2] Olmsted was referring to the design for Franklin Park, but he might as easily have been discussing the Fens, the Arboretum, or any of his other plans. Both statements reveal Olmsted's collaborative method of working, both with a partner and with his client.

Olmsted's design process can best be grasped by a close examination of the five parks of the emerald necklace. Each has a different kind of site, a differ-

ent function, and a different visual effect. All are well documented; at least nine-tenths of the original drawings survive, as well as extensive correspondence and published reports. By looking at the studies upon studies and essays upon essays and reading the related correspondence, one can arrive at a reasonably clear understanding of Olmsted's intentions.

This chapter deals with the earliest studies for the parks, the most revealing of which are those for the Fens, the Arboretum, and Franklin Park, all challenging design problems. In the case of the Fens, Olmsted was presented with a site that had long since lost its original landscape character and consisted almost entirely of polluted water. His solution was to accept the engineering problem as the governing factor in his design and to restore salt marsh vegetation to the reclaimed land. The Arboretum site, by contrast, had considerable natural advantages; the major difficulty was to install a tree museum according to a hierarchical order while maintaining an informal effect. At Franklin Park Olmsted found the gentle, pastoral scenery he loved best. What he accomplished there can best be described as design by subtraction; by removing buildings, boundary walls, and other discordant elements, he revealed and emphasized the natural beauty of the site. He provided for subsidiary recreational activities in the Ante-Park so that they would not intrude into the park proper.

Before examining the studies for these three parks, we should look at Olmsted's relationship with his clients and at his general methods of proceeding with a design. Comparison with the customary practices of an architect is helpful in this context.[3]

For the Boston park system, Olmsted's clients were the city of Boston and the town of Brookline. Although his direct dealings were with the varying three-man boards of park commissioners, Olmsted clearly felt that his ultimate responsibility was to the citizens they represented. The large, expensive, and very visible public works produced by his efforts would directly affect not only his own generation but also their descendants. Beyond his broad commitment to the public, Olmsted had to make sure that both boards negotiated effectively with other municipal and town bodies, were able to raise sufficient funds and on occasion initiate legislation. Olmsted described the first board of Boston commissioners as "three gentlemen of notable position and character, of great commercial ability, liberal and public spirited."[4] The same could be said of the Brookline commissioners and the later Boston boards. The significant fact is that the governing bodies of Boston and Brookline were prepared to follow the recommendations of these exemplary gentlemen.

An interesting facet of Olmsted's relationship with the Boston commissioners is that he rarely suggested sites to them. With his finely tuned sensitivity to public opinion and his conviction that the public was his ultimate client, he may not have wanted it to appear that such important decisions were being imposed from without. Olmsted frequently rejected sites, and he almost always suggested revisions in boundaries, but when a new park was being chosen, he acted with extreme caution. This was evident at the very beginning of the park movement in 1869, when Olmsted carefully avoided comment on any of the various park schemes. The Muddy River was broached as a "suggestion" in the Olmsted plan of 1880, and he probably had good reason to believe that it would be well received. In some cases, it is very difficult to tell whether Olmsted did or did not suggest a site. Without making a formal proposal, he may have simply dropped a few words into a receptive ear.[5]

Normally a client first approaches an architect with a project for which there is a specific program: for example, a parish may need a church seating so many people, costing so much money and meeting certain liturgical requirements. Although the architect may help the client work out the details, the client generally has a fairly good idea of what he needs. By contrast, when a city's park commissioners first approached Olmsted, they often knew only that their city wanted a "park." Olmsted had to help them understand what a park was and to decide whether they really needed a park or some other kind of public ground. If their need was really for a park in Olmsted's sense of the word, he had to be constantly on guard to see that they did not turn it into something else. Olmsted described his chronic predicament to the architect, Henry Van Brunt:

Suppose that you had been commissioned to build a really grand opera house; that after the construction work had been nearly completed and your scheme of decoration fully designed, you should be instructed that the building was to be used on Sundays as a Baptist Tabernacle, and that a suitable place must be made for a huge organ, a pulpit and a dipping pool. Then at intervals afterwards, you should be advised that it must be so refitted and furnished that parts of it would be used for a court room, a jail, a concert hall, hotel, skating rink, for surgical cliniques, for a circus, dog show, drill room, ball room, railway station and shot tower?[6]

The Boston park commissioners said they wanted a park in the Back Bay, but it turned out that what they really needed was a storage basin for the flood waters of Stony Brook and the Muddy

River. Olmsted helped them reconcile these two needs, although the result was not what he would call a park. For the Arnold Arboretum, on the other hand, Olmsted was given a very detailed and strict program: a museum that would include every kind of tree that could be grown in the Boston climate, planted in a prescribed sequence but with a natural effect. Fulfilling this program must have been quite a challenge.

Franklin Park, the only true park of the Boston system, was a classic case of the difficulties Olmsted described to Van Brunt. Because he had the support of the park commissioners, Olmsted was fairly successful in keeping circuses and surgical cliniques out of the park during his active career. He was able, for example, to persuade Mayor Matthews not to turn part of it into a rallying ground for labor and religious groups. But after his retirement, the park commissioners and the city succumbed to the tendency to treat the park as just so much space, to be used any way they wanted.

After a program is formulated, the architect or landscape architect works out a design on paper. The drawings for the Boston park system fall generally into the same three categories as architectural drawings: preliminary studies and plans, presentation drawings, and working drawings. Before he could begin, however, Olmsted needed to have a topographical survey, showing existing contours, buildings, and important groups of trees, prepared by an engineer. The topographical survey was lithographed in quantity and served as a base map for the first preliminary studies. Only a very simple and schematic plan, such as the first Muddy River plan, could be prepared without a topographical survey. In such a case, an ordinary city map served as the base.

While an architect's first studies for a building are often tiny sketches, Olmsted, using the topographical map as a base, generally had to work on a large scale from the very beginning. His first studies were usually for roadway and path systems and were drawn either on tracing paper as an overlay or directly on the topographical map in contrasting colors. Sometimes studies were made for divisions of space within a park to accommodate the functions required by the client's program: distribution of the tree collection in the Arboretum, the organi-

zation of various recreational areas in Franklin Park. Both kinds of initial studies on base maps are two-dimensional and deal either with circulation or with the distribution of internal space; they correspond to an architect's preliminary ground plans, normally the first step in the design of a building. (As Olmsted himself pointed out, there is no equivalent in landscape architecture to architects' elevations.)[7] After the basic road pattern and divisions of space had been worked out, the firm prepared numerous tracing-paper studies of internal details— intersections, paths, ponds, and so on. Generally these are plans only, although some include contours.

Only a handful of the more than a thousand drawings for the Boston park system are signed by Olmsted or can otherwise be firmly attributed to him. Most of the later ones are by Jones or Langdon, and some are initialed or signed by John Olmsted, Eliot, or Codman. It is probably safe to assume that at least some of the many unsigned early drawings for the Fens, Arboretum, and Franklin Park are by Olmsted. Nevertheless, it is hard to avoid the conclusion that much of the time Olmsted produced only the most preliminary of drawings. Visitors to Richardson's home/office on Cottage Street came away with vivid memories of the architect drawing sketch plans, often in bed.[8] By contrast, Charles Eliot in his diaries frequently describes Olmsted meeting with clients or writing reports but says not one word about Olmsted at the drafting table. While Olmsted generated design concepts and did some rough drawing, he was apparently even less likely than Richardson to participate in the later phases of graphic design. Warren Manning's memoirs confirm this supposition: "Mr. Olmsted was not a finished draughtsman . . . He would make rapid sketches and plans with indications on surveys and verbal and written explanations which enabled his office aides to interpret his intent."[9]

When the preliminary studies were complete, Olmsted would present his clients with a plan or plans for approval. The lithographed preliminary, general, and revised plans for the Boston parks (or, strictly speaking, the ink-on-linen plans from which the prints were made) were all presentation plans, although Olmsted rarely referred to them as such.

Since Olmsted regarded his relationship with his client as a continuing dialogue, the presentation of the first plan was not so much an effort to "sell" him that plan as to offer a stimulus to further discussion and a still better plan. When Vaux and Olmsted entered the Central Park competition, their set of presentation drawings included several pairs of perspective sketches, showing views of the park as it would appear before and after construction. By 1878, and probably long before that, Olmsted had abandoned perspective views and any attempt at realistic representation as "delusive."[10] His presentation or "show" plans were simply elaborate maps—rendered, it is true, with particular neatness and care.

In his meetings with clients, Olmsted relied heavily on oral presentation and written reports. The writing of reports was, for him, intimately related to the process of graphic design. As John put it:

He *can't* take writing easily. He must worry over it till the moment when it is delivered and he can alter no more. It would be useless to re-typewrite the report until the last possible moment, except as an aid to him in getting a fresh view of it—just as an architect alters details at each successive drawing—seeing them in a fresh light when newly or differently rendered. To put his writing in type helps him to realize how it will strike the reader.[11]

When the commissioners had approved his plans, Olmsted did not consider his job done. His ultimate client, the public, still had to be convinced. The reports were always included in the commissioners' publications, but Olmsted generally printed at least a few sentences of explanation on the plan itself. For Franklin Park, he went to the extent of writing a kind of synopsis of his report, which was printed beside the plan (Figure 41). The lithographed plan cum explanation was posted, at his request, at various points within the park.

The early studies for the Fens and the Muddy River Improvement are quite different from those for projects in which most of the existing topography was to be retained. Since there were no solid contours to speak of in the Fens, no topographical

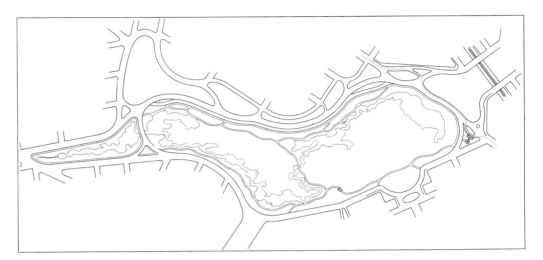

Figure 99
First of two alternate studies for the Back Bay Fens presented to the Boston park commissioners, fall 1878.

map was made. Olmsted apparently used an outline map of the boundaries of the proposed park as a base to prepare studies of details and of the entire area of the park.[12] By the fall of 1878, he had reached the point of preparing show plans.

The first two "essays" for the Fens that Olmsted presented to the commissioners were alternate plans, drawn in ink on linen and carefully prepared with colored backings. Neither covered the total area that was included in the final Fens plan. The simpler of the two (Figure 99) seems to include only the area from the present Boylston Street Bridge (the road crossing the park at the left of the railroad on the right side of the drawing) to Tremont Entrance, now called Evans Way, near the present Gardner Museum (extreme left). It shows a narrow, winding stream that does not take up a very large proportion of the park. The second study (Figure 100) shows a much more complicated and extensive waterway, with peninsulas and islands, extending from the railroad tracks to the present Brookline Avenue (at the top of the drawing). Several small shelters and a more elaborate system of paths are also shown. Both studies include an interesting arrangement of inner and outer parkways similar to those eventually constructed on part of the Brookline side of the Muddy River. In Figure 99 these are shown on the side of the present Park Drive (top); in Figure 100, on the side of the present Fenway (bottom).

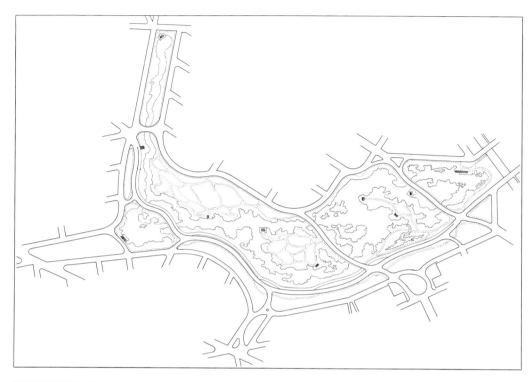

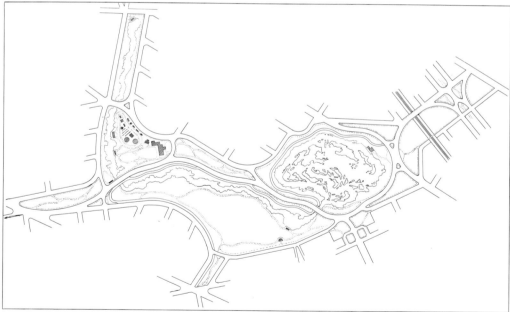

Figure 100 (top)
Second alternate study.

Figure 101 (bottom)
Third Fens study.

These drawings are clearly labeled "Studies for the Back Bay Park Presented to the Commissioners." Since there is no correspondence concerning these studies, and the meeting at which they were presented is not recorded in the minutes of the Boston Park Department, it is impossible to say exactly why the commissioners were not satisfied with them. On October 24 Olmsted presented a third plan (Figure 101), which has many features in common with the final, executed plan. The configuration of the Boylston Street Bridge appears much as it does today. The plan extends to Beacon Street (extreme right of drawing), although not all the way to the Charles River, since it was then anticipated that the Embankment would extent to this point. The formal entrances to the park at Westland and Huntington avenues are almost exactly as finally constructed, and the arrangement of the waterway is closer to the final version. A puzzling feature of this drawing is a complex of several buildings of unknown purpose and varying sizes and shapes near Tremont Entrance.

The park commissioners were prepared to accept this plan, but the city engineer confirmed Olmsted's misgivings about its practicality, and Olmsted began recasting the design. Armed with a plan showing the contour of hard bottom in the Back Bay (a substitute, to some extent, for a topographical survey), Olmsted and John in December 1878 prepared quantities of tracing-paper studies, mostly for Beacon Entrance.[13] A detailed preliminary plan for Beacon Entrance and a preliminary plan for the entire Back Bay park were presented to the commissioners in January and February 1879. The preliminary plan for the entire park was accompanied by a sheet of cross sections of the shore at various points. Except for the intersection with Commonwealth Avenue, both preliminary plans are almost identical with the plan that was lithographed and published in the commissioners' annual report for 1879 (Figure 31, discussed fully in Chapter IV). A later plan (Figure 102), published in 1887, shows minor changes to the original design, including the widening of Longwood Entrance as a smooth transition to the start of the Muddy River Improvement.

The Arnold Arboretum posed equally difficult design problems, but of an entirely different nature. It was the first arboretum in the United States, and both Sargent and Olmsted were determined that it should be outstanding artistically as well as botanically. Before examining Olmsted's studies for this part of the park system, it is necessary to look briefly at the history of the arboretum as a scientific phenomenon and as a landscape design type.

The first documented arboretum appears to have been that of Henry Compton (1632–1713), bishop first of Oxford and then of London, who installed on his grounds at Fulham on the Thames what was then the most varied collection of trees in England. Although Bishop Compton's arboretum was remarkably complete for the time, it was not intended to be a comprehensive collection; that is, he did not try to grow every tree that could survive the cli-

Figure 102
Map of the Back Bay Fens, 1887.

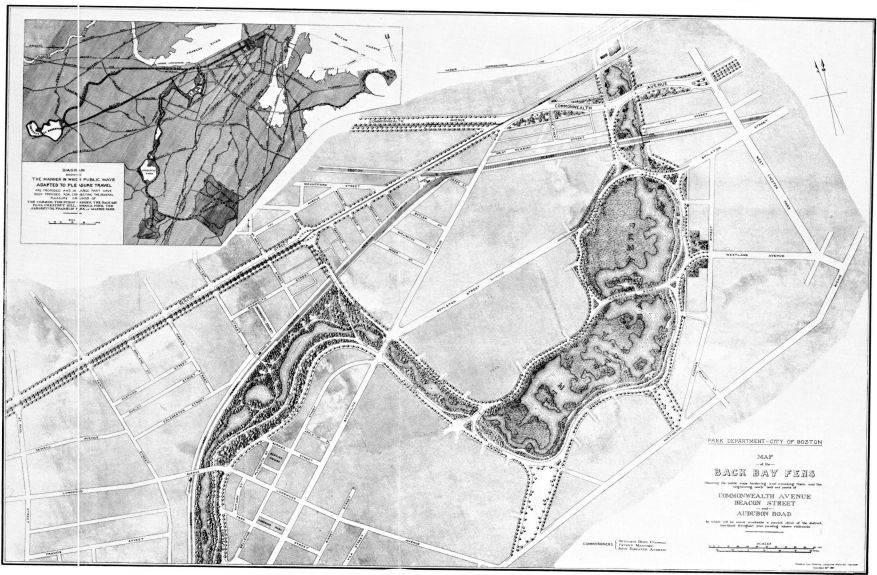

mate. Scientific interest in trees exactly paralleled the development of the private landscaped parks of eighteenth-century England, such as those designed by Capability Brown and Humphrey Repton. Two arboretums of the time that were noted for the diversity of their plantings were those of Archibald Campbell, Duke of Argyle, at Whitton, Middlesex, and of Archibald Russell, Duke of Bedford, at Woburn Abbey, Bedfordshire.[14]

In the United States, as we saw earlier, amateur horticulturists and tree enthusiasts were often also gentlemen landscape gardeners. Boston and its suburbs, the Hudson River Valley, and the suburbs of Philadelphia were famous for their many landscaped estates featuring exotic trees and other horticultural rarities. Mount Auburn Cemetery in 1831 became the first large public ground to be planted with a wide variety of specimen trees, many of them from the gardens of Henry A. S. Dearborn's Brinley Place in Roxbury. Here too, although the trees were identified, no attempt was made either to have a comprehensive collection or to plant the trees in a systematic order.[15]

The fifty or so years immediately preceding the establishment of the Arnold Arboretum were a period of enormous growth in the science of botany, particularly in taxonomy. By the early nineteenth century the "artificial" order of the Linnaean system, which involved categorizing trees by the number of male and female plant parts, was being gradually replaced by a "natural" system based on morphological similarities. The publication of Darwin's *Origin of Species* in 1859, rather than upsetting previous work in botany, instead provided a theoretical framework for a classification system that had been in practical use for many years.[16]

As the natural system became accepted and grew increasingly sophisticated, it was only logical that there should be an interest in planting trees according to the new order. Although the Arnold Arboretum was the first in the United States, it was preceded by at least three important unexecuted projects—one by A. J. Downing, one by Olmsted and Vaux, and one by H. W. S. Cleveland. All were planned according to the natural order, but each offered a different solution to the design problems posed by that choice. The first, Downing's project for the Boston Public Garden, around 1841, was

briefly discussed in Chapter I. Downing had the smallest area to work with, and his design solution was the simplest: he proposed to arrange the trees along the boundaries of the twenty-two acre Public Garden. Although Downing mentions that he prepared an actual plan showing the precise location of each tree, this plan seems to have been lost, and we have only his brief description in a letter.[17] We do not know how large a collection he planned, but space limitations would probably have precluded a very large variety.

The most important of the three plans from the point of view of the later design of the Arnold Arboretum was Olmsted and Vaux's own unexecuted project for an arboretum in Central Park. This arboretum appeared on the "Greensward" plan of 1858 (Figure 103, a detail of Figure 14) and was discussed in their "Descriptive Guide to the Arboretum," submitted with the "Greensward" plan and report. Located at the northeast corner of Central Park, the arboretum was to have contained forty acres of land and would have been limited to American trees, although, as the designers pointed out, the park as a whole would contain numerous examples of most trees, native and foreign, likely to thrive in New York City (but not planted in the natural, or any other, botanical order). The words below, written in 1858, might describe the Arnold Arboretum, designed more than two decades later:

The principal walk is intended to be so laid out, that while the trees and shrubs bordering it succeed one another in the natural order of families, each will be brought, as far as possible, into a position corresponding to its natural habits, and in which its distinguishing characteristics will be favorably exhibited. At the entrance, marked "W" on the plan, we place the Magnoliaceae, associating with them the shrubs belonging to the orders Ranunculaceae, Anonoceae, Berberidaceae, and Cistaceae. The great beauty of these families entitles them, if no other reasons prevailed, to a very prominent place on our grounds. In pursuing the path which enters here, we find on our right the order Tiliaceae, with the shrubs belonging to the orders Rutaceae, Anacardiaceae, and Rhamnaceae. On each side of the walk groups succeed, composed wholly of the order Sapindaceae. Next on the right, planted on high ground, among large rocks, we come to the natural order, Leguminosae, distinguished for the beauty of its forms and the lightness of its foliage, and not less in some species for the exquisite fragrance and delicacy of its blossoms.

At the next turn of the path, we come upon the Rosaceae. The shrubs of this order being very beautiful, we have placed many of them singly, as well as in thickets between, and over, the large masses of rock, which here occur on both sides.[18]

Comparison with a modern map of the Arnold Arboretum (Figure 35) shows an almost exact correspondence with the Central Park proposal. Magnolias and tulip trees (Magnoliaceae) are shown near the main entrance (Jamaica Plain Gate, at the right of the plan). A little farther on to the right are the lindens (Tiliaceae). The main drive then passes through trees not mentioned in the Central Park proposal, but on the right the tree legume (Leguminosae) slope soon appears, with the shrub collection to the left beyond the next turn in the road. Shrub roses planted as a hedge on either side of the walk appear today almost exactly as they did in 1905 (Figure 104).

We need scarcely look further for a prototype for the Arnold Arboretum, but a proposal made by H. W. S. Cleveland in 1869 is also relevant. He suggested that Chicago acquire additional parkland in the form of a gigantic boulevard or circumferential parkway 300 feet wide and 14 miles long, girdling the city and connecting the three large park systems already projected. Since the land was flat and lacked natural topographical interest, he advised planting the parkway as an arboretum, an idea he may have derived from the miniature arboretum planted in the central strips of the Avenue de l'Impératrice in Paris.[19]

Cleveland's aim, like that of Olmsted and Sargent, was to combine the science of botany with the art of the landscape gardener. In the Central Park plan and in the Arnold Arboretum as executed, Olmsted for the most part concentrated each collection on one side of the road, alternating from side to side along its entire length. By contrast, Cleveland envisioned his boulevard as passing through each collection, submerging the traveler first in maples, then in oaks, and so on, all displayed in great masses. Unlike Downing's or Olmsted and Vaux's projects, which were limited to fairly constricted sites, the grandiose scale of Cleveland's

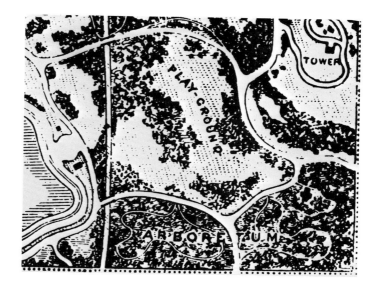

Figure 103
Proposed arboretum in Central Park. Detail of Olmsted and Vaux's Greensward plan of 1858 (Figure 14).

Figure 104
Meadow Road and rose hedge, Arnold Arboretum, 1905.

scheme would have permitted a comprehensive collection of a type not found anywhere in the world.

From Downing's description, we know only that he intended to distribute his arboretum trees around the boundaries of the rectangular Public Garden. On such a small site, this suggests a formal treatment, perhaps even malls similar to those surrounding the Common. Despite Downing's later preeminence as the leading spokesman for the Picturesque school of landscape gardening, this solution would have been entirely logical under the circumstances. Olmsted and Vaux used an irregular plan in keeping with the design of the rest of Central Park. However, there was only one main path, thus assuring, as in the case of Cleveland's plan, that the visi-

tor would see the collections in the proper sequence.

Although Olmsted never wrote a report for the Arnold Arboretum and there is no correspondence relating to the early stages of the design, the evolution of the plan becomes quite clear when the more than 160 drawings for this park are studied chronologically.[20] This total includes 78 early studies—a much greater number than for the contemporaneous Back Bay Fens. Of these, 31 are studies for the layout of the roads and 24 for the distribution of the tree collections. The large number of studies probably reflects at least three circumstances: the complexity of the design problem, Sargent's tenacious perfectionism, and the fact that five years elapsed

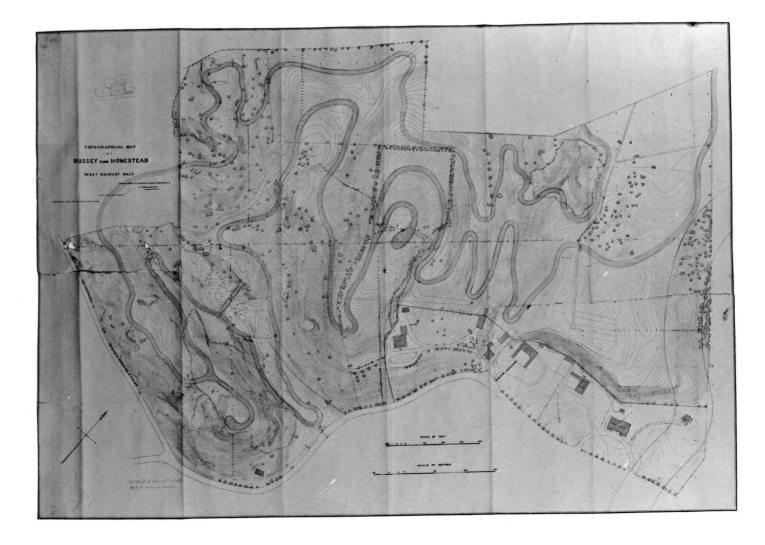

Figure 105
Study for roads in the Arnold Arboretum, circa 1878.

between the first studies and the beginning of construction.

Olmsted began "getting the plan" of the Arnold Arboretum as soon as the topographical map was completed in the summer of 1878. After the boundaries had been adjusted and some additional land purchased, he had 137 acres at his disposal. Since the problems of circulation and distribution of the collections were so intimately related, they had to be worked out together. The distribution studies are not planting plans in the usual sense of the word, for they come at the beginning rather than the end of the design process, and they are therefore discussed here rather than in Chapter XIII.

The first circulation studies, of which Figure 105 is a typical example, show a single winding road of almost tortuous complexity. In most of the drawings there are only two entrances, one at either end. This type of road system is, on the one hand, an extreme example of a characteristic Olmsted plan, adapted from Paxton and other English designers. From an aesthetic point of view, such a circulation system gives the illusion of great space and provides a multiplicity of views. On the other hand, "the longest possible road" and similar studies were a response to the very real problem of providing access to a huge number of trees in the correct natural order. The elimination of branch roads ensured that visitors would not be diverted into unrelated collections.

Of the many English landscape gardeners who influenced Olmsted, at least one, J. C. Loudon (1783–1843), had dealt with a similar design problem, although on a diminutive scale.[21] Loudon was an established writer and editor on horticultural matters and a leading exponent of the "gardenesque" school, which exploited new and exotic plant materials. Loudon designed Derby Arboretum in 1839; while not intended to be comprehensive, this collection accommodated 802 species on only eleven acres. Even tinier, at three acres, was his plan for a public garden in an unidentified English corporate town (Figure 106), which has a single writhing path, similar to the "longest possible road."

If the Arnold Arboretum had been executed according to the Loudonesque road schemes of the early studies, visitors would have been forced either to traverse the entire collection or to turn back and

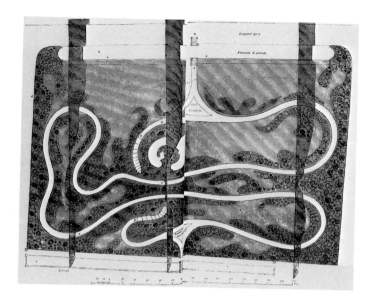

Figure 106
Plan for a public garden by John Claudius Loudon, 1836.

retrace their steps. Olmsted must eventually have realized that on a site of 137 acres this was impractical. It should be pointed out, however, that the Arboretum road, now restricted to foot traffic, was originally intended for carriages. Thus, the early long-road studies were a translation of Loudon's type of plan from a pedestrian to a vehicular scale. Today the Arboretum still has only one main road, but there are several entrances and thus several choices of route (see Figure 35). There is also a side road to the top of Bussey Hill, which appears in the early studies; a similar road on Hemlock Hill also appears in the studies but was later abandoned. As the studies advanced, the road was simplified and became less convoluted, a development that was related to the progress of the distribution studies.

The earliest of these studies, which were done at the same time as the first long-road drawings on the topographical map, showed a solution similar to Cleveland's, with each collection arranged on both sides of the main road. Later distribution studies and the final planting plan of 1886 (Figure 107) show a system similar to that proposed by Olmsted for Central Park, with collections for the most part alternating on opposite sides of the road. This plan, besides being more interesting visually, provided much greater freedom in arranging the available space, making it no longer necessary to have such a

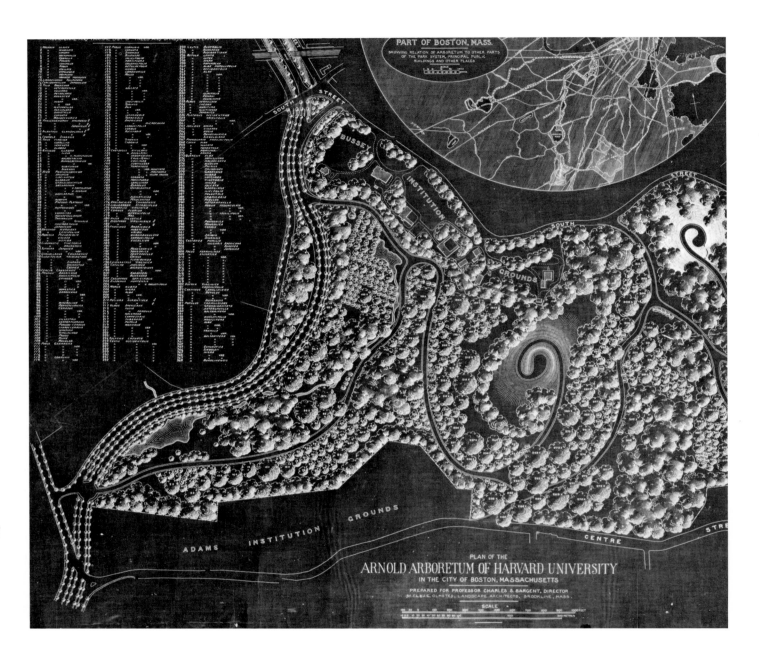

Figure 107
General plan of the Arnold
Arboretum, showing the
final distribution of the
tree collections. Blueprint,
1886.

contorted road plan. In Figure 108, a detail from one of the later distribution studies, we can also see the close correspondence between the Arboretum plantings and the Central Park project. Starting at the lower left-hand corner of the plan, the road first passes through several species of maple (*Acer*) and some of the natural woods. On the right the tree legume slope then appears, containing groups of honey locust, Kentucky coffee tree, yellowwood,

and locust (*Gleditsia, Gymnocladus, Cladrastis,* and *Robinia,* respectively) with large groupings of hawthorn, pear, and cherry (*Crataegus, Pyrus,* and *Prunus*), all members of the rose family, on the left. Around the curve in the road are groups of ash, catalpa, mulberry, elm, and birch (*Fraxinus, Catalpa, Morus, Ulmus,* and *Betula*), each representing a different botanical family.

Today these trees are found in the same general

areas shown on the study, but the precise arrangement is different. Ashes and catalpas still grow on the slope of Bussey Hill, but from an early date the dominant feature of this part of the road has been the lilac collection (see Figure 37). The numerous members of the rose family would have been too cramped in the space originally allotted to them, although many are found near the place shown on the study—crab apples, for example, are located just off the plan on the other side of the road. However, as the design evolved, most of this space was devoted to the shrub collection (Figure 109), which contains many plants of the rose family. Certain collections grew beyond all reasonable predictions. Hawthorns (*Crataegus*) became a special study for Sargent.[22] As he added to this collection, it was moved to the Peter's Hill tract, where it soon preempted much of the space. Many new trees and shrubs have, of course, been added since the original plantings, including a collection of Chinese trees on Bussey Overlook, on land formerly reserved by the city of Boston.

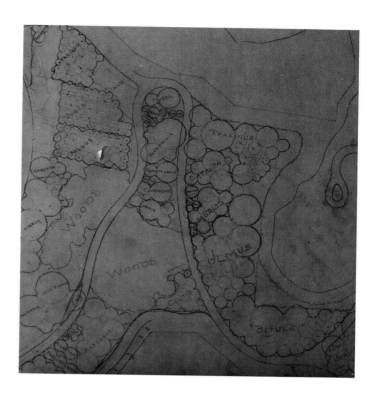

Figure 108
Study for the distribution of trees (detail), August 1885.

Figure 109
View of the shrub collection from Bussey Hill, 1905.

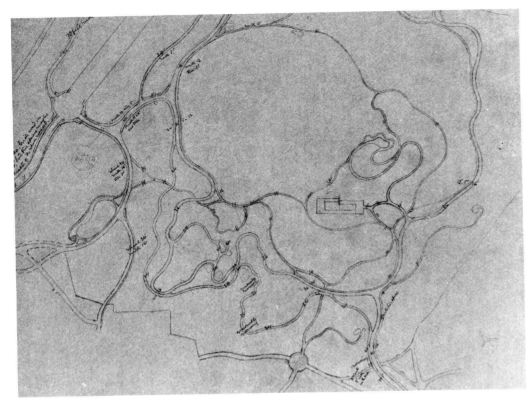

Figure 110
Study for road and pathway systems, Franklin Park, January 2, 1885.

Figure 111
Study for the Overlook in Franklin Park by John C. Olmsted, August 6, 1885.

At Franklin Park, Olmsted had a site that was exactly suited to its purpose. But the park was large, and the circulation system, although less rigid than that required for the Arboretum, was complex. The program also called for the inclusion of other functions besides the country park proper. For these reasons, numerous studies were necessary before the General Plan (Figure 41) was realized in 1885.

Olmsted followed the same method as he had for the Arboretum studies. The topographical map was printed in quantity, but in this case it was marked off in horizontals and verticals so that details could be enlarged and worked on individually. The grid was also useful for the extensive field photography done in Franklin Park before and during construction; the location of most of these photographs is indicated by grid coordinates. The earliest studies, for the road and pathway systems, were drawn directly on the topographical map. Although color was sometimes used, it does not stand out sufficiently clearly from the base map to allow reproduction here. However, a tracing-paper overlay study (Figure 110) of most of the area of the park, done in January 1885, illustrates the meticulous attention to detail required even at an early stage of the design process. By April the basic outlines of the plan had been established. Olmsted presented to the commissioners a preliminary study, which indicated roads, walks, bridle paths, Country Park, Greeting, and Playstead in essentially their final positions.[23] Over the next several months the plan was painstakingly adjusted and refined. During the design development stage, the Olmsted firm concentrated on specific areas of the park: sometimes whole sections, such as the Wilderness, but more frequently details of such sections.

The first part of the park to receive intensive study was the Playstead. A schematic plan without contours drawn by John Olmsted was shown to commissioners Dean and Maguire in July 1885.[24] It was accepted, and John worked out further details over the summer. Figure 111 shows one of his studies for the Playstead Overlook, drawn in pencil over a portion of the squared-off topographical map.

At Franklin Park Olmsted was not altering the basic character of the scenery but merely emphasizing its positive features, which required no major topographical changes. The minor alterations he did

Figure 112
Grading the Playstead,
1887.

make generally consisted of removing inappropriate elements. As Olmsted expressed his design aims for Franklin Park:

The intention is to make no change in any of the present leading features of the ground except with the purpose of giving a fuller development, aggrandizement, and emphasis to what are regarded as the more interesting and effective existing elements of the scenery, and of taking out or subordinating elements that neutralize or conflict with those chosen to be made more of.[25]

Olmsted's design by subtraction is more clearly illustrated by photographs than by drawings. Figure 112 shows the Playstead being graded in 1887. On the topographical map of 1884 the Playstead site appears as an open field, marked only by a few trees near a former property line. The Playstead and all low-lying sections of the park required extensive drainage and minor contour changes, but the construction crews worked around the existing trees. In the finished design (Figure 113), we see an ap-

Figure 113
The Playstead completed.

parently natural level field, with the best of the elms remaining, although a vista has been opened up to the south toward the Blue Hills. Figures 114 and 115, showing Ellicottdale during and after construction, illustrate a similar process. Here there were many more trees and numerous stone boundary walls, which were apparently being dismantled when the earlier photograph was taken. Carefully chosen trees and some natural stone outcroppings were kept as part of the landscape design, as we can see in Figure 115.

These three examples—the Back Bay Fens, Arnold Arboretum, and Franklin Park—demonstrate how Olmsted and his firm solved widely varying problems of site, program, and design in order to "get the plan" of a park. The next step was the preparation of working drawings and the actual construction.

Figure 114
North side of Ellicottdale
during construction, 1890.

Figure 115
North side of Ellicottdale
completed.

XI

Building
the Parks

◆

For more than twenty years the sites of the Boston parks were full of men and their horse-drawn machines, digging, filling, draining, and grading, as the plans Olmsted had so meticulously "gotten" moved from paper to actuality. In the course of this work, over 2,000 acres of the city were reshaped, the channels of two streams were altered, solid land was created from parts of the Charles River and Boston Harbor, and miles of roads and pathways were built. It was the largest construction project in the history of the city, surpassing even the filling of the Back Bay.

The engineering of the Boston park system falls into three categories: sanitary engineering, topographical engineering, and the construction of roads, all of which come under the general heading of civil engineering.[1] In sanitary engineering, the most difficult technical problems Olmsted confronted were the control of the waters of Stony Brook and the Muddy River in the Fens and the related problem of the Muddy River valley in Boston and Brookline. Olmsted's ingenious solutions for these two parks will be examined in some detail. We shall also look briefly at the unglamorous but important activity of drainage, as seen especially in the Arnold Arboretum and Franklin Park.

Unlike the work of sanitary engineering, which occurs mostly underground, the results of topographical engineering, shaping the contours of the land, are highly visible aesthetic components of any landscape design. In the Boston park system the Fens and the lower valley of the Muddy River were completely recontoured. Finally, the building of roads, walks, and bridle paths was an essential part of the construction of all the parks; we shall examine primarily the roads of the Fens, Franklin Park, and Arnold Arboretum.

After Olmsted, John Olmsted, and senior designers such as Percy Jones and James Langdon had developed the design of the parks and before construction could begin, numerous detailed working drawings had to be prepared. Some of these were drawn by Jones and Langdon, but most are attributed to men who seem to have been transitory members of the firm, probably junior draftsmen or apprentices. Detailed specification writing was not apparently a standard practice at this time. The city or town engineer was told in a general way what would be required and was given detailed drawings from which to make an estimate. The lack of such specifications placed great responsibility on the men who supervised the construction of the parks.

On private projects Olmsted's chiefs of construction and planting directed the work. For the park system several work forces had to be coordinated, and successful execution depended on a complicated chain of command. Construction was done either by contract, as in the case of the Muddy River Improvement or, more commonly, by the city engineer's department. Engineering work and the construction of bridges were supervised by the engineer in charge; construction of park buildings was supervised by the city architect's office and the consulting architects. These men were in turn supervised by John or another member of the Olmsted firm. Olmsted himself paid frequent visits to the park sites. When he was out of town for prolonged periods, as happened in 1892, he kept in close touch with John by letter.

Olmsted was always careful to explain the difference between his profession and the related but distinct professions of engineering, architecture, and horticulture. While members of these professions worked collaboratively with him on all his projects, he was always concerned that there be no confusion between his role and theirs. As he explained to a correspondent:

A Landscape Architect needs to be fairly well-informed in Engineering and in Architectural Science, but he does not need to be an Engineer and Architect. We study, sometimes very laboriously, engineering and architectural schemes to fit into our plans, but we do so only to establish conditions of the problems that we require Engineers and Architects to resolve.[2]

He further felt that engineers, by training and by temperament, were unsuited to the practice of landscape architecture: "It has appeared to me that the training of an Engineer was most adverse to facility in the exercise of constructive imagination . . . A good Engineer is nearly always impatient of [the] indefiniteness, unlimitedness and mystery which is the soul of landscape."[3]

This chapter will amply illustrate the extent to which Olmsted consulted with engineers and relied on their technical advice. He disagreed with them only when they tried to interfere with his design concept, and this happened rarely. In working out his solutions to the Fens and the Muddy River, Olmsted conferred with City Engineer Joseph P. Davis and his successor, Henry Wightman. The engineer in charge of all work on the Boston park system during this whole period was E. W. Howe. His

Figure 116
Clearing fields near the
Circuit Drive, Franklin
Park, 1890.

counterpart in Brookline was Alexis H. French, engineer to the town.

All of the parks required extensive site preparation before construction could begin. In Franklin Park land was cleared and the stone boundary walls that criss-crossed woods and fields dismantled (Figures 114, 116, and 117).[4] At Jamaica Pond and Franklin Park, large houses had to be removed. (In many cases, these were sold at auction and moved elsewhere, rather than being demolished.) Parks built largely on made land, such as Charlesbank, Wood Island Park, Marine Park, and Charlestown Playground, required months, in some cases years, of filling. The Back Bay Fens was also built on made land, but here the water was relatively shallow, and the site had to be laboriously dredged. Figure 118 shows the dredging of the northern basin in 1882.

Olmsted's third scheme for the Back Bay park (see Figure 101) was stalled when an initial meeting called at Olmsted's request between himself, the city engineer, the superintendent of sewers, and Commissioners Dalton, Coolidge, and Gray led to an impasse after four hours of discussion. Olmsted, however, continued to meet with the city engineer for several weeks and eventually came up with a plan that satisfied both the engineering and the landscape requirements of the site. As Olmsted reconstructed his conversations with Davis in a talk before the Boston Society of Architects, they took the form of a rather one-sided Socratic dialogue:

Can sewage matter be kept out of the basin? Answer, yes, by intercepting sewers.

But the ordinary flow of the streams will yet be often foul; can this flow, except in the emergencies for which the basin is needed, be kept out of it? Answer, yes, by conduits of moderate dimensions laid outside the basin.

That being the case, can the basin when not required for its main purpose be kept clean and sweet? Answer, yes, by flooding it as far as necessary for the purpose with salt water, letting this move in and out enough to avoid stagnation.

But suppose we go to the very expensive expedient of high retaining walls, will not the deposit that will occasionally be made above these, when the water subsides after a flood, leave a slime upon them offensive both to

Figure 117
Removing a boulder on Circuit Drive, 1893.

the eye and the nose, and would not their aspect be in all respects unpleasant? Answer, it could not be otherwise.

Sloping earthen banks instead of masonry would answer the purpose of holding the water, what would be the objection to them? Answer, the slope would need to be as nearly level as that of a sea beach, or, to be pitched with stone in all that part liable to be flooded and for some part above it. Otherwise, it would be undermined and washed out by the waves beating against it. Such a slope for the masonry depth would require a great space of ground and it would not have a pleasing appearance. Moreover such a lining of stone would be open to the same objections as a vertical wall of stone.

Suppose the wash of waves could be avoided, the lining of stone dispensed with and the margin of the water be made inoffensive, could a basin of sufficient extent be formed within the area now under control of the Park Department? By calculation it was found that it could.

By taking care that there shall nowhere be any great breadth of water for the wind to act upon, we may avoid the liability to waves of destructive forces. By taking care that the slope of the bank between high and low water level shall be at an inclination of about 1 to 6; by making the breadth of ground to be flooded during freshets so great that the difference between high and low water need not exceed four feet and by providing for a growth of foliage on the banks, not liable to be flooded with salt water, that will obscure the margin, should we not have a result that would serve all the engineering requirements as well as they would be served in a basin of masonry and be much less objectionable on the score of taste?

Answer. We should.

Figure 118
Dredging the northern basin, Back Bay Fens, 1882.

And would not a basin of this character cost much less than a basin of masonry?
Answer. It would.[5]

The apparatus that was eventually constructed to regulate the water level in the Fens and the flow of the Muddy River and Stony Brook worked almost exactly as described in this conversation and functioned perfectly while it was in operation. First, intercepting sewers were built to remove the problem of sewage. Second, although the Muddy River appeared to empty into the Fens at Brookline Avenue, the entire flow of this river was to be diverted to the Charles in a covered conduit. Regulating Stony Brook was a more complicated matter. Olmsted decided, for both practical and aesthetic reasons, to keep the Fens a salt marsh. Since allowing fresh water to empty into salt creates an unattractive slime, the ordinary flow of Stony Brook,

normally quite small, was also diverted through a covered conduit into the Charles.

The gate chamber between Stony Brook and the Fens was arranged so that when the water level in the brook rose above the level of the water in the Fens, which would generally happen only in the spring when abnormally high tides coincided with heavy rain, a pair of gates would automatically open into the Fens. By flooding the salt marsh, the thirty acres normally covered by water could be increased to fifty acres without raising the water level more than a few feet. As the tide dropped, the extra water would empty out into the Charles over a dam under Beacon Street. Gates in the dam regulated the tide in the Fens, which normally rose only a foot between low and high water. The gate chamber at Stony Brook also included a sluiceway through which larger amounts of salt water could be admitted periodically at high tide through the Stony

Brook conduit to prevent stagnation. It was also possible to empty the Fens entirely if that should be necessary. The apparatus worked completely automatically and was thoroughly equipped with safety features, so that if one part of the mechanism failed to operate, back-up devices would take over.[6]

Olmsted's engineering solution for the Muddy River Improvement was a logical outgrowth of his plan for the Fens. At the end of 1880 Olmsted resumed his Socratic dialogue with the city engineer:

The plans for the Basin having been adopted, I asked . . . what are your plans for dealing with the Muddy River above the Basin?
We have none.
What are you likely to have there eventually—a big conduit of masonry to carry the flood, several miles in length and intercepting pipes for the sewerage from both sides?
That is not unlikely.
Such an arrangement will be very costly and will be delayed many years because of its cost. Meantime and before many years the Muddy River valley will be very dirty, unhealthy, squalid. No one will want to live in the neighborhood of it. Property will have little value and there will grow up near the best [illegible] district of the city an unhealthy and pestilential neighborhood.
All that is not improbable.
Why not make an open channel there and treat the banks of it as we [illegible] to treat the banks of the Basin. Would not that be an economical move?
I don't see but it would.
Then the roads leading up that valley to Jamaica Pond would be the beginning of a Parkway leading from the Back Bay to the Arboretum and West Roxbury Park.
They might be.
Suppose then that we put our two professional heads together again and see if we can't make a practicable plan for that purpose and get the city to adopt it.
Agreed.
And from that conference came this plan which you will see is essentially an extension of the Back Bay Plan, and has been fully adopted by [illegible] Brookline and Boston.[7]

The flood- and tide-regulating devices Olmsted proposed for the Muddy River in 1880 were similar, although somewhat less complex, than those al-

ready under construction in the Fens. Intercepting sewers were installed to carry off the wastes that had formerly emptied directly into the river. Although the original plan for the Fens was to divert the entire flow of the Muddy River to the Charles by a covered conduit, this conduit was not built until after the Charles River dam was constructed in 1910. When Olmsted wrote his first Muddy River report in 1880, he clearly intended to continue the salt water scenery of the Fens up as far as Tremont Street in the Muddy River Improvement. The proposed method for admitting salt water to the river was not explicitly described, but it could have entered either from the Fens, as had always been the case, or from the Charles at high tide through the conduit. In the Fens the normally salt water of the basin received the fresh water of Stony Brook only on the relatively rare occasions when heavy floods coincided with extremely high tides. Leverett Pond, on the other hand, was planned as a fresh-water pond that could occasionally store the flood waters of the salt Muddy River.[8]

The decision to make the Muddy River Improvement an entirely fresh-water park was apparently motivated by aesthetic rather than by practical considerations. By 1882 Olmsted was describing its lower valley (the Muddy River section) as the fresh-water counterpart to the salt-marsh landscape of the Fens.[9] Quite apart from the question of whether it was essential as a storage basin, Leverett Pond was an important landscape feature of the Muddy River Improvement. To assure that the pond received an abundant supply of water, the flow from Jamaica Pond through Ward's and Willow ponds was supplemented by the Brookline Town Brook, diverted into Leverett Pond through a conduit. At the northern (Tremont Street) end of the pond, a dam was constructed to limit the flow into the Muddy River. To the south of Leverett Pond, the smaller ponds were connected by a narrow stream, and a series of little boulder dams was built across the stream to hold back enough water "to show."[10]

Another aspect of sanitary engineering is drainage. Throughout the park system miles of drainage pipes were laid. These were especially necessary in the low-lying sections of Franklin Park, particularly near the eastern end of the Country Park at Nazingdale. Similarly, the meadow in the Arnold Arboretum had to be drained before it could be used for planting at all.

Topographical engineering was an important part of the construction of all the parks. In the Arnold Arboretum and Franklin Park only light grading was done, except in the vicinity of roads and

Figure 119 (top)
Grading study of banks, Beacon Entrance, Back Bay Fens, by John C. Olmsted, February 18, 1882.

Figure 120 (bottom)
Grading plan for Beacon Entrance by John C. Olmsted, March 3, 1882.

walks, and the natural contours of the land were retained. Similarly, at Jamaica Park Olmsted kept the kettle holes and other contours formed by glaciers millions of years earlier. By contrast, the entire Back Bay Fens and the lower valley of the Muddy River were rebuilt. All parts of the Fens that were neither salt marsh nor water were minutely graded under the direction of E. W. Howe, the engineer in charge. According to John Olmsted, the grading plans prepared by the Olmsted office, "with one-foot contours, which showed every irregularity of the surface desired to simulate a natural appearance [were] implicitly and mechanically followed by the engineers of the City Engineer's office in setting stakes for the guidance of the foremen in charge of the distribution of the filling."[11] Figure 119 shows an 1882 grading plan for the part of Beacon Entrance between Commonwealth Avenue and Boylston Street; this plan has five-foot contours and is marked "superseded." Figure 120 is the final grading plan, with one-foot contours, for all of Beacon Entrance. Both plans are in John's hand, according to the plans catalog at the Olmsted National Historic Site, Brookline.

Work on the Fens progressed systematically, starting at Beacon Entrance. By the end of 1885 approximately two-thirds of the Fens had been dredged and filled; Beacon Entrance had been completely constructed and planted; the northern basin was almost finished, although the marsh meadow and some of the planting were not complete; and the marsh meadow in the southern basin had just been started. Figure 121 shows the progress of work on the Fens to December 31, 1885.

Construction work did not begin on the Muddy River Improvement until 1890, ten years after Olmsted's first Muddy River "Suggestion" had been published and approved. Although both the city and town were eager to begin construction, the Boston commissioners' hands were tied until more funds became available. Brookline, however, lost no time in starting to excavate and fill on its side of the river. As soon as the state legislature authorized the boundary change in May 1890, the Brookline commissioners advertised for bids, awarded contracts, and promptly went to work. (They had first asked Olmsted's advice on whether they could start before Boston.) Figure 122 shows grading in progress.

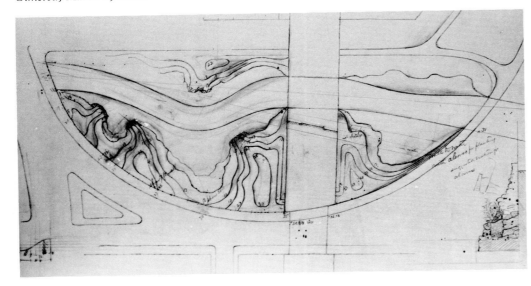

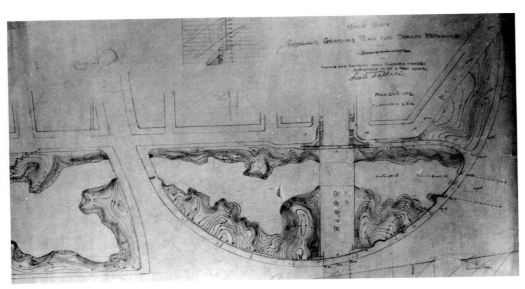

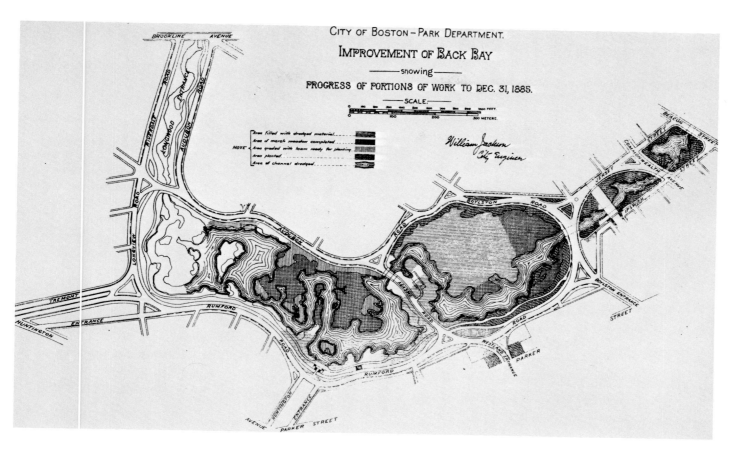

CITY OF BOSTON—PARK DEPARTMENT.

IMPROVEMENT OF BACK BAY

——showing——

PROGRESS OF PORTIONS OF WORK TO DEC. 31, 1885.

——SCALE.——

William Jackson
City Engineer

Figure 121
Plan of the Back Bay Fens,
showing progress of work
to December 31, 1885
(William Jackson, City Engineer).

Figure 122
Grading in progress, about
1891, on the Muddy River
Improvement near Long-
wood Avenue, looking
downstream toward Bos-
ton.

Figure 123
Grading nearly complete,
spring 1892, from approxi-
mately the same point of
view as Figure 122.

With the exception of the section between Brookline Avenue and Tremont Street, where the wooden houses on Downer Street were left standing for the time being, the entire length of the Brookline side was contracted for. The area was filled with gravel to a depth of about three and a half feet, then the gravel was covered with mud, excavated from the new river channel, and loam. Delays in negotiating an exchange of land between the town and the Boston and Albany Railroad Company held up the completion of work in the Longwood area. The engineers also discovered that the soil was "semi-liquid" in this area and could only be kept out of the newly excavated channel by a timber bulkhead. Elsewhere, gravel dikes were sufficient. By early 1892 Brookline had completed excavating, filling, grading, loaming, and manuring and was ready to begin planting. The engineering work on the Boston side, begun in 1891, was largely completed by 1893.[12]

On the Boston side considerable picturesque, wooded upland was incorporated into the com-

Figure 124
Construction of the Long-
wood section of the
Muddy River Improve-
ment, spring 1892.

pleted park, but there was little on the Brookline side that was worth saving. As in the Fens the land was minutely recontoured according to detailed grading plans. This process is dramatically illustrated in a series of photographs taken by the Olmsted firm in the spring of 1892, when the work on the Brookline side was almost complete. Two sections of the park—Longwood and Leverett Pond—are illustrated here.[13]

In designing Longwood, the Olmsted firm had to provide a sequestered riverside environment under rather difficult circumstances. The city was close at hand and visible. The park boundaries were extremely narrow on both sides, and railroad trains rattled past and discharged passengers several times a day. To provide a sense of intimacy and seclusion, Olmsted used several simple devices. To hide the railroad and muffle its noises, a continuous mound of earth, later densely planted, was raised between the tracks and the path along the river (to the left in Figures 122 and 123). Two small islands were constructed in the river (Figure 124) and when planted, these blocked out most of the city buildings that had been visible from Longwood Avenue. Two railroad stations that were less than 1,500 feet apart created a dangerous situation, since schoolboys frequently got out of the train at one stop and ran to catch it at the next. Arrangements were made with the Boston and Albany Railroad Company, which had the contract for filling this section of the park, to take down these stations and build a new one at a better location. Chapel Street, the new road running in front of the station, was graded by the railroad company at its own expense.[14]

Leverett Pond, in marked contrast to Longwood, was the only part of the Muddy River Improvement wide enough to allow broad views and a sense of spaciousness. Most of the area of the original cattail swamp was dredged for the pond, although room had to be provided on the Brookline side for two drives, the projected street railway, and a footpath. Figure 125 shows Leverett Pond in a relatively early stage of construction about 1891; the buildings are on the approximate site of the present Brook House in Brookline. To vary the shores of the pond, tiny islands and numerous little coves and inlets, one of which was crossed by a footbridge, were constructed. Figure 126 shows Leverett Pond almost

complete. Most of the inexpensive wooden houses (shown in both photographs) were apparently outside the boundaries of the park and were left standing. The existing broad meadow near Leverett Pond on the Boston side (not visible in the construction photographs) was retained with little change.

Figure 125 (top) Leverett Pond under construction about 1891.

Figure 126 (bottom) Construction of Leverett Pond nearly complete, with some planting done on the Brookline side to the left, circa 1892.

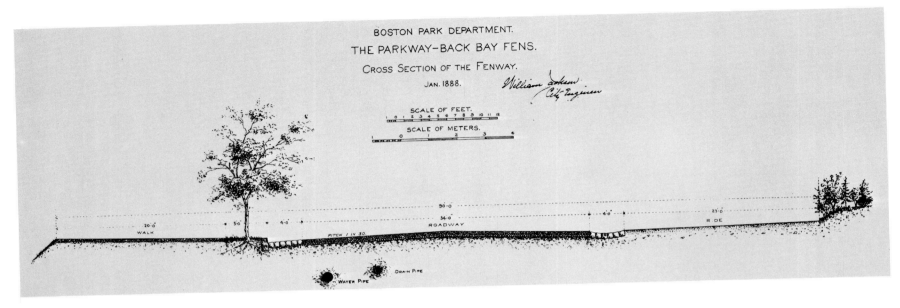

Figure 127
Cross section of the Fen-
way, 1888 (William Jack-
son, City Engineer).

Figure 128
Construction of the drive
in the Arnold Arboretum,
circa 1892.

Possibly more time, money, and manpower went into the building of the roads, walks, and bridle paths of the Boston parks than into any other construction activity. In 1901 the commissioners estimated that there were over thirty-five miles of driveways, over fifty-seven miles of walks, and over eight miles of bridle paths in the park system, not all of which were complete.[15] Along with roadways and paths within the parks, the construction included the entire length of the parkway from the Fens to Franklin and Marine parks. So massive was this project that the final link, the Strandway in South Boston, was not completed until well into the twentieth century. Figure 127 shows a cross section of the Fenway, with flanking walk and bridle path. In the foreground of Figure 128, showing construction of the drive in the Arnold Arboretum about 1892, work is in progress near the main entrance from the Arborway. A derrick is lifting stones, probably for construction of the culvert that runs under the drive at this point. Farther back, a steam roller is going over the newly surfaced road, while to the right is the just completed administration building. Figure 129 is a close-up view of a steam roller used on the park drives.

The methods and machines used in constructing the Boston parks were the customary ones of the day. Even Olmsted's solution for controlling the

Figure 129
A steamroller used in constructing the park drives.

waters of the Back Bay Fens was not remarkable in the strictly technological sense; he modified a standard engineering scheme into an appropriate landscape design. The brilliance of his solution lay in his synthesis of the practical and the aesthetic, rather than in any engineering innovation as such. However, in terms of the sheer scale of the project, the detail of the working drawings (as shown, for example, in the grading plans for the Fens), and the care shown in both supervision and execution, the construction of the Boston park system was indeed an extraordinary enterprise.

XII

The "Furniture" of the Boston Parks

———————◆———————

IN 1894 Olmsted wrote to City Architect Edmund M. Wheelwright, describing the plans then in progress for the Franklin Park Refectory as "subordinate and auxiliary to the design of a larger work, as a staircase or a balcony or a porch would be to the general design of a building . . . This refectory building is a minor part of the park; a piece of furniture, as it were, of the park. We are the designers of the park."[1]

The buildings in the Boston park system range in size and importance from a small open shelter on the Riverway to the large and elaborate Head House at Marine Park. Most were designed with the assistance of the best Boston architects of the period. At Olmsted's insistence, even plans for bridges, generally considered the province of the civil engineer, were reviewed by architects as well.

The list of Boston firms that played a part in the design of the "furniture" of the park system is impressive: it begins with H. H. Richardson; continues with his successors, Shepley, Rutan and Coolidge; and includes such firms as C. Howard Walker, R. Clipston Sturgis, Rotch and Tilden, and Hartwell and Richardson, as well as City Architects Arthur H. Vinal and E. M. Wheelwright. Richardson designed two bridges, a gatehouse, and a fountain for the Fens and three temporary shelters in Franklin Park. Nearly all of the remaining bridges in the park system, as well as some minor buildings, were designed by Shepley, Rutan and Coolidge. The other architects worked primarily on the shelters in Franklin, Marine, and Wood Island parks and at Charlesbank.[2]

In what sense did these important firms "design"

structures that Olmsted considered "subordinate" to his own, larger work of park design? There is no question that Olmsted firmly rejected the notion held by most of the older generation of landscape gardeners that his was primarily an ornamental art and subsidiary to architecture. Nevertheless, when he designed the grounds of a building that was the main feature of an entire composition, he carefully and sensitively adapted his design to suit its style. As he expressed it: "We often have to make our art becomingly secondary to the magnification of the art of architecture; to help out the motive of an architectural work. We have done so sometimes with a degree of success for which the designers of buildings have been grateful."[3]

In the case of parks, however, the situation was reversed: the entire design was Olmsted's, and the bridges and other structures were merely details of the whole composition. As he explained patiently to Wheelwright (who was then overseeing the design for the Franklin Park Refectory, which Hartwell and Richardson were preparing from preliminary sketches provided by the Olmsted firm):

The view upon which we proceeded in making these sketches was not the usual view upon which an architect proceeds. The building was regarded as a detail of, and a secondary matter to, a design for a work not of building; the usual process of an architect being reversed . . . In this case it is not a building that is to be made; it is an anti-building; a retreat from buildings. There should be the least show possible of building consistent with convenience and a frank avowal of purpose and an honest use of building materials.[4]

Most architects, including H. H. Richardson and the firm of Shepley, Rutan and Coolidge, submitted gracefully to the reversal of their usual relationship with the landscape architect. Wheelwright and the firm of Hartwell and Richardson, however, either did not understand Olmsted's point of view or refused to accept it. The Franklin Park Refectory was one of the few structures in the Boston park system with which the Olmsted firm was dissatisfied.[5]

As he tried to explain to Wheelwright, Olmsted felt that in site, shape, size, and architectural design, buildings within a park should harmonize with and be completely subordinate to the scenery. He always

recommended that restaurants and administration or service buildings be located on the outskirts, and he preferred that shelter buildings be located in secluded spots and constructed of materials such as weathered shingles or rough, gray stone, whose colors would blend with the surroundings. Frequently he planned for the buildings to be covered with vines. They were generally only one story high and had low-pitched roofs, often of thatch or with an undulating surface. Olmsted considered park bridges to be architectural rather than engineering works, and he required that they also harmonize with the scenery. His preferred material for them was boulders.[6]

In a letter cited in Chapter XI, Olmsted explained that his firm laboriously worked out architectural and engineering schemes for their projects, but only "to establish conditions of the problems that we require Engineers and Architects to resolve."[7] This evaluation is overly modest. The preliminary plans for all but two of the Boston park structures were designed either by John Olmsted or under his direction, and practically all were constructed closely following his plans.[8] It is true that the firm required that their architectural plans, at least for major structures, be reviewed and approved by either the city architect or a consulting architect, or both. Sometimes the consulting architect merely approved an Olmsted plan without altering it at all. In the case of many of the smaller granite bridges in the Muddy River Improvement, for example, Shepley, Rutan and Coolidge merely blueprinted the Olmsted plan and stamped it with their office stamp. Often they made only minor changes or worked out ornamental details, although for the more monumental structures, their design contribution was substantial. But the boulder arches and bridges, such as the Agassiz Bridge in the Back Bay Fens, were constructed directly from the Olmsted firm's plans, without a consulting architect.[9]

The working drawings for the bridges were prepared by the city engineer's office, those for the buildings by the city architect's office. The Olmsted firm generally asked the consulting architect to visit the site periodically, although the city engineer's or architect's office had primary responsibility for supervising construction.

In this chapter we shall examine in some detail the architecture of the Fens, with a particularly close look at the Boylston Street Bridge—a major Olmsted/Richardson collaboration and the first important structure to be built in the Boston parks. There are also many significant bridges and buildings in the Muddy River Improvement and Franklin Park, and we shall consider briefly the buildings in the Arnold Arboretum and Marine Park.

Beacon Entrance was the first section of the Back Bay Fens to be designed in detail, the first to be constructed, and the first to be planted. It posed significant architectural problems because five bridges were needed in a relatively small area. Questions immediately arose concerning the proper siting, design, and materials for the bridges and also the role of the Olmsted firm vis à vis the city engineer, the city architect, and consulting architects. These questions were to recur throughout the history of the park system, especially in Franklin Park and the Muddy River Improvement.

Three of the necessary bridges—those carrying Beacon Street, Commonwealth Avenue, and the Boston and Albany railroad tracks across Beacon Entrance—crossed at a low elevation and were relatively inconspicuous. Designed by the city engineer's office, these were simple deck bridges with pile and timber foundations and abutments and piers of ashlar masonry.[10] The other two bridges were quite a different matter. The Boylston Street Bridge and, to a lesser degree, the bridge over the railroad tracks were focal points of the Fens. Still standing today, although half buried in foliage and dwarfed by the Charlesgate interchange, the Boylston Street Bridge (Figure 130) remains the most famous structure in any of the Boston parks.[11]

Although the Boylston Street Bridge is not mentioned in correspondence or in Park Department reports and minutes until 1880, the archives at the Olmsted National Historic Site contain an earlier record: a sheet of tracing-paper studies for Beacon Entrance dated December 1878, which includes two tiny sketches for a single arched span (Figure 131). These little studies, like the series of which they are a part, are unsigned and uncatalogued, but there can be little doubt that they represent the Boylston Street Bridge and must have been drawn by either Olmsted or John.

In January 1880 Olmsted sent City Engineer Davis a diagram, showing the positions of the bridges in Beacon Entrance, as an enclosure in a letter. Olmsted and Davis had apparently had a difference of opinion over the materials of the Boyl-

Figure 130
The Boylston Street Bridge, Back Bay Fens, 1901.

Figure 131
Sketches for the Boylston Street Bridge by F. L. or J. C. Olmsted, December 1878. Illustrated at approximately the same size as original.

Figure 132
Preliminary panoramic
sketch for the Boylston
Street Bridge by the Rich-
ardson office, possibly in
H. H. Richardson's hand,
circa 1880.

ston Street Bridge, revealing a basic divergence in their points of view. Olmsted sent a copy of the letter to Commissioner Dalton, to whom he railed against the "habitual drift of the engineering mind," which constantly led Davis to the commonplace. He warned Dalton against letting Davis "find opportunities for backing away from the more refined purposes of your undertaking." Davis's motives, according to Olmsted, were not intentional or even conscious, but "to an engineer, bridges are engineering works." At the end of the letter, Olmsted asked Dalton for Richardson's assistance in designing the bridge.[12]

The letter to Davis included a long and emphatic paragraph on the importance of the Boylston Street Bridge:

The Boylston Bridge will be the most conspicuous object in all the scheme. It will be forced on the attention above and below and on each side. It will dominate everything and be seen from Charles River to Parker Hill. People will rest and linger upon it and look at it more closely than anything else on the Bay. A natty, formal elegant structure would put all the rural elements of the Bay out of countenance. It would be a discord. The bridge must, if possible, have a rustic quality and be picturesque *in material* as well as in outlines and shadows . . . The more the real structure is evident the better. I would like an arch of Roxbury Puddingstone or an arch of boulders or of rough field stones with voussoirs of cut stone or brick; or an arch wholly of cheap rough brick. I would much prefer wood to iron . . . Let us have iron anywhere else if economy requires but on Boylston Street, I think I would always prefer a brick arch or arches at the same cost.[13]

Richardson's sketch for the Boylston Street Bridge (Figure 132) does indeed show it as "the most conspicuous object in all the scheme," as does a bird's-eye photograph of the completed Fens taken in the late nineties (Figure 32). In the Richardson perspective, the principal arch over water appears much as it does in the tiny Olmsted firm studies of 1878, but the bridge is flung far to the right in a viaductlike arrangement of successive arches, terminating in the bridge over the railroad. This scheme is not as different from the executed bridge as it first appears. With one exception, the additional arches were never constructed (they would probably have been concealed by planting if they had), but the bridge was extended by a curved retaining wall that connected it with the railroad bridge.[14]

The choice of material continued to be a subject of dispute. Davis wanted iron for reasons of economy. Olmsted would have preferred brick or even wood, but as he told the Boston Society of Architects, his first intention was to use boulders. According to Olmsted, "Mr. Richardson fell in with this idea," and his first plans for the arch were for "a very picturesque structure of fieldstone."[15] In a later memorandum Olmsted referred again to specific drawings for the bridge—those prepared by his own firm as well as Richardson's drawing submitted to the commissioners—which showed it faced with boulders.[16]

The Richardson perspective sketch shown in Figure 132 does not indicate boulders or any other material (unless the wavy lines can be interpreted as a rough surface). Unfortunately, it and the tiny

1878 sketches are the only surviving early drawings for the bridge. (The Richardson sketch is undated but is clearly a preliminary study.) The commissioners and the city engineer—by this time Henry Wightman had succeeded Davis—were both reluctant to use boulders, and to Olmsted's disappointment, the bridge was ultimately built of seam-faced Cape Ann granite. A later elevation prepared by the Richardson firm (now in the Richardson archives at Houghton Library, Harvard University) for a blind arch in the northwest wing wall plainly shows the change of material. Partly because of delays in shipping the stone and grout, construction of the bridge and retaining wall took four years, 1880 to 1884;

Figure 133 shows them about half finished in 1882. Olmsted was pleased with the outlines and color of the Boylston Street Bridge, but he felt it would have "suited the circumstances better if it had not been quite so nice."[17]

Few people today would consider it too "nice." As executed, the bridge has a sculptural elegance that would surely have been diminished had it been constructed of fieldstone. Although Richardson's original concept, like Olmsted's, seems to have been for a boulder bridge, he undoubtedly made subtle changes in the design (such as the "tourelles," or projecting bays, attributed to Richardson by John Olmsted) once the stone was finally decided on.[18]

Figure 133
Boylston Street Bridge and retaining wall under construction, 1882.

Richardson was the consulting architect for three other structures in the Fens. Although the Olmsted drawings include no studies for the bridge over the railroad tracks, the Richardson collection at Houghton contains what are presumably four alternate elevations for this bridge—two showing iron trusses and two for suspension bridges. Since none of the four has any resemblance to the finished bridge (seen at the far right in Figure 32), the statement made by John in his letter to Baxter, that Richardson was responsible only for the "railing, lamps, etc." of this bridge, is probably accurate. A sheet of details, possibly in Richardson's hand, for the ironwork of the railroad bridge (Figure 134) agrees almost exactly with a detail of the bridge photographed shortly before its demolition in 1965 (Figure 135).[19]

Two rather mystifying Richardson projects are the Stony Brook Gatehouse near Huntington Entrance, which was executed, and a fountain in the Fens, which was apparently never constructed. No drawings survive for either project. The Gatehouse is firmly attributed to Richardson in the records of the Boston Park Department and also in John's letter to Baxter. The fountain is attributed to Richardson in an entry in the plan catalog at the Olmsted National Historic Site. Richardson submitted plans for the Gatehouse to the park commissioners at the same meeting as the plans for the Boylston Street Bridge, but the Gatehouse plans were approved immediately. The Gatehouse is a very simple structure of Roxbury puddingstone. Standing directly beside it today is an almost exact replica built in 1905 after the Stony Brook outlet was enlarged to a double channel. At that time the old Gatehouse was moved a short distance and placed on a new substructure (Figure 136).[20]

Although the drawing for the fountain appears to be lost (or misfiled in the vast archives in Brookline), there is a card in the plan catalog for a tracing-paper drawing labeled "Richardson's Fountain Plan" and dated 12 January 1885 (Back Bay Fens, Plan no. 28). There is no description of the fountain nor any indication of its proposed location in the Fens.

The Agassiz Bridge was constructed directly from John's plans by the engineers. It is located near the junction of Agassiz Road, which separates

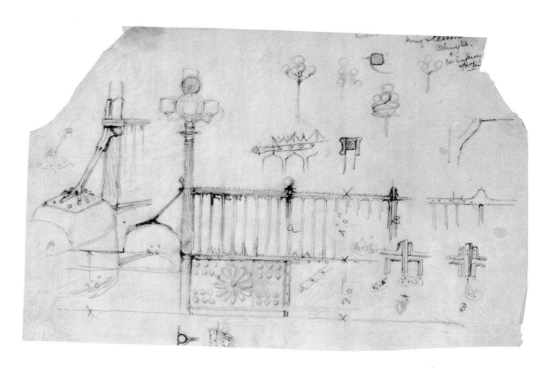

Figure 134
Details of metalwork for the bridge over the railway. Sketch from the Richardson office, possibly in H. H. Richardson's hand.

Figure 135
The bridge over the railway (detail), as it appeared in 1963, shortly before demolition.

Figure 136 (top)
The Stony Brook Gate-
house being moved, 1905.

Figure 137 (bottom)
Elevation, plan, and sec-
tion for the Agassiz Bridge
by the Boston City Archi-
tect's office, March 1887.

the northern and southern basins of the Fens, and Audubon Road (now Park Drive). In John's words:

Agassiz Road, which crosses the main basin of the park, was dipped down to the lowest possible elevation to keep open the view through the length of the park . . . Agassiz Bridge was designed with five small arches . . . partly for picturesque effect, but partly as

expressing the greater accommodations seemingly needed for the waterway, which had to pass the floods of Stony Brook rapidly during the low stages of the tide. Not being necessarily an imposing mass of masonry like Boylston Bridge, it was designed in an ultra-picturesque style, almost suggesting the interesting effect of a partly ruined, but still standing and useful, ancient piece of comparatively unskilled masonwork.[21]

For such a bridge, boulders were the obvious choice. Two sketches for the Agassiz Bridge have survived, neither by John. The first drawing (Figure 137) is dated March 1887, and the plan catalog at the Olmsted National Historic Site notes that it was received from the city architect, Arthur Vinal. Vinal's drawing shows a bridge with a parapet of random ashlar and a substructure entirely of boulders. This strange solution to the controversy over the use of boulders versus cut and finished stone was fortunately not adopted. The second plan (Figure 138), drawn by Percy Jones, presumably from John's sketches, shows a boulder bridge, just as it was executed and as it stands today. As in Vinal's drawing, a space is left for planting, but a projecting bay over the central arch unites the two stages of the bridge. The Agassiz Bridge was constructed of boulders from the boundary walls then being dismantled at Franklin Park. Each boulder was numbered *in situ* and then assembled in the Fens according to the plan.[22] The planting space between the two stages and all the crevices between the stones were stuffed with earth and planted with "creepers."

The three remaining bridges in the Fens can be discussed more briefly. The Huntington Entrance Bridge (Figure 139) over the Stony Brook storm outlet was designed by C. Howard Walker from preliminary plans by John Olmsted. Constructed of brown brick in "the Italian style," it reflected the formal character of Huntington Entrance in contrast with the informality of the Fens proper. It stood for approximately ten years. Fen Bridge and the culvert under Brookline Avenue were simple boulder affairs and, like the Agassiz Bridge, were constructed by the engineers directly from John's plans.[23]

As in the Back Bay Fens, bridges were the most important architectural works of the Muddy River

Figure 136 (top)
The Stony Brook Gatehouse being moved, 1905.

Figure 137 (bottom)
Elevation, plan, and section for the Agassiz Bridge by the Boston City Architect's office, March 1887.

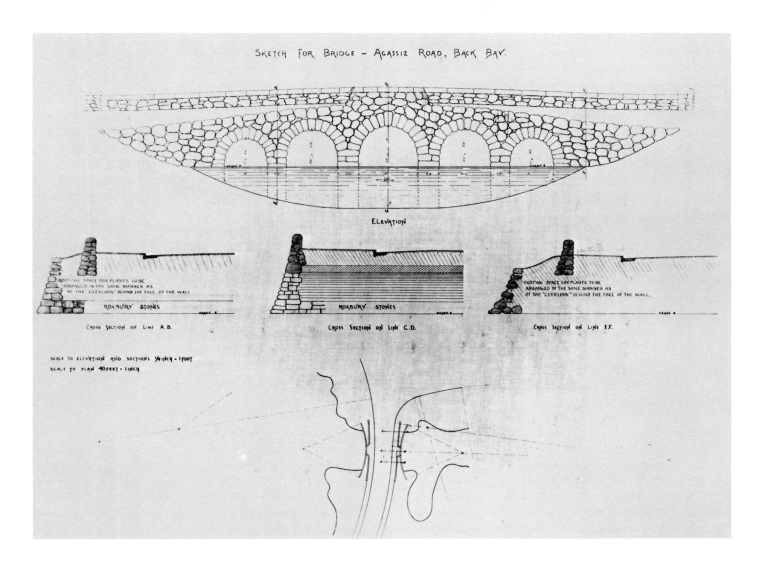

Figure 138
Elevation, plan, and sections for the Agassiz Bridge by Percy R. Jones of the Olmsted office, March 1887.

Improvement and the only ones still standing, besides a small circular shelter on the Riverway at Longwood. Of the seventeen bridges that originally spanned the Muddy River and the coves and streams of Leverett Park, most remain. They range in size from the monumental Longwood Avenue Bridge to several diminutive footbridges near Ward's Pond. With the exception of half a dozen small boulder footbridges, all are of seam-faced granite and were designed by Shepley, Rutan and Coolidge from preliminary plans by the Olmsted firm. (After 1891 Shepley, Rutan and Coolidge were consulting architects for most of the park bridges.)[24]

The Muddy River bridges are remarkably consistent in style and blend admirably with the riverside scenery. The earliest sketches by the Olmsted firm, however, show that the landscape designers had something rather different in mind. Their original intention was to design the bridges in varying but harmonious styles and to use a greater variety of materials. Consistency of style may have been the choice of a member of the Shepley firm, but consistency of material was the decision of Charles Sargent of the Brookline Park Commission.

The relationship between the Olmsted and Shepley firms can be seen clearly in the evolution of the

Figure 139
The Stony Brook Bridge,
1901.

Figure 140
Rough study by John C.
Olmsted for culvert from
Willow Pond to Leverett
Pond in the Muddy River
Improvement, May 18,
1890.

designs for three minor bridges in the Muddy River Improvement. As early as 1890 John had made a study for a culvert opening between Willow and Leverett ponds (Figure 140). This, the only such architectural sketch by John to have survived, shows a modest, three-arched structure; it was built almost exactly as drawn. When the final plans for this culvert were made in 1892, John wrote a letter to Shepley, Rutan and Coolidge, explicitly delineating their role as consulting architects. A day earlier John had left plans for three masonry structures at the Shepley office. The first two, a small footbridge and the culvert, were drawn in ink. John explained that if there was nothing wrong or disagreeable-looking architecturally about these two structures, all the Shepley firm had to do was return the plans with their approval. The third structure, a footbridge at the head of Leverett Pond, was larger and more conspicuous. This plan John left in pencil so that the architects could make any changes they thought advisable.[25]

In November and December 1890 the Olmsted firm made preliminary plans for four other bridges. Figure 141, drawn by Jones, is a study for the bridge near Chapel Station. Although it was constructed finally in seam-faced granite, in this plan the bridge is shown as a wrought-iron structure of elaborate and elegant design. Plans were also made for two small footbridges leading to an island near Brookline Avenue. In the firm's plans, each bridge had a distinctive style, although boulders were indicated for both. The footbridge next to Brookline Avenue (Figure 142) used a primitive type of post and lintel construction, while the bridge near Bellevue Street (Figure 143) had a single arch and a protruding bay on one side. Plans were also made for a boulder bridge at Bellevue Street (not illustrated).

The Chapel and Bellevue Street bridges had to be built jointly by Boston and Brookline, and Boston did not yet have an appropriation for them. The two small footbridges lay entirely in Brookline, however, and the Brookline commissioners decided to build them as soon as grading was completed in that section of the park. On the plan for one of these little bridges is the notation: "Mr. Sargent will be back 22 August." Mr. Sargent must have returned slightly earlier than expected, for on August 19, 1891, an unsigned editorial, entitled "Architectural Fitness" appeared in *Garden and Forest*.[26] Written at Sargent's suggestion, by Mrs. Van Rensselaer, the editorial criticized the boulderwork in some of the Boston structures. Olmsted replied in an unpublished statement addressed to Sargent ("His Omniscient Editorial Majesty"), defending his use of boulders.[27] In both editorial and response, the stonework of the Muddy River bridges was the actual, although unacknowledged, issue.

The gist of Mrs. Van Rensselaer's criticism was that boulderwork was too rude and unsophisticated for an urban park, which was "one of the most complicated and refined of the artistic creations of mankind . . . A park," she maintained, "must depend for the most part upon nature for its charm,

but it must also conspicuously depend upon art; and it is trite to say that when art is set to work its activity should be frankly and clearly confessed."[28] She deplored the overly rustic appearance of the Agassiz Bridge, which she felt suffered greatly by comparison with "the carefully finished surface" of Richardson's Boylston Street Bridge. In his rebuttal Olmsted explained that the "single, simple, sweeping arch" praised in the editorial was indicated in his firm's first design for the bridge, that both he and Richardson had preferred boulders, and that

Figure 141
Preliminary study by Percy R. Jones for footbridge near Chapel Station. Elevation and plan, December 18, 1890.

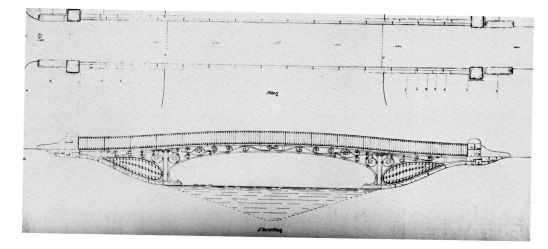

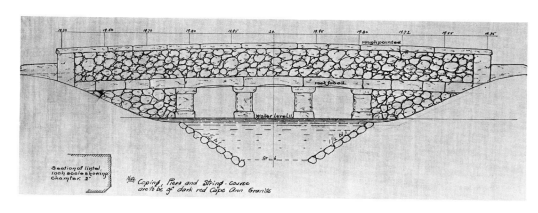

Figure 142
General design for footbridge west of Brookline Avenue by Percy R. Jones. Elevation, November 26, 1890.

finished stone had been substituted at the insistence of the park commissioners. He concluded:

It is one thing to use the handiest stone in the vicinage in an undressed condition, to form blocks for sustaining . . . veiling forms of foliage, and quite another to use it with the affected and paroting motives which your Majesty justly characterizes. It will nowhere appear that your servant has ever used it in the manner that you impute to him, nor will it be found that he has followed any fashion in his use of it: on the contrary, it will be found that fashion staggered years behind him.[29]

It is clear that Olmsted was directing his reply to Sargent and that he did not hold Mrs. Van Rensse-

Figure 143
General design for foot-bridge east of the Bellevue Street Bridge by James G. Langdon. Elevation, November 28, 1890.

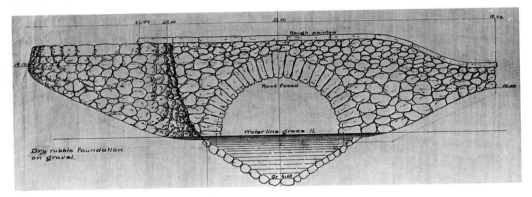

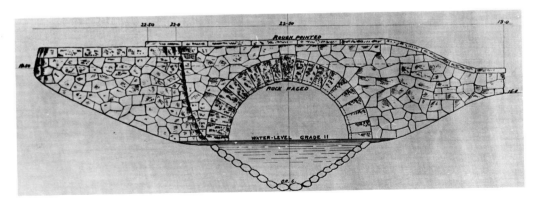

Figure 144
Revised sketch for foot-bridge east of the Bellevue Street Bridge by Percy R. Jones. Elevation, August 20, 1891.

laer entirely responsible for the views expressed in the editorial. Two years later Mrs. Van Rensselaer reprinted "Architectural Fitness" in her book *Art Out-of-Doors*. Although she made minor revisions, the criticism of boulderwork remained. Olmsted was enthusiastic about the book as a whole but remarked on the "Architectural Fitness" essay: "The comment in your book on boulder work in the Boston Parks is wholly wrong as to its facts and also wrong as to its theory of motives. I think Profr. Sargent much to blame for having misled you at first and still more wrong, if he knew that you were to reprint the article, in not having guarded you against a repetition of the misinformation he had given you."[30] He then described Sargent, who was nineteen years his junior, as "the most obstinate and implacably 'set' old man I have ever known. If he were as young and pliant as I am his usefulness would be far greater—great as it is. A good natured and liberal minded man too. Singulary contradictory."[31]

While this verbal scuffle was going on, Percy Jones was at work revising the plans for the little footbridges near Brookline Avenue. Two of his sketches, dated August 20, 1891, show the basic design of the bridges unaltered but with random rubble stonework substituted for boulders (Figure 144). This compromise between rusticity and urbanity did not really please anyone. When consulted, C. Howard Walker advised random ashlar, which appeared in the next pair of plans, dated August 29 (Figure 145).[32] These were forwarded to Shepley, Rutan and Coolidge along with the plans for the Bellevue Street and Chapel bridges and the culverts under Brookline Avenue and Tremont Street. The only change made by the Shepley firm in the footbridge east of Bellevue Street was to introduce a stepped coping at either end (Figure 146). However, they apparently did not like the primitive little footbridge near Brookline Avenue as designed by the Olmsted firm (see Figure 142) and suggested a single arch instead. It was constructed according to the latter plan.

The Tremont and Bellevue Street, Brookline Avenue, and Chapel bridges went through similar metamorphoses. All ended up as seam-faced granite structures, although boulders were originally planned for the first three and wrought iron for the last.[33] By 1892, however, the materials controversy had been resolved.

The finest group of bridges in the Muddy River Improvement are those in the Longwood area. These were expensive as well as handsome structures and were not built until the mid- and late nineties. Chapel Bridge, the original plan of which is shown in Figure 141, spans the Muddy River at its narrowest point and is connected by a flight of steps to another bridge (not illustrated), which spans the bridle path. Between the bridle path and the Riverway is a circular stone shelter, also designed by Shepley, Rutan and Coolidge. Several of these round rain shelters were planned for Leverett and Jamaica parks but were never built. Although wrought iron was abandoned for Chapel Bridge, alternate studies (located at the Olmsted National Historic Site, not illustrated here) were made by Shepley, Rutan and Coolidge in 1893 for an iron railing. (The Shepley draftsman with a touch of humor added an elegantly dressed, top-hatted gentleman to the drawing of the more elaborate railing, and a threadbare figure to that of the starkly plain railing.) The railing as executed did not follow either plan (Figure 147).

For years Longwood Avenue had crossed the Muddy River over an unpretentious wooden bridge. A special appropriation was needed for a new stone bridge, and as a result construction did not begin until 1898. The earliest surviving design for this bridge is an elevation done by Percy Jones in May 1889 (not illustrated because it is very faded). This study is similar in its basic concept, if not in all details, to the bridge that was constructed almost ten years later. A central arch spanned the Muddy River, and smaller side arches apparently penetrated the bridge completely to allow uninterrupted foot traffic along the riverside paths. Stairs were also provided on each side for pedestrians. On the Brookline side the railroad passed under another arch. No material is indicated in this rough elevation. A perspective view published by Shepley, Rutan and Coolidge in 1895 (Figure 148) is an elaboration of Jones's basic concept. In the Shepley firm perspective, the central arch has been broadened considerably to allow foot passage on either side of the river. The side arches, presumably for pedestrians, in Jones's drawing have become blind

arches and are partially concealed behind elaborate twin stairways.

As executed (Figure 149), the Longwood Avenue Bridge is a rather stripped-down version of the architects' original plan. The blind arches, the stairway on the Boston side, and the medallions in the spandrels of the main arch were all eliminated, and the stairway on the Brookline side was simplified. In

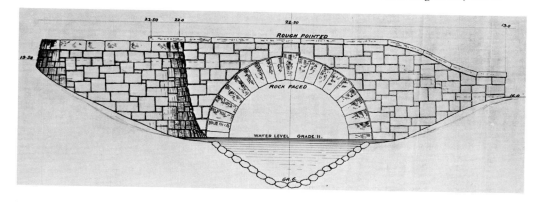

*Figure 145
Revised sketch for foot-bridge east of the Bellevue Street Bridge, showing random ashlar stonework as finally constructed. Elevation, August 29, 1891.*

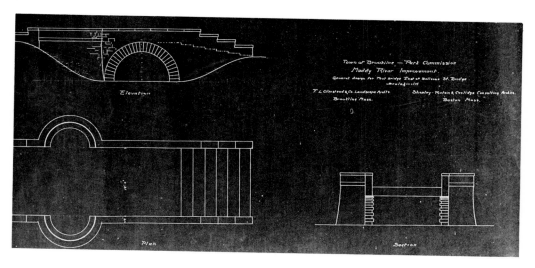

*Figure 146
General design for foot-bridge east of the Bellevue Street Bridge. Elevation, plan, and section, September 16, 1891. (Blueprint, F. L. Olmsted and Co. and Shepley, Rutan and Coolidge.)*

Figure 147
Footbridge near Chapel
Station, 1901.

spite of these modifications, made undoubtedly for the sake of economy, the Longwood Avenue Bridge is still a most imposing structure. Sylvester Baxter described it as follows:

In contrast to the almost sublime reticence of the Boylston Bridge, this work of Richardson's successors is marked by a striking elegance of treatment . . . Where the Richardson Romanesque structure depends upon massive proportions combined with absolute simplicity of surface, the Longwood Bridge is conceived in the Renaissance spirit. It complements massive harmony with a sort of melodic grace; it accents and emphasizes surface character with rich lines and clean-cut projections.[34]

In retrospect the boulder controversy seems a tempest in a teapot. The compromise that was finally settled upon—to use boulders for minor bridges and seam-faced granite for important ones —was generally satisfactory. The complete uniformity of style is slightly more questionable. As executed, the Muddy River bridges all appear to be different versions of the same bridge. The general effect is extremely tasteful but perhaps a little too low-keyed. Admirable as they now are, Chapel Bridge and the footbridge near Brookline Avenue

Figure 148
Longwood Avenue Bridge,
perspective view, 1895.
(Shepley, Rutan and Coo-
lidge, Consulting Archi-
tects.)

would probably be more interesting structures had they been executed according to the original plans.

The Arnold Arboretum is entirely surrounded by a stone wall, necessitating gates for the various entrances. Designs for these were prepared by the Olmsted firm, generally without the assistance of architects. Sylvester Baxter attributed the South Street Gate to H. H. Richardson, although this structure is not mentioned in John's letter of 1898.[35] While it is entirely possible, in terms of date and style, that this gate was designed by Richardson, firm documentation is lacking. The Arboretum also contains three simple boulder culverts—its only bridges—designed by John Olmsted.[36]

For most of the first two decades of the Arboretum's existence, Sargent administered its affairs from Cambridge or Brookline. After he relinquished the directorship of the Harvard Botanic Garden in 1879, he moved his personal collection of herbarium specimens to an empty house on the grounds of Holm Lea. His own botanical books were also moved there and to this day form the nucleus of the Arboretum library.[37] In 1890 Hollis H. Hunnewell donated money for a combined library, herbarium, museum, and administration building for the Arboretum, which was designed by the firm of Longfellow, Alden and Harlow.[38] Since the building was to be erected on part of the land reserved to Harvard University just inside the main entrance to the Arboretum, this was not considered a park structure, and the Olmsted firm had no part in its design. Alexander Wadsworth Longfellow, who had studied architecture at Massachusetts Institute of Technology and the Ecole des Beaux-Arts in Paris and had also worked in Richardson's office, designed a handsome brick building (Figure 150) in a subtly Richardsonian idiom, somewhat reminiscent of Sever Hall in Harvard Yard (see also Figure 128).

Just beyond the Arboretum a massive granite viaduct was built from plans by Shepley, Rutan and Coolidge to carry the New York, New Haven, and Hartford Railroad lines over the Arborway. The Forest Hills Viaduct was one of several railroad bridges built on this part of the line in the late 1890s, but because of its location over part of the

Figure 149
Longwood Avenue Bridge,
1901.

Figure 150
The Arnold Arboretum
Administration Building,
1903.

park system, it was the only one to be designed by an architectural firm. It has five arches, corresponding to each division of the parkway: a side road, walk, drive, bridle path, and side road.[39]

As in the Fens and the Muddy River Improvement, bridges and arches were important features of Franklin Park, but this park also contained several buildings. The Olmsted firm planned them with great care to harmonize with the park's rural scenery, and most were executed closely following their original plans.

Franklin Park was opened to the public in the summer of 1883, even before all of the land had been acquired. The first structures to be built were three small temporary shelters, apparently identical, designed by H. H. Richardson and completed the following year.[40] No drawings or photographs of these "pavilions," as they were labeled on the 1884 topographical map, remain, but it can be assumed

that they were small, inexpensive, and architecturally unpretentious. While it may seem peculiar that Richardson, then at the height of his career, should have agreed to design temporary park shelters, accepting such a commission is consistent with his oft-quoted comment that "I'll plan anything a man wants, from a cathedral to a chicken coop."[41] Had he not died in 1886 it is likely that Richardson would have continued to collaborate with Olmsted on many or even all of the later park structures.

The next building designed for Franklin Park, the Playstead Shelter (Figure 151), was attributed by John to Olmsted himself:

The Overlook shelter in Franklin Park was very completely designed, in accordance with our usual custom, in this office, and is the one building on the whole park system to which my father gave so much thought that the design may fairly be called his. The working drawings were prepared by the City Architect of that date, Arthur H. Vinal. I think the only feature of the building

Figure 151
The Playstead Shelter,
Franklin Park, 1889.

for which Mr. Vinal is responsible as a matter of design is the introduction of the two stone columns to support the roof and the roof trusses, and, of course, the details of moulding, etc. We not only furnished the preliminary plans for the building, but also the model for the undulations in the roof.[42]

Except for some very rough sketches drawn by Olmsted on wrapping paper, the preliminary plans John refers to appear to be lost.

The Playstead was the first part of Franklin Park to be constructed. The boulder terrace, which served as a natural platform for viewing sports, was planned by Olmsted as an integral part of the park and appears on the 1886 lithograph (see Figures 41 and 42); it was designed by John, following his father's detailed written instructions.[43] The shelter building, now unfortunately destroyed except for its massive foundations, was designed in 1887 and completed in 1889. Although the graphic evidence is incomplete, an important letter and memorandum from Olmsted to Vinal strongly support John's attribution. After receiving Vinal's drawings, Olmsted felt that the building did not appear sufficiently rustic and "barn-like."[44] His suggestions to Vinal, similar to those given to John earlier for the terrace, specify dimensions, materials, and disposition of interior spaces, as well as the general character of the design.[45] In the basement the young players could run in from the field directly to their lockers and washrooms through an arch in the boulder terrace. Most of the main floor was devoted to a "buffet," consisting of two soda fountains and facilities for serving hot drinks. A station and changing rooms for the park police were also provided. One of Olmsted's stipulations was that the central space on the main floor be open to the roof with exposed rafters.

Because of its low-slung proportions and its surface of rough stone and weathered shingles, the Playstead Shelter blended unobtrusively with the park scenery, despite its relatively large size. The same qualities—horizontal emphasis and simplicity of surface, frequently shingled—were characteristic of the best American domestic architecture of the period. Olmsted's Franklin Park Playstead Shelter ranks with the house William Ralph Emerson designed for himself in Milton, Massachusetts, in

1886 and with McKim, Mead and White's W. G. Low House in Bristol, Rhode Island, of 1887 as masterpieces of the last phase of the shingle style.[46]

The Valley Gate (Figure 152), which separated the Country Park and the Ante-Park, was under construction at the same time as the Playstead Shelter. It was designed by C. Howard Walker of the firm of Walker and Best as a charming informal structure in the Olmsted boulder style.[47] Although the outer portions remain standing in derelict condition, the inner chambers and the sliding, wrought-iron gate have long since disappeared. Similar in style were several rustic fountains in the Playstead and elsewhere in the park, designed by the Olmsted firm.

Although all of the original buildings in Franklin Park are now demolished or ruinous, the arches and bridges remain. These include the boulder Ellicott Arch under Circuit Drive, designed in the late eighties by John Olmsted, and two bridges over Scarboro Pond and the Forest Hills Entrance Arch, all designed in the early nineties by Shepley, Rutan and Coolidge.[48] Of these, the Forest Hills Entrance is undoubtedly the finest. This was intended to be the termination of the Arborway and the park's principal entrance. An arch was necessary because the road to Forest Hills Cemetery intersected the parkway at this point, and it was obviously desirable to separate the two types of traffic. In the perspective drawing shown in Figure 153, pleasure carriages are entering the park, while below them a funeral cortège is on its way to the cemetery, each ceremonial procession—that of life and that of death—passing well out of view of the other.

Two small shelters and a refectory were also constructed in Franklin Park in the early 1890s. Ellicott House, primarily a place for the tennis players on Ellicottdale to change their clothing, was designed with boulder walls by the firm of Rotch and Tilden.[49] A shelter on Schoolmaster Hill with extensive arbors was provided for picnickers. According to John, this shelter was a building "which my father studied out with great particularity and for which he is more responsible than I am."[50] The roof, however, was designed by City Architect Edmund M. Wheelwright and was a disappointment to Olmsted.

The disagreement between the Olmsted firm and

Figure 152
The Valley Gate, Franklin
Park, 1889.

Figure 153
Forest Hills Entrance,
Franklin Park, perspective
view, 1893. (Shepley,
Rutan and Coolidge, Con-
sulting Architects.)

Wheelwright over this roof presaged a more serious clash a few years later over the design of the Refectory. Olmsted had his heart set on thatched roofs for both cottages, and for the Schoolmaster Hill Shelter he wanted one of especially intricate design. (He had used such roofs before in Prospect Park.) Initially, Wheelwright went along with the idea of thatch, but he insisted on simplifying and formalizing the design. When Olmsted received this news while traveling in England in the spring of 1892, he wrote to John:

About the thatched roof I shall hope that I may be able to talk to the city architect before it is proceeded with and to show him some photographs . . . the structure on Franklin Park had besides its essential utilitarian purpose a dramatic purpose and the planning of its utilitarian structure was designed to be . . . adjusted, accommodated, humored, to the dramatic purpose. I am sure that considering its purpose calling for a variety of cells and passages, and its situation, within the edge of a wood on a crooked, rocky declivity with other rocky wooded ground secluding it, adaptation to scenic effect is reasonably to be had in view in a much greater degree than in ordinary architectural work even of a domestic and cottage character. If the plan does not admit of such a roof as I designed then the plan is defective and I would have the architect show how supports, etc. should be provided consistently or without injury to the utilitarian purpose. That my curve and quiddle, twist, undulation, hog's back, dormers, gable and pent that I had proposed may be brought into a cottage roof naturally and with no purpose but to accomplish the purposes of a thatched roof over a purely utilitarian structure below, [and that] every sort of play of light and shade may happen even when there is no purpose of scenic or picturesque effect, we have seen much evidence during the last few days (I write after passing through Devonshire and the New Forest). We have seen outward curves and inward curves, roofs steep at the bottom, steep at the top, ogee sections of any variety, etc., all manner of undulations on buildings of all classes, where certainly there had been no aim but convenience, comfort and economy; where the last thing thought of was a quaint or fantastic effect . . . After seeing what I did yesterday, my conviction is that the roof as planned is not . . . eccentric and quaint enough for the place. I certainly must have it complicated with mosses and apparent outworks of ivy and other foliage.[51]

(A drawing of more than a year earlier by James G. Langdon of the Olmsted firm, Figure 154, shows a thatched roof of irregular outline but hardly "eccentric or quaint.") Olmsted commented that if an ordinary form of roof were what he had wanted, shingles would have been perfectly suitable, adding somewhat plaintively: "But may we not be a little humorous?"[52]

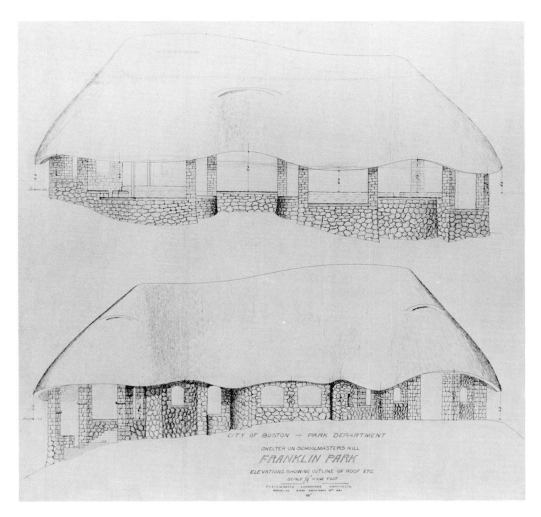

Figure 154
Elevations for the shelter on Schoolmaster Hill, Franklin Park, by James G. Langdon, December 12, 1890.

Humor seems not to have been Wheelwright's strong point, for a few months later the design for a "formalized" roof was approved by the board at his recommendation.[53] In October of 1892 thatch was still to be used for both cottages, but when estimates came in for the "best quality hand thrashed Rye straw," Wheelwright objected.[54] Feeling that thatch was too expensive and would not be durable, he persuaded the park commissioners to use an ogee tile roof instead, which, he maintained, would "be picturesque in a different way."[55] Both cottages were subsequently roofed with tile. Photographs of the Schoolmaster Hill Shelter as built (Figure 155),

show a roof of "rigid and stiff" outline, as John described it, that does not seem to belong to the building below.[56] Ironically, Wheelwright's roof has burned, while Olmsted's walls, although now an abandoned shell, are more or less intact.

Hartwell and Richardson were approached as consulting architects for the Refectory in September 1891, after the Olmsted firm had prepared preliminary sketches. Apparently Olmsted had not known these architects previously: he remarked to John that he "thought they promised well . . . [and] will take all desirable guidance if you get hold of them soon enough."[57] John's impression was also that

Figure 155
Schoolmaster Hill Shelter
as built, 1897.

"Hartwell and Richardson fully appreciate our ideas of subordinating the architecture to the landscape."[58]

The Refectory was to be the largest building in Franklin Park and was sited, according to Olmsted's usual practice with refectories, near the park boundaries—in this case, just inside the Blue Hill Avenue Entrance.[59] The Olmsted firm's preliminary design was for a one-story building with a partial second story and an upper-level deck covered with awnings and canopies. Olmsted hoped that the style could be reminiscent of "Syrian or Persian houses . . . of the simpler antecedent types out of which Moorish architecture has been developed," similar to houses he had seen in eastern Mexico.[60] He wanted narrow terra-cotta columns (he drew an example) to support a trellis on a terrace overlooking the Country Park.

Hartwell and Richardson's preliminary plans were presented to the board in March 1892 but were not approved for more than a year.[61] By February 1894, detailed plans were under way and City Architect Wheelwright was also involved. His suggestions were markedly out of character with the original concept, prompting the letter quoted at the beginning of this chapter, in which Olmsted compared the Refectory's place in the park scheme to that of a piece of furniture planned as part of the

design of a building.[62] Olmsted's efforts were to no avail, for according to John, the Refectory as built (Figure 156) was "a marked violation of our instructions and wishes as to the relation of the design to the landscape. We did not intend to have the building of light-colored terra cotta, nor so showy in its details."[63] Although John described the building as having been done "with considerable interference as to design by City Architect E. M. Wheelwright," he held Hartwell and Richardson equally responsible, reversing his initial impression of them:

Wheelwright is not . . . artistic in his appreciation of the landscape surroundings and desires rather to make stunning and picturesque effects which will draw attention to the building separately instead of making it a part of the design of the park. This criticism is far more applicable to Hartwell and Richardson's Refectory. It was perfectly obvious in my conferences with them that they absolutely disregarded our ideas as to harmonizing the building with the landscape. Their whole idea seemed to be to make the most stunning building possible with the appropriation available. This is a general fault with the majority of the architects we have had to deal with.[64]

As a designer of park structures, Wheelwright appears the villain of the piece, both in the original correspondence and in John's retrospective letter to Sylvester Baxter. Yet Wheelwright was an intelligent, well-educated, and versatile architect, whose work was highly regarded by such critics as Charles Eliot Norton and Baxter himself.[65] Many of the municipal structures he designed as city architect are still attractive and useful today. His chief flaw, naturally a crucial one for the Olmsteds, was that he lacked sensitivity to landscape. His Head House (Figure 157) at Marine Park, modeled after a German Rathaus, struck John as "fussy and picturesque for such broad simple landscape surroundings."[66] However, Wheelwright's design (unexecuted) for a shelter and look-out at Castle Island (Figure 158) would have been a far more successful park structure than either the Head House or the Franklin Park Refectory. The drawing shows a low, rambling building flanked by two lighthouse-like towers, much in the spirit of some of the best shingle-style seaside houses.[67] This shelter—apparently never

Figure 157
Head House, Marine Park,
designed by Edmund M.
Wheelwright, City Architect, 1897.

CITY OF BOSTON
SHELTER AND LOOK-OUT AT CASTLE ISLAND
EDMUND M. WHEELWRIGHT · CITY ARCHI

Figure 158
Proposed shelter and look-
out at Castle Island,
Marine Park. Perspective
view, 1895, from the office
of Edmund M. Wheel-
wright, City Architect.

constructed because of the financial retrenchment of the mid-nineties—would have shown Wheelwright in a much more positive light.

Despite the relative failure of the Marine Park Head House, the Refectory, and Schoolmaster Hill Shelter, most of the structures in the Boston system succeed admirably as park "furniture." That Olmsted was able to convince such a diverse group of architects to subordinate their designs to his own is a tribute to his persuasive powers and to the respect he evoked from colleagues in related professions.

XIII

Plant Materials
and Design

———◆———

THE final stage of Olmsted's design process was the preparation of planting plans and selection of plant materials. The extent of such work varied greatly, from the entirely new plantings required by the Back Bay Fens, the lower valley of the Muddy River, and the parkways, to the judicious care and augmentation of existing trees necessary at Jamaica Pond and parts of Franklin Park.

Olmsted felt that his own knowledge of horticulture was deficient, so he relied for advice on many people, including botanists, such as Sargent, and his own staff, especially Warren H. Manning and John Olmsted. Manning, who managed the horticultural side of the office from 1889 to 1895, has left us an invaluable first-hand account of how Olmsted selected plant materials with the help of more botanically expert colleagues. Manning recalled:

While he could not identify the major part of the vegetation in any locality, he did have a most intimate knowledge of the landscape values of plants. For example, at Biltmore there was a woodland along the side of the main entrance road where he wanted a ground cover that would give glinting light effects on leaf tops and wide leaf shadows. Our dialogue was about like this:

"Rhubarb?"—I suggested.

"No—leaf too coarse and wrinkled."

"Hellebore?"

"No—leaf too deeply cut and dull."

"Large-leaved Saxifrage?"

"Yes—that's the ideal plant for the place."

At another point he asked me about gray-leaved

plants as he wanted a color gradation in grays to give longer perspective values in a vista.

"Silver-leaved Willow?"—I suggested.

"No—too tall and broadspreading."

"Olive?"

"No—not hardy enough."

"Hippophae?"

"No—too low and bushy."

"Russian Olive?"

"Yes—that's just the thing."[1]

Clearly, although Olmsted was not entirely comfortable with scientific plant names and by himself could not always select the plants he needed, he knew exactly what he wanted in terms of visual effect. With the help of Sargent, John, Eliot, Manning, and others, he was able to orchestrate his landscape compositions.

For the Boston parks, however, Olmsted depended most on the horticultural skills of William L. Fischer. Born in 1819 in Karlsruhe, Germany, Fischer began his career as a landscape gardener working in the gardens of the University of Heidelberg and the royal park of Sans Souci, near Potsdam. After he emigrated to England, he was employed in the gardens of the Royal Horticultural Society and, under Joseph Paxton, on the Duke of Devonshire's estates at Chatsworth and in Scotland. In 1849 he came to the United States, where he had his own horticultural business in New York City for ten years. He then became foreman gardener for the New York Park Department and later superintendent gardener of Central Park. Ultimately he was in charge of all the plantations, propagating establishments, and nurseries of Central, Riverside and Morningside parks. In 1884 Olmsted persuaded him to come to Boston to be his second in command in horticultural matters for the park system. As in New York, he was employed by the Park Commission, not by the Olmsted firm.[2]

As assistant landscape gardener, Fischer was responsible for the plantings in all of the Boston parks after 1884. In general the Olmsted firm would prepare detailed planting plans for a project, then strongly recommended that the client retain gardeners who would execute these plans without deviation. Fischer, whom Olmsted regarded as a designer as well as executor, and who apparently preferred to work without plans, was the one exception to the firm's policy. Aside from a tree-planting plan for the Back Bay Fens, which Fischer prepared himself shortly after his arrival in Boston and which was stipulated in Olmsted's first contract, detailed planting plans exist only for the Brookline side of the Muddy River, outside of Fischer's jurisdiction, and for the Arnold Arboretum and the Beacon Entrance to the Fens, both of which predated Fischer's appointment.

The unfortunate fact is that the horticultural aspect of the Boston parks is documented much less fully than the other aspects. Except for oaks, beeches, and other long-lived trees, few of the original plants remain. Old photographs illustrate the general effect of Olmsted's design, but few show trees and shrubs clearly enough for exact identification. Furthermore, the plantings were extensively revised from 1897 on, so only photographs taken before that date can be considered reliable evidence of what Olmsted had in mind.[3] Some correspondence exists concerning plant materials and design, but much of it deals with isolated crises and controversies and may give a somewhat distorted view of normal procedure. There is simply no information about what happened, horticulturally speaking, on an ordinary day when there were no crises or controversies.

In this chapter we shall look primarily at the plantings of the Fens and the Muddy River Improvement and more briefly at Franklin Park and the parkway. First, however, it is necessary to discuss some general characteristics of Olmsted's planting style.

By Olmsted's time the "gardenesque" style of landscape design described by J. C. Loudon in the early nineteenth century was in its heyday. The gardenesque exploited the full range of new plant materials that became available during this period; small-scale effects featuring exotic and unfamiliar plants were characteristic of the fashion. Large-scale scenic composition and the imitation of "nature" were for the most part forgotten. It was an era of parterres, bedding out, and elaborate constructions made of living plants.[4] The gardenesque style was favored by most private estate gardeners and by many public park superintendents as well, among them William Doogue, superintendent of common

Figure 159
Washington Monument,
Boston Public Garden,
1888. Surrounding the
equestrian statue is a for-
mal Victorian carpet bed
designed by William
Doogue, Superintendent of
Common and Public
Grounds.

contrived areas of planting that invite close inspection could be used successfully in smaller public squares and botanical gardens. This was one basis for his distinction between parks and other types of public grounds and between urban beauty and the beauty of rural scenery. He also used predominantly native plant materials, both because he was generally imitating "nature" (a New England salt marsh, a riverbank) and because he did not want the enjoyer of rural scenery to be distracted by conspicuously unusual plants. However, he did use carefully chosen foreign plants in small quantities or in situations where they would not be a distraction.

and public grounds in Boston in the 1880s.[5] Figure 159 shows a typical planting by Doogue near the equestrian statue of Washington in the Boston Public Garden.

The worst excesses of the gardenesque, particularly when used in large public parks, were anathema to Olmsted. Throughout his career he practiced a modified version of the Capability Brown pastoral style, varying this with frequent picturesque "passages." He did not, however, arbitrarily impose styles on a site but instead generally chose a treatment consistent with the original character of the land. In a few cases, such as the Back Bay Fens, this approach amounted almost to a restoration in today's sense of the word.

In any kind of design, Olmsted's first concern was to achieve visual unity; he thought in terms of the organization of space, perspective, and vistas. As we have seen in Manning's account, he frequently created intentionally what in painting would be called atmospheric perspective, placing dark, intricate forms of foliage in the foreground, with simpler and lighter forms farther away.[6] Olmsted generally planted very densely, but he was always careful to maintain open views. Since his greatest concern was a unified composition, details that stood out as separate effects could only dilute his larger scheme, and this was his chief objection to the gardenesque. He fully recognized that small

The site of the Back Bay Fens had been, before its gradual stagnation and pollution in the early nineteenth century, a large natural salt marsh. Olmsted's plan for the Fens was in part a restoration of that marsh. This choice committed him to a planting program so innovative that it literally had no precedent. First, he had to determine which kinds of grasses and reeds would grow in salt marsh conditions in the northern and southern basins. Then he had to select low-growing plants—wild flowers, vines, ground-cover plants, and shrubs of various sizes—that would grow in close proximity to salt water in Beacon Entrance and in similar locations elsewhere in the Fens. The third and most conventional problem was to select trees for the borders of the basin.

When complete, the Fens appeared to be a natural salt marsh around which a city had happened to grow, which was exactly what Olmsted intended. But to an observer looking closely, even without knowledge of the tide- and flood-regulating mechanisms, there were many noticeable differences between the Fens and a natural salt marsh. For all its beauties, a salt marsh can seem monotonous and rather inhospitable: impassable at high tide and slimy at low tide. To avoid having high, bare mud banks exposed at low tide, Olmsted decided to limit the rise and fall of the tide to only a foot. He also chose a far greater variety of plants than would normally grow in such a confined area. For the marsh itself, he was limited to a few grasses mingled with "slashes of golden-rods and asters."[7] Immediately above, on the steep slopes of Beacon Entrance and of both basins, a variety of salt-tolerant wild flowers and shrubs was planted. Around the borders of the park, out of the reach of salt spray, many kinds of shrubs and shade trees were arranged to form a transitional zone between the urban residential districts surrounding the Fens and the informal scenery within it. There were no lawns and no turf at all, except on the margins of the roads.[8]

While this planting was "naturalistic," it was certainly not natural. The distinction is an important one. John Olmsted described the Fens plan: "As is usual in park designing in the naturalistic style, more variety of scenery was compressed into the design than would ordinarily be found in nature."[9]

Although Beacon entrance was the first part of the Fens to be actually planted, the most immediate problem was the choice of salt-marsh grasses, on whose success would depend the success of the entire scheme. If they could not be made to grow in the basins, the mud banks would erode, and a masonry storage basin would probably be necessary. Some time early in 1879, when Olmsted was working on the studies preceding the preliminary plan submitted in February, he asked Sargent for advice on salt-marsh plants. As in the earlier quoted conversation with Manning, Olmsted knew the precise landscape effect he wanted but was unsure of scientific names:

There are two broad dimensions of beauty of vegetation in tidal lands

1. that of which I know as salt meadows, the beauty of which is in the complete occupation of nearly level surfaces by a short fine grass—in lawnlike breadth and repose. This is a salt hay grass. I don't know its botanical name.

2. that of taller, graceful moving reeds, rushes and sedges, in which interest may lie much in the variety and contrast of forms and tints.[10]

Olmsted had noticed that the short, fine salt hay normally grew near the elevation of ordinary high water, where its roots would be only occasionally covered by salt water. Of "the taller and coarser vegetation," he had observed two classes, one growing where it would be covered much of the time by salt water and the other rarely reached by the tide

but moistened at the roots by infiltration at high tide. He asked Sargent the botanical names of a few plants that would normally predominate at various elevations of high and low water and with which he could reasonably expect to succeed.[11]

The two plants that normally predominate in salt marshes are salt-meadow grass or salt hay (*Spartina patens*) and salt-marsh cordgrass (*Spartina alterniflora*), a taller grass, which grows along the edges of salt creeks and is about half covered by water at high tide. These are clearly the first two grasses described by Olmsted. Several kinds of taller grasses, rushes, and sedges grow above the high water line, including black grass (*Juncus gerardi*) and several sedges (*Cyperus polystachyos* var. *texensis* and others), both frequently mentioned by Olmsted.[12] Since the difference between high and low water was only one foot, these grasses and sedges could be planted closer together than they are usually found in natural salt marshes. By 1886, when Olmsted addressed the Boston Society of Architects, the salt grasses had already proved successful, although the entire marsh was not yet planted. They were grown both by seed and by transplanting sods, both methods being equally reliable.[13]

Beacon Entrance, planted in the spring of 1884, was the most exposed part of the Fens. In winter it was raked by strong winds from the Charles, and in summer it baked in heat reflected from the encircling bridges and retaining walls. Even without the complication of planting near salt water, it would have been a considerable challenge to establish plants here. Olmsted avoided ornamental shade trees because they would have been damaged by wind and because he wanted to keep open the important view from the Boylston Street Bridge to the Charles and the reverse view from Commonwealth Avenue Bridge under the Boylston Street Bridge to the northern basin. On the higher parts of the site he used pines, spruce, red cedar, prostrate juniper, and birches. The ground was very steep (see grading plan, Figure 120), and no grass was used, except for a thin band of sedge between high and low water. Olmsted provided a thick cover of low-growing shrubs, vines, and flowers, which in time were to clothe the slopes with a "dense, close, self-protecting, hardy chaparral."[14]

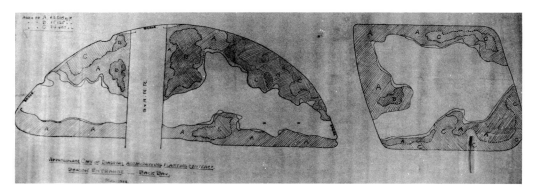

Figure 160
Diagram that accompanied the planting contract for Beacon Entrance, Back Bay Fens, March 1884.

ing at Back Bay to be heeled in over the winter. It is difficult to describe the Beacon Entrance planting very exactly, for the only existing planting plan (Figure 160) has no key, and although there are numerous plant lists, they do not always use complete botanical names. Of the various lists, the most useful is probably Charles Eliot's, recorded in his diary during his apprentice days, for he included not only Temple's plants, but those received from other nurseries.[16] By comparing these lists, the planting plan in Figure 160 can be at least partially reconstructed (see Plant List 1).

The most striking thing about the Beacon Entrance lists is the sheer quantity of plants—more than 100,000 shrubs, vines, and flowers in a space of only two and half acres. Equally extraordinary is the variety; many more kinds of shrubs and wild flowers were used than would seem necessary. The reason for both quantity and variety was that the planting was innovative and experimental. Since Olmsted did not expect that all the plants would live, he used many kinds of similar plants, so that if one kind died, another might still provide the same visual effect. He also anticipated thinning the thriving plants later.[17]

Most of the shrubs, vines, and wild flowers were

Olmsted had misgivings about planting even unusually hardy shrubs under the bleak conditions of Beacon Entrance, but a Cambridge nurseryman, F. L. Temple, approached him with what appeared to be ideal qualifications for the job. Temple had studied the problems of establishing plants under poor conditions on the New England seacoast, and he brought letters of recommendation from landscape gardeners testifying to his success. In November 1883 Temple signed a contract with the Boston Park Commission to provide most of the plants for Beacon Entrance, do the planting, and supervise it for three years.[15] Plants soon began arriv-

---

Plant List 1. Suggested key for Figure 160, Beacon Entrance planting plan, Back Bay Fens.[a]

Letter on plan	Location	Plants
A	On the margin of the water and along the shores above common flood but subject to spray	Sea lavender, golden rod, asters, beach peas, beach plum, sea buckthorn, tamarix, virginia rose
B	Exposed dry slopes	Bayberry, sweet fern, dyer's greenwood, Oregon holly grape, bearberry, mountain cranberry, raspberry, blackberry, swamp dewberry, dwarf gray willow; vines and ground-cover plants, such as periwinkle, clematis, and Japanese honeysuckle, planted among them
C	On high ground, on the knolls, and along the base of the wall	White and red pines, white spruce, red cedar, white and dwarf birch; prostrate juniper; nursery shrubs, such as barberry, privet, summersweet, viburnum
—	Unmarked strip along water	Salt sedge

a. No formal plant lists exist for Beacon Entrance. The plants listed here are taken from Olmsted's letters to F. L. Temple, from Temple's contract, and from Charles Eliot's Weekly Notebook. See also the grading plan for Beacon Entrance, Figure 120.

native to New England, but there were some exceptions. Two plants used in quantity were dyer's greenwood (*Genista tinctoria*), native to Europe and western Asia but sometimes naturalized in the eastern United States, and mahonia (probably *Mahonia aquifolium* or Oregon holly grape), a plant of the Pacific Northwest, which had been brought east by the Lewis and Clark expedition.[18] "Tamarisk," one of the plants listed by Olmsted, may have been five-stamen tamarix (*Tamarix pentandra*), a hardy salt-resistant plant from southwestern Europe and central Asia, which had been introduced to this country that same year (1883). Still another was sea buckthorn (*Hippophae rhamnoides*), a Eurasian plant introduced in colonial times. Most of the plants used in quantity, however, were New England seaside shrubs such as bayberry (*Myrica pensylvanica*) and beach plum (*Prunus maritima*). It is evident that Olmsted wanted a "wild" effect with native plants predominating, but he did not attempt to reproduce nature exactly, and he frequently used other plants that would be likely to grow under the conditions of Beacon Entrance and that would not look noticeably exotic.

While Olmsted did not expect all of the plants at Beacon Entrance to thrive, he was dismayed by what actually happened. By 1885 it was obvious that many of the plants were not doing well. Olmsted certified his approval of Temple's work that spring only after Temple had planted several thousand additional shrubs. Hardly had the new shrubs been installed, however, than they too died. A count taken in the spring of 1886 showed that most of the shrubs planted within a few feet of the water's edge had died. Some on higher ground had also succumbed. The only plants in thriving condition were commercial ornamental shrubs provided by the Park Department, all on high ground, and wild flowers, put in chiefly for temporary effect. Olmsted admonished Temple: "The mere loss of so many plants is the smallest part of the disaster. The whole design is a wreck."[19]

It is not clear why the planting failed. Presumably Temple was at least partly at fault, in spite of the rigors of the situation. In his talk before the Boston Society of Architects, Olmsted speculated that the plants between the salt sedge and a line about three feet above might have been killed by salt water carried upward by capillary attraction,

but he also mentioned that he had had no proper organization for the work, "being dependent on a contractor."[20] There are no plans, plant lists, or correspondence for the second planting of Beacon Entrance, which must have been done under W. L. Fischer's supervision and which appears to have been successful. A photograph of Beacon Entrance taken ten years after the "disaster" (Figure 161) shows a dense growth of shrubs and trees similar to those described in Olmsted's letters, although it is impossible to identify specific plants.

One of Fischer's first tasks after his appointment in 1884 may have been to draw the tree-planting plan for the northern basin, a detail of which is illustrated in Figure 162. The plan shows an interest-

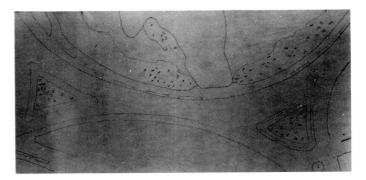

Figure 161
Beacon Entrance, looking toward the Boylston Street Bridge, 1896.

Figure 162
Tree planting plan for the northern basin, Back Bay Fens, by W. L. Fischer, circa 1885. Detail near the Boylston Street Bridge.

Plant List 2.   Key for Figure 162, tree planting plan by W. L. Fischer for the northern basin, Back Bay Fens, circa 1885.[a]

Number on plan	Scientific name[b]	Common name
1	*Pinus strobus*	Eastern white pine
2	*Pinus resinosa*	Red pine
3	*Pinus cembra*	Swiss stone pine
4	*Ailanthus altissima (glandulosa)*, female	Tree of heaven
5	*Gleditsia triacanthos*	Common honey locust
6	*Quercus coccinea*	Scarlet oak
7	*Salix alba*	White willow
8	*Quercus rubra*	Northern red oak
9	*Quercus alba*	White oak
10	*Quercus prinus*	Chestnut oak
11	*Acer rubrum*	Red maple
12	*Acer saccharinum (dasycarpum)*	Silver maple
13	*Acer platanoides*	Norway maple
14	*Acer saccharum (saccharinum)*	Sugar maple
15	*Quercus macrocarpa*	Bur oak
16	*Quercus velutina (tinctoria)*	Black oak
17	*Betula pendula (alba)*	European birch
18	*Betula lenta*	Sweet birch
19	*Betula papyrifera (papyracea)*	Paper birch
20	*Betula nigra*	River birch
21	*Quercus phellos*	Willow oak
22	*Fraxinus americana*	White ash
23	*Robinia pseudoacacia*	Black locust
24	*Cladrastis lutea (Virgilia lutea)*	American yellow wood

a. No quantities are given with this key. On the plan, oaks and pines are used predominantly.

b. Obsolete names used by Fischer are given in parentheses. Modern botanical names are from Alfred Rehder, *Bibliography of Cultivated Trees and Shrubs* (Jamaica Plain, Mass.: Arnold Arboretum of Harvard University, 1949).

ing and imaginative choice of trees (see Plant List 2), which probably reflected Fischer's wide background in Europe and at Central Park. No quantities are given, but oaks and pines appear most frequently on the plan. As in the case of Beacon Entrance, native plants predominate, particularly the North American oaks, pines, maples, and birches. A few European and Asiatic trees were planted, including Swiss stone pine (*Pinus cembra*), Norway maple (*Acer platanoides*), and tree of heaven (*Ailanthus altissima*), a tree of Chinese origin, now considered a weed but used ornamentally in the nineteenth century.[21] Other American trees that are not very common in New England, such as willow oak (*Quercus phellos*) and American yellow-wood (*Cladrastis lutea*), were also used.

Some of the original trees still survive, but their placement seems to indicate that Fischer did not follow his own planting plan exactly.[22] Between the trees and the marsh grasses in the northern basin, shrubs were planted thickly, as at Beacon Entrance. The same style of planting was continued in the southern basin (Figure 163) and Longwood Entrance, seen about 1895 in Figure 164. Perhaps better than any other photograph, this view illustrates what Olmsted described as the "waving, fenny verdure, the meandering water, the blooming islets, the border of trees and underwood" and the "tufty, ruffled and mysteriously intricate" foliage of the Fens.[23]

Fischer was in charge of the later plantings of the Fens, the Boston side of the Muddy River Improvement, and countless smaller projects, but he is most intimately associated with Franklin Park. As part of his salary, he was provided with a house on the park, near Morton Street, where he and his family lived for twelve years. This building, the old Thomas residence, also housed the Olmsteds' field office for design and superintendence, so Fischer was literally living with the firm, or at least a branch of it. (When he retired, he moved to the Forest Hills section of Jamaica Plain, only a stone's throw away from the park. One of his sons, William E. Fischer, continued to work as a gardener at Franklin Park for several years after his father's retirement.)[24]

Olmsted had great confidence in Fischer's intuitive and improvisatory method of working and gave him unusual freedom to design the details of the work he executed. Olmsted seemed to feel that his own role was to provide the "leading motives" for Fischer to follow, to select the "predominating" plant materials, and to protect Fischer from harassment by the engineers and the commissioners. When he was out of town, he repeatedly wrote to his partners, urging them to provide the best possible conditions for Fischer:

You can trust Fischer to design details better than you can design them yourself, *provided he understands the general principles of design* to which local particulars are to be subordinate and is not disconcerted by failure of facilities for doing what he will want to *at the right time.* Within reasonable limits he must be allowed his own

Figure 163
A cove in the Back Bay Fens, 1894.

Figure 164
Longwood Entrance, Back Bay Fens.

way and you must, from day to day, see that Howe and Cook (and Sargent and the Mayor) are not interfering with him . . . Howe and the engineers need to be constantly punched up to have suitable preparations for him. They cannot appreciate his necessities and are always inclined to make light of conditions which are absolutely essential to his working to good advantage.[25]

Nevertheless, a precise assessment of Fischer's contribution to Franklin Park, and to the Boston park system in general, is made very difficult by the skimpiness of available documentation. Besides the general problems with documentation mentioned at the beginning of this chapter, there are other com-

Plant List 3. Plants to be used on the Overlook Terrace, Franklin Park.[a]	
Scientific name	Common name
Euonymus radicans	Trailing euonymus
[Ampelopsis species]	Ampelopsis
Rhus aromatica	Fragrant sumac
[Rosa species]	Dwarf, small-leafed roses of compact and horizontal habit of growth
Berberis thunbergii	Japanese barberry
Rosa multiflora	Japanese rose
Rosa centifolia var. parvifolia (Rosa parvifolia)	Burgundy cabbage rose
Rosa rugosa	Rugosa rose
[Berberis species]	Barberry
[Smilax species]	Catbrier or common greenbrier
Genista tinctoria	Dyer's greenwood
Rhus copallina	Shining sumac
Comptonia peregrina	Sweet fern
Myrica	Wax myrtle?
Sedum	Stonecrops
Sempervivum	Hen and chickens

a. Letter from Olmsted to Fischer, July 21, 1887, OP.

plications. Because Olmsted was usually able to come to an understanding with Fischer through site conferences, there is little correspondence between the two men. We also know that Olmsted purposely avoided giving Fischer overly specific instructions so as not to "check his spontaneity."[26] There are, however, a few important letters to Fischer about Franklin Park, most concerning the planting of the Overlook Terrace. Besides explaining this particular plantation, they shed quite a bit of light on the relationship between Olmsted and his master gardener.

In the spring of 1887 Olmsted conferred very fully with Fischer "on the ground" about the permanent planting on and near the Terrace. Since this was to be the first planting at Franklin Park, he followed up the conference with a long written statement describing the function of the Terrace. Olmsted did not want to disguise altogether the new construction, but he wanted to "avoid anything like a horizontal streak across the landscape and to subordinate the artificial elements as much as practicable to the natural."[27]

On the boulder wall Olmsted wanted "plants of a *naturally snug, close growth,*" such as climbing euonymus, *Ampelopsis,* fragrant sumac, and dwarf small-leafed roses. He stressed that it was "very desirable to avoid the character of the ordinary artificial garden 'rockery' and to have the whole affair appear *old* and 'natural,' that is to say, resembling places where, near ledges and ancient stone walls, there has been an interesting *spontaneous* growth."[28] Although Olmsted mentioned many specific plants in this letter (see Plant List 3), he did not include any formal list and left the exact choice of plants and detailed design pretty much to Fischer's discretion.

The Overlook planting led to the only documented disagreement between Olmsted and Fischer. As at Beacon Entrance, many herbaceous perennials were put in for temporary effect while the permanent plantations were "coming on." By 1889 it seemed to Olmsted that the permanent shrubs and vines had grown sufficiently that the flowering perennials along the base of the Overlook wall could be removed, but he found that Fischer intended the Overlook flowers (as well as a similar display in the Fens) to be permanent. Again Olmsted followed up the conversation in writing, referring Fischer to his letter of two years earlier and asking him to remove the flowers gradually. He assured his master gardener that he did not want Fischer to do something he felt to be in positively bad taste but concluded:

As to the question of good taste, we often see ladies very splendidly dressed with jewels and bright ribbons and flowers and agree that it is in good taste. We see other ladies dressed quietly without jewelry or any finery of color or material, and we agree that they also are dressed in good taste. If the difference between us is a difference between two ideas, each of which is in good taste, then I think that I have a right to ask you to adopt my more modest rather than your more splended preference.[29]

Fischer replied in a slightly hurt tone that he had only meant to show nature "in holy day dress."[30] The differences seem to have been successfully resolved, for a photograph of the base of the Overlook taken about 1890 (Figure 165) does not show a "broad or high display of flowers" but the "vines and creepers and small salient and out-thrusting bushes" desired by Olmsted for the permanent effect.[31]

The only other letter from Olmsted to Fischer concerning plantings in Franklin Park is a straightforward statement of his views about planting the rocky slope north of the Ellicott Arch. Olmsted again enumerated suitable plants for the lower and higher parts of the slope (Plant List 4), but he left it to Fischer to determine the exact kinds and quantities of each. He also indicated that Fischer could use a few foreign plants as long as they did not have conspicuous flowers and foliage and would not "materially affect the native character of the main body of foliage."[32] There is no photograph of this particular slope after planting. However, Figure 166, a view of the Ellicott Arch in 1892, showing a dense, intricate, yet carefully proportioned planting, gives us a good general picture of the kind of work done by Fischer under Olmsted's direction. As at the Overlook Terrace and Agassiz Bridge in the Fens, a close and finely textured array of small shrubs, vines, and ground-cover plants were stuck into the crevices of the boulders—some of them dripping down over the arch opening—and planted

Figure 165
Planting in the rear of the Overlook, Franklin Park.

nearby. Rhododendrons, which Olmsted sometimes used for their foliage rather than their flowering effect, are seen at the left.[33]

In the early 1890s trees were ordered for the Boston parkways, to be kept in the city nursery until they were large enough to plant in their permanent places. The order lists show that instead of the northern red oak (*Quercus rubra*) eventually planted along almost all of the parkways, the Olmsted firm originally intended each parkway to have its own distinctive tree species. The Fenway, apparently the only parkway planted before 1896, had Norway maples (*Acer platanoides*), but in 1893 the firm planned to augment these with sugar maples (*Acer saccharum*). Audubon Road (Park Drive) was planted with red maples (*Acer rubrum*) and white ash (*Fraxinus americana*), which were replaced with Norway maples in 1898.[34] For other parts of the parkway, they chose the following: Riverway, American linden (*Tilia americana*); Jamaicaway, northern red oak (*Quercus rubra*); Dorchesterway, buckeye (*Aesculus glabra*); Strandway, ori-

Plant List 4.   Plants to be used on the slope north of the Ellicott Arch, Franklin Park[a]

Low planting		Higher planting	
Scientific name	Common name	Scientific name	Common name
Rose virginiana (lucida)	Virginia rose and other low wild roses	[*Ligustrum* species]	Privet
		[*Berberis* species]	Barberry
Buxus canadensis	Box	*Rosa eglanteria*	Sweetbrier
Myrica cerifera	Wax myrtle	*Rhus copallina*	Shining sumac
Vaccinium corymbosum	Highbush blueberry	*Cercis canadensis*	Eastern redbud
Clethra alnifolia	Summersweet	*Cornus alternifolia* and others	Alternate-leaved and other dogwoods
Spiraea tomentosa	Hardhack		
Spiraea salicifolia	Willowleaf spirea	*Viburnum acerifolium*	Mapleleaf viburnum
Potentilla fruticosa	Bush cinquefoil	*Viburnum cassinoides*	Witherod
Symphoricarpos orbiculatus (vulgaris)	Indian currant or coralberry	*Quercus prinoides*	Dwarf chinkatin
		Prunus pumila	Sand cherry
Rhus aromatica	Fragrant sumac	*Lindera benzoin (Laurus benzoin)*	Spicebush
Diervilla lonicera (trifida)	Dwarf bush honeysuckle		
Ceanothus americanus	New Jersey tea	*Rhododendron nudiflorum (Azalea nudiflora)*	Pinxterbloom
Amelanchier canadensis alnifolia (dwarf)	Serviceberry		
		Smilax rotundifolia	Common greenbrier
Genista tinctoria	Dyer's greenwood		
Lonicera sempervirens	Trumpet honeysuckle		
Lonicera coerulea	Sweetberry honeysuckle		
Lonicera ciliata	Fly honeysuckle		
Vitis indivisa	Grape		

a. Letter from Olmsted to Fischer, Sept. 30, 1889, OP.

ental plane (*Platanus orientalis*); and Arborway, cucumber tree (*Magnolia acuminata*) or tulip tree (*Liriodendron tulipifera*.)[35] Tulip trees and cucumber magnolias, while they are splended native trees, are unusual choices for parkways. They may have been selected to signal the approach of the Arboretum, for they are the first trees in the natural order and the first to be seen when entering the main gate on the Arborway.

Most of the trees along the parkways, the "line" trees as they were generally called, were planted in the late 1890s under John A. Pettigrew's superintendency. In 1897 and 1898 Pettigrew planted the American lindens ordered by the Olmsted firm along the Riverway but continued the red oaks from Huntington Avenue at the beginning of the Jamaicaway all the way to Franklin Park. The Arborway was differentiated by the addition of shrub roses in the loam spaces between the trees.[36] Figure 167 shows the Arborway as it appeared in 1903, looking toward Franklin Park with the Forest Hills Viaduct in the distance.

Figure 166
Planting at the east front of the Ellicott Arch, Franklin Park, 1892.

Figure 167
Young oaks and shrub roses on the Arborway, 1903.

At the Muddy River Improvement, Brookline was approximately a year ahead of Boston in all phases of construction and by the spring of 1892 was ready to plant. This is the only part of the park system for which a complete set of planting plans—studies, preliminary plans, and working drawings—was made.[37] The entire series was done within six weeks during March and April 1892. The first plan was simply a collection of field notes and jottings by John Olmsted, which he wrote down on a print of the revised Muddy River plan. At this stage of the design process, John was concerned with the relationship between spaces and masses, not with specific plants or details of color and texture. Vistas were indicated by arrows, and plants were shown only as trees, shrubs, or grass.

From these rough notes Warren Manning made five sheets of large-scale drawings on tracing paper. The sight lines were indicated more precisely and the massing shown in more detail, but specific plants were still not identified. Manning used a rough key corresponding to John's categories: tall trees; shorter trees; high, medium, and low shrubs. The next set of plans, made after the plant list had been decided on, were done by James Langdon. For the final plans, Langdon translated the rough key used in the earlier plans into specific plants.

For the Muddy River, as for the Fens, the plants Olmsted selected were predominantly native not only to the United States but specifically to New England. However, the plant lists for both parks included a small number of trees and shrubs of foreign origin, and this group became a subject of controversy between Sargent and the Olmsted firm. Like the Muddy River boulder controversy, the plant materials controversy is first mentioned in an editorial in *Garden and Forest*. In 1888 a one-paragraph column, probably by Sargent, appeared in its pages:

It is not easy to explain why certain plants look distinctly in place in certain situations and why other plants look as distinctly out of place in the same situations. This is a matter which nature has perhaps settled for us . . . We have become accustomed to see certain plants adapted by nature to fill certain positions in combination with certain other plants in a given region; and that all attempts to force nature, so to speak, by bringing in alien elements from remote continents and climates, must inevitably produce inharmonious results. Landscape gardeners have rarely paid much attention to this subject."[38]

Olmsted replied, "The law seems to me to have been laid down that the introduction of foreign plants in our scenery is destructive of landscape repose and harmony. No exception was suggested."[39] He pointed out that the incongruous and jarring effect of foreign plants mixed with native would normally be noticed only by an unusually sophisticated observer and in some cases only by a botanist.

The Olmsted firm originally recommended that the planting of both sides of the Muddy River be done by the Boston planting force under Fischer's direction. Their recommendation, it seems, was ignored, for in the fall and winter of 1891–1892 Sargent ordered plants of his own choice for Brookline and made plans to hire his own superintendent.[40]

Late in March Olmsted left for a six-month stay in Europe, but before he went, he checked and approved the plant lists and rough planting plans made by John and Manning. Olmsted had been out of the country only a few days when Sargent dropped in on John. The visit was a disconcerting experience for John, who wrote an account of it to Codman, then in Chicago. In brief, Sargent asked to review the lists and plans for Brookline. When given the plant list, he crossed out a third of the trees and a quarter of the shrubs. Practically all of the foreign trees and shrubs, all of what Sargent considered "garden" plants (most of which were also foreign), and all shrubs with showy flowers were struck out. A few items were eliminated because of their susceptibility to diseases and pests. John argued that the plant list had been approved by his father and that, although he was willing to make some substitutions, particularly for horticultural reasons, he could not strike off every foreign plant that Sargent objected to. Sargent responded with an ultimatum: if John would not follow his directions, Sargent no longer wanted the firm's services. John refused to accept dismissal from one member of the commission and decided to wait until the entire board met.[41]

Codman, who, it will be remembered, was Sargent's nephew, promptly replied that "it will probably be best to resign our position rather than to allow our design to be so injured and cut to pieces as Professor Sargent proposes."[42] He recommended finishing the plans without concession to Sargent's views and submitting them to the entire Board. There is no recorded response from Olmsted until July, when he wrote simply, "I am sorry for mishaps at . . . the Brookline Parkway."[43] The plant list Sargent edited so vigorously is still in the files at the Olmsted National Historic Site in Brookline (see the Appendix, Lists A and B). A few days after the confrontation, John sent Sargent the first sheet of the Brookline planting plan and a revised list with half of the plants Sargent had objected to crossed out. Olmsted had gone over the plant list three times before he left for Europe, and John felt he could make no further omissions "without serious injury to the design and without danger of being false to the views and principles which have governed him as a landscape designer."[44]

Sargent delivered no further ultimatums but simply bided his time. The previous fall and winter he had ordered large quantities of several trees, shrubs, and vines (plants indicated by an asterisk in the Appendix, List A). The only foreign plants on the list were Japanese barberry (*Berberis thunbergii*), for which, according to John, Sargent had a special liking, and the European brier-rose (*Rosa eglanteria*). These plants, together with some of those ordered by the firm, were used for the Brookline planting.[45]

The planting of the Boston side in the spring of 1893 apparently went smoothly, but the record is much less complete than for Brookline. In the fall of 1892 Olmsted wrote frequently to John from Asheville, North Carolina (where he was supervising work on G. W. Vanderbilt's estate, Biltmore) about the Boston planting. He wanted skeleton plans ready by the time he came home so that he could write instructions on them: "My idea is to . . . [state] what should 'predominate,' then turn them over to Fischer with instructions to have . . . greater variety of detail and to be less cramped with reference to foreign plants etc. Professor Sargent's hobbies." In a spirit of some competitiveness, he added: "We ought to take care to secure quite as good plants as he obtained from nurseries . . . the same species, plants one year later."[46] The skeleton plans requested by Olmsted are in the vaults at the Olmsted National Historic Site, but nothing is marked on them except the same rough categories used in the early Brookline plans. Many years later, John recalled that his father and Fischer had done the planting of the Boston side by eye and that no planting plans in the usual sense of the word were ever prepared.[47]

How serious were the differences between Olmsted and Sargent? Olmsted's list was already heavily weighted with native trees and shrubs, particularly several species of native oaks, maples, birches, dogwood, hawthorn, sumac, and viburnum. Most of the plants eliminated by Sargent were foreign: Lombardy poplar, Siberian crab apple, European mountain ash, golden rain tree, as well as many shrubs. Olmsted had intended, however, to use these plants very sparingly: only two or three specimens were ordered of most foreign species. Sargent's excisions of native trees seem even more arbitrary. A few of these, such as slippery elm (*Ulmus fulva*), were struck out for horticultural rea-

sons, but it is difficult to understand why Sargent eliminated such beautiful native trees as the cucumber magnolia (*Magnolia acuminata*), the sweet gum (*Liquidambar styraciflua*) and the common honey locust (*Gleditsia triacanthos*). The Kentucky coffee tree (*Gymnocladus dioicus*) and Carolina silverbell (*Halesia carolina*) may have been left out because their normal range is in the southeastern part of the country, although they are hardy in Boston.[48] Because of "Professor Sargent's hobbies," the Brookline planting is somewhat more monotonous than it might otherwise have been—a result that was largely, although not entirely, independent of the native/foreign controversy.

Although all the shrubs and many of the trees planted in the early 1890s have long since died, mature, handsome specimens of oaks and other long-lived trees can still be found in this park. These show that Olmsted and Fischer used considerable latitude in making Boston agree with Brookline. In Boston, in the Longwood area alone, some of the less common native oaks, such as bur oak and swamp white oak, together with sweet gum and cucumber magnolias, may be seen, while the Brookline side is still dominated by Sargent's favorites, the northern red and white oaks.

It is understandable that Sargent, as a botanist, should have been unusually sensitive to the native habitats of trees and correspondingly disturbed by combinations which appeared to him to "force nature." At the Arboretum, of course, forcing nature was the whole point, since any tree or shrub, whatever its origin, that could thrive in the Boston area was grown there. Sargent also grew many foreign trees and shrubs at Holm Lea. As an arboriculturist, he generally advised against the landscape use of any tree, native or foreign, that was not entirely free of pests or diseases and that could not be relied upon to survive for many decades.

At the other extreme, Fischer, when left to his own devices, tended more toward the gardenesque, in that he liked flowering plants and those of foreign origin. His preferences, while in good taste, were sometimes more "splendid" than Olmsted, or certainly Sargent, would have liked. While he was still in charge of the firm, Olmsted, who was the soul of tact, was apparently able to deal with both men in a friendly manner, to use fully the talents of both, and to make his own preferences prevail—a middle ground between Sargent's rigorously purist philosophy and Fischer's "gardenesque" leanings.

Olmsted retired in September 1895. In January 1897, the position of assistant landscape gardener was abolished, and Fischer, who was seventy-seven, retired. After July 1897 the Olmsted firm served more as occasional consultants than as a consistent, controlling force in the affairs of the Park Department.[49] Sargent appears to have taken the firm's place, serving as an unpaid advisor in landscape design and arboriculture for the entire park system. Fischer's duties and those of the engineer in charge, E. W. Howe, who left the Park Department at the same time, were taken over by Superintendent John Pettigrew, who seems to have been hired at Sargent's recommendation.[50]

Some of the changes to the park system made in the late 1890s at Sargent's recommendation were: the filling up of the natural history pools in the Muddy River Improvement; the decision not to complete the Greeting in Franklin Park; destruction of various retaining and other walls at Jamaica Park and elsewhere; wholesale removal of all exotic plants from the park system; and vigorous thinning and "use of the axe" in Franklin Park, the Fens, and the Boston side of the Muddy River Improvement. Because of public outcry over work done under the new dispensation, the Park Department was investigated by a committee of the Board of Aldermen in 1900. Although the commissioners, Sargent, and Pettigrew were exonerated, there appears to have been some justification for the accusation that Sargent was altering Olmsted's plan. Of the two people who could have clarified the matter, Frederick Law Olmsted was not in a position to testify because he was then a patient at McLean Hospital in Belmont, Massachusetts, and John Olmsted chose not to.[51]

There was probably also some basis for the feeling that Fischer, in his last year or so with the department, had used more exotic plants than were compatible with the original plan and had not "used the axe" sufficiently.[52] Fischer seems to have been responsive only to Olmsted, and without Olmsted's mediating presence, it was almost inevitable that Sargent and Fischer, with their opposing horticultural views, should find themselves on a collision course.

It was also inevitable that Sargent should win, for he had both a forceful personality and a position of power. His considerable abilities as a gentleman landscape gardener at Holm Lea and as co-author of the Arboretum plan have already been discussed in Chapter IV. But as a designer of parks he had some serious limitations. In the letter just cited, Olmsted remarked not only on Sargent's "too cramped" exclusions of foreign plants but also on the need for "greater variety of detail." Although John Olmsted did not testify at the 1900 hearing, he wrote a report ten years later that confirms this view. Of Franklin Park, he says:

Where trees have been planted in the more open parts of the park, the work has been well done and the selection of sorts is admirable. The predominating use of the native oaks is particularly to be commended. . . . In general, the trees . . . are too uniformly spaced and too much like a succession of individual wide-branched specimens to look as natural as they should . . . There is opportunity for endless invention and contrivance to add effects of naturalness and variety . . . not only in this park but in others where naturalistic landscape is attempted. It would be well to constantly aim to please the artist. Few artists are attracted to well developed, round headed, healthy trees, almost evenly spaced, as appealing subjects for a picture. What most pleases the horticulturist seldom suits the artist. He looks either for large effects of color or mass, with prevailing harmony but some limited contrast of form or color or light or shade, or else he looks for picturesque, small local effects, with some deep shadow or a high light, or a dash of brilliant color, or a crooked gnarled trunk, or a mossy hole and fern-covered decaying stump. The arboricultural work done of late years on the parks cannot be too highly praised. It is perhaps the best in the country . . . but the artistic side of park planting has not been quite what it should be.[53]

John also commented on the tendency in the Boston parks to use the same predominant trees and shrubs in all parts of the system, a trend he attributed to "excessive attention to the arboricultural and economical side of the business of planting and too little to the artistic side," and he cautioned against categorically refusing to use trees of doubtful hardiness or resistance to disease in "an irregular mixed plantation," where they might have a valuable, if temporary, landscape effect.[54]

Like Sargent, Olmsted disliked fussy and contrived horticultural effects in a naturalistic park. But well-designed "variety of detail" of massing, color, and texture, which enhanced rather than detracted from his total composition, was an intrinsic part of his planting style, as can be seen particularly well in the 1892 planting plan and early photographs of the Muddy River Improvement. Here, as at Beacon Entrance in the Fens, the ground was densely planted with trees, shrubs, and vines, in expectation of later thinning. Wide expanses of grass were generally avoided in the Muddy River planting, partly because of the expense of hand mowing and partly because Olmsted did not want what he called a "lawnlike" effect. By today's standards, the sheer number of plants and the density with which they were planted are remarkable, but the care taken in the massing of trees and shrubs was so meticulous that the views across water and valley, which were such an integral feature of the design, were always kept open.

Figure 168 is a detail from the final planting plan for the section of the Muddy River near the Longwood Avenue Bridge. (For the plant list, see the Appendix.) Figures 169 and 170, photographs taken in 1896, only four years after planting, show the Muddy River looking downstream and upstream from the Longwood Avenue Bridge. In both views, the mound between the riverside path and the railroad (shown under construction in Figures 122 and 123) has been planted solidly with at least five or six different kinds of shrubs in intricately interwoven groups. The same method of planting can be seen in another detail of the 1892 plan (Figure 171), showing the Brookline shore of Leverett Pond. Pond Avenue was planted with American elms (*Ulmus americana,* number 12 on the plan), and a thick screen of shrubbery was planted between the avenue and the park proper. In Figure 172, a view taken about 1895, of Leverett Pond looking from Brookline toward Boston, the "general correspondence" between the two shores of the pond is apparent. This photograph also shows particularly well how skillfully Olmsted could combine dense planting with broad, open vistas.

Throughout his life, the pastoral scenery of En-

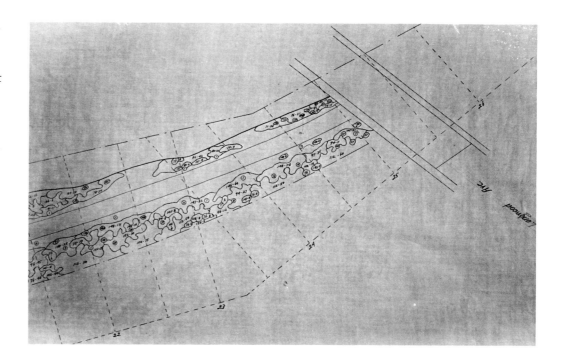

Figure 168 (top)
Planting plan of the
Brookline side of the
Muddy River Improvement
by James G. Langdon,
April 9, 1892. Detail near
the Longwood Avenue
Bridge.

Figure 169 (bottom)
View downstream from the
Longwood Avenue Bridge,
1896.

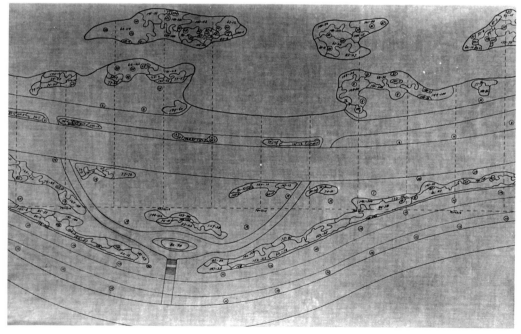

Figure 170 (top)
View upstream from the
Longwood Avenue Bridge,
1896.

Figure 171 (bottom)
Planting plan of the
Brookline side of the
Muddy River Improvement
by James G. Langdon,
April 13, 1892. Detail of
the shore of Leverett Pond,
including islands.

gland was a continuing inspiration to Olmsted. During the spring and summer of 1892, while the Muddy River was being planted, he revisited England and France. This trip, intended as recuperation from the crushing demands of the Chicago World's Columbian Exposition, turned out, in spite of Olmsted's ill health, to be a period of study and observation that benefited not only his work in Chicago, but the landscaping of Biltmore and the Boston parks as well.[55] He saw again the English landscape that had moved him as a young man to write: "The country—and such country!—green, dripping, glistening, gorgeous! We stood dumb-stricken by its loveliness, as, from the bleak April and bare boughs we had left at home, broke upon us that English May—sunny, leafy, blooming May—in an English lane."[56]

More than forty years later, he wrote, in a quieter tone but no less eloquently: "Such is the advantage of a temperate and moist climate, there is nothing in America to be compared with the pastoral or with the picturesque beauty that is common property in England. I cannot go out without being delighted. The view before me as I write, veiled by the rain, is just enchanting."[57] In July Olmsted spent a week cruising on the Thames and studying its riverside scenery, particularly the several varieties of willows, about which he wrote at great length to his partners.[58] While these observations were applicable chiefly to the Chicago Exposition, they had an obvious affinity with the work then in progress on the Muddy River.

After Olmsted returned home in the fall of 1892, he spent most of his limited strength on the World's Fair and Biltmore for the rest of that year and most of 1893.[59] He was painfully aware of his growing frailty and thought increasingly of his eventual retirement. During this period he wrote to John and to Charles Eliot, evaluating his own recent career and the "good will capital" he would leave to them and to Frederick, Jr. In these valedictory letters, Olmsted maintained repeatedly the importance of the Boston municipal and metropolitan park systems, stressing particularly the Muddy River—and even more specifically, its planting:

I would have you decline any business that would stand in the way of doing the best for Boston all the time, and . . . the most critical circumstance of all our busi-

Figure 172
Leverett Pond from Brook-
line, looking toward
Boston.

ness at the moment is the Muddy River Improvement . . . don't fail to see that the Muddy River work is well-ordered from day to day. The aims are novel, the conditions are novel. You cannot trust to usage.[60]

Our reputation is still to be made in such dealings with public pleasure roads outside of "parks," and in such "wild" public grounds, as those that we are now first to engage with about Boston . . . And our first stroke of

importance in this sort of work is that *now being made* on Muddy River. Twenty years hence you will be looking back to Muddy River as I do to Central Park.[61]

For Olmsted, the selection and design of plant materials at the Muddy River, the other Boston parks, and elsewhere, far from being a decorative adjunct to landscape architecture, lay at the heart of his creative process.

EPILOGUE

◆

Let it not be for present delight, nor for present use alone; let it be such work as our descendants will thank us for, and . . . say "See! This our fathers did for us."

—Ruskin, *The Seven Lamps of Architecture,* quoted in *Notes on the Plan of Franklin Park*

The Arnold Arboretum, 1980.

Olmsted:
The Second Century

———◆———

THE Boston park system, product of Olmsted's artistic maturity, is only now entering its second century. Recognized from the time of its completion as one of Olmsted's masterpieces and acclaimed as a cultural achievement comparable to its contemporaries the Museum of Fine Arts and the Boston Symphony, the park system was misunderstood and misused during much of the twentieth century. During the late 1960s and the 1970s, however, renewed recognition and support for parks became a national phenomenon that rode the crest of the environmental movement. Now that environmental values are being severely challenged, the "Olmsted Renaissance," as one historian has called it, still shows no sign of slackening.[1]

Throughout this book the emphasis has been on the history of the Boston parks during their design and construction, although subsequent physical changes to the individual parks have been described briefly in Part II. Figures 173 through 178 show the emerald necklace and its parks as they appear today from the air. But the fate of the Boston system in the twentieth century should be examined more closely, for it was not unique. Rather, it was paralleled in every American city to some extent.

In Boston by the end of the nineteenth century, two trends in park planning had emerged—both from Olmsted's office—which eventually replaced the large urban country parks. One was the metropolitan park system and the other the playground.

Figure 173
The Back Bay Fens, April 1982, showing the outline of Olmsted's plan intact. Later changes include the Charlesgate Interchange over Beacon Entrance (right); victory gardens and fire department headquarters opposite Westland Entrance in the northern basin; and a memorial, rose garden, and ballfield in the southern basin opposite the Museum of Fine Arts (lower left). Compare with Figures 31 and 102. At the upper left is the beginning of the Muddy River Improvement, including the parking lot in its first link.

Relatively few cities seem to have adopted metropolitan or regional park systems on the scale of Boston's, although Olmsted's successor firm designed extensive outer park systems, exploiting river valleys and other natural topographical features, in Cleveland, Seattle, and Washington, D.C.[2] The National Park System, developed between 1872 and 1929 but havings its origins in Olmsted's efforts on behalf of Yosemite in the early 1860s, also illustrates the growing emphasis on the conservation of natural scenic wonders in remote areas, as opposed to the creation of "natural" pastoral landscapes in the city.[3]

Charlesbank, on the other hand, had numerous progeny, although with the exception of Wood Island, no other Boston park provided all of the activities of the original model. Instead, Charlesbank's diverse functions were parceled out among more specialized sites: the playground, the sand court, and the neighborhood resting place. New York and Chicago established "model playgrounds" in the early 1890s, and by 1900 at least a dozen cities had playgrounds of some type, provided generally through private philanthropy. Between 1903 and 1905, Chicago opened ten parks and playgrounds of less than ten acres, designed by Olmsted Brothers

Figure 174
The Muddy River Im-
provement, April 1982.
Compare with Figure 50.
Beacon Street runs diago-
nally through Brookline,
shown in the upper half of
the photograph. In the
upper left corner, opposite
the Brookline Reservoir, is
Olmsted's subdivision of
Fisher Hill (Figure 88).

in variants of the Charlesbank prototype. Similar small neighborhood parks began to appear across the country, equipped with gymnasiums, sand boxes, running tracks and, increasingly, ball fields and swimming pools. As at Charlesbank, activities were supervised by professional recreation leaders. Few were landscaped as sensitively as Charlesbank and the small Chicago parks, and such amenities as boundary berms and sweeps of grass gradually disappeared.[4]

The wilderness reservation and the inner-city recreational ground were not antithetical to the country park; they simply supplemented it. But

there was undoubtedly a tendency for park commissioners, occupied as they were with very different concerns, to lose sight of the importance of their large city parks. In general, however, these parks were still heavily used and meticulously maintained in the first decades of this century.

In the 1930s, there arose a new tendency that caused serious damage to most of the nation's nineteenth-century parks. In New York City, this era is identified with the career of Park Commissioner Robert Moses, who, paradoxically, accomplished much in adding land to the New York park system (6,000 acres between 1934 and 1940), updating old playgrounds, renovating badly neglected smaller parks, and building parkways.[5] However, in New York and elsewhere, an overriding emphasis was placed on providing large-scale facilities for active recreation, with little awareness of the design integrity of historic parks—a trend that continued for almost thirty years. Baseball, football, swimming, and basketball grew immensely in popularity during this period, and certainly it was necessary to provide space for them somewhere in the city. But all too often the new facilities were put into the older parks, where they destroyed the intended landscape effect and disrupted the delicate balance of function planned by the original designers. Passive recreation was largely ignored; the assumption seemed to be that the world was divided into athletes and spectators. Numerous such intrusions in the Boston parks

—the stadium in Franklin Park, the skating rink on the Riverway—have already been described.

Not all the blame for the widespread deterioration of parks during this period can be placed on the trend toward active recreation. Heavy automobile traffic had by this time become a serious problem. In some parks traffic patterns were modified effectively.[6] In many others, parkways and interior roads were widened, and high-speed throughways were allowed to cut across parks.[7] Particularly after World War II, the neighborhoods around most city parks changed radically as the middle class moved to the suburbs. There was a gradual decline in maintenance and an increase in vandalism and crime. The final stage was the selling—or even giving away—of parkland for commercial or institutional purposes. Thus Boston found itself with a hospital in Franklin Park and a private parking lot replacing the first link of the Muddy River.

The Olmsted renaissance occurred on both a scholarly and a popular level. Rediscovery of Olmsted by historians began in the 1950s and has grown greatly in the past decade. Renewed appreciation of his parks and a more widespread understanding of his life and work have been discernible since the mid-1960s but reached a high point in the early 1970s, prompted by exhibitions and other observances of the sesquicentennial of Olmsted's birth in 1972 and by the American Bicentennial in 1976. Olmsted's second entry into national consciousness was obviously spurred by the environmental movement. However, response to his example was multifaceted; as has been pointed out, his career was relevant as well to other major reform movements of the 1960s and 1970s.[8]

In those decades there was new impetus for the conservation of large wilderness areas, but because land was scarce and expensive, inner-city "vest pocket" parks, tot lots, and plazas became the characteristic landscape forms.[9] Many of these small parks were heavily architectural and involved little or no use of plant materials. Examples in Boston include Copley Square, Government Plaza, and Waterfront Park.

"Open space" became the catchword of the day, and all unbuilt areas of whatever type within or near a city were seen as part of an open-space system, whether or not they were physically connected.

Figure 175
Jamaica Pond, May 1982. The open land on the left is outside the park boundaries (see Figure 56). It includes, clockwise from lower left, the Hellenic College site; part of the Sargent estate, a low-density subdivision built in the 1920s on Holm Lea; and the Cabot estate with cluster condominiums on part of the land. The high-rise building, upper right, is Jamaicaway Towers.

Figure 176
The Arnold Arboretum,
April 1982, showing the
original tract, Peters Hill,
and later additions; com-
pare with Figures 34 and
35. The dark areas are
Hemlock Hill and the con-
ifer collections, contrasting
with the deciduous tree
collections just leafing out.

An imaginative, though still unrealized, plan of the early 1970s was the Charles-to-Charles: a proposal to treat the Olmsted park system, other publicly owned grounds, and private estates as a continuous corridor from the Charles River at the Fens to its link upstream in Newton, all to be connected by trails and paths for hiking, bicycling, and cross-country skiing.[10] This was to be accomplished primarily by conservation easements rather than by large-scale acquisition of land. Another project, now partially achieved, was for public acquisition of the Boston Harbor Islands and their development as nature reserves and limited recreational sites.[11]

Historic urban parks were at first viewed simply as more open space. However, awareness of their unique qualities and special problems grew for a variety of reasons. Citizen groups, such as the Friends of the Public Garden and the Franklin Park Coalition, were formed during these years and began publicizing their parks. Information on Olmsted and historic parks began to appear in newspaper and magazine articles, brochures, guide maps, and other accessible media. After the passage of the National Historic Preservation Act of 1966, state and local historical commissions were established. Although architectural inventories and designations were the

Figure 177
Franklin Park, April 1982. Later additions to the plan (see Figure 41) include Shattuck Hospital, upper left; White Stadium, upper right; and the zoo, redesigned from the Greeting (lighter portions are new construction). To the left of the park is a portion of Forest Hills Cemetery.

chief function of these agencies, there was increasing emphasis on historic districts rather than individual buildings and on parks. In Boston the Common, Public Garden, and the Olmsted park system from the Fens through Franklin Park were placed on the National Register of Historic Places by the early 1970s. Master plans and historic restoration proposals were discussed. In New York, but not in Boston, park curators and later administrators were appointed.

During the same years the condition of the parks became a matter of widespread concern, and numerous volunteer cleanups were held. There was a resurgence of interest in individual, back-to-nature sports, and once again hikers, bicyclists, and horseback riders were an everyday sight in the parks. Outdoor concerts, plays, and ballets were staged; in Boston, most were limited in size—the Elma Lewis Playhouse-in-the-Park at Franklin Park and the City of Boston Summerthing events—rather than mega-performances of the type held in Central Park. (Large "happenings" in Boston generally take place on the Charles River Esplanade or on the Common.) Many deteriorating neighborhoods near the parks improved as families moved back to the city. Antihighway and antiautomobile crusades prevented the building of the Inner Belt, which would have destroyed one whole end of the Fens, and succeeded in limiting traffic in some of the parks. In the Southwest Corridor, an area that was to have been a highway, a new eighty-acre linear park has been planned to stretch from the Back Bay to the Forest Hills section of Jamaica Plain.[12]

Current economic cutbacks and antienvironmental policies are a source of great concern to park advocates. However, the achievements of the past few years have been substantial. As a result of a campaign of nearly a decade by many individuals and groups, Congress in 1980 authorized the National Park Service to acquire the Olmsted house and office at 99 Warren Street, Brookline, together with the complete graphic archives of the firm. In the same year the National Association for Olmsted Parks, an organization dedicated to the preservation of the hundreds of parks across the country designed by Olmsted and his successors, was formed.

Figure 178
Marine Park, Castle Island, and the Strandway (now Day Boulevard), April 1982. Compare with Figure 62.

The protection of urban parks has never been easy, as Olmsted's own career amply illustrates. Nevertheless, certain problems today are especially critical. One is simple economics: public funds have dried up at every level of government. Until recently, federal programs have been available to help support capital improvement to parks. Now, with some programs eliminated and others drastically cut, private sources appear to be the only avenue. Private fund raising has already been done with considerable success in some cities and would seem a logical course for Boston to follow.[13] On the local level, park maintenance, already minimal in most Massachusetts communities, has declined still further with the passage of a state law limiting local property taxes to 2½ percent of assessed valuation.

There continues to be controversy over what kinds of activities are appropriate in parks. Nearly all of the activities Olmsted allowed in his country parks would today be classified as passive. However, active versus passive recreation is a relatively new concept. Franklin Park, with its Country Park and Ante-Park and its provision for a wide range of activities within each division, is organized on the basis of a hierarchy of spaces and uses. Olmsted seems to have been concerned less with the strenuousness of an activity than with its potential for physically damaging the parks or for interfering with the average park user's full enjoyment of the landscape. While leisurely strolling is clearly passive and football clearly active, there are gray areas in between. As a sport becomes more popular, it is pursued more intensely and becomes more difficult to contain.

One interesting exception is tennis, a sport associated with Olmsted parks but one that has left little permanent mark on them. After lawn tennis was patented in England in 1874, it caught on quickly in this country and was played in Prospect and Franklin parks (see Figure 45). In its early years, tennis was more of a pastime than a sport: equipment was simple, rules informal, and little

more exertion was needed than for croquet. (Part of its appeal lay in the fact that, like croquet, it could be played by men and women together.) During the early decades of the twentieth century, lawn tennis became highly organized and competitive, but it was generally played in private clubs. Thus, despite the popularity of tennis both in Olmsted's day and our own, large-scale tennis facilities in parks are rare.[14]

In general, however, a sudden spurt in the popularity of an activity completely alters its impact on a park. The solitary, early-morning jogger seems entirely appropriate anywhere. However, packs of grimly determined runners leave no space for walking, and the atmosphere they generate is hardly tranquil. In Central Park the path around the reservoir has been set aside exclusively for such serious running. While for many decades there has been a clear trend toward increased athleticism, fashions in individual sports are impossible to predict. Labels of "active" and "passive" are perhaps less important than an awareness of the effects of any given recreational activity on a particular park.

Crime in the parks is another complex issue. Local cutbacks have again made increased police protection unlikely. However, educating the public in a few simple precautions would accomplish much. Serious crime rarely occurs in the daytime or when the parks are being heavily used. In Central and Prospect parks, park rangers have been introduced. Like Olmsted's "Park Keepers," the rangers have an educational and supervisory role. They do not have police powers, but they have radio contact with police, and their presence is a deterrent to vandalism and crime.

The Boston park system, like the great majority of Olmsted's designs, has reached the century mark shabby but in salvageable condition. That this is so testifies both to Olmsted's artistic genius and to the enduring human need for the refreshment of grass, trees, water, and unconfined space.

Appendix

Notes

List of Illustrations

Index

APPENDIX

Muddy River Improvement
Plant Lists

———◆———

All lists are in the Olmsted firm archives at the Olmsted National Historic Site, Brookline, Massachusetts. Outdated botanical names are given in parentheses. Modern botanical names are obtained from Alfred Rehder, *Bibliography of Cultivated Trees and Shrubs* (Jamaica Plain, Mass.: Arnold Arboretum of Harvard University, 1949); and Harlan P. Kelsey and William A. Dayton, *Standardized Plant Names,* 2d ed. (Harrisburg, Pa.: J. Horace McFarland for the American Joint Committee on Horticultural Nomenclature, 1942). For native habitats (the issue between Sargent and the Olmsted firm), see Donald Wyman, *Trees for American Gardens* (New York: Macmillan, 1965); Donald Wyman, *Shrubs and Vines for American Gardens* (New York: Macmillan, 1969); Charles Sprague Sargent, *Manual of the Trees of North America,* 2 vols. (1922; reprint ed., New York: Dover Publications, 1965); and Harold William Rickett, *Wild Flowers of the United States,* vol. I, *The Northeastern States* (New York: New York Botanical Garden, McGraw-Hill, 1966).

A question mark indicates that the quantity is unclear, or it is unclear whether the plant has been struck out, or the common name cannot be determined (original lists are handwritten). In List A, plants ordered by Sargent, fall 1891, are indicated by an asterisk; plants deleted from the April 1892 plant list by Sargent but reinstated by John Olmsted are indicated by a dagger.

A. Brookline and Boston, 1892 and 1893.

Number on plan	Scientific name	Common name	Total no., Brookline	Total no., Boston
1*	*Quercus rubra*	Red oak	305	400
2*	*Quercus alba*	White oak	205	360
3	*Quercus coccinea*	Scarlet oak	19	25
4	*Quercus palustris*	Pin oak	12	16
5	*Quercus macrocarpa*	Bur oak	5	7
6	*Quercus bicolor*	Swamp white oak	5	7
7	*Quercus prinus*	Chestnut oak	12	16
8*	*Acer saccharum (saccharinum)*	Sugar maple	200	260
9	*Acer saccharinum (dasycarpum)*	Silver maple	30	40
10	*Acer rubrum*	Red maple	30	40
11	*Acer negundo*	Box elder	10	13
12*	*Ulmus americana*	American elm	136	175
14	*Ulmus thomasii (racemosa)*	Rock elm	5	7
17	*Sassafras albidum (officinalis)*	Common sassafras	5	7
18	*Juniperus virginiana*	Eastern red cedar	10	13
19	*Fagus grandifolia (ferruginea)*	American beech	36	50
21	*Nyssa sylvatica (multiflora)*	Black tupelo	10	13
23	*Betula nigra*	River birch	18	24
24	*Betula lenta*	Sweet birch	5	7
25	*Betula lutea*	Yellow birch	10	13
27	*Betula papyrifera*	Paper birch	5	7
28	*Celtis occidentalis*	Hackberry	5	7
29	*Fraxinus americana*	White ash	15	20
30	*Liriodendron tulipifera*	Tulip tree	10	13
31†	*Magnolia acuminata*	Cucumber tree	10	13
35	*Platanus orientalis*	Oriental plane tree	10	13
36	*Populus deltoides (monolifera)*	Eastern cottonwood	5	7
37†	*Populus nigra italica (P. nigra pyramidalis)*	Lombardy poplar	15	20
38	*Salix alba vitellina*	Yellowstem willow	10	13
39	*Salix alba sericea (S. alba argentea)*	?	13	13
40	*Salix alba f. chermesina (S. alba britzensis)*	Redstem willow	12	?
41	*Salix babylonica*	Babylon weeping willow	12	16
42	*Tilia americana*	American basswood	5	7
45	*Ostrya virginiana (virginica)*	Eastern hophornbeam	10	13
46	*Carpinus caroliniana (americana)*	American hornbeam	5	7
60*	*Cornus florida*	Flowering dogwood	300	400
61*	*Cornus alternifolia*	Alternate-leaved dogwood	1,040	1,350
62*	*Cornus racemosa (paniculata)*	Gray dogwood	1,320	1,700
63	*Cornus sanguinea*	Bloodtwig dogwood	603	800
64	*Cornus amomum (sericea)*	Silky dogwood	180	240
65	*Cornus sericea (stolonifera)*	Red osier dogwood	600	800

A. Brookline and Boston, 1892 and 1893 (*continued*).

Number on plan	Scientific name	Common name	Total no., Brookline	Total no., Boston
66	*Crataegus crus-galli*	Cockspur thorn	?	?
67	*Crataegus pedicellata (coccinea)*	Scarlet hawthorn	251	330
68	*Ptelea trifoliata*	Hoptree	150	200
70	*Acer spicatum*	Mountain maple	75	100
71	*Lonicera japonica repens (L. flexuosa)*	Hardyleaf Japanese honeysuckle	710	1,000
72	*Lindera benzoin*	Spicebush	800	1,000
73†	*Rosa multiflora*	Japanese rose	230	300
74?†	*Calycanthus floridus*	Carolina allspice	350	500
75†	*Kerria japonica*	Kerria	800	1,100
76*	*Rosa virginiana (lucida)*	Virginia rose	8,000	10,700
77	*Rhus aromatica (canadensis)*	Fragrant sumac	2,150	2,800
78*	*Parthenocissus quinquefolia (Ampelopsis quinquefolia)*	Virginia creeper	512	700
79*	*Celastrus scandens*	American bittersweet	409	550
80	*Clethra alnifolia*	Summersweet	2,400	3,200
82*	*Myrica cerifera*	Wax myrtle	1,820	2,400
83	*Cephalanthus occidentalis*	Buttonbush	330	400
84	*Ceanothus americanus*	New Jersey tea	1,115	1,500
85	*Potentilla fruticosa*	Bush cinquefoil	2,000	2,700
86†	*Rosa wichuraiana*	Memorial rose	500	700
87	*Viburnum acerifolium*	Mapleleaf viburnum	230	300
88	*Viburnum cassinoides*	Witherod	10	13
89	*Viburnum dentatum*	Arrowwood	300?	400?
90	*Viburnum lentago*	Nannyberry	75	100
91	*Viburnum nudum*	Smooth witherod	50	65
92	*Viburnum opulus*	European cranberrybush	105	140
93	*Viburnum prunifolium*	Black haw	315	400
94	*Ligustrum vulgare*	Common privet	1,900	5,000
96*	*Berberis vulgaris*	Common barberry	1,300	1,700
97*	*Berberis thunbergii*	Japanese barberry	1,800	2,400
98	*Physocarpus opulifolius (Spiraea opulifolia)*	Eastern ninebark	250	330
99	*Akebia quinata*	Fiveleaf akebia	300	400
100	*Menispermum canadense*	Common moonseed	250	350
101	*Parthenocissus quinquefolia hirsuta (Amelopsis quinquefolia radicans or radicantissima)*	Variety of Virginia creeper	?	?
104	*Lonicera japonica repens (Lonicera flexuosa)*	Hardyleaf Japanese honeysuckle	1,000	1,400
105	*Lycium barbarum*	Barbary matrimony vine	650	900
107	*Hamamelis virginiana*	Common witch hazel	325	400
112	*Rhus typhina*	Staghorn sumac	800	1,000
113	*Salix pentandra*	Laurel willow	15	20

A. Brookline and Boston, 1892 and 1893 (*continued*).

Number on plan	Scientific name	Common name	Total no., Brookline	Total no., Boston
115	*Baccharis halimifolia*	Groundsel bush	?	?
116†	*Colutea arborescens*	Bladder senna	150	200
117	*Ilex verticillata*	Winterberry	260	340
118†	*Ligustrum ibota*	Ibota privet	150	200
119	*Lonicera fragrantissima*	Winter honeysuckle	385	425
120?†	*Lonicera morrowi*	Morrow honeysuckle	370	490
121?†	*Lonicera tatarica*	Tatarian honeysuckle	60	80
122?†	*Lonicera xylosteum*	European fly honeysuckle	70	85
123	*Alnus firma*	?	?	?
124	*Amelanchier canadensis*	Shadblow serviceberry	150	200
125	*Chionanthus virginicus*	Fringetree	?	?
128	*Aronia arbutifolia (Pyrus arbutifolia)*	Red chokeberry	25	30
129	*Rhus copallina*	Shining sumac	175	225
130*	*Sambucus canadensis*	American elder	200	260
132	*Staphylea trifolia*	American bladdernut	?	?
133*	*Comptonia peregrina asplenifolia (Comptonia asplenifolia)*	Sweet fern	1,000	1,400
134	*Diervilla lonicera (trifida)*	Dwarf bush-honeysuckle	50	70
135	*Genista tinctoria*	Dyer's greenwood	650	900
136	*Hypericum kalmianum*	Kalm Saint Johnswort	450	600
137	*Leucothoë racemosa*	Sweet bells	100	133
138	*Myrica gale*	Sweet gale	150	200
139*	*Rosa carolina*	Carolina rose	500	700
140*	*Rosa eglanteria (rubiginosa)*	Sweetbrier	550	700
141	*Rubus odoratus*	Flowering raspberry	900	1,200
142	*Salix tristis*	Dwarf gray willow	2,000	2,700
143	*Spiraea salicifolia*	Willowleaf spirea	50	70
144	*Spiraea tomentosa*	Hardhack	150	200
145	*Symphoricarpos albus laevigatus (racemosus)*	Snowberry	575	700
146	*Symphoricarpos albus (pauciflorus)*	?	600	800
147	*Symphoricarpos orbiculatus (vulgaris)*	Indian currant or coralberry	1,850	2,400
148	*Xanthorhiza simplicissima (apiifolia)*	Yellowroot	7,750	10,400
150	*Shepherdia canadensis*	Russet buffaloberry	10	15
151	*Rubus hispidus*	Swamp dewberry	3,000	4,400
152*	*Rhamnus catharticus*	Common buckthorn	1,150	1,500

B. Plants deleted by Sargent from April 1892 plant list for Brookline side:
St. Mary's Street to Cumberland Avenue.

No. on plan	Scientific name	Common name	Total no. deleted
13	*Ulmus fulva*	Slippery elm	14
15	*Morus alba*	White mulberry	1
16	*Abies alba*	Silver fir	3
20	*Koelreuteria paniculata*	Goldenrain tree	?
22	*Betula pendula* (*alba*)	European birch	?
26	*Betula populifolia*	Gray birch	3
32	*Liquidambar styraciflua*	Sweet gum	5
33	*Gleditsia triacanthos*	Common honey locust	1
34	*Gymnocladus dioicus*	Kentucky coffeetree	1
43	*Tilia?*	Linden?	?
44	*Cercis canadensis*	Eastern redbud	?
47, 109	*Sorbus aucuparia* (*Pyrus aucuparia*)	European mountain ash or rowan tree	3
48	*Sorbus decora* (*Pyrus americana*)	Showy mountain ash	2
69	*Alnus incana*	Speckled alder	?
81	*Acanthopanax sieboldianus* (*Aralia pentophylla*)	Five-leaf acanthopanax	49
95	*Ligustrum ovalifolium*	California privet	811?
102	*Clematis virginiana*	Virgin's bower	?
103	*Clematis vitalba*	Traveler's joy	?
106	*Halesia carolina* (*tetraptera*)	Carolina silverbell	13?
108	*Prunus cerasifera* (*mirobolona*)	Myrobalan plum	1
110	*Malus baccata* (*Pyrus baccata*)	Siberian crab apple	2
111	*Rhus glabra*	Smooth sumac	?
114	*Zanthoxylum americanum*	Common prickly ash	?
126	*Physocarpus opulifolius* (*Spiraea opulifolia*) (kept in as 98)	Eastern ninebark	?
127	*Prunus maritima*	Beach plum	?
131	*Spiraea* x *vanhouttei*	Vanhoutte spirea	80?
149	*Elaeagnus multiflorus* (*longipes*)	Cherry elaeagnus	5

C. Additional plants ordered by Olmsted firm for Brookline, 1893.

No. on plan	Scientific name	Common name	Total no.
153	*Vinca minor*	Periwinkle	500
154	*Rhododendron viscosum (Azalea viscosa)*	Swamp azalea	150
155	*Rhododendron nudiflorum (Azalea nudiflora)*	Pinxterbloom	150
156	*Rhododendron canadense (Rhodora canadensis)*	Rhodora	300
157	*Lysimachia nummularia*	Moneywort	500
158	*Caltha palustris*	Marsh marigold	500
159	*Saponaria officinalis*	Bouncing bet	200
160	*Iris kaempferi*	Japanese iris	400
161	*Iris sibirica*	Siberian iris	400
162	*Lythrum salicaria roseum (L. roseum superbum)*	Rose loosestrife	300
163	*Adiantum pedatum*	American maidenhair fern	400
164	*Dennstedtia punctilobula (Dicksonia punctiloba)*	Hay-scented fern	400
165	*Osmunda claytoniana*	Interrupted fern	200
166	*Onoclea sensibilis*	Sensitive fern	200
167	*Athyrium felixfemina (Asplenium felix foeminia)*	Lady fern	300
168	*Osmunda cinnamomea*	Cinnamon fern	350
169	*Pteretis nodulosa (Onoclea struthiopteris)*	Ostrich fern	300
170	*Ajuga genevensis*	Geneva bugle	500
171	*Woodwardia virginica*	Virginia chainfern	500
172	*Aster novae-angliae*	New England aster	300
173	*Trillium grandiflorum*	Large white trillium	350
174	*Aster undulatus*	Wave aster	550
175	*Cardamine pratensis*	Cuckooflower or lady's smock	300
176	*Acorus calamus*	Sweet flag	200
177	*Anemone canadensis (pennsylvanica)*	Meadow anemone	700
178	*Geranium maculatum*	Wild geranium	700
179	*Yucca filamentosa*	Common yucca or Adam's needle	100
180	*Boltonia latisquama*	Violet boltonia	150
181	*Cassia marilandica*	Wild senna	30
182	*Coreopsis lanceolata*	Lance coreopsis	300
183	*Erigeron speciosus*	Oregon fleabane	200
184	*Myosotis scorpioides (palustris)*	True forget-me-not	300

Notes

Abbreviations

BDA — *Boston Daily Advertiser*

BET — *Boston Evening Transcript*

FLL — Frances Loeb Library, Graduate School of Design, Harvard University, Cambridge, Massachusetts

OP — Olmsted Papers, Library of Congress, Washington, D.C.

OAP — Olmsted Associates Papers, Library of Congress

RBPD — Records, Boston Park Department (manuscript minutes and other records from 1875 on), Boston Department of Parks and Recreation, Boston City Hall.

I. *Topographical Development of Boston, 1630–1878*

1. The basic source is Walter Muir Whitehill's classic *Boston: A Topographical History,* 2d. ed., enlarged (Cambridge, Mass.: Harvard University Press, 1968). Also essential for the study of late nineteenth-century Boston are Bainbridge Bunting, *Houses of Boston's Back Bay* (Cambridge, Mass.: Harvard University Press, 1967), and Sam Bass Warner, Jr., *Streetcar Suburbs: The Process of Growth in Boston, 1870–1900,* 2d ed. (Cambridge, Mass.: Harvard University Press, 1978).

2. All nine states of the Bonner map, except for a presumptive fourth state, are illustrated in John W. Reps, "Boston by Bostonians: The Printed Plans and Views of the Colonial City by its Artists, Cartographers, Engravers, and Publishers," in *Boston Prints and Printmakers, 1670–1775,* ed. Walter Muir Whitehill (Boston: Colonial Society of Massachusetts, 1973), 3–56.

3. Whitehill, *Boston,* 75–78.

4. John Koren, *Boston, 1822 to 1922, The Story of Its Government and Principal Activities During One Hundred Years* (Boston, 1922; City Document no. 39-1922), 6–15. See also James M. Bugbee, *The City Government of Boston* (Baltimore: Johns Hopkins University, 1887).

5. Oscar Handlin, *Boston's Immigrants: A Study in Acculturation,* rev. ed., enlarged (Cambridge, Mass.: Harvard University Press, 1959).

6. Whitehill, *Boston,* 88–94, 100.

7. Bunting, *Back Bay,* 1, and chap. 8, "The Back Bay Area as an Example of City Planning," 361–399. As Bunting explains, although the Back Bay had been filled earlier along Charles Street and for a few blocks of Beacon and Boylston streets, these were extensions of existing neighborhoods. There had also been sporadic filling of the Public Garden area with city refuse, but the land was not brought up to street level until the late 1850s.

8. Margaret Supplee Smith, "Boston's South End," in *Victorian Boston Today: Ten Walking Tours,* ed. Pauline Chase Harrell and Margaret Supplee Smith (Boston: New England Chapter, Victorian Society in America, 1975), 12–25. See also Whitehill, *Boston,* chap. 6, "The Flight from the South End," 119–140. Also valuable is Margaret Supplee Smith, "Between City and Suburb: Architecture and Planning in Boston's South End," Ph.D. Dissertation, Brown University, 1976, 5–9, 70–71.

9. For the attribution of the Back Bay plan to Arthur Gilman, see "Arthur Gilman," in *Sketches of Men of Mark; Written by the Best Talent of the East* (New York: New York and Hartford Publishing Co., 1871), 817–821.

10. M. A. DeWolfe Howe, *Boston Common: Scenes from Four Centuries* (Cambridge, Mass.: Riverside Press, 1910), 45–46.

11. The best source for the Public Garden is Christopher R. Eliot, "The Boston Public Garden," *Proceedings of the Bostonian Society* (1939), 27–45.

12. Abel Bowen's projected development of the Back Bay, originally published in 1825 in some issues of Dr. Caleb H. Snow's *A History of Boston,* is reproduced in Whitehill, *Boston,* 145.

13. Letter from John Cadness, quoted in Marshall

Pinckney Wilder, "The Horticulture of Boston and Vicinity," in *The Memorial History of Boston,* ed. Justin Winsor (Boston: Ticknor and Co., 1881), IV, 615–617.

14. A. J. Downing to John Jay Smith, Nov. 15 (1841?, partly illegible), manuscript letter in the collection of the Library Company of Philadelphia, now on long-term loan to the Historical Society of Pennsylvania. The relevant portion reads: "I have been employed to a very considerable extent this season in giving designs for laying out grounds both in the neighborhood of Boston and New York, and landscape gardening bids fair to become a profession in this country. I have given a plan which it is probable may be carried out for a large public garden at Boston, 22 acres in extent, in which the boundary is an arboretum scientifically arranged according to the natural system. I prepared lists of the trees and indicated the precise places where they were to be planted on the plan, and sincerely hope it may be carried out." I am grateful to George B. Tatum, professor of art history at the University of Delaware, for bringing this letter to my attention. Downing's plan has been lost, and no mention of it has been found in any source other than the letter cited. However, his description, including exact acreage, clearly refers to the Public Garden, and the date, even if approximate, makes sense.

15. *Report of the Joint Committee on Public Lands in Relation to the Public Garden* (Boston: City Doc. no. 18-1850).

16. For a full explanation of the complicated Tripartite Agreement of 1856, see Bunting, *Back Bay,* 363–364.

17. Wilder, "Horticulture of Boston and Vicinity," 618–640. See also *History of the Massachusetts Horticultural Society, 1829–1878* (Boston, 1880), 1–54.

18. The Mount Auburn bibliography is as follows: Jacob Bigelow, *A History of the Cemetery of Mount Auburn* (Boston and Cambridge, 1860); *History of the Massachusetts Horticultural Society,* 55–84; John W. Reps, *The Making of Urban America: A History of City Planning in the United States* (Princeton: Princeton University Press, 1965), 325–330; Albert Fein, "The American City: The Ideal and the Real," in *The Rise of an American Architecture,* ed. Edgar Kaufmann, Jr. (New York: Praeger, 1970), 81–83; Bainbridge Bunting and Robert H. Nylander, *Survey of Architectural History in Cambridge, Report Four: Old Cambridge* (Cambridge, Mass.: Cambridge Historical Commission, 1973), 69–72. For information on the two most important founding members, see D[onald] C. P[eattie] and J[ohn] F. F[ulton], "Jacob Bigelow," *Dictionary of American Biography* (New York: Charles Scribner's Sons, 1936), I, 257–258; and H. W. H[oward] K[nott], "Henry A. S.

Dearborn," *Dictionary of American Biography*, III, 176–177. See also Caroline H. Dall, *In Memoriam: Alexander Wadsworth* (Washington: May 7, 1898).

19. *History of the Massachusetts Horticultural Society*, 85–96. I am grateful to Arthur Krim of the Massachusetts Historical Commission for sharing with me the results of his research in progress on Mount Auburn Cemetery; we found that we had come independently to the same conclusions about the collaborative nature of the Mount Auburn design.

20. *History of the Massachusetts Horticultural Society*, 96–118.

21. Warner, *Streetcar Suburbs*, 163–165.

22. Warner, *Streetcar Suburbs*, 132–141.

23. [Robert Morris Copeland], Editorial, *BDA*, Oct. 16, 1873.

II. The Making of a Landscape Architect

1. The principal biographical source is Laura Wood Roper, *FLO: A Biography of Frederick Law Olmsted* (Baltimore: Johns Hopkins University Press, 1973). Other biographical studies and surveys of Olmsted's work published between 1922 and the present include: Frederick Law Olmsted, Jr., and Theodora Kimball, eds., *Frederick Law Olmsted, Landscape Architect, 1822–1903 (Forty Years of Landscape Architecture: Being the Professional Papers of Frederick Law Olmsted, Senior)*, 2 vols. (New York: G. P. Putman's Sons, 1922, 1928), reissued in 1 vol. (New York: Benjamin Blom, 1970); Albert Fein, ed., *Landscape into Cityscape: Frederick Law Olmsted's Plans for a Greater New York City* (Ithaca, N.Y.: Cornell University Press, 1968); Julius Gy. Fabos, Gordon T. Milde, and V. Michael Weinmayr, *Frederick Law Olmsted, Sr., Founder of Landscape Architecture in America* (University of Massachusetts Press, 1968); Albert Fein, *Frederick Law Olmsted and the American Environmental Tradition* (New York: George Braziller, 1972); Elizabeth Stevenson, *Park Maker: A Life of Frederick Law Olmsted* (New York: Macmillan, 1977); Charles Capen McLaughlin and Charles E. Beveridge, eds., *The Papers of Frederick Law Olmsted*, vol. I, *The Formative Years, 1822–1852* (Baltimore: Johns Hopkins University Press, 1977); and Charles E. Beveridge, Charles Capen McLaughlin, and David Schuyler, eds., *The Papers of Frederick Law Olmsted*, vol. II, *Slavery and the South, 1852–1857* (Baltimore: Johns Hopkins University Press, 1981). For Olmsted's early years, Charles E. Beveridge, *Frederick Law Olmsted, the formative years, 1822–1865*, Ph.D. dissertation, University of Wisconsin, 1966 (Ann Arbor: University Microfilms, 1969) is highly recommended.

2. Olmsted, Autobiographical Fragment A, OP, in McLaughlin and Beveridge, *Papers*, I, 98–113.

3. Olmsted, Autobiographical Fragment B, OP; in McLaughlin and Beveridge, *Papers*, I, 117. At the time Olmsted lived with him in Andover, Mass., Barton was studying for the ministry at Andover Theological Seminary and teaching mathematics at Phillips Academy (Claude M. Fuess, *An Old New England School: A History of Phillips Academy, Andover* [Boston: Houghton Mifflin, 1917], 210). Olmsted's study with Barton seems to have involved at least a nominal enrollment at Phillips Academy, for he was recorded as a member of the class of 1838, Teachers' Seminary, which later became the English Department (Archives, Phillips Academy, Andover, Mass.; and Fuess, *Old New England School*, 300). However, when Barton went to his first church in Collinsville, Conn., Olmsted went with him.

4. All extant letters written by Olmsted during his China voyage are in McLaughlin and Beveridge, *Papers*, I, 132–190.

5. Olmsted to Charles Loring Brace, June 22, 1845; Olmsted to John Hull Olmsted, June 23, 1845, OP; both in McLaughlin and Beveridge, *Papers*, I, 215–220. See also Roper, *FLO*, 35–48.

6. Roper, *FLO*, 49–65. For Olmsted's correspondence during this period, see McLaughlin and Beveridge, *Papers*, I, 225–334.

7. Roper, *FLO*, 57.

8. Olmsted to John Olmsted, Feb. 29 (Mar. 1), 1850, OP; in McLaughlin and Beveridge, *Papers*, I, 337–341.

9. [Frederick Law Olmsted], *Walks and Talks of an American Farmer in England*, 2 vols. in 1 (New York: Dix, Edwards and Co., 1852), illustrated with woodcuts by M. Field from sketches by Olmsted. Although Olmsted and his companions spent several weeks in other European countries, the book deals only with his visit to England.

10. [Olmsted], *Walks and Talks*, I, 79. For Birkenhead Park, see George F. Chadwick, *The Park and the Town: Public Landscape in the 19th and 20th Centuries* (New York: Praeger, 1966), 68–71. Chadwick gives the area of the park as 125 acres and the area set aside for building lots as 101 acres.

11. [Olmsted], *Walks and Talks*, I, 81. The emphasis in Olmsted's.

12. [Olmsted], *Walks and Talks*, I, 133.

13. [Olmsted], *Walks and Talks*, I, 99.

14. An American Farmer [Frederick Law Olmsted], "The Phalanstery and Phalansterians, by an Outsider," *New York Daily Tribune*, July 29, 1852. For the North American Phalanx and Fourierism in the United States,

see Dolores Hayden, *Seven American Utopias: The Architecture of Communitarian Socialism, 1790–1975* (Cambridge, Mass.: MIT Press, 1976), 148–185. For a discussion of the influence of Fourierism on Olmsted, see Fein, *Frederick Law Olmsted,* 8–10, 15–18.

15. Frederick Law Olmsted, *A Journey in the Seaboard Slave States, with Remarks on Their Economy* (New York: Dix and Edwards, 1856); Olmsted, *A Journey Through Texas; or, a Saddle-Trip on the Southwestern Frontier* (New York: Dix, Edwards and Co., 1857); Laura Wood Roper, "Frederick Law Olmsted and the Western Texas Free-Soil Movement," *American Historical Review* 56 (Oct. 1950), 58–64; Frederick Law Olmsted, *A Journey in the Back Country* (New York: Mason Brothers, 1860). The three southern books were then condensed and published in one volume as *The Cotton Kingdom: A Traveller's Observations on Cotton and Slavery in the American Slave States* (London: Sampson Low, Son & Co.; New York: Mason Brothers, 1861 [2 vols.]). Beveridge, McLaughlin, and Schuyler, *Papers,* II, 81–321, 397–456, includes Olmsted's personal and professional correspondence concerning the South and all of his significant newpaper articles and other statements on the subject not published in the original three volumes or the 1861 abridged version. Especially useful also are the introduction (1–39) by Beveridge, and Appendix II, 463–482, which consists of annotated itineraries of Olmsted's southern journeys from 1852 to 1854. For contemporary reactions to Olmsted's southern writings, see Laura Wood Roper, "Frederick Law Olmsted in the 'Literary Republic,'" *Mississippi Valley Historical Review* 39, no. 3 (December 1952), 459–482. See also Stevenson, *Park Maker,* 112–131.

16. Beveridge, McLaughlin, and Schuyler, *Papers,* II, 322–376, includes correspondence concerning this phase of Olmsted's life. See also Roper, *FLO,* 109–123; Laura Wood Roper, "'Mr. Law,' and *Putnam's Monthly Magazine:* A Note on a Phase in the Career of Frederick Law Olmsted," *American Literature* 26 (March 1954), 88–93.

17. Frederick Law Olmsted, "The Beginning of Central Park: A Fragment of Autobiography" (ca. 1877), in Fein, *Landscape into Cityscape,* 49–62. See also Roper, *FLO,* 124–134; Henry Hope Reed and Sophia Duckworth, *Central Park: A History and a Guide* (New York: Clarkson N. Potter, 1967); and Elizabeth Barlow, *Frederick Law Olmsted's New York,* with illustrative portfolio by William Alex (New York: Praeger, 1972).

18. Olmsted, "Beginning of Central Park," in Fein, *Landscape into Cityscape,* 61.

19. Roper, *FLO,* 135–142.

20. Frederick Law Olmsted and Calvert Vaux, "Description of a Plan for the Improvement of the Central Park: 'Greensward,'" (1858; reprint, 1868), reprinted in Fein, *Landscape into Cityscape,* 63–88, quote on 67.

21. Olmsted and Vaux, "'Greensward'" in Fein, *Landscape into Cityscape,* 73–75.

22. George F. Chadwick, *The Works of Sir Joseph Paxton* (London: Architectural Press, 1961). For Edensor, see Nikolaus Pevsner, *The Buildings of England: Derbyshire* (London: Penguin Books, 1953), 129–131.

23. For Downing, see the memoir by George W. Curtis prefacing a posthumous edition of Downing's *Rural Essays* (New York: 1853), xi–lviii; and George B. Tatum, *Andrew Jackson Downing: Arbiter of American Taste, 1815–1852,* Ph.D. dissertation, Princeton University, 1950. (Ann Arbor: University Microfilms, 1950). For Vaux, see John David Sigle, comp., "Bibliography of the Life and Work of Calvert Vaux," *Papers of the American Association of Architectural Bibliographers* (Charlottesville, Va.: University Press of Virginia, 1968), V, 69–93.

24. Uvedale Price, *Three Essays on the Picturesque,* (London: J. Mawman, 1810), vol. I.

25. Price, *Three Essays,* I, 102; the emphasis is Price's. He went on to say that although "to *create* the sublime is above our contracted powers . . . we may sometimes heighten, and at all times lower its effects by art." It could be argued that Olmsted's efforts for the conservation of Yosemite, the Mariposa Big Tree Grove, and Niagara Falls were his contribution to the Sublime. Proper management of these scenic wonders would ensure that their effects would not be "lowered" by either art or neglect. The best modern discussion is Walter John Hipple, Jr., *The Beautiful, the Sublime and the Picturesque in Eighteenth-Century British Aesthetic Theory* (Carbondale, Ill.: University of Southern Illinois Press, 1957), 83–98 and 202–223. The basic primary sources, besides Price, are Edmund Burke, *A Philosophical Enquiry Into the Origins of Our Ideas of the Sublime and the Beautiful* (London: R. and J. Dodsley, 1757), and William Gilpin, *Remarks on Forest Scenery and Other Woodland Views (Relative Chiefly to Picturesque Beauty), Illustrated by Scenes of New Forest in Hampshire,* 3 vols. (London: R. Blamire, 1791).

26. Nikolaus Pevsner, "The Genesis of the Picturesque," *The Architectural Review* 96 (1944); in collaboration with S. Lang, "A Note on Sharawaggi," *The Architectural Review* 106 (1949); "Richard Payne Knight," *The Art Bulletin* 31 (1949); "Uvedale Price," *The Architectural Review* 95 (1944); all reprinted in Nikolaus Pevsner, *Studies in Art, Architecture and Design* (New York: Walker and Co. 1968), I, 78–137.

27. Humphrey Repton in *The Landscape Gardening*

and Landscape Architecture of the Late Humphrey Repton, ed. John C. Loudon (London, 1840), 30. Repton was in partnership with the architect John Nash for a few years, ending in 1802. Regent's Park in London, designed by Nash in 1811, is sometimes incorrectly attributed to Repton. See Chadwick, *The Park and the Town,* 29–32. See also John Summerson, *The Life and Work of John Nash, Architect* (Cambridge, Mass.: MIT Press, 1980), 58–74, and Edward Hyams, *Capability Brown and Humphrey Repton* (New York: Charles Scribner's Sons, 1971), 165–174.

There is a curious parallel between the early lives of Repton and Olmsted in that both tried many occupations before settling down to landscape design in their mid-thirties. (Hyams, *Brown and Repton,* 115–126.)

28. Nikolaus Pevsner, "Humphrey Repton," *The Architectural Review* 102 (1948), reprinted in Pevsner, *Studies,* I, 138–155.

29. Olmsted to Vaux, Nov. 26, 1863, OP.

30. Olmsted to Vaux, Nov. 26, 1863, OP.

31. Olmsted to Vaux, Nov. 26, 1863, OP. For Vaux's reaction to this letter, see Calvert Vaux to Henry W. Bellows, Feb. 25, 1864, OP; in Olmsted and Kimball, *Frederick Law Olmsted,* II, 78–79. Vaux accepted Olmsted's description of their respective contributions but felt that Olmsted's knowledge of "agriculture in its finer sense," which was not mentioned in Olmsted's letter, balanced his own technical knowledge in architecture.

32. Roper, *FLO,* 138–139 and 261–262.

33. For Haussmann and the rebuilding of Paris, see David H. Pinkney, *Napoleon III and the Rebuilding of Paris* (Princeton: Princeton University Press, 1958), and Howard Saalman, *Haussmann: Paris Transformed* (New York: George Braziller, 1971). The parks of Paris are best described in Jean Alphand's own book, *Les Promenades de Paris,* 2 vols. (Paris: J. Rothschild, 1873); and in William Robinson, *The Parks, Promenades and Gardens of Paris* (London, 1869).

Alphand, an engineer by profession, had begun work on the Bois de Boulogne by 1857. In a later letter Olmsted revealed that the Central Park Commissioners had considered importing either Alphand or Joseph Paxton to design the park before deciding on the competition (Olmsted to the Board of Commissioners of Central Park, Jan. 22, 1861, OP; in Olmsted and Kimball, *Frederick Law Olmsted,* II, 311). There seems to be no record that the commissioners actually approached either designer.

34. Olmsted and Kimball, *Frederick Law Olmsted,* I, 8; Olmsted to Henry Hill Elliott, September 1860, OP. In 1876–1877 Olmsted presented a similar curvilinear

plan for laying out parts of Westchester County that had recently been annexed to New York City and later became part of the Bronx. See Frederick Law Olmsted and J. James R. Croes, "Document no. 72 of the Board of the Department of Public Parks" (1876) and Olmsted and Croes, "Document no. 75 of the Board of the Department of Public Parks" (1877), both in Fein, *Landscape into Cityscape,* 349–382. The first report contains one of Olmsted's most important statements on community design and his most scathing attack on the grid system.

35. Roper, *FLO,* 156–232.

36. Roper, *FLO,* 233–290.

37. Roper, *FLO,* 271–290. Roper reconstructed the suppressed Yosemite report from an incomplete manuscript found many years later and from excerpts in contemporary newspapers. See Frederick Law Olmsted, "The Yosemite Valley and The Mariposa Big Trees: A Preliminary Report" (1865), with an Introductory Note by Laura Wood Roper, *Landscape Architecture* 43, no. 1 (October 1952), 12–25.

38. Vaux to Olmsted, June 3 [1865], OP.

39. Vaux to Olmsted, May 10, 1865, OP.

40. Olmsted to Vaux, Aug. 1, 1865, Calvert Vaux Papers, Manuscript Division, New York Public Library. This letter is not entirely consistent with other statements by Olmsted concerning his role as an artist. For two earlier letters that touch on the same matter, see Olmsted to the Board of Commissioners of the Central Park, May 20, 1858, and Jan. 22, 1861, OP; both in Olmsted and Kimball, *Frederick Law Olmsted,* II, 50 and 310, respectively.

41. Norman T. Newton, *Design on the Land* (Cambridge, Mass.: Harvard University Press, 1971), 277–278. Frederick Law Olmsted and Calvert Vaux, "Preliminary Report to the Commissioners for Laying Out a Park in Brooklyn, New York: Being a Consideration of Circumstances of Site and Other Conditions Affecting the Design of Public Pleasure Grounds" (1866), reprinted in Fein, *Landscape into Cityscape,* 95–127.

42. Frederick Law Olmsted and Calvert Vaux, "Report of the Landscape Architects and Superintendents to the President of the Board of Commissioners of Prospect Park, Brooklyn," (1868); "Document no. 50 of the Board of the Department of Public Parks: A Preliminary Study by the Landscape Architect(s) of a Design for the Laying Out of Morningside Park," (1873); "General Plan for the Improvement of Morningside Park," (1887); Frederick Law Olmsted, "Document No. 60 of the Board of the Department of Public Parks: Report of the Landscape Architect Upon the Construction of Riverside Park and Avenue," (1875); all are in Fein, *Landscape*

Into Cityscape, 129–164, 333–341, 441–457, and 343–348.

43. Roper, *FLO,* 342–343.

44. Roper, *FLO,* 344–348. See Katherine McNamara, entry on Weidenmann in *Dictionary of American Biography* (New York: Charles Scribner's Sons, 1936), X, 605–606.

45. Frederick Law Olmsted, "The Spoils of the Park: With a Few Leaves from the Deep-Laden Note-books of 'A Wholly Unpractical Man,'" (1882), in Fein, *Landscape into Cityscape,* 391–440. See also Roper, *FLO,* 348–362; and Fein, *Frederick Law Olmsted and the American Environmental Tradition,* 47–52.

III. The Boston Park Movement

1. *Gleason's Pictorial Drawing Room Companion* 4, no. 9 (Feb. 26, 1853), 137 and 143.

2. City of Boston, *Report of Committee on the Improvement of the Public Garden* (Oct. 31, 1859, City Document no. 63-1859), 7 and 3.

3. The winning design for the Public Garden was published in *Ballou's Pictorial Drawing-Room Companion* 17, no. 23 (Dec. 3, 1859), 359. George F. Meacham (1831–1917) was a member of the Harvard class of 1853. In Boston he designed the Hotel Huntington and several Back Bay houses, but no other landscape works by him are known. For Meacham, see *BET,* Dec. 4, 1917; Boston Architectural Index, Fine Arts Dept., Boston Public Library.

4. Report of James Slade, City Engineer, in City of Boston, *Report of Committee on the Public Garden* (July 9, 1860, City Doc. no. 57-1860), 5–8. Slade's earlier plan is referred to in an order of the Board of Aldermen (Aug. 8, 1859, City Doc. no. 63-1859), 2. For changes in the design of the Public Garden, see also Frederick Law Olmsted, *Notes on the Plan of Franklin Park and Related Matters,* published as a supplement to: City of Boston, *Eleventh Annual Report of the Board of Commissioners of the Department of Parks for the Year 1885* (City Doc. no. 26-1886), 76–77.

5. See Jon Alvah Peterson, "The Origins of the Comprehensive Planning Ideal in the United States, 1840–1911," Ph.D. dissertation, Harvard University, 1967, 65–133.

6. Albert Fein, "The American City: The Ideal and the Real," in *The Rise of an American Architecture,* ed. Edgar Kaufmann, Jr. (New York: Praeger, 1970), 93.

7. City of Boston, *Public Parks in the City of Boston: A Compilation of Papers, Reports and Arguments Relating to the Subject* (Oct. 21, 1880, City Doc. no. 125-1880), 3–16.

8. *BDA,* Nov. 2, 1869; [Horace William Shaler Cleveland], *The Public Grounds of Chicago: How to Give Them Character and Expression* (Chicago: Charles D. Lakey, 1869). For discussions of Cleveland (1814–1900), see Roy Lubove, introduction to H. W. S. Cleveland, *Landscape Architecture as Applied to the Wants of the West* (Pittsburgh, Pa.: University of Pittsburgh Press, 1965); Norman T. Newton, *Design on the Land: The Development of Landscape Architecture* (Cambridge, Mass.: Harvard University Press, 1971), 308–317; and John Brinckerhoff Jackson, *American Space: The Centennial Years, 1865–1876* (New York: W. W. Norton, 1972), 73–79.

9. [Cleveland], *Public Grounds of Chicago,* 9. The "we are surrounded by parks" argument, seemingly begun by Cleveland, turns up persistently until the mid 1870s. On Nov. 10, 1869, an editorial in the *BET* opposed parks for Boston, using this argument as its basis.

10. City of Boston, *Report and Accompanying Statements and Communications Relating to a Public Park for the City of Boston* (Dec. 20, 1869, City Doc. no. 123-1869); *BDA,* Nov. 6, 1869; *BET,* Nov. 6 and 10, 1869; excerpts from the testimony are also found in City Doc. no. 125-1880.

11. Reprinted in Elizur Wright, *Appeals for the Middlesex Fells and the Forests,* with a sketch of what he did for both by his daughter, Ellen Wright (Medford, Mass.: Medford Public Domain Club, 1893), 3–9; as well as City Doc. no. 123-1869. In the reprint the date is incorrectly given as 1867.

12. *BDA,* Dec. 4 and 18, 1869; Uriel H. Crocker to Joint Special Committee, in City Doc. no. 123-1869; *Map and Description of Proposed Metropolitan Park for Boston* (Boston, 1870). The last is Crocker's project published anonymously with the plan drawn probably by Col. Francis L. Lee, a Boston landscape gardener who favored the project. For Crocker, see Samuel S. Shaw, "Memoir of Uriel H. Crocker," *Proceedings of the Massachusetts Historical Society* 39 (1905), 554–565.

13. *BDA,* Dec. 18, 1869. This second letter to the *Advertiser* is unsigned but was probably written either by Crocker or by Lee for Crocker. The content closely parallels that of the first letter and the later anonymous report. The letter of Dec. 18 was accompanied by a rough plan (figure 23), which differs in a few points from that published in 1870. In 1871 a most peculiar plan was published anonymously; it proposed an avenue beginning at Warren Square and passing *through* the Old Granary Burial Ground to a point just beyond the Common; see *Boston in the Future: Its Park Grounds and a Grand Avenue through the City* (Boston: 1871).

14. *BDA,* Apr. 26, 1871, reprinted in Wright, *Appeals,* 9–12.

15. James T. Fields to Olmsted, Nov. 15 and 25,

1869, OP; Edward Everett Hale to Olmsted, Nov. 24, 1869, OP; Uriel H. Crocker to Olmsted, Feb. 13, 1870, OP; Charles G. Loring to Olmsted, Feb. 20, 1870, OP; Robert Morris Copeland to Olmsted, Dec. 3, 1869, OP; James Haughton to Olmsted, n.d. (probably early Jan. 1870), OP. Edward Everett Hale also preached a Thanksgiving Day sermon, "The People's Park," in which he quoted from a letter and a report by Olmsted (*BDA*, Nov. 20, 1869).

For Fields, see W. S. Tryon, *Parnassus Corner: A Life of James T. Fields, Publisher to Victorians* (Boston: Houghton Mifflin Co., 1963). For Hale, see Jean Holloway, *Edward Everett Hale: A Biography* (Austin: University of Texas Press, 1956). For Loring, see Charles Henry Pope, assisted by Katherine Peabody Loring, *Loring Genealogy* (Cambridge, Mass.: Murray and Emery, 1917), 264–265. For Copeland, see note 21, below. James Haughton of Haughton, Perkins and Co., Dry Goods Jobbers, is listed in the Boston City Directories from 1830 through 1873. He lived in the Back Bay and on Avon Street in Brookline. He may have moved out of state in 1873, since neither he nor his business is listed in the 1874 Directory; his death is not recorded in the Massachusetts Vital Records; and his name is not found in local obituary indexes.

16. Henry Villard to Olmsted, Dec. 8, 1869, OP; Haughton to Olmsted, Jan. 28 and Feb. 14, 1870, OP. Haughton's letter of Jan. 28 expressed concern that Olmsted had misconstrued the request to appear before the House Judiciary Committee: he had hoped that Olmsted's familiarity with the subject would make an impression on the committee, not that he would be an advocate of any particular scheme or project. Olmsted was a member and officer of the American Social Science Association. See Laura Wood Roper, *FLO: A Biography of Frederick Law Olmsted* (Baltimore: Johns Hopkins University Press, 1973), 317.

17. Olmsted, *Public Parks and the Enlargement of Towns* (Cambridge, Mass., 1870), reprinted in *Civilizing American Cities: A Selection of Frederick Law Olmsted's Writings on City Landscapes,* ed. S. B. Sutton (Cambridge, Mass.: MIT Press, 1971), 52–99; *BDA*, Feb. 26, 1870; *BET*, Feb. 26, 1870. This lecture may have been the article rejected by the *Atlantic Monthly* because it was not of general interest. According to Fields, Olmsted had sent an essay on social science instead of a brief article (Fields to Olmsted, Dec. 8, 1869, OP).

18. Olmsted, *Public Parks,* 68. Olmsted's predictions concerning the future growth of Boston can be contrasted with Cleveland's assumption that Boston's growth would remain static, in *The Public Grounds of Chicago* (portion on "What Boston May Do," quoted in the *BDA* editorial of Nov. 2, 1869).

19. Commonwealth of Massachusetts, *Acts of the General Court,* 1870, chap. 283.

20. *BDA,* Nov. 8 and 9, 1870; City Doc. no. 125-1880, 16–17.

21. *BDA,* Dec. 2, 1869. For Copeland see his obituary (*BDA,* Mar. 30, 1874); also see the reminiscences of his associate, Ernest W. Bowditch (unpublished, privately owned typescript, kindly made available to me by Nathaniel Bowditch of Philadelphia and now owned by the Essex Institute, Salem, Mass.); and Ellen Weiss, "Robert Morris Copeland's Plans for Oak Bluffs," *Journal of the Society of Architectural Historians* 34, no. 1 (March 1975), 60–66. Little is known about Copeland, who appears to have been an important figure in the development of American landscape architecture in spite of his death at a relatively early age. He was born in Roxbury in 1830 and graduated from Harvard College in 1851. His best-known executed project is Oak Bluffs on Martha's Vineyard in Massachusetts. He seems never to have executed any parks on the scale of his Boston municipal and metropolitan park projects. According to his obituary, Copeland had "done much in the way of laying out and ornamenting private grounds, but his ambition was for work on a grander scale." Bowditch's reminiscences also tell us that Copeland was the brother-in-law of Charles F. Dunbar, editor of the *Boston Daily Advertiser,* and that he wrote editorials for the paper. Except in the case of the Dec. 2, 1869, editorial, which he sent to Olmsted, and an editorial of Mar. 12, 1870, Copeland did not initial his columns, although it is tempting to attribute many editorials of this period to him. It seems almost certain, for example, that he wrote the editorial of Nov. 2, 1869, which quotes extensively from his former partner, Cleveland.

22. Robert Morris Copeland, *The Most Beautiful City in America: Essay and Plan for the Improvement of the City of Boston* (Boston: Lee and Shepard, 1872). For an excellent discussion of the essay, see Jackson, *American Space,* 131–135. Copeland wrote one other book, *Country Life: A Handbook of Agriculture, Horticulture and Landscape Gardening* (Boston: John P. Jewett and Co., 1859).

23. *BDA,* Oct. 16 and 24, 1873. Both editorials contain many passages whose content and phraseology echo *The Most Beautiful City in America.*

24. *BDA,* Oct. 24, 1873.

25. City Doc. no. 125-1880, 16–17.

26. *BDA,* June 13 and 17, 1874.

27. For Bowditch (1850–1918), see his obituary (*Milton Record,* May 25, 1918) and his unpublished reminiscences. He was born in Brookline, studied engineering at Massachusetts Institute of Technology, and later settled in Milton. There was a direct line of profes-

sional descent from H. W. S. Cleveland through R. M. Copeland to Bowditch. Cleveland and Copeland had been partners from about 1855 until Cleveland left Boston for Chicago in 1869. In 1871 Copeland asked Bowditch to do his engineering work, although they were never formally partners. After Copeland's death in 1874, Bowditch took over his landscape gardening practice. In order to preserve the firm name, he took Copeland's brother, Franklin, into partnership, but Franklin appears to have been a silent, or at least a nondesigning, partner, and this relationship was severed after a few years. Bowditch laid out the grounds of the resort community of Tuxedo Park, New York, and of many private estates in Newport, Rhode Island; Lenox, Mass.; and elsewhere. Suburban subdivisions were one of his specialties, and he designed many in and around Boston and Cleveland, Ohio. He also designed the Cleveland park system and the grounds of the State House wings in Boston. He continued with his engineering practice also, doing much surveying, including some for the Olmsted firm, and designing sewage systems for Milton and other towns. Bowditch, like Copeland, is a relatively unknown figure in the history of American environmental design whose work should be thoroughly explored and evaluated.

28. *BDA,* June 24, 1874.

29. Ernest W. Bowditch, "Rural Parks for Boston" (Boston, Jan. 9, 1875).

30. For Paris, see Chapter II, note 33, and Sigfried Giedion, *Space, Time and Architecture: The Growth of a New Tradition,* 5th ed. (Cambridge, Mass.: Harvard University Press, 1967), 739–775. See also Baron Georges Haussmann, *Mémoires,* (Paris: Victor-Havard, 1890), II, 232–234, for an account of one of Haussmann's few unexecuted projects: a continuous greenbelt to replace the fortifications of 1840 and connect the Bois de Boulogne and the Bois de Vincennes. For Vienna, see E. A. Gutkind, *International History of City Development,* vol. II, *Urban Development in the Alpine and Scandinavian Countries* (New York: Free Press, 1965), 64 and 88; and Carl E. Schorske, *Fin-De-Siècle Vienna: Politics and Culture* (New York: Alfred A. Knopf, 1980), 24–115.

31. Robert Fleming Gourlay, *Plans for Beautifying New York and For Enlarging and Improving the City of Boston* (Boston: Crocker and Brewster, 1844), 37.

32. Cleveland, *Public Grounds.* Portions on "What Boston May Do" were quoted in [R. M. Copeland?], Editorial, *BDA,* Nov. 2, 1869.

33. Michael P. Conzen and George K. Lewis, *Boston: A Geographical Portrait* (Cambridge, Mass.: Ballinger, 1976), 5–9. Besides considering the historical and geographical sources of the Copeland/Bowditch plan, one should probably not discount the universal psychological appeal of the circle as a symbol of wholeness and completion.

34. Davenport had a certain vested interest in the matter, since he was the principal owner of the Cambridge riverfront property. See Cambridge Historical Commission, *Report Three: Cambridgeport* (Cambridge, Mass.: Cambridge Historical Commission, 1971), 31–32. Because of successive alterations, the chronology of Davenport's various plans (generally undated) is very difficult to disentangle.

35. City of Boston, *Report on the Establishment of a Public Park* (Dec. 3, 1874, City Doc. no. 105-1874).

36. City Doc. no. 125-1880, 22–34; George A. Shaw, *Speech in the Common Council of the City of Boston, March 25, 1875, on the Subject of Public Parks* (Boston, 1875). For Hugh O'Brien, see *The Story of the Irish in Boston,* ed. James Bernard Cullen (Boston: James B. Cullen and Co., 1889), 216–218, For Shaw, see his obituary (*BET,* July 22, 1882).

37. Commonwealth of Massachusetts, *Acts of the General Court,* 1875, chap. 185.

38. Roger B. Merriman, *Memoir of Charles Henry Dalton* (Cambridge, Mass., 1909).

39. *BET* and *BDA,* Aug. 17, 18, 19, and 20, 1886. In the summer of 1886, Gray was found to have embezzled a total of about $500,000 from three corporations of which he was treasurer: the Atlantic Cotton Mills, the Indian Orchard Mills, and the Ocean Mills. This revelation came as a complete surprise to everyone, including presumably Charles Dalton, who was then president of the first two companies. On Aug. 16, 1886, Gray disappeared. His body was found a few days later in the Blue Hills, where he had shot himself.

40. T. Jefferson Coolidge, *Autobiography* (Boston: Houghton Mifflin, 1923); John T. Morse, Jr., "Memoir of T. Jefferson Coolidge," *Massachusetts Historical Society Proceedings* 54 (October 1920–June 1921), 141–149.

41. RBPD, July 30, 1875–Mar. 16, 1876. The records of the Boston Park Department in its first decade are very terse, seldom giving more than the barest facts. The newspapers give supplementary information on the hearings, with some of the testimony printed verbatim: *BDA,* Sept. 10, 1875 (general hearing); *BDA,* Oct. 15, 1875 (Crocker); *BDA,* Oct. 22, 1875 (Bowditch); *BDA,* Oct. 30, 1875 (general hearing); *BDA,* Nov. 5, 1875 (Richard H. Dana on the Charles River Embankment); *BDA,* Nov. 23, 1875 (G. Washington Warren on the Back Bay) and *BDA,* Nov. 27, 1875 (Shebnah Rich on the South Bay).

42. Dalton to Olmsted, Oct. 18, 1875, OP; Dalton to Olmsted, Nov. 3, 1875, OP; Olmsted to Dalton, Nov. 5, 1875, OP; and Dalton to Olmsted, Nov. 15, 1875,

OP. (The two men may have met earlier in connection with the Sanitary Commission, but there seems to be no record of such a meeting.) Coolidge describes the events of these months in his *Autobiography,* 81–82. The following spring Dalton requested a bill from Olmsted, but Olmsted's reply indicated that he did not feel sure that Dalton regarded his visits "thus far as 'business.'" The charge for these preliminary visits may have been incorporated into a later payment. (Olmsted to Dalton, Apr. 8, 1876, and Dalton to Olmsted, Apr. 11, 1876, OAP). For Olmsted's informal relationship with the park commission at this time, see also Olmsted to T. L. Livermore, Feb. 4, 1892, OP.

43. RBPD, Mar. 31 and Apr. 1, 1876; Olmsted to Dalton, Apr. 8, 1876, OP.

44. City of Boston, *Second Report of Board of Commissioners of the Department of Parks* (Apr. 24, 1876, City Doc. no. 42–1876), reprinted in *Franklin Park Coalition Bulletin* (January 1981, whole issue). The report contains an acknowledgment (38) of Olmsted's advice, which had been sought on "the general scheme, rather than upon the minor details." Dalton's authorship is given by Merriman ("Memoir of Charles Henry Dalton," 21) and by Coolidge (*Autobiography,* 82). The commissioners' first annual report (City of Boston, *First Report of the Board of Commissioners of the Department of Parks* [Jan. 10, 1876, City Doc. no. 12-1876]) had been little more than a statement of progress.

45. *Parks for the People: Proceedings of a Public Meeting held at Faneuil Hall, June 7, 1876* (Boston, 1876), quotation from speech of Richard Dana, Jr.

46. City of Boston, *Report of the Joint Standing Committee on Common and Public Grounds on the Establishment of Public Parks* (June 26, 1876, City Doc. no. 72-1876).

47. City Doc. no. 125-1880, 42-156. A major speech by Hugh O'Brien was published separately (Hugh O'Brien, *Public Parks; Speech in the Board of Aldermen, May 21, 1877* [Boston, 1877]); H. H. Richardson to Olmsted, Nov. 26, 1876, office archives of Shepley, Bulfinch, Richardson and Abbott, Boston; Proceedings of the Common Council of Nov. 16, 1876, probably sent to Olmsted by Dalton, OP; City of Boston, *Second Annual Report of the Board of Commissioners of the Department of Parks for the City of Boston, for the year 1876* (Jan. 11, 1877, City Doc. no. 10-1877); RBPD, Feb. 2, 1877 (the Park Commission did not meet between Feb. 24 and July 30, 1877); H. H. Richardson to Olmsted, May 13, 1877, OAP.

Another aspect of O'Brien's policies as alderman during these stringent times is given in Walter Muir Whitehill, *Boston Public Library: A Centennial History* (Cambridge, Mass.: Harvard University Press, 1956),

104–109. O'Brien apparently justified his support of appropriations for parks by extreme economy in other areas, notably the Public Library. I am grateful to the late Francis Moloney for bringing this source to my attention.

48. City Doc. no. 125-1880, 135–156; John C. Olmsted, "The Boston Park System," *Transactions of the American Society of Landscape Architects* (1899–1908), 45–46; RBPD, July 30–Dec. 29, 1877; City of Boston, *Sixth Report of the Board of Commissioners of the Department of Parks for the City of Boston* (Dec. 29, 1877, City Doc. no. 104-1877).

49. RBPD, Jan. 8–Mar. 1, 1878; City of Boston, *Third Annual Report of the Board of Commissioners of the Department of Parks for the City of Boston for the Year 1877* (Jan. 28, 1877, City Doc. no. 16-1878); Dalton to Olmsted, May 6, 1878, OP; Olmsted to Dalton, May 8 and 13, 1878, OP (quotation from letter of May 13; the emphasis is Olmsted's).

50. Olmsted to Dalton, May 13, 1878, OP.

51. RBPD, June 3, 1878; *BDA,* May 30 and 31, 1878; *BET,* May 31 and June 4, 1878; "The Boston Park Plans," *American Architect and Building News* (June 8, 1878), 202; Ernest Bowditch, unpublished reminiscences. The Boston City Directory for 1878 gives the following occupations and addresses for the few competitors who are mentioned by name in the above articles:

Bowditch and Copeland: E. W. Bowditch, landscape gardener, 60 Devonshire, and Franklin Copeland, landscape gardener, 13 Doane.
Hermann Grundel, florist, 3053 Washington.
Frederick M. Hersey, civil engineer, 7 Court Square.
Lee and Curtis: Francis L. Lee, landscape gardener, and Joseph H. Curtis, civil engineer, 16 Pemberton Square.
George F. Loring, draughtsman, City Surveyor's Office, City Hall.

The article in the *American Architect* also mentions the plan of Edward P. Adams of Medford, who is not listed in the Boston Directory. In his reminiscences, Ernest Bowditch incorrectly gives a "Mr. Doogue" as the winner of the competition. This may have been William Doogue, who later became Superintendent of Common and Public Grounds. George Meacham, who had designed the Public Garden, was still practicing architecture, but no plan by him is mentioned.

IV. Pioneering Projects: The Fens and the Arboretum

1. Frederick Law Olmsted and Calvert Vaux, "Report of the Landscape Architects and Superintendents to the President of the Board of Commissioners of Prospect

Park, Brooklyn" (1868); "Document no. 50 of the Board of the Department of Public Parks: A Preliminary Study by the Landscape Architect(s) of a Design for the Laying Out of Morningside Park" (1873); "General Plan for the Improvement of Morningside Park" (1887); all in Albert Fein, ed., *Landscape into Cityscape: Frederick Law Olmsted's Plans for a Greater New York City* (Ithaca, N.Y.: Cornell University Press, 1968), 129–164, 333–341, 441–457.

2. Victoria Post Ranney, *Olmsted in Chicago* (Chicago: R. R. Donnelley and Sons, 1972), 15–39.

3. Laura Wood Roper, *FLO: A Biography of Frederick Law Olmsted* (Baltimore: Johns Hopkins University Press, 1973), 384–385. See also August Heckscher, *Open Spaces: The Life of American Cities* (New York: Harper and Row, 1977), 203–206. For Dorsheimer, see M[illedge] L. B[onham], Jr. entry on Dorsheimer, *Dictionary of American Biography* (New York: Charles Scribner's Sons, 1936), III, 387. Dorsheimer was associated with at least five H. H. Richardson commissions, three of which were also Olmsted collaborations (James F. O'Gorman, *Henry Hobson Richardson and His Office: Selected Drawings* [Cambridge, Mass.: Harvard College Library, 1974], 122–124, 188–190).

4. Roper, *FLO,* 361–362.

5. Roper, *FLO,* 364–365.

6. Information on the history of the Back Bay salt marsh is found in John and Mildred Teal, *Life and Death of the Salt Marsh* (New York: Audubon/Ballantine, 1969), 234–239. The section on the birth and death of a hypothetical New England salt marsh (7–49) is also useful.

7. John C. Olmsted, "The Boston Park System," *Transactions of the American Society of Landscape Architects* 1 (1899–1908), 46; Julius Gy. Fabos, Gordon T. Milde, and V. Michael Weinmayr, *Frederick Law Olmsted, Senior: Founder of Landscape Architecture in America* (University of Massachusetts Press, 1968), 57–58; Roy Mann, *Rivers in the City* (New York: Praeger, 1973), 205–207.

8. Augustine H. Folsom (1845–1926) lived and had his photographic studio on Parker Hill in Roxbury. Folsom seemed to specialize in views of suburban houses in and around Boston, photographed with remarkable sensitivity to the building's total setting. The largest collection of Folsom's photographs is at the Print Department of the Boston Public Library.

9. The most valuable source for the early history of the design of the Back Bay Fens is an after-dinner talk by Olmsted to the Boston Society of Architects (of which he had been made an honorary member) in 1886: "The [illegible] Problem and Its Solution," n.d., OP (draft).

Olmsted addressed the society on April 2, 1886, according to William D. Austin, "A History of the Boston Society of Architects in the Nineteenth Century" (Aug. 1942), II, chap. 13, p. 11 (unpublished manuscript at the Boston Athenaeum). Austin also says of this meeting that twenty members were present at dinner and four after dinner. The complete text of the talk is found in Cynthia Ridgway Zaitzevsky, "Frederick Law Olmsted and the Boston Park System," doctoral dissertation, Harvard University, 1975, Appendix IV, 295–306.

10. RBPD, June 3, 1878.

11. Olmsted, "The Problem," OP; Olmsted to Dalton, Nov. 5, 1878, OP; Olmsted to Davis, Dec. 26, 1878, OP; RBPD, Dec. 10, 1878. In the records of the Boston Park Department, no commission meetings are noted between Sept. 27 and Dec. 10, 1878, probably meaning that they met only informally.

12. Frederick Law Olmsted, "Report of the Landscape Architect Advisory," in City of Boston, *Fifth Annual Report of the Board of Commissioners of the Department of Parks for the Year 1879* (City Doc. no. 15-1880), 6–16; Olmsted to Dalton, Dec. 9, 1879, OP. *The American Architect and Building News* (Mar. 20, 1880), 117–118, received Olmsted's plan and report for the Back Bay with little enthusiasm.

13. Olmsted, "Report of the Landscape Architect Advisory," in City Doc. no. 15-1880, 6–16.

14. Olmsted, "Report of the Landscape Architect Advisory," in City Doc. no. 15-1880, 12.

15. Frederick Law Olmsted, "Report of the Landscape Architect Advisory," in City of Boston, *Ninth Annual Report of the Board of Commissioners of the Department of Parks for the Year 1883* (City Doc. no. 9-1884), 16–20; Frederick Law Olmsted, "Report of the Landscape Architect Advisory," in City of Boston, *Tenth Annual Report of the Board of Commissioners of the Department of Parks for the Year 1884* (City Doc. no. 7-1885), 13–16.

16. City of Boston, *Annual Reports of the Board of Commissioners of the Department of Parks,* 1900–1910, especially the reports of John A. Pettigrew, superintendent. John C. Olmsted, "Verbatim Notes and Summary Notes of a Perambulatory Tour through the Boston Park System with Pettigrew," 1910, typescript (xerox) FLL; Olmsted Brothers, "Report," in City of Boston, *Annual Report of the Board of Commissioners of the Department of Parks for the Year 1910,* 48–62.

17. Arthur A. Shurtleff in consultation with Olmsted Brothers, "Report on the Fens," Nov. 1921, typescript, FLL; Arthur A. Shurtleff, *Special Report* (Boston: Dept. of Parks, 1925), 8–13; Arthur A. Shurtleff, *Future Parks, Playgrounds and Parkways* (Boston: Dept. of

Parks, 1925), 47; Mann, *Rivers in the City,* 215. The changes in the Back Bay Fens after 1895 are covered in more detail in Zaitzevsky, "Olmsted and the Boston Park System," 152–159. For the damming of the Charles River, see "Boston's Charles River Basin: An Engineering Landmark," *Journal of the Boston Society of Civil Engineers Section/ASCE 67,* no. 4 (Summer 1981, special issue).

18. It is to be hoped that some of the effects of almost three-quarters of a century of neglect and misunderstanding of this major segment of the Boston park system can yet be reversed. In recent years the Boston Park Department has made efforts to improve maintenance, and it has adopted a new master plan for the Fens done by Carol R. Johnson and Associates, Landscape Architects, of Cambridge.

19. S. B. Sutton, *Charles Sprague Sargent and the Arnold Arboretum* (Cambridge, Mass.: Harvard University Press, 1970), 3–8.

20. Sutton, *Sargent,* 8–21.

21. Hugh M. Raup, "Notes on the Early Uses of Land Now in the Arnold Arboretum," *Bulletin of Popular Information,* Arnold Arboretum, series 4, vol. 3, nos. 9–12 (Dec. 23, 1935), 41–74.

22. The "worn-out farm" quote is found in C. S. Sargent, "The First Fifty Years of the Arnold Arboretum," in *Journal of the Arnold Arboretum* 3, no. 3 (January 1923), 130. The public use of Bussey Farm is mentioned in Harriet Manning Whitcomb, *Annals and Reminiscences of Jamaica Plain* (Cambridge, Mass.: Riverside Press, 1897), 52–53, 57. W. H. Channing also describes an expedition to Bussey's woods with Margaret Fuller (R. W. Emerson, W. H. Channing and J. F. Clarke, *Memoirs of Margaret Fuller Ossoli* [1884; reprint ed., New York: Burt Franklin, 1972], II, 34–35).

23. James Arnold's "suburban seat" at New Bedford was visited by A. J. Downing (Downing, *A Treatise on the Theory and Practice of Landscape Gardening adapted to North America,* 6th ed. [New York: A. O. Moore & Co., 1859], 41). For Emerson, see Robert C. Waterston, *Memoir of George Barrell Emerson, LL.D.* (Cambridge, Mass.: John Wilson and Son, 1884). Emerson was related to Arnold by marriage.

24. George B. Emerson to the Reverend Dr. Peabody, Mar. 31, 1869, Harvard University Archives; quoted in full in Hugh M. Raup, "The Genesis of the Arnold Arboretum," *Bulletin of Popular Information,* Arnold Arboretum, series 4, vol. 8, no. 1 (Apr. 26, 1940), 7.

25. Sutton, *Sargent,* 22–49; A. Hunter Dupree, *Asa Gray, 1810–1888* (Cambridge, Mass.: Harvard University Press, 1959), 343–344, 348–350.

26. Text of the Arnold indenture in Sargent, "The First Fifty Years," 127–129.

27. Sargent to Olmsted, June 26, 1874, OP. See also Sargent to Olmsted, July 5, 1874, OP.

28. Olmsted to Sargent, July 8, 1874, OP.

29. In his history ("The First Fifty Years," 130–131), Sargent stated that Olmsted was laying out the Boston park system in 1873 and that Olmsted had originated the idea of including the Arboretum—errors that have been passed along by all later historians of the Arboretum, including Sutton. Lapse of memory after fifty years seems the only explanation, since the original correspondence is unambiguous. For Sargent's fund raising, see Sutton, *Sargent,* 53–54.

30. C. S. Sargent, "Report," in City Doc. no. 15-1880, 22.

31. Sutton, *Sargent,* 55–63.

32. C. S. Sargent, "Report of the Director of the Arnold Arboretum," in *Annual Reports of the President of Harvard College,* 1877–1886. The drawings for the Arboretum at the Olmsted National Historic Site, Brookline, are discussed in Cynthia Zaitzevsky, "Report," in William Alex, "Survey-Inventory of the Frederick Law Olmsted Office, Estate and Contents, Brookline, Massachusetts," submitted to the National Endowment for the Arts, 1973–1974, 86–104.

33. C. S. Sargent, "Report," in City Doc. no. 15-1880, 21–22. Olmsted's only published discussion of the Arboretum consists of a few sentences in a report on the entire park system: "Report of the Landscape Architect Advisory," in *Seventh Annual Report of the Board of Commissioners of the Department of Parks for the City of Boston for the Year 1881* (City Doc. no. 16-1882), 27, reprinted in S. B. Sutton, ed., *Civilizing American Cities: A Selection of Frederick Law Olmsted's Writings on City Landscapes* (Cambridge, Mass.: MIT Press, 1971), 226.

34. Holm Lea is described, and the design of its grounds attributed to Sargent, in M. G. Van Rensselaer, "A Suburban Country Place," *Century Magazine* 54, no. 1 (May 1897), 3–17. This is probably also the estate referred to in M. G. Van Rensselaer, *Art Out-Of-Doors* (New York: Charles Scribner's Sons, 1893), 35–39. By the late 1890s Sargent had virtually transformed the estate begun by his father. Holm Lea also incorporated the twenty-acre property of Thomas Lee on Jamaica Pond, which in Downing's day had been famous for its rare imported rhododendrons and mountain laurel (Downing, *Theory and Practice,* 40).

35. The establishment of scientific arboretums in England also evolved from the parks and private tree collections of wealthy, horticulturally inclined amateurs. See

William T. Stearn, "From Medieval Park to Modern Arboretum: The Arnold Arboretum and Its Historic Background," *Arnoldia* 32, no. 5 (September 1972), 173–197.

36. O'Gorman, *Richardson and His Office,* 4, 176.

37. Van Rensselaer, *Art Out-Of-Doors,* rev. ed. (1925), 444–445. For this edition, Mrs. Van Rensselaer added three chapters, including one on the Arnold Arboretum, under the heading "Thirty Years Later."

V. "Franklin Park and Related Matters"

1. Frederick Law Olmsted, *Notes on the Plan of Franklin Park and Related Matters,* published as a supplement to City of Boston, *Eleventh Annual Report of the Board of Commissioners of the Department of Parks for the Year 1885* (City Doc. no. 26-1886). Olmsted's *Notes* are reprinted in part in S. B. Sutton, ed., *Civilizing American Cities: A Selection of Frederick Law Olmsted's Writings on City Landscapes* (Cambridge, Mass.: MIT Press, 1971), 233–262. Parts II and III are reprinted in *Franklin Park Coalition Bulletin,* nos. 4 and 5 (November 1978–January 1979), whole issue. The quote is from the original edition, p. 42. (Cited hereafter as *Notes.*)

2. City of Boston, *Second Report of Board of Commissioners of the Department of Parks* (April 24, 1876, City Doc. no. 42-1876), 30–31, reprinted in *Franklin Park Coalition Bulletin* (January 1981, whole issue), 27–28.

3. City Doc. no. 42-1876, 31.

4. Olmsted to Charles H. Dalton, May 17, 1881, OP.

5. John Koren, *Boston, 1822 to 1922, The Story of Its Government and Principal Activities During One Hundred Years* (Boston, 1922; City Doc. no. 39-1922), 6–15; James M. Bugbee, *The City Government of Boston* (Baltimore, Johns Hopkins University, 1887), 44–56.

6. See Geoffrey Blodgett, *The Gentle Reformers: Massachusetts Democrats in the Cleveland Era* (Cambridge, Mass.: Harvard University Press, 1966), for a vivid and detailed account of the events of 1884 and their consequences. For further information on Patrick Maguire, see James Bernard Cullen, ed., *The Story of the Irish in Boston* (Boston: James B. Cullen and Co., 1889), 412–413, and Blodgett, *Gentle Reformers,* 59, 141–144; for John F. Andrew, see Edmund March Wheelwright, "Memoir of the Hon. John Forrester Andrew, LL.B.," *Publications of the Colonial Society of Massachusetts,* vol. III, *Transactions, 1895–1897* (Boston,

1900), 351–374, and Blodgett, *Gentle Reformers,* 25–26, 64–65; for Benjamin Dean, see *South Boston Bulletin, Apr. 17, 1897.*

7. Blodgett, *Gentle Reformers,* 61–63, 141; For the Irish in Boston, see also Barbara Miller Solomon, *Ancestors and Immigrants: A Changing New England Tradition* (Cambridge, Mass.: Harvard University Press, 1956), especially chap. 3.

8. Charles Eliot Norton to Olmsted, Mar. 5, 1885, OP. For Norton, see Kermit Vanderbilt, *Charles Eliot Norton, Apostle of Culture in a Democracy* (Cambridge, Mass.: Harvard University Press, 1959).

9. Olmsted to Norton, May 2, 1885, OP; Norton to Olmsted, May 3, 1885, OP; Olmsted to William McMillan, Mar. 16, 1885, OP. For the political background of the Boston parks and of Franklin Park in particular, see Geoffrey Blodgett, "Frederick Law Olmsted: Landscape Architecture as Conservative Reform," *Journal of American History* 62, no. 4 (March 1976), 883–887.

10. RBPD, Apr. 29 and July 22, 1885; Olmsted to Norton, July 27, 1885, OP; Norton to Olmsted, July 30, 1885, OP.

11. RBPD, Sept. 12, 1885.

12. Frederick Law Olmsted, "Remarks about a Difficulty Peculiar to the Park Department of City Governments, Addressed, upon Invitation, to the New England Club, 26th January 1889," in City of Boston, *Fourteenth Annual Report of the Board of Commissioners of the Department of Parks for the Year 1888* (City Doc. no. 72-1889), 34.

13. Commonwealth of Massachusetts, *Acts of the General Court,* 1875, chap. 185, sec. 5–12; City Doc. no. 42-1876, 6–10.

14. The records of the Boston Park Department during the entire period attest to the expensive suits over land which, to judge from the minutes of their meetings, absorbed a very large part of the commissioners' time. See especially [Samuel Elwell Sawyer], *History of the West Roxbury Park: How Obtained, Disregard of Private Rights, Absolute Injustice, Arbitrary Laws, Right of Eminent Domain, 1873–1887* (Gloucester, Mass., 1887). Eventually, it became necessary to raise money under the Park Loan to pay for much of the construction as well as for acquisition of land. For the loans outside the city debt limit, see Wheelwright, "John F. Andrew," 358–359, and Nathan Matthews, Jr., *The City Government of Boston, A Valedictory Address to the Members of the City Council, January 5, 1895* (Boston, 1895), 112–116. The 1886 loan was held up in the board of aldermen until January 1887 because, according to Olmsted, the Republican aldermen were afraid to trust

the Democratic commissioners with the funds. During
this period, work was suspended on Franklin Park and
all the other parks. Olmsted to Charles Eliot, Feb. 25
and July 20, 1886, OP; City of Boston, *Twelfth Annual
Report of the Board of Commissioners of the Department of Parks for the Year 1886* (City Doc. no. 24-
1887), 13–14; RBPD, Jan. 7, 1887.

15. RBPD, Jan. 30 and Feb. 10, 1886.

16. *Notes, 51–52.*

17. *Notes, 57–58.* Olmsted described the Ante-Park
as a "fore-court, portico, and reception room, with
minor apartments opening from them for various special
uses." (*Notes, 52*). The concept is similar to that expressed repeatedly by the Renaissance architect and
theorist Leone Battista Alberti in his ten books on architecture (originally *De Re Aedificatoria*), published in English by T. Edlin (London, 1726); Alberti applied the
concept both to individual houses and to city plans. The
Franklin Park plan is unusual even for Olmsted in its extensive provision for a wide variety of recreational functions as well as for enjoyment of rural scenery, the primary purpose. The other activities are carefully grouped
in hierarchical order so that they do not impinge on the
central space (the great meadow) of the Country Park.

18. *Notes, 58–59.*

19. *Notes. 53–57.* Even on the periphery of the
Country Park—in the Wilderness, on Schoolmaster Hill,
and in Ellicottdale—Olmsted provided for relatively
quiet recreational uses, such as horseback riding, picnicking, and lawn tennis. He apparently did not see these as
conflicting with enjoyment of scenery.

20. *Notes, 49–50.* For Emerson's connection with
the site, see Richard Heath, "Ralph Waldo Emerson in
Franklin Park," *Franklin Park Coalition Bulletin* no. 12
(May 1980, whole issue).

21. *Notes, 63–65.*

22. *Notes, 62–63.*

23. George F. Chadwick, *The Park and the Town:
Public Landscape in the 19th and 20th Centuries* (New
York: Praeger, 1966), 68–71. The scale should be borne
in mind when comparing the two parks: Birkenhead is
less than half the size of Franklin Park, thus making its
plan appear simpler, at least on paper.

24. Chadwick, *The Park and the Town,* 68. At Birkenhead, Regent's Park, and elsewhere in England it was
common practice to set aside space on the borders and
even within the park for house lots, the sale of which
would help pay for the park. Olmsted's view was that
private development just outside the park would occur
naturally and that the additional revenue from taxes
would defray park costs.

25. John C. Olmsted, "The Boston Park System,"

*Transactions of the American Society of Landscape Ar-
chitects* 1 (1899–1908), 52.

26. Norman T. Newton, *Design on the Land: The
Development of Landscape Architecture* (Cambridge,
Mass.: Harvard University Press, 1971), 299. The high
hill in the heart of the central open space in Franklin
Park that Newton refers to does indeed detract from the
effectiveness of that space. However, the hill does not
appear on the 1884 topographical map or on any of the
early plans and is therefore neither a natural hill nor part
of Olmsted's concept. Although the grading plans for the
reconstruction of the golf course in the 1930s have not
yet been discovered, it seems likely that the hill was
added at that time.

27. *Notes, 62.*

28. For such a point of view, see John Brinckerhoff
Jackson, *American Space: The Centennial Years, 1865–
1876* (New York: W. W. Norton and Co. 1972), 217–
218, and Sam Bass Warner, Jr., review of Laura Wood
Roper, *FLO: A Biography of Frederick Law Olmsted,* in
New Republic 170, no. 29 (Mar. 23, 1974), 29–30.

29. Frederick Law Olmsted, *Public Parks and the
Enlargement of Towns* (Cambridge, Mass.: Riverside
Press, 1870), reprinted in Sutton, *Civilizing American
Cities,* 52–99.

30. Frederick Law Olmsted, *Mount Royal* (New
York: G. P. Putnam, 1881), reprinted in part in Sutton,
Civilizing American Cities, 197–220.

31. Olmsted, *Mount Royal,* in Sutton, *Civilizing
American Cities,* 219.

32. *Notes, 42.*

33. *Notes, 42.*

34. *Notes, 43.*

35. *Notes, 43.*

36. *Notes, 43.*

37. *Notes, 46.*

38. Olmsted, *Public Parks,* in Sutton, *Civilizing
American Cities,* 81. For an excellent discussion of the
pastoral ideal as shown chiefly in literature, see Leo
Marx, *The Machine in the Garden: Technology and
the Pastoral Ideal in America* (London: Oxford University Press, 1964).

39. Charles E. Beveridge, "Frederick Law Olmsted's
Theory of Landscape Design," *19th Century* 3, no. 2
(Summer 1977), 39–40, and Charles E. Beveridge, *Fred-
erick Law Olmsted, the Formative Years, 1822–1865,*
Ph.D. dissertation, University of Wisconsin, 1966 (Ann
Arbor: University Microfilms, 1969). 15–17. See also Jo-
hann Georg ritter von Zimmerman, *Solitude Considered,
with Respect to Its Influence Upon the Mind and the
Heart,* trans. J. B. Mercier (New London, Conn., 1807)
and Horace Bushnell, "Unconscious Influence," in *Ser-*

mons for the New Life (New York: Charles Scribner, 1858), 186–205.

40. William Wordsworth, "Lines Composed A Few Miles Above Tintern Abbey on Revisiting the Banks of the Wye During A Tour, July 13, 1798," first published in William Wordsworth and Samuel Taylor Coleridge, *Lyrical Ballads* (1798), lines 41–49.

41. Wordsworth, "Tintern Abbey," lines 30, 25–26.

42. Wordsworth, "Tintern Abbey," lines 76–78, 158.

43. Ralph Waldo Emerson, "Nature," first published anonymously in 1836, collected in *Nature, Addresses and Lectures, AND Letters and Social Aims* (Boston: Houghton Mifflin, 1929), 16.

44. Emerson, "Nature," 8.

45. Laura Wood Roper, *FLO: A Biography of Frederick Law Olmsted* (Baltimore: Johns Hopkins University Press, 1973), xiv.

46. Olmsted, *Public Parks,* in Sutton, *Civilizing American Cities,* 75. Sam Bass Warner, Jr., has proposed a theory describing three American attitudes toward nature, based on different branches of the Judeo-Christian religious tradition. One attitude, based on Genesis 1:28, gives man dominion over the rest of creation. The second attitude, expressed in the writings of the nineteenth-century romantics and transcendentalists and still alive today, contrasts man and nature, city and country, to the disadvantage, Warner feels, of both man and city. A third attitude, based on Isaiah, 11:6–8, stresses man's harmony with nature rather than his conquest of or separation from it. Warner groups Olmsted with the romantics and transcendentalists (all of them, in his view, anti-man and anti-city). While Olmsted's attitude toward nature obviously has much in common with that of the romantics and transcendentalists, it should be clear from the cited passage and from many similar statements by Olmsted that he belongs in the third category, "the Peaceable Kingdom" (Sam Bass Warner, Jr., *The Way We Really Live: Social Change in Metropolitan Boston since 1920* [Boston: Trustees of the Public Library, 1977], 52–55).

47. Olmsted, *Public Parks,* in Sutton, *Civilizing American Cities,* 65–66.

48. Frederick Law Olmsted and Calvert Vaux, "Preliminary Report to the Commissioners for Laying Out a Park in Brooklyn, New York: Being a Consideration of Circumstances of Site and Other Conditions Affecting the Design of Public Pleasure Grounds" (1866), in Albert Fein, ed., *Landscape into Cityscape: Frederick Law Olmsted's Plans for a Greater New York City* (Ithaca, N.Y.: Cornell University Press, 1968), 100–101.

49. *Notes,* 106. See Beveridge, "Olmsted's Theory of Landscape Design," 39–40, and Charles C. McLaughlin,

"Frederick Law Olmsted's Parks: Antiques or Urban Necessities?" *National Association for Olmsted Parks Newsletter* 1, no. 1 (Fall/Winter 1980–1981), 7–10.

50. Franklin's heirs contested the will, and there was lengthy litigation. Eventually, the money went to found the Franklin Union, now the Franklin Institute, a technical school (*Boston Globe,* Jan. 24, 1979). Olmsted planned only a limited zoo of native animals, to be located in Long Crouch Woods, and in the late 1880s the city entered negotiations with the Boston Natural History Society for a lease of the land. Even at this early date, Olmsted was concerned about the type of zoo planned by the society (Olmsted to Mr. Ross, Mar. 5, 1889, OP; Olmsted to A. Hyatt, Mar. 24, 1889, OP; Olmsted to Prof. Hyatt, May 6, 1889, OP; Olmsted to M. D. Ross, n.d., OP). In these letters he reiterated that only native animals should be used and that the border of unbuilt land in Long Crouch Woods should be 100 feet wide. ("Even a child would enjoy more peeping into an old rabbit warren," he wrote in the letter of March 24 to Mr. Hyatt, "than in staring into a cage of sulky lions.") Apparently nothing came of these negotiations. In 1911 Arthur A. Shurtleff designed an extensive zoo in the Long Crouch Woods, Greeting, Deer Park, and Sargent's Field areas, which was only partially constructed (Arthur A. Shurtleff, "The Franklin Park 'Zoo,' Boston," *Architectural Review* [March 1912], 28–32). Currently the Boston Zoological Society is planning a major expansion within these areas.

51. RBPD, Dec. 5, 1890.

52. Olmsted to Thomas L. Livermore, Feb. 4, 1892, OP. Although the Olmsted firm did studies and prepared a general plan for Franklin Field in 1891 (before the land was actually purchased by the city), draining the peat meadow that formed a large part of it proved more difficult than expected, and the plan was not adopted immediately. The firm's later studies for Franklin Field are limited to site plans for athletic buildings and so on, and it is unclear whether the general plan was ever adopted. The electrification of Boston's street railway system in the late 1880s may have been a factor in the city's final decision to purchase Franklin Field, although it obviously came too late to influence the choice of the Franklin Park site. An existing horse railway line, the Highland Street Railway, terminated at Grove Hall in Dorchester and then was extended to Franklin Park. In 1887 this line was consolidated with the West End Street Railway Company and electrified. By 1898 another extension was made to Franklin Field. See Geoffrey Blodgett, "Frederick Law Olmsted: Landscape Architecture as Conservative Reform," *Journal of American History* 62, no. 4 (March 1976), 885–886.

53. August Heckscher with Phyllis Robinson, *Open*

Spaces: The Life of American Cities (New York: Harper and Row, 1977), 161–191.

54. A study done in 1981 by the Boston Police Department shows that Franklin Park's crime rate is no higher than in the other parts of the system. Most of the violent crime takes place in the late evening or early morning hours and has little to do with normal daytime use of the park. I am grateful to John Herbert of the Boston Police Department for making this study available to me.

55. Olmsted to Calvert Vaux, Nov. 26, 1863, OP.

56. William H. C. Walker and Willard Brewer Walker, *A History of World's End* (Milton, Mass.: Trustees of Reservations, 1973). World's End and the Trustees of Reservations are discussed more thoroughly in Chapter VIII.

57. The Coalition's membership includes local organizations and individuals, as well as many out-of-towners. It has built on the work done by the Franklin Park Advisory Committee in the early 1970s and particularly on the pioneering efforts of Elma Lewis, director of the Elma Lewis School of Fine Arts. Besides lobbying for better conditions in the park, the Coalition publishes a bulletin and a newsletter and sponsors lectures and slide presentations. I am grateful to Richard Heath, president of the Franklin Park Coalition, for much help with the final section of this chapter.

VI. The Emerald Necklace Completed

1. The only pre-Olmsted representations of the Muddy River area that I have located are a print that appeared originally in *Gleason's Pictorial* in 1855 and is reproduced in John Gould Curtis, *History of the Town of Brookline, Massachusetts* (Boston: Houghton Mifflin, 1933), opp. 170, and a photograph from about 1890 in the Brookline Public Library. The former shows Brookline from the corner of Tremont and Heath streets (now Huntington and South Huntington avenues) in Roxbury, and the latter shows the Muddy River near Longwood. Neither is very useful as a visual record.

2. For the early history of the hamlet of Muddy River, see Curtis, *Brookline,* 1–15, 61–63. Neil Jorgenson, *A Guide to New England's Landscape* (Barre, Mass.: Barre Publishers, 1971), is recommended for discussion of the natural landscape in the vicinity of Boston.

3. Frederick Law Olmsted, "Suggestions for the Improvement of Muddy River," in City of Boston, *Sixth Annual Report of the Board of Commissioners of the Department of Parks for the Year 1880* (City Doc. no. 12-1881), 13–17, published also by the Brookline Park Commissioners in Town of Brookline, *Reports* for the

year ending Jan. 31, 1881, 170–175, reprinted in S. B. Sutton, ed., *Civilizing American Cities: A Selection of Frederick Law Olmsted's Writings on City Landscapes* (Cambridge, Mass.: MIT Press, 1971), 228–233.

4. Olmsted, "Suggestions," in Sutton, *Civilizing American Cities,* 228–230; John C. Olmsted, "The Boston Park System," *Transactions of the American Society of Landscape Architects* 1 (1899–1908), 49–50. For the history of the Longwood area, see Anne Wardwell, "'Longwood' and 'Cottage Farm' in Brookline," in *Victorian Boston Today: Ten Walking Tours,* ed. Pauline Chase Harrell and Margaret Supplee Smith (Boston: New England Chapter, Victorian Society in America, 1975), 56–69. Plans by Alexander Wadsworth, civil engineer for the subdivision of Longwood and Cottage Farm (about 1852), are in the Map Collection of the Brookline Public Library.

5. "Report of Committee on Muddy River Improvement," in Town of Brookline, *Reports* for the year ending Jan. 31, 1881, 169–176. The full publication history of this report and plan is given above, n. 3.

6. Curtis, *Brookline,* 279–283; Alfred D. Chandler, "Brookline: A Study in Town Government," *New England Magazine* (August 1893), 777–796; Andrew J. Downing, *A Treatise on the Theory and Practice of Landscape Gardening adapted to North America,* 6th ed. (New York: A. O. Moore & Co., 1859), 40–41; James F. O'Gorman, *Henry Hobson Richardson and His Office: Selected Drawings* (Cambridge, Mass.: Harvard College Library, 1974), 2–5.

7. For information on Lawrence, see *The Chronicle* (Brookline), Mar. 3, 1903; for Lyman, see Charles Francis Adams, "Memoir of Theodore Lyman," *Proceedings of the Massachusetts Historical Society,* second series, vol. 2 (1907), 147–177, and Henry Lee, "Theodore Lyman" in John T. Morse, Jr., *Memoir of Henry Lee* (Boston: Little, Brown, 1905), 410–412; for Whitney, see *The Chronicle,* Jan. 27, 1923, and Sam Bass Warner, Jr., "Residential Development of Roxbury, West Roxbury and Dorchester, Massachusetts, 1870–1900," unpublished dissertation, Harvard University, 1959, 68–74; for Lincoln, see *The Chronicle,* Dec. 3, 1925. Sargent's domination of the Brookline Park Commission and the disagreements between Sargent and the Olmsted firm on architectural and plant materials are discussed in Chapters XII and XIII.

8. Reports of the Park Commissioners, in Town of Brookline, *Reports,* for the years 1880–1895.

9. City of Boston, Board of Commissioners of the Department of Parks, *Report on Proposed Sanitary Improvement of Muddy River* (Oct. 24, 1881, City Doc. no. 130-1881).

10. Reports of the Park Commissioners, in Town of

Brookline, *Reports,* for the years 1881–1888; Alfred D. Chandler to Olmsted, Feb. 10, 1881, Olmsted National Historic Site, Brookline.

11. F. L. Olmsted and Co., "Report to the Brookline Park Commissioners," in Town of Brookline, *Report* for the year ending Jan. 31, 1890, 257–264.

12. Olmsted, "Suggestions," in Sutton, *Civilizing American Cities,* 229–231.

13. Frederick Law Olmsted, "Report of the Landscape Architect Advisory," in City of Boston, *Seventh Annual Report of the Board of Commissioners of the Department of Parks for the Year 1881* (City Doc. no. 16-1882), reprinted in Sutton, *Civilizing American Cities,* 224.

14. The attribution of Christ's Church, Longwood, to Gilman comes from an undated print of the church in the Boston Athenaeum collection. The print is entitled "Christ's Church in Brookline—Longwood, The First of the Union of Churches in the Spirit of Charity," and small letters under the image identify A. Gilman, Architect, and L. H. Bradford & Co., Lith.

15. Olmsted, "Report," in City Doc. no. 16-1882, reprinted in Sutton, *Civilizing American Cities,* 226.

16. Francis S. Drake, *The Town of Roxbury* (Roxbury, Mass.: privately printed, 1878), 405–406.

17. Olmsted to C. H. Dalton, Apr. 8, 1876, OP; City of Boston, *Second Report of the Board of Commissioners of the Department of Parks* (Apr. 24, 1876, City Doc. no. 42-1876), 28, reprinted in *Franklin Park Coalition Bulletin* (January 1981, whole issue), 26–27.

18. Walter Muir Whitehill, "Francis Parkman as Horticulturist," *Arnoldia* 33, no. 3 (May–June 1973), 169–182; Mason Wade, *Francis Parkman, Heroic Historian* (1942; reprint ed., Hamden, Conn.: Archon Books, 1972), 442–443. In contrast to the Muddy River Improvement, Jamaica Pond in its pre-Olmsted period is documented by numerous fine photographs, some of which are shown here. Photographs can be found in the Boston Public Library Print Department, the Society for the Preservation of New England Antiquities, and the Jamaica Plain Tuesday Club. The Olmsted National Historic Site in Brookline has many construction and post-construction site photographs.

19. [John C. Olmsted?], "Report of Olmsted Brothers," in City of Boston, *Thirty-sixth Annual Report of the Board of Commissioners of the Department of Parks for the Year Ending January 31, 1911,* p. 65.

20. For the history of the Pinebank site, see Cynthia Zaitzevsky, "Pinebank: The History of a Site and a Building," in Richard White, "Feasibility Study: Pinebank Recreation Building," Mar. 30, 1979, 4–16, unpublished report deposited in the Boston Redevelopment

Authority Library. See also Cynthia Zaitzevsky, "Victorian Jamaica Plain," in Harrell and Smith, *Victorian Boston Today,* 80–81. Pinebank, the boat house, and the Parkman Memorial are discussed here rather than in Chapter XII, because the first is pre-Olmsted, and the last two are post-Olmsted structures.

21. Harold Kirker and David Van Zanten, "Jean Lemoulnier in Boston, 1846–1851," *Journal of the Society of Architectural Historians* 31, no. 3 (October 1972), 204–208.

22. Margaret Henderson Floyd, "A Terra-Cotta Cornerstone for Copley Square: Museum of Fine Arts, Boston, 1870–1876, by Sturgis and Brigham," *JSAH* 32, no. 2 (May 1973), 88–90.

23. Cynthia Zaitzevsky in Richard White, *Planning for Preservation of the Boathouse Roof, Olmsted Park System, Jamaica Pond Boathouse, Jamaica Plain, Mass.* (Washington, D.C.: Heritage Conservation and Recreation Service, 1979), 7–9.

24. Michael Richman, *Daniel Chester French: An American Sculptor* (New York: Metropolitan Museum of Art for the National Trust for Historic Preservation, 1976), 97–102.

25. Cabot Estate Open Space Task Force, "Report," Sept. 23, 1971, unpublished report deposited in the Boston Redevelopment Authority Library.

26. Olmsted, Memorandum ("Cut of City Point and Castle Island"), Dec. 1, 1883, OP.

27. John C. Olmsted, "The Boston Park System," 55; "Park Statistics to January 31, 1896," in City of Boston, *Annual Report of the Board of Commissioners of the Department of Parks for the Year 1895* (City Doc. no. 22-1896), 33–34. Quote from Olmsted to Sargent, Feb. 7, 1891, OP.

28. Largely because of too-frequent interruption by access roads, Norman T. Newton does not consider Olmsted's Boston parkway a "parkway" in the twentieth-century sense of the word. However, Newton describes the more recent type, citing the New York Bronx River Parkway as the first example, as "a strip of land dedicated to recreation and the movement of pleasure vehicles (passenger, not commercial automobiles). The parkway was *not* itself a road, it *contained* a roadway. The strip of land was not just a highway with uniform grassy borders; it was of significantly varying width, depending on immediate topographic and cultural conditions" (Norman T. Newton, *Design on the Land: The Development of Landscape Architecture* [Cambridge, Mass.: Harvard University Press, 1971], 597). This description fits the emerald necklace very closely, especially its contiguous portion (Fens, Muddy River, and Jamaica Park). Newton points out that without limited access,

the older Olmsted parkway does not *function* as a parkway in the modern sense, but in concept the two are practically identical.

29. Columbia Road was laid out by the Street Department rather than by the Park Department, and the Olmsted firm served as consultants rather than designers. The drawings for Columbia Road at the Frederick Law Olmsted National Historic Site, Brookline, consist only of a set of blueprints received from the Street Department, although a lithograph was published under the firm's name. The firm was not particularly happy with Columbia Road (John C. Olmsted, "The Boston Park System," 54).

30. The parkway, at least from the Muddy River to the end of the Arnold Arboretum, is fairly intact. The first section of the Fens, as I pointed out in Chapter IV, has been almost completely obliterated by the Charlesgate interchange, and the last link of the Arborway, from the Arboretum to Franklin Park, has been covered up by a concrete overpass. A new Southwest Corridor linear park has been planned to end at Forest Hills Station on the Arborway, and some of the landscaping will be restored.

VII. Small Parks, Playgrounds, and Unexecuted Projects

1. The Gourlay plan is illustrated in Walter Muir Whitehill, *Boston: A Topographical History,* 2d ed., enlarged (Cambridge, Mass.: Harvard University Press, 1968), fig. 81, p. 146.

2. City of Boston, *Second Report of the Board of Commissioners of the Department of Parks* (April 24, 1876, City Doc. no. 42-1876), 15–18, reprinted in *Franklin Park Coalition Bulletin* (January 1981, whole issue), 14–16.

3. "Report of the Landscape Architects on the Extension of the Charles River Embankment," in City of Boston, *Nineteenth Annual Report of the Board of Commissioners of the Department of Parks for the Year 1893* (City Doc. no 25-1894), 40–45; City of Boston, *Twentieth Annual Report of the Board of Commissioners of the Department of Parks for the Year 1894* (City Doc. no. 25-1895), 47–51; Olmsted to Charles Eliot, Nov. 10, 1894, OP; Eliot to Olmsted, Mar. 21, 1895, OP; F. L. Olmsted, Jr., "Neighborhood Pleasure-Grounds in Boston," *Harper's Weekly* 61, no. 2140 (Dec. 25, 1897), 1290. For the later history of the embankment, see James L. Bruce, "Filling In of the Back Bay and the Charles River Development," *Proceedings of the Bostonian Society* (1940), 25–38, and Eugene C. Hultman,

"The Charles River Basin," *Proc. Bos. Soc.* (1940), 39–48.

4. In 1880 the population of Ward 8, the West End, was 12,800, many of whom were immigrants. See Department of the Interior, Census Office, *Statistics of the Population of the United States at the Tenth Census, June 1, 1880* (Washington: Government Printing Office, 1883), 210. Microfilms of the original census sheets for Boston and all of New England, located at the Boston Public Library, give age, occupation, place of birth, place of parents' birth, and other statistics, such as illiteracy and chronic disease.

5. City of Boston, *Fifth Annual Report of the Board of Commissioners of the Department of Parks for the Year 1879* (City Doc. no. 15-1880), 18. RBPD, Feb. 12 and 18, 1881; Jan. 27, 1882; Apr. 25, 1883; and May 25, 1883.

6. Frederick Law Olmsted, "Report on the Charles River Embankment ('Charlesbank')," in City of Boston, *Twelfth Annual Report of the Board of Commissioners of the Department of Parks for the Year 1886* (City Doc. no. 24-1887), 15–17.

7. Sylvester Baxter, *Boston Park Guide Including the Municipal and Metropolitan Systems of Greater Boston* (Boston: L. Maynard, 1896), 33.

8. George W. Spindler, *The Life of Karl Follen* (Chicago: University of Chicago Press, 1917), 126–137. Follen's method of instruction was derived from that of Frederick Lewis Jahn, originator of modern gymnastics, who established the first gymnasium (*Turnplatz*) in Berlin in 1811.

9. "Report on Charlesbank Gymnasiums," in City of Boston, *Seventeenth Annual Report of the Board of Commissioners of the Department of Parks for the Year Ending January 31, 1892* (City Doc. no. 26-1892), 49–53. For Dudley Sargent, see *Dictionary of American Biography* (New York: Charles Scribner's Sons, 1935), VIII, 355–356. The Olmsted firm made a model of Charlesbank Gym, which was exhibited by the Turnerbund in the World's Columbian Exposition (RBPD, Oct. 16, 1893).

10. Geoffrey Blodgett, entry on Kate Gannett Wells in *Notable American Women,* ed. Edward T. James et al. (Cambridge, Mass.: Harvard University Press, 1971), III, 563–565.

11. Joseph Lee, "Playgrounds, Beaches and Baths," in *Fifty Years of Boston: A Memorial Volume,* ed. Elisabeth M. Herlihy (Boston: Boston Tercentenary Committee, 1932), 673.

12. Baxter, *Boston Park Guide,* 37.

13. Kate Gannett Wells et al., "Report of the Committee of the Massachusetts Emergency and Hygiene As-

sociation in Charge of the Women's Gymnasium at Charlesbank," in City Doc. no. 25-1894, 88–90. The detailed yearly reports of this committee of "well known ladies," as they were referred to, are a fascinating social record.

14. Baxter, *Boston Park Guide,* 35.

15. Lee, "Playgrounds, Beaches and Baths," 676. Originally, playing on this grassy area was not allowed, but around the turn of the century, it was encouraged, even though such heavy use made upkeep more difficult.

16. Frederick Law Olmsted, "Report on Wood Island Park," in City of Boston, *Tenth Annual Report of the Board of Commissioners of the Department of Parks for the Year 1884* (City Doc. no. 7-1885), 21–22; Baxter, *Boston Park Guide,* 37–38.

17. *Statistics of . . . the Tenth Census, 1880,* 210; *East Boston; Boston 200 Neighborhood History Series* (Boston: Boston 200 Corporation, 1976), 8–11; Richard Heath, "'La Montagnella': A History of Wood Island Park," *East Boston Community News,* Aug. 7, 1979; obituary of Pauline Bromberg, *Boston Globe,* Aug. 14, 1981.

18. Baxter, *Boston Park Guide,* 38; F. L. Olmsted, Jr., "Neighborhood Pleasure-Grounds in Boston," 1290; *Atlas of the City of Boston: Charlestown and East Boston* (Philadelphia: G. W. Bromley and Co., 1922), pl. 14.

19. The slow progress of construction of Charlestown Playground is documented in the city engineer's reports in the park commissioners' annual reports from 1892 to 1902. Its layout when complete is shown in *Atlas: Charlestown and East Boston,* pl. 16.

20. Lee, "Playgrounds, Beaches and Baths," 677.

21. Quoted in [Charles W. Eliot], *Charles Eliot, Landscape Architect* (Boston: Houghton Mifflin, 1902), 485–486.

22. Olmsted, Olmsted and Eliot [Charles Eliot], "Report of the Landscape Architects," in City Doc. no. 25-1895, 73–77, reprinted in [Eliot], *Charles Eliot,* 484–485; F. L. Olmsted, Jr., "Neighborhood Pleasure-Grounds in Boston," 1290. Commissioner Paul Kendricken may have been responsible for the formal treatment of the North End Park terrace. Eliot wrote that Kendricken sketched in such a terrace, and the firm was formally ordered to prepare a new plan based on his idea (Charles Eliot to John Olmsted, June 29, 1894, OAP).

23. *Atlas of the City of Boston: Boston Proper and Back Bay* (Philadelphia: G. W. Bromley and Co.), 1895 ed., pl. 4; 1898 ed., pl. 7; 1902 ed., pl. 7.

24. *BET,* Sept. 19, 1895.

25. Linda Fitzpatrick, "Highland Park, Roxbury: Report and Proposal," unpublished report, Planning Dept., Boston Redevelopment Authority, February 1968, depos-

ited at the office of the Boston Landmarks Commission, Boston City Hall.

26. Lee, "Playgrounds, Beaches and Baths," 677–678; Mayor Josiah Quincy, "Inaugural Address," 1897 (City Doc. no. 1-1897), 14–20. Mayor Quincy's enthusiasm sometimes led him to act prematurely and, in the words of Charles Eliot, "pile half-hatched plans for playgrounds" on the park commissioners (Charles Eliot to John C. Olmsted, Nov. 27, 1896, OAP.

27. City of Boston, *Report of the Park Commissioners upon the Expediency of Securing Land around the Parker Hill Reservoir to Serve as a Park* (City Doc. no. 97-1893); John C. Olmsted, "The Boston Park System," *Transactions of the American Society of Landscape Architects* 1 (1899–1908), 49; Commonwealth of Massachusetts, *Report of the Board of Metropolitan Park Commissioners* (Dec. 1911, Public Doc. no. 48-1912), 115–119.

28. Frederick Law Olmsted, "'A Healthy Change in the Tone of the Human Heart' (Suggestions to Cities)," *Century Magazine* new series, vol. 10 (1886), 964.

29. Frederick Law Olmsted, "Report of the Landscape Architect Advisory," in City of Boston, *Thirteenth Annual Report of the Board of Commissioners of the Department of Parks for the Year 1887* (City Doc. no. 14-1888), 52–63, reprinted in Commonwealth of Massachusetts, *Report of the Board of Metropolitan Park Commissioners* (January 1893, House no. 150), 131–142. Olmsted to Mariana G. Van Rensselaer, May 17, 1887, OP.

30. Robert Douglas to Olmsted, Sept. 5 and 10, 1887, OP; J. S. Fay to Olmsted, Sept. 25, 1887, OP; Douglas to Olmsted, Dec. 1887, OP; Douglas to Boston Park Commission (contract), Dec. 1887, OP.

31. F. W. Brewer to Olmsted, Mar. 31, 1888, OP, and Charles Eliot to John C. Olmsted, July 26, 1895, OP. The Harbor Islands are currently receiving considerable attention almost a hundred years after Olmsted's "Suggestions." The Metropolitan District Commission, which since 1920 has absorbed the Metropolitan Park Commission, is gradually improving those islands owned by the Commonwealth, and boat service is available to most of the islands during the summer. Their history and present condition, as well as proposals for their use, are covered in an excellent publication: Metropolitan Area Planning Council, *Boston Harbor Islands Comprehensive Plan* (Boston: Massachusetts Department of Natural Resources, 1972).

VIII. Plans for Greater Boston

1. Charles Sargent and Frederick Law Olmsted to Charles Dalton, on replanting the central greens of Com-

monwealth Avenue, Nov. 29, 1880, OP; S. B. Sutton, *Charles Sprague Sargent and the Arnold Arboretum* (Cambridge, Mass.: Harvard University Press, 1970), 307–310; Olmsted, Olmsted, and Eliot to Paul Kendricken, Apr. 2, 1894, OAP; Olmsted, Olmsted, and Eliot to the Boston park commissioners, July 30, 1894, OAP.

2. John Charles Olmsted, "The Boston Park System," *Transactions of the American Society of Landscape Architects* 1 (1899–1908), 44 and 47. It has always been assumed that it was Olmsted who chose to deflect the line of Commonwealth Avenue west of Massachusetts Avenue; according to John Olmsted, the engineer in charge was responsible, and in John's eyes at least, it was not a fortunate decision. The Park Commission reports are not completely clear on the point of tearing up the portion of Commonwealth Avenue between the Fens and Kenmore Square, but that section was definitely redesigned during this period (F. L. Olmsted and Co. to G. F. Joyce, Sept. 20, 1891, OP).

3. Weekly Notebook of Charles Eliot, entries for May 24 and July 9, 1884, Charles Eliot Collection, FLL.

4. Comparison of plates in the 1897 and 1909 editions of *Atlas of the City of Boston: Brighton* (Philadelphia: G. W. Bromley and Co.) shows the progress of construction and the final plan. See also Sylvester Baxter, Scrapbook of articles contributed to the *Boston Sunday Herald* in 1904, with Baxter's manuscript corrections for a projected book on the civic improvement of Boston, (Boston Public Library, Rare Book Department), 26–27; *Mayor's Message Relative to the Importance of Providing Appropriations for Commonwealth Avenue . . .* (City Doc. no. 157-1891); *Message of the Mayor Relative to the Completion of Commonwealth Avenue* (City Doc. no. 189-1892); and *Report of Special Committee on Subject of Construction of Commonwealth Avenue* (City Doc. no. 139-1894).

5. *Beacon Street: Its Improvement in Brookline by Connection with Commonwealth Avenue* (Brookline, 1887); John Gould Curtis, *History of the Town of Brookline, Massachusetts* (Boston: Houghton Mifflin, 1933), 297–300; Sam Bass Warner, Jr., "Residential Development of Roxbury, West Roxbury and Dorchester, Massachusetts, 1870–1900," unpublished dissertation, Harvard University, 1959, 68–74.

6. F. L. and J. C. Olmsted, "Draft of Report Accompanying Preliminary Plan for Widening Beacon Street," Oct. 28, 1886, OP; and typescript of report on Beacon Street, Nov. 24, 1886, OP; F. L. and J. C. Olmsted, "The Beacon Street Plan," *The Chronicle* (Brookline), Dec. 4, 1886.

7. A. Alphand, *Les Promenades de Paris* (Paris: J. Rothschild, 1873), I, 237. According to Alphand, the strips on the Avenue de l'Impératrice were planted as a miniature arboretum, with all the rare tree and shrub species that could be grown in Paris, but these were destroyed in the siege of Paris in 1870–1871.

8. Olmsted apparently first used this type of parkway plan in his design for Eastern Parkway, Brooklyn, in 1868. Unter den Linden in Berlin, also a major approach to a large rural park, was an influence, along with the Avenue de l'Impératrice. See Frederick Law Olmsted and Calvert Vaux, "Report of the Landscape Architects and Superintendents to the President of the Board of Commissioners of Prospect Park, Brooklyn" (1868), reprinted in Albert Fein, ed., *Landscape into Cityscape: Frederick Law Olmsted's Plans for a Greater New York City* (Ithaca, N.Y.: Cornell University Press, 1968), 157–159.

9. Quoted in George R. Collins, "The Ciudad Lineal of Madrid," *Journal of the Society of Architectural Historians* 18, no. 2 (May 1959), 38. See also George R. Collins, "Linear Planning throughout the World," *JSAH* 18, no. 3 (October 1959), 74–93, for Soria's influence on later planners.

10. Douglass Shand Tucci, *Built in Boston: City and Suburb* (Boston: New York Graphic Society, 1978), 101–130.

11. RBPD, Apr. 15, 1887.

12. Cynthia Zaitzevsky, "Frederick Law Olmsted in Brookline: A Preliminary Study of His Public Projects," *Proceedings of the Brookline Historical Society* (1975–1978), 42–65.

13. Zaitzevsky, "Frederick Law Olmsted in Brookline," 52–54.

14. Zaitzevsky, "Frederick Law Olmsted in Brookline," 60–62.

15. A. D. Chandler, "The Proposed Brookline Parkway Including the Reservoir: A Statement," reprinted from *The Chronicle*, Dec. 27, 1902.

16. William H. C. Walker and Willard Brewer Walker, *A History of World's End* (Milton, Mass.: Trustees of Reservations, 1973), 2–3.

17. Walker and Walker, *World's End*, 11–13. For Brewer, see *BET*, Sept. 26, 1893.

18. Opinion of Dr. Wilmon Brewer, cited in Stephen F. Calhoun, Jacob G. Braun, and Kenneth I. Helphand, "World's End Reservation, Hingham, Massachusetts: A Master Plan," unpublished, copy deposited at FLL, 1971, n.p.

19. F. W. Brewer to Olmsted, Mar. 28, 1888, OP.

20. Walker and Walker, *World's End*, 35–39.

21. F. L. Olmsted and Co. to Philip A. Chase, chairman of the Park Commission of Lynn, Mass., in City of Lynn, *First Annual Report of the Park Commissioners for the Year Ending December 31, 1889*, 10–12.

22. Charles Eliot, "Report of the Landscape Archi-

tect," in Commonwealth of Massachusetts, *Report of the Board of Metropolitan Park Commissioners* (January 1893, House no. 150), 93. See also Sylvester Baxter, *Boston Park Guide Including the Municipal and Metropolitan Systems of Greater Boston* (Boston: L. Maynard, 1896), 59–63; and Nathan Mortimer Hawkes, *In Lynn Woods with Pen and Camera* (Lynn, Mass.: Thomas P. Nichols, 1893).

23. Charles Eliot, Letter to the Editor on the Waverley Oaks, *Garden and Forest* 3, no. 106 (Mar. 5, 1890), 118.

24. [Eliot], *Charles Eliot*, 316–350; Olmsted to Eliot, May 20, 1890, OAP.

25. For the metropolitan park system, see Norman T. Newton, *Design on the Land: The Development of Landscape Architecture* (Cambridge, Mass.: Harvard University Press, 1971), 318–336. See also Geoffrey Blodgett, *The Gentle Reformers: Massachusetts Democrats in the Cleveland Era* (Cambridge, Mass.: Harvard University Press, 1966), 125–126.

26. For Baxter, see his obituary (*Boston Herald*, Jan. 29, 1927); George R. Collins and Christiane Crasemann Collins, *Camillo Sitte and the Birth of Modern City Planning*, Columbia University Studies in Art History and Architecture no. 3 (New York: 1965), 138; and Albert Fein, *Frederick Law Olmsted and the American Environmental Tradition* (New York: George Braziller, 1972), 60–61. In later life Baxter took Robert Frost under his wing. Frost described Baxter as "a lovely old boy [who] quite took possession of me while I was in Boston. When he wasn't actually with me like Mary's lamb he was keeping track of me by telephone. I believe he is doing for me on principle. He's got me on his conscience" (Lawrance Thompson, *Robert Frost: The Years of Triumph, 1915–1938* [New York: Holt, Rinehart and Winston, 1970], 22).

27. Commonwealth of Massachusetts, *Report of the Board of Metropolitan Park Commissioners* (January 1893, House no. 150); [Eliot], *Charles Eliot*, 351–357, 380–415, 420–473, 487–545, 557–631, 646–741.

28. Olmsted to Partners (John Olmsted and Charles Eliot), Oct. 28 and Nov. 1, 1893, OP.

IX. The Olmsted Firm in Brookline

1. Olmsted recounted the circumstances of his move to Brookline in a talk given to the Brookline Club, "The History of Streets," in 1889, which was reviewed and summarized in *The Chronicle* (Brookline), Mar. 2, 1889. An incomplete and undated draft copy of this talk is in OP.

2. H. H. Richardson to Olmsted, Feb. 6, 1883, OP.

3. Nina Fletcher Little, *Some Old Brookline Houses* (Brookline: Brookline Historical Society, 1949), 93–95.

4. Laura Wood Roper, *FLO: A Biography of Frederick Law Olmsted* (Baltimore: Johns Hopkins University Press, 1973), 390–391; William Alex, "A Survey—Inventory of the Frederick Law Olmsted Office—Estate and Contents, Brookline, Massachusetts," unpublished report prepared for the National Endowment for the Arts, 1973–74, deposited at FLL, pp. 18–20 and figs. 3 and 4.

5. James F. O'Gorman, *H. H. Richardson and His Office: Selected Drawings* (Cambridge, Mass.: Harvard College Library, 1974), 4–13. The house, built in 1803, still stands, but the Coops were demolished shortly after Richardson's death, when his successor firm, Shepley, Rutan and Coolidge, moved downtown.

6. Paul R. Baker, *Richard Morris Hunt* (Cambridge, Mass.: MIT Press, 1980), 26–44.

7. Richard Chafee, "The Teaching of Architecture at the Ecole des Beaux-Arts," in *The Architecture of the Ecole des Beaux-Arts*, ed. Arthur Drexler (New York: Museum of Modern Art, 1977), 61–110; Richard Chafee, "Richardson's Record at the Ecole des Beaux-Arts," *Journal of the Society of Architectural Historians* 36, no. 3 (October 1977), 175–88.

8. Chafee, "The Teaching of Architecture at the Ecole des Beaux-Arts," 88–89. The only exception to the separation of an architect's atelier from his office occurred if the patron had only one student. In this case the student would generally work in the architect's professional office and might be employed by him as well as working under his supervision on the competition programs set by the Ecole.

9. Baker, *Richard Morris Hunt*, 98–107.

10. O'Gorman, *Richardson*, 10; Mariana Griswold Van Rensselaer, *Henry Hobson Richardson and His Works* (1888; reprint ed., Park Forest, Ill.: Prairie School Press, 1967), 123–131.

11. Olmsted to Frederick Law Olmsted, Jr., Jan. 7, Feb. 3 and 15, 1895, OP. By "post-graduate," Olmsted meant that his apprentices had completed a college undergraduate course, with some later study in engineering, botany, and horticulture, not that they had an undergraduate degree in architecture or landscape architecture.

12. "John Charles Olmsted: A Minute on His Life and Service," *Transactions of the American Society of Landscape Architects* 2 (1909–1921), 104–107; and Emanuel Tillman Mische, "In Memoriam: John Charles Olmsted," *Parks and Recreation* 3 (April 1920), 52–54. I am grateful to the late Harry Perkins and Mrs. Perkins for sharing with me and William Alex their personal memories of John Olmsted in an interview at their home

in New Hampshire on Sept. 26, 1973. From 1901 to 1951 Mr. Perkins was the clerk in charge of organizing and filing all the drawings at Olmsted Brothers. Mrs. Perkins was secretary and bookkeeper during part of the same period. Because Olmsted and his stepson always referred to each other as "father" and "son," I have followed that usage here.

13. Notebooks of Charles Eliot, 1883–1884, Charles Eliot Collection, FLL; [Charles W. Eliot], *Charles Eliot, Landscape Architect* (Boston: Houghton, Mifflin, 1902), 32–34; Norman T. Newton, *Design on The Land: The Development of Landscape Architecture* (Cambridge, Mass.: Harvard University Press, 1971), 318–336.

14. Weekly notebook of Charles Eliot (first entry is May 6, 1883; other important entries include May 6, Aug. 19, Sept. 9 and 30, Nov. 11, Dec. 16, 20, and 30, 1883, and Jan. 6, Feb. 3, Mar. 23 and 30, Apr. 13 and May 11, 1884; quotation is from entry of May 11, 1884); [Eliot], *Charles Eliot,* 34–44; Roper, *FLO,* 390–391.

15. Olmsted to John C. Olmsted, Dec. 6, 1884, OP.

16. Obituary of Henry Sargent Codman, *BET,* Jan. 14, 1893. [Eliot], *Charles Eliot,* 50–203; Newton, *Design on the Land,* 319–320. Partial listing of correspondence between Olmsted and his traveling apprentices (all in OP): Eliot to Olmsted, Dec. 19, 1885, Eliot to John Olmsted and H. S. Codman, Feb. 13, 1886, Olmsted to Eliot, Feb. 25, 1886, Eliot to John C. Olmsted, May 25 and June 5, 1886, Olmsted to Eliot, Oct. 28, 1886, Codman to Olmsted, Jan. 1, 1888, Codman to Olmsted, Mar. 20, 1888, Codman to Olmsted, Apr. 30, 1888, Codman to Olmsted, July 25, 1888, Codman to Olmsted, Aug. 8, 1888, Codman to Olmsted, Nov. 2, 1888.

17. Olmsted to Charles Brace, Jan. 18, 1890, OP.

18. Olmsted to Frederick Law Olmsted, Jr., Sept. 5, 1890, OP.

19. For *Garden and Forest,* see S. B. Sutton, *Charles Sprague Sargent and the Arnold Arboretum* (Cambridge, Mass.: Harvard University Press, 1970), 131–133, and Roper, *FLO,* 404–405. During its first ten months of publication, *Garden and Forest's* offerings included: several signed articles by Mrs. Van Rensselaer, including a seven-part series titled "Landscape Gardening"; many unsigned editorials on various aspects of landscape architecture, some of which are definitely by Mrs. Van Rensselaer—they appear in her book *Art Out-Of-Doors* (New York: Charles Scribner's Sons, 1893)—and others of which are probably by her; two short articles ("Plan for a Small Homestead" and "Terrace and Verandah—Back and Front") and a letter to the editor by Olmsted; four articles, including a three-part series on

cemeteries by John Olmsted; an article by Codman on the squares of Paris; and one by Eliot on the parks and squares of American cities.

For biographical information on Mrs. Van Rensselaer, see the entry by Talbot Hamlin in *Dictionary of American Biography* (New York: Charles Scribner's Sons, 1936) X, 207–208, and the entry by James Early in *Notable American Women,* ed. Edward T. James et al. (Cambridge, Mass.: Harvard University Press, 1971), III, 511–513.

20. All quotations in this paragraph are from Olmsted to George W. Curtis, Aug. 22, 1891, OP.

21. Olmsted to John Olmsted, Feb. 17, 1893, OP.

22. Olmsted to Mariana Van Rensselaer, May 22, 1893, OP.

23. Olmsted to George W. Curtis, Aug. 22, 1891, OP.

24. For Edward Bolton, see the unpublished reminiscences of Ernest Bowditch, ca. 1917, in the Essex Institute, Salem, Mass., n.p. For Warren Manning, see Newton, *Design on the Land,* 385–386 and 388–389, and the Manning Family Association Papers, Special Collections, University of Lowell Library, Lowell, Mass. I am again grateful to the late Harry Perkins and Mrs. Perkins for their recollections of Jones and Langdon in our conversation of Sept. 26, 1973. I have been unable to find obituaries or other biographical information about these two men.

25. Roper, *FLO,* 332–334; quotation from memorandum of Mar. 4, 1890, OP.

26. Memorandum of Mar. 4, 1890, OP.

27. Olmsted to Ariel Lathrop, July 7, 1890, OP.

28. Articles of agreement between Olmsted and the Boston Park Commission, Dec. 1878, OP. In 1885, when his contract with the Boston Park Commission was being extended to include Franklin Park, Olmsted had to remind the commissioners that he could not "sell" the Franklin Park plan unless provision were made for him to superintend its "elaboration" over a three-year period. As he put it: "I did not intend to submit two propositions but one proposition in two clauses" (Olmsted to Charles Dalton, Feb. 9, 1885, OAP).

X. *"Getting the Plan"*

1. Olmsted to John Olmsted, Dec. 6, 1884, OP.

2. Olmsted to Charles Dalton, Aug. 26, 1884, OAP.

3. Richardson's design process is thoroughly discussed in James F. O'Gorman, *Henry Hobson Richardson and His Office: Selected Drawings* (Cambridge, Mass.: Harvard College Library, 1974), 1–36.

4. Olmsted, "The [illeg.] Problem and Its Solution,"

n.d. [Apr. 2, 1886], OP (draft). Olmsted's talk before the Boston Society of Architects was delivered a few months before the discovery of William Gray, Jr.'s embezzlements. (See Chapter III, note 39.)

5. The only time Olmsted insisted on the inclusion of a site for the Boston park system was when he urged the commissioners and the mayor to purchase Franklin Field, which, he argued, was a necessary satellite to Franklin Park.

6. Olmsted to Van Brunt, Jan. 22, 1891, OP.

7. Olmsted to Charles Dalton, May 13, 1878, OP.

8. W. A. Langton, "The Method of H. H. Richardson," *The Architect and Contract Reporter* 63 (Mar. 9, 1900), 156–158. Discussed in O'Gorman, *Richardson,* 19–25.

9. Warren H. Manning, Draft Autobiography, Manning Family Association Papers, Special Collections, University of Lowell Library, Lowell, Mass., p. 20.

10. Olmsted to Charles Dalton, May 13, 1878, OP.

11. John Olmsted to Calvert Vaux, Sept. 22, 1887, OP.

12. These tracing-paper studies are in poor condition and thus have not been photographed and illustrated here.

13. Olmsted, "The Problem," OP. The plan showing the contour of hard bottom (Back Bay Fens, Plan no. 1a, Dec. 4, 1878) was apparently provided as a result of the conversations with the city engineer.

14. William T. Stearn, "From Medieval Park to Modern Arboretum: The Arnold Arboretum and Its Historic Background," *Arnoldia* 32, no. 5 (September 1972), 179–180, 192–195.

15. *History of the Massachusetts Horticultural Society, 1829–1878* (Boston, 1880), 87.

16. S. B. Sutton, *Charles Sprague Sargent and the Arnold Arboretum* (Cambridge, Mass.: Harvard University Press, 1970), 38–39.

17. See Chapter I, note 14.

18. Frederick Law Olmsted and Calvert Vaux, "Descriptive Guide to the Arboretum, as Proposed in 'Greensward' Plan, 1858," in *Frederick Law Olmsted, Landscape Architect, 1822–1903,* ed. Frederick Law Olmsted Jr., and Theodora Kimball (1922–1928; reprint ed., New York: Benjamin Blom, 1970), 335. A more general discussion of the proposed arboretum in Central Park is found in the body of the "Greensward" report, also reprinted in Olmsted and Kimball, *Olmsted,* 231–232. Olmsted and Kimball reproduce the 1868 reprint of the "Greensward" report.

19. [Horace William Shaler Cleveland], *The Public Grounds of Chicago: How to Give Them Character and Expression* (Chicago: Charles D. Lakey, 1869), 13–19.

For the planting of the Avenue de l'Impératrice, see Chapter VIII, note 7.

20. Cynthia Zaitzevsky, "An Analysis of the Drawings at Olmsted Associates, Brookline, Mass.," in William Alex, "Survey-Inventory of the Frederick Law Olmsted Office, Estate and Contents, Brookline, Massachusetts," unpublished report deposited at FLL, 1973–1974, pp. 91–93, 101–102.

21. George F. Chadwick, *The Park and the Town: Public Landscape in the 19th and 20th Centuries* (New York: Praeger, 1966), 53–65.

22. Sutton, *Sargent,* chap. 11, "*Crataegus:* A Thorny Problem," 279–298.

23. Franklin Park Plan no. 11: "Preliminary Study Shown Commissioners, April 6, 1885," colored pencil on topographical map (Olmsted National Historic Site, Brookline); RBPD, Apr. 7, 1885 (records meeting at which Olmsted presented plan).

24. Franklin Park Plan no. 13: "Study for Playstead Shown Commissioners Dean and Maguire 3 July 1885," John C. Olmsted, draftsman, pencil on tracing paper (Olmsted National Historic Site, Brookline).

25. Frederick Law Olmsted, *Notes on the Plan of Franklin Park and Related Matters,* published as a supplement to: City of Boston, *Eleventh Annual Report of the Board of Commissioners of the Department of Parks for the City of Boston for the Year 1885* (City Doc. no. 26-1886), 61.

XI. Building the Parks

1. See James Kip Finch, *The Story of Engineering* (Garden City, N.Y.: Anchor Books, 1960), chap. 13, "American Civil Engineering in the 19th Century," 257–300.

2. Olmsted to George W. Curtis, Aug. 22, 1891, OP.

3. Olmsted to Curtis, Aug. 22, 1891, OP.

4. The stone walls in New England mark the boundaries of former cultivated fields. By Olmsted's day, many of these had been abandoned for years and had reverted to second-growth woods; see Neil Jorgensen, *A Guide to New England's Landscape* (Barre, Mass.: Barre Publishers, 1971), 228–233, and Betty Flanders Thomson, *The Changing Face of New England* (Boston: Houghton Mifflin, 1977), 19–32.

5. Frederick Law Olmsted, "The [illeg.] Problem and Its Solution," n.d., OP (draft). Olmsted gave the talk on April 2, 1886, according to William D. Austin, "A History of the Boston Society of Architects in the Nineteenth Century," August 1942, unpublished manuscript

at the Boston Athenaeum, vol. II, chap. 13, p. 11. The complete text of Olmsted's talk is found in Cynthia Ridgway Zaitzevsky, "Frederick Law Olmsted and the Boston Park System," unpublished doctoral dissertation, Harvard University, 1975, Appendix IV, 295–306.

6. The most complete account of the Fens flood-control apparatus is found in E. W. Howe, "The Back Bay Park, Boston," speech read before the Boston Society of Civil Engineers, Mar. 16, 1881, OP.

7. Olmsted, "The Problem," OP. By 1880 Henry Wightman had replaced Davis as city engineer. See also Olmsted to Wightman, Dec. 13, 1880.

8. Frederick Law Olmsted, "Suggestions for the Improvement of Muddy River," in City of Boston, *Sixth Annual Report of the Board of Commissioners of the Department of Parks for the Year 1880* (City Doc. no. 12-1881), 13–16, reprinted in *Civilizing American Cities: A Selection of Frederick Law Olmsted's Writings on City Landscapes*, ed. S. B. Sutton (Cambridge, Mass.: MIT Press, 1971), 228–233.

9. Frederick Law Olmsted, "Report of the Landscape Architect Advisory," in City of Boston, *Seventh Annual Report of the Board of Commissioners of the Department of Parks for the Year 1881* (City Doc. no. 16-1882), 24–28, in Sutton, *Civilizing American Cities*, 224.

10. John C. Olmsted, "The Boston Park System," *Transactions of the American Society of Landscape Architects* 1 (1899–1908), 50.

11. John Olmsted, "The Boston Park System," 47.

12. Reports of City Engineer William Jackson, in the *Reports* of the Boston park commissioners for 1890–1894; Reports of Alexis H. French, civil engineer, in *Reports* of the Brookline Park Commissioners for the same years.

13. See Norman T. Newton, *Design on the Land: The Development of Landscape Architecture* (Cambridge, Mass.: Harvard University Press, 1971), Figs. 207–212, for other views of the Muddy River Improvement.

14. John Olmsted, "The Boston Park System," 49–50; F. L. Olmsted and Co., "Report to the Brookline Park Commissioners," in Town of Brookline, *Report for the Year Ending January 31, 1890,* 260–262. John Olmsted to A. H. French, June 4, 1890, OAP; John Olmsted to C. S. Sargent, Aug. 8, 1890, OAP; F. L. Olmsted and Co. to T. L. Livermore, Oct. 9, 1890, OAP. (Sargent was a director of the Boston and Albany Railroad Company as well as a member of the Brookline Park Commission.)

15. "Park Statistics," in City of Boston, *Annual Report of the Board of Commissioners of the Department of Parks for the Year Ending January 31, 1901* (City Doc. no. 27-1901), 63.

XII. *The "Furniture" of the Boston Parks*

1. Olmsted to Edmund M. Wheelwright, Feb. 17, 1894, OAP.

2. Attributions for most of the structures in the Boston parks are given in a letter from John Olmsted to Sylvester Baxter, dated Jan. 17, 1898, FLL, reprinted in Cynthia Zaitzevsky, "The Olmsted Firm and the Structures of the Boston Park System," *Journal of the Society of Architectural Historians* 32, no. 2 (May 1973), 171–174, cited hereafter as John Olmsted to Baxter in "Structures." Baxter had apparently requested the information for a series of articles titled "Architectural Features of the Boston Parks," *American Architect and Building News,* July 16, 1898, 19–20; Aug. 13, 1898, 51–52; and Sept. 10, 1898, 83–84. In these articles Baxter repeated much of John's information almost verbatim.

3. Olmsted to Wheelwright, Feb. 17, 1894, OAP.

4. Olmsted to Wheelwright, Feb. 17, 1894, OAP.

5. John Olmsted to Baxter in "Structures," 172. For Wheelwright, see Francis W. Chandler, ed., *Municipal Architecture in Boston from Designs by Edmund M. Wheelwright, City Architect, 1891 to 1895,* 2 vols. (Boston, 1898); T[albot] H[amlin], entry on Wheelwright in *Dictionary of American Biography* (New York: Charles Scribner's Sons, 1936) X, 61–62; Henry F. Withey and Elsie Rathburn Withey, *Biographical Dictionary of American Architects (Deceased)* (Los Angeles: Hennessey and Ingalls, 1956), 648–649; Vincent J. Scully, Jr., *The Shingle Style and the Stick Style,* rev. ed. (New Haven: Yale University Press, 1971), 106–108, n. 51; and Cambridge Historical Commission, *Report Three: Cambridgeport* (Cambridge, Mass.: Cambridge Historical Commission, 1971), 33–34. For Hartwell and Richardson, see Susan Maycock Vogel, "Hartwell and Richardson: An Introduction to Their Work," *Journal of the Society of Architectural Historians* 32, no. 2 (May 1973), 132–146.

6. Olmsted to William Martin Aiken, Sept. 17, 1891, OAP.

7. Olmsted to George W. Curtis, Aug. 22, 1891, OP.

8. John Olmsted to Baxter in "Structures," 171–172.

9. John Olmsted to Baxter in "Structures," 172–173.

10. E. W. Howe, "The Back Bay Park, Boston," speech read before the Boston Society of Civil Engineers, Mar. 16, 1881, 132–133, OP.

11. For the Boylston Street Bridge, see Mariana G. Van Rensselaer, *Henry Hobson Richardson and His Works* (1888; reprint ed., Park Forest, Ill.: Prairie School Press, 1967), 72; Henry-Russell Hitchcock, *The Architecture of H. H. Richardson and His Times* (Cambridge, Mass.: MIT Press, 1966), 213–215; and James F. O'Gorman, *Henry Hobson Richardson and His Office: Selected Drawings* (Cambridge, Mass.: Harvard College Library, 1974), 193.

12. Olmsted to Dalton, Jan. 24, 1880, OP.

13. Olmsted to Davis, Jan. 24, 1880, OP. The emphasis is Olmsted's.

14. O'Gorman, *Richardson*, 194–195.

15. Frederick Law Olmsted, "The [illeg.] Problem and Its Solution," n.d. [April 2, 1886], OP (draft).

16. Frederick Law Olmsted, "A Few Annotations, For Private Use Only, upon 'Architectural Fitness,' Humbly Submitted to the Consideration of His Omniscient Editorial Majesty, by His Prostrate Servant, F. L. O.," 1891, OP and OAP; published in Zaitzevsky, "Park Structures," 170–171. Cited hereafter as F. L. Olmsted in "Structures."

17. RBPD, July 5 and 11, Oct. 24, Nov. 26, and Dec. 12, 1881; O'Gorman, *Richardson,* 194. The construction history of the Boylston Street Bridge is found in the fifth through tenth annual reports of the Boston Park Commission (City Doc. nos. 15-1880, 12-1881, 16-1882, 20-1883, 9-1884, and 7-1885). Quotation from Olmsted, "The Problem," OP.

18. John Olmsted to Baxter in "Structures," 172. A possible prototype for the Boylston Street Bridge is shown in W. G. Hoskins, *The Making of the English Landscape* (Harmondsworth: Penquin Books, 1955), pl. 65, p. 255, an illustration of two arched stone bridges over an eighteenth-century canal.

19. O'Gorman, *Richardson,* 193–195; John Olmsted to Baxter in "Structures," 172.

20. RBPD, July 5, 1881; John Olmsted to Baxter in "Structures," 171. For the later Gatehouse and the moving of the earlier one, see Appendix E, "Report of the Deputy Superintendent of the Sewer Division," in City of Boston, *Annual Report of the Street Department for the Year 1905* (City Doc. no. 40-1906), 82–274. The Richardson Gatehouse is the northerly one.

21. John C. Olmsted, "The Boston Park System," *Transactions of the American Society of Landscape Architects* 1 (1899–1908), 48.

22. Baxter, "Architectural Features," *AABN* (July 16, 1898), 19.

23. John Olmsted, "The Boston Park System," 48–49; Sylvester Baxter, *Boston Park Guide Including the Municipal and Metropolitan Systems of Greater Boston* (Boston, 1896), 7; John Olmsted to Baxter in "Structures," 172.

24. John Olmsted to Baxter in "Structures," 172–173.

25. F. L. Olmsted and Co. to Shepley, Rutan and Coolidge, June 3, 1892, OP.

26. [Mariana G. Van Rensselaer], "Architectural Fitness," *Garden and Forest* (Aug. 19, 1891), 385–386, reprinted in Zaitzevsky, "Park Structures," 168–170. Cited hereafter as Van Rensselaer in "Structures."

27. F. L. Olmsted in "Structures," 170–171.

28. Van Rensselaer in "Structures," 169.

29. F. L. Olmsted in "Structures," 171. Earlier in the same memorandum, Olmsted stated that "Richardson's work at North Easton was conceived after he had examined two works of rough-hewn stones and boulders, built in Central Park twenty years before. (This upon the point of following a fashion set by him.)" and that "Mr. Richardson not only countenanced, approved and cooperated in the use of rough stone with the intentions with which it has everywhere been used in the Fens and in Franklin Park; not only used boulders, roughly in a bridge opening from the principal street of a village into the approach of a mansion of cut stone, the mansion being near at hand and in view; but he introduced such boulders, valiantly and conspicuously projecting from bodies of flat masonry, where they could not be draped by creeping foliage, and this in a monumental structure (the tower of the church at Malden) and he was proud that he had done so, calling attention, admiringly, to those stones in the latter part of his life" (170–171).

The "bridge" must refer to the Ames Gate Lodge in North Easton (1880), and the church must be Grace Church in Medford, Mass. (1867), since there is no church by Richardson in Malden. The two "works of rough-hewn stones and boulders" in Central Park were probably boulder bridges in the wooded northern half of the park. Olmsted thus appears to have set the "fashion" for the use of boulders in bridges, but Richardson seems to have been the first to have used them in buildings.

30. Olmsted to M. G. Van Rensselaer, Sept. 23, 1893, OP. "Architectural Fitness" was reprinted with minor revisions in Mariana G. Van Rensselaer, *Art Out-Of-Doors* (New York: Charles Scribner's Sons, 1893), 191–201, and in later editions. For the edition that came out in 1925, Mrs. Van Rensselaer, then aged seventy-four, added a section called "Thirty Years Later." It is clear from her comments ("The unfit use of rough fieldstones or boulders in constructions large and small has no longer the vogue it had for a time . . .")

that Mrs. Van Rensselaer was always more in agreement with Sargent than with Olmsted on boulders (*Art Out-Of-Doors* [New York: Charles Scribner's Sons, 1925], 390). See also her rather lukewarm comments on the Ames Gate Lodge (Van Rensselaer, *Henry Hobson Richardson and His Works*, 103–104).

31. Olmsted to Van Rensselaer, Sept. 23, 1893, OP.

32. C. H. Walker to Mr. Olmsted, Aug. 23, 1891, Olmsted National Historic Site, Brookline.

33. For the Brookline Avenue Bridge, see RBPD, Oct. 7, 1891.

34. Baxter, "Architectural Features," *AABN* (July 16, 1898), 20.

35. Baxter, "Architectural Features," *AABN* (Aug. 13, 1898), 51.

36. John Olmsted to Baxter in "Structures," 173.

37. S. B. Sutton, *Charles Sprague Sargent and the Arnold Arboretum* (Cambridge, Mass.: Harvard University Press, 1970), 64.

38. Sutton, *Sargent*, 134–136; City of Boston Building Department, permit to build, dated Sept. 14, 1891, Longfellow, Alden and Harlow, architects, L. D. Wilcutt, builder. Longfellow, Alden and Harlow also designed the herbarium addition to the rear of the original building in 1909. Basement and foundation plans for the original building from Longfellow's office are found at the Olmsted National Historic Site in Brookline, while the Arnold Arboretum owns a complete set of blueprints for the herbarium addition. For Longfellow, see Margaret Henderson Floyd, ed., *An Introduction to Alexander Wadsworth Longfellow* (Boston: Museum of Fine Arts, Department of American Decorative Arts, in press).

39. City of Boston, *Twenty-Third Annual Report of the Board of Commissioners of the Department of Parks, for the Year Ending January 31, 1898* (City Doc. no. 24-1898), 48; Cynthia Zaitzevsky, Nikita Zaitzevsky, and Calvin F. Opitz, "Four Bridges on the Providence Division of the New Haven Railroad—Boston, Massachusetts," July 3, 1980, unpublished report and photographic documentation submitted to the Historic American Engineering Record and deposited at the Library of Congress, 10–12. The Forest Hills railroad viaduct is scheduled to be demolished as part of the MBTA's Southwest Corridor Project.

40. City of Boston, *Tenth Annual Report of the Board of Commissioners of the Department of Parks for the Year 1884* (City Doc. no. 7-1885), 30. These shelters (marked "pavilions") appear on the 1884 topographical map. "Sanitoria" were also provided, so this was not their function. That they were clearly intended to be temporary is indicated by the fact that one was located on the Playstead Overlook, one at the top of Scar-

boro Hill (eventually built as a carriage concourse), and one almost on top of the Greeting. No plans for these have been found in either the Olmsted or Richardson archives. They were apparently lost as early as 1892, when the Olmsted firm asked Howe to look for them (FLO and Co. to E. W. Howe, June 1, 1892, OAP).

41. H. H. Richardson to J. J. Glessner, in conversation, ca. 1885, in J. J. Glessner, "The Story of a House," 1923, unpublished, quoted in Hitchcock, *Richardson*, 328.

42. John Olmsted to Baxter in "Structures," 171. In the first (1896) edition of his *Boston Park Guide* (p. 21), Sylvester Baxter misattributed the Playstead Overlook Shelter to C. Howard Walker. In the 1898 edition an errata sheet (p. 79) reflects John's letter, and Baxter changed the attribution of the shelter to Frederick Law Olmsted. The undulation in the roof referred to by John was on the opposite side of the building from that visible in Figure 151.

43. John Olmsted to Baxter in "Structures," 173; Frederick Law Olmsted, Draft of Memoranda on the Playstead Terrace with Sketches, July 30, 1885, OP.

44. Olmsted to Arthur H. Vinal, Sept. 27, 1887, OP.

45. [Frederick Law Olmsted], Playstead Lodge, Franklin Park, Data and Suggestions for Architect, Sept. 27, 1887, OP.

46. Scully, *The Shingle Style*, 113–154; Cynthia Zaitzevsky, *The Architecture of William Ralph Emerson, 1833–1917* (Cambridge, Mass.: Fogg Art Museum, 1969), 22–23.

47. John Olmsted to Baxter in "Structures," 173; City of Boston, *Fourteenth Annual Report of the Board of Commissioners of the Department of Parks, for the Year 1888* (City Doc. no. 72-1889), 19.

48. John Olmsted to Baxter in "Structures," 173.

49. John Olmsted to Baxter in "Structures," 173.

50. John Olmsted to Baxter in "Structures," 172. John also indicates (173) that he and Eliot designed the terraces on Schoolmaster Hill and that the working drawings were prepared by the city architect's department.

51. Olmsted to John Olmsted, from Torquay, England, May 15, 1892, OP.

52. Olmsted to John Olmsted, May 15, 1892, OP.

53. Olmsted to partners, from Chislehurst, England, July 24, 1892, OP.

54. RBPD, Oct. 24, 1892.

55. FLO and Co. to E. M. Wheelwright, Oct. 28, 1892, OAP; E. M. Wheelwright to Boston park commissioners, Oct. 24, 1892, in RBPD, Oct. 31, 1892; RBPD, Nov. 21, 1892.

56. John Olmsted to Baxter in "Structures," 173.

57. RBPD, Sept. 4, 1891; quotation from Olmsted to John Olmsted, Sept. 8, 1891, OP.

58. John Olmsted to Olmsted, Sept. 18, 1891, OAP.

59. Olmsted to William Martin Aiken, Sept. 17, 1891, OAP.

60. Olmsted to John C. Olmsted, Sept. 8, 1891, OP.

61. FLO and Co. to Hartwell and Richardson, Mar. 4, 1892, OAP; RBPD, July 3, 1893.

62. Olmsted to E. M. Wheelwright, Feb. 17, 1894, OAP.

63. John Olmsted to Baxter in "Structures," 173.

64. John Olmsted to Baxter in "Structures," 173–174.

65. Norton quoted in the preface to Chandler, *Municipal Architecture in Boston;* Sylvester Baxter, scrapbook of articles contributed to the *Boston Sunday Herald* in 1904, with Baxter's manuscript corrections for a projected book on the civic improvement of Boston, Boston Public Library, Rare Book Department. Baxter's initial reaction to the Refectory was negative. He thought it "too prosaic for the location—too blocky, *urban* and business-like, something like a pumping station. It seemed to me a lighter, more graceful design was required for the purpose—one that should suggest a fête champêtre, and summer uses" (Baxter to Olmsted, Mar. 16, 1892, OAP).

66. John Olmsted to Baxter in "Structures," 173. The panels of the Marine Park Head House contained decorative designs in sgraffito, executed by Max Bachmann after sketches by himself and Wheelwright (Baxter, *Boston Park Guide,* 31; Chandler, *Municipal Architecture in Boston,* 41–43).

67. Chandler, *Municipal Architecture in Boston,* 44.

XIII. Plant Materials and Design

1. Warren H. Manning, Draft Autobiography, Manning Family Association Papers, Special Collections, University of Lowell Library, Lowell, Mass., p. 20.

2. Olmsted to the Boston park commissioners, Oct. 7, 1884, OAP; Fischer's obituary, *Jamaica Plain News,* Nov. 25, 1899.

3. City of Boston, Special Committee of the Board of Aldermen on Investigation of the Park Department, *Majority and Minority Reports,* with testimony, closing arguments of counsel and exhibits (City Doc. no. 115-1900). Much of the testimony (which was recorded verbatim) in this investigation deals with the changes made in the plantings after 1897. The planting revisions are also documented in the superintendent's reports in the yearly reports of the Boston park commissioners from 1897 through 1912.

4. George F. Chadwick, *The Park and the Town: Public Landscape in the 19th and 20th Centuries* (New York: Praeger, 1966), 53–65; Rudy J. Favretti and Joy Putman Favretti, *Landscapes and Gardens for Historic Buildings: A Handbook for Reproducing and Creating Authentic Landscape Settings* (Nashville, Tenn.: American Association for State and Local History, 1978), 45–63.

5. The Department of Common and Public Grounds had jurisdiction over the smaller public grounds of the city. In 1912 the Park Department merged with this department and the departments of music and baths. In 1920 they were joined by the Cemetery Department. See Charles W. Eliot II, "The Boston Park System," in *Fifty Years of Boston: A Memorial Volume,* ed. Elisabeth M. Herlihy (Boston: Boston Tercentenary Committee, 1932), 662. For Doogue, see James Bernard Cullen, ed. and comp., *The Story of the Irish in Boston* (Boston: James B. Cullen and Co., 1889), 356–357.

6. Charles E. Beveridge, "Frederick Law Olmsted's Theory of Landscape Design," *Nineteenth Century* 3, no. 2 (Summer 1977), 38–43.

7. Frederick Law Olmsted, "Report of Landscape Architect Advisory," in City of Boston, *Fifth Annual Report of the Board of Commissioners of the Department of Parks for the City of Boston for the Year 1879* (City Doc. no. 15-1880), 10–12, 15.

8. Frederick Law Olmsted, "Report of Landscape Architect Advisory," in City of Boston, *Ninth Annual Report of the Board of Commissioners of the Department of Parks for the City of Boston for the Year 1883* (City Doc. no. 9-1884), 17–19. At exactly the same time that he was developing the Fens plan, Olmsted was working on a much smaller but somewhat analogous project in Newport, which was apparently never executed; see F. L. Olmsted, *Preliminary Report on the Improvement of Easton's Beach* (Boston: Franklin Press: Rand, Avery and Co., 1883), 5–9.

9. John C. Olmsted, "The Boston Park System," *Transactions of the American Society of Landscape Architects* 1 (1899–1908), 48.

10. Olmsted to Sargent, Jan. 27, 1879, OP.

11. Olmsted to Sargent, Jan. 27 and 29, 1879, OP. The replies to both these letters appear to be lost.

12. The plants in this paragraph are discussed in John and Mildred Teal, *Life and Death of the Salt Marsh* (New York: Audubon/Ballantine, 1969), chap. 7, "The Dominant Spartinas," 84–101; and Loren C. Petry, *A Beachcomber's Botany* (Chatham, Mass.: Chatham Conservation Foundation, 1968), 29–31, 114–152.

13. Frederick Law Olmsted, "The [illeg.] Problem and Its Solution" [Apr. 2, 1886], OP (draft).

14. Olmsted, "Report of Landscape Architect Advisory," in City Doc. no. 9-1884, 19; Frederick Law Olmsted, "Report of Landscape Architect Advisory," in City of Boston, *Tenth Annual Report of the Board of Commissioners of the Department of Parks for the Year 1884* (City Doc. no. 7-1885), 13–16.

15. Olmsted to F. L. Temple, Aug. 21, 1883, OP; Olmsted to Temple, Mar. 15, 1886, OP; RBPD, Dec. 1, 1883 (contract dated Nov. 24, 1883).

16. Weekly Notebook of Charles Eliot, entry of Dec. 2, 1883, FLL.

17. Olmsted to Temple, Aug. 21, 1883, and Mar. 7, 1884, OP. By crowding permanent plants and less valuable "nurse" plants very close together, Olmsted was following common nineteenth-century planting practice. When the permanent plants were well established, the nurse plants were removed. Even trees were planted this way, although there was often a public outcry over the removal of nurse trees. See F. L. Olmsted and J. B. Harrison, *Observations on the Treatment of Public Plantations, More Especially Relating to the Use of the Axe* (Boston, 1889).

18. For information on the plants mentioned in this paragraph, see Donald Wyman, *Shrubs and Vines for American Gardens* (New York: Macmillan, 1969), which describes most of the plants listed in the plant list for Beacon Entrance. For the flowers, see Harold R. Hinds and Wilfred A. Hathaway, *Wildflowers of Cape Cod* (Chatham, Mass.: Chatham Press, 1968) and Petry, *A Beachcomber's Botany*.

19. Olmsted to Temple, Mar. 15, 1886, OP.

20. Olmsted, "The Problem," OP. Many years later Sargent maintained that the planting failed because it consisted mostly of insufficiently tried, foreign plants, which he had only recently introduced at the Arboretum (City Doc. no. 115-1900, testimony of Charles Sprague Sargent, p. 1415). However, the only plant at Beacon Entrance that seems to fit into this category is *Tamarix pentandra*. Of the plants mentioned by Olmsted in the letter cited in note 19, all that were planted near the water perished, regardless of whether they were native or foreign; the only survivors were on high ground and included many foreign "garden" shrubs. Temple later supplied over 9,000 trees for the planting of Beacon Street, Brookline ("A Walk in Shady Hill Nurseries," *American Garden* 9, no. 5 [May 1888], 208A-B).

21. Olmsted to John Olmsted, Sept. 11, 1884, OP. The trees mentioned in this paragraph and listed in the plant list are described in Donald Wyman, *Trees for American Gardens* (New York: Macmillan, 1965).

22. Surveys by the Arnold Arboretum of the trees in the Fens and the Muddy River Improvement indicate that many of the original trees remain, although not always in the places shown on the planting plan, and that additions and substitutions were apparently made to Fischer's list. See Martha Dahlen, "Willow Oak (*Quercus phellos*): A Fenway Jewel," *Arnoldia* (September/October 1973), 292–294; and Richard E. Weaver, Jr., "A Group of Outstanding Goldenrain Trees (*Koelreuteria paniculata*) along Boston's Fenway," *Arnoldia* (May/June 1974), 134–135.

23. Olmsted, "Report of Landscape Architect Advisory," in City Doc. no. 15-1880, 11–12; Olmsted to Temple, Aug. 21, 1883, OP.

24. *Boston City Directories,* 1885–1916.

25. Olmsted to Partners from Biltmore, North Carolina, Nov. 1, 1893, OP.

26. Olmsted to Henry Sargent Codman from Chislehurst, England, July 30, 1892, OP.

27. Olmsted to Fischer, July 21, 1887, OP. For the Overlook and its planting, see also "The Listener" column, *BET*, June 5, 1889, and Olmsted's draft response (Olmsted to "Listener," n.d. OP).

28. Olmsted to Fischer, July 21, 1887, OP. The emphasis is Olmsted's. It should be noted that the roses he recommends here and elsewhere are not hybrids but various species of shrub roses, native and foreign, generally with small flowers and a limited period of bloom.

29. Olmsted to Fischer, Aug. 6, 1889, OP.

30. W. L. Fischer to Olmsted, Aug. 9, 1889, OAP. For Olmsted's reply, see Olmsted to Fischer, Aug. 11, 1889, OP.

31. First quotation from Olmsted to Fischer, Aug. 6, 1889, OP; second from Olmsted to "Listener," n.d., OP.

32. Olmsted to Fischer, Sept. 30, 1889, OP. In 1890 the firm wrote to Fischer, asking him to use more native trees and shrubs in Franklin Park, noting also that these were often difficult to find in nurseries. (F. L. and J. C. Olmsted to Fischer, Mar. 7, 1890, OP.)

33. Olmsted discusses the foliage effects of rhododendrons and other plants more frequently grown for their flowers in Olmsted to Fischer, Aug. 11, 1889, OP.

34. John A. Pettigrew, "Report," in City of Boston, *Twenty-fourth Annual Report of the Board of Commissioners of the Department of Parks for the Year Ending January 31, 1899* (City Doc. no. 24-1899), 20–21. Pettigrew was an Englishman with a background in botany and extensive experience in managing parks in this country. See Cynthia Zaitzevsky, "John A. Pettigrew, Park Superintendent," Introduction to "The Planting of Franklin Park: Selected Park Department Reports," *Franklin Park Coalitin Bulletin* (July 1981), 1–5; testimony of John A. Pettigrew, in City Doc. no. 115-1900, 1101–1102; and Pettigrew's obituary in the *Boston Her-*

ald, July 3, 1912. For the replanting of Audubon Road, see also City Doc. no. 115-1900, testimony of Charles Sprague Sargent, pp. 1414–1415.

35. Tree list for the Boston parkways, Sept. 11, 1893, Olmsted National Historic Site, Brookline. The same order also included ash to be planted on Audubon Road, Norway maple for Seaver Street bordering Franklin Park, and tree of heaven (female) for Marine Park.

36. Reports of John A. Pettigrew, in City of Boston, *Twenty-third Annual Report of the Board of Commissioners of the Department of Parks for the Year Ending January 31, 1898* (City Doc. no. 24-1898), 22, and in City Doc. no. 24-1899, 21. A planting order list dated Sept. 3, 1896, at the Olmsted National Historic Site, Brookline, indicates that the firm was still intending to use tulip trees and cucumber trees on the Arborway and had ordered 550 of each, to be delivered the following spring. The Arborway, with a central park drive and two side roads, needed four rows of trees. The firm may have planned to use the tulip trees—much the taller of the two types—on the inner parkway, and the cucumber magnolias at the sides.

37. These plans, because of their large size and fine detail, are extremely difficult to read when reduced, so that only two examples, details of the final planting plans, have been illustrated here.

38. Editorial, *Garden and Forest* (Aug. 1, 1888), 266. The editorial also specifically criticized the use of "garden shrubs" (lilac, forsythia, mockorange) in juxtaposition with native, "wild" plants at Prospect Park.

39. Olmsted, Letter to the Editor, *Garden and Forest,* Oct. 24, 1888, 418–419.

40. F. L. Olmsted and Co. to Henry M. Whitney, Sept. 7, 1891, OAP; A. H. French to F. L. Olmsted and Co., Jan. 28, 1892, Olmsted National Historic Site, Brookline; F. L. Olmsted and Co. to A. H. French, Jan. 30, 1892, OAP; and John Olmsted to C. S. Sargent, Mar. 19, 1892, OAP.

41. John Olmsted to Henry Codman, Apr. 4, 1892, OP. See also Report of Visit, Feb. 6, 1892, OAP.

42. H. S. Codman to John Olmsted, Apr. 7, 1892, Olmsted National Historic Site, Brookline.

43. Olmsted to Partners, July 24, 1892, OP.

44. F. L. Olmsted and Co. to C. S. Sargent, Apr. 9, 1892, OAP.

45. It appears that the detailed planting plans were interpreted rather freely, presumably by Sargent, who must have supervised the planting himself. Early in 1893, when plans were being made for completing the planting in Boston and Brookline, John went over the previous season's planting and checked it carefully against the original plan. The plan is covered with exasperated comments in John's handwriting, such as, "An immense amount of *Cornus sericea* has been used far in excess of the amount called for on plan." See Muddy River Improvement, Plan no. 133, Feb. 8, 1893, Olmsted National Historic Site (copy of planting plan from Washington Street to Cumberland Avenue, Brookline, with field notes on changes, errors, etc., in planting).

46. Olmsted to John Olmsted, Nov. 27, 1892, OP.

47. John Olmsted, "Verbatim Notes and Summary Notes of Perambulatory Tour through the Boston Park System with Pettigrew," 1910, summary notes from tour of October 7, typescript (xerox), FLL, 2. Warren Manning apparently had something to do with the planting of the Boston side too. He recollects in his autobiography that "a controversy arose between Professor Sargent and Mr. Olmsted about the character of the planting along the stream between Brookline and Boston. Professor Sargent wanted dominantly New England plants while Mr. Olmsted wanted suitable exotic varieties added. The detailed plans which I made were a suitable compromise, with the Brookline side of the stream carrying out in general Professor Sargent's idea and the Boston side Mr. Olmsted's." (Manning, Draft Autobiography, University of Lowell, 22) In the late 1890s, the Boston side was replanted to conform with Brookline (City Doc. no. 115-1900, testimony of Raban V. Knuepfer, 678–684). Knuepfer was a gardener.

48. For the trees mentioned here, see Wyman, *Trees for American Gardens.*

49. RBPD, Sept. 28, 1896, to Apr. 13, 1897.

50. City Doc. no. 115-1900, Majority Report, p. 8; and testimony of Charles Sprague Sargent, 1395–1431, and of John A. Pettigrew, 1101–1105.

51. City Doc. no. 115-1900. Besides the testimony of Sargent, Pettigrew, and Knuepfer previously cited, the following are particularly relevant to the change in planting policy and to Sargent's role: testimony of Charles E. Stratton, Jr., chairman of the Park Commission, 5–46; of William R. Jeffery, a Park Department employee, 57–105; and of Fischer's son, William E. Fischer, 372–421; as well as the closing argument of former Mayor Nathan Matthews, Jr., counsel for the park commissioners, 1486–1580.

52. Olmsted, Olmsted and Eliot [Charles Eliot] to Mr. E. C. Hodges, Jan. 4, 1897, in City Doc. no. 115-1900, Exhibit 133, 1461–1464. This letter was reprinted, with Fischer's name deleted, in [Charles W. Eliot], *Charles Eliot: Landscape Architect* (Boston: Houghton Mifflin, 1903), 690–694.

53. "Report of the Olmsted Brothers," in City of Boston, *Thirty-sixth Annual Report of the Board of Commissioners of the Department of Parks for the Year*

1910 (City Doc. no. 25-1911), 82–84. In 1910 the park commissioners engaged John Olmsted and Frederick Law Olmsted, Jr., to determine whether the original Olmsted plan was being adhered to. The result was the "perambulatory tour with Pettigrew" cited in note 47 and a very detailed report on all parts of the park system, which, although signed by both men was almost certainly written by John.

54. Report of the Olmsted Brothers," in City Doc. no. 25-1911), 84.

55. Laura Wood Roper, *FLO: A Biography of Frederick Law Olmsted* (Baltimore: Johns Hopkins University Press, 1973), 435–443.

56. [Frederick Law Olmsted], *Walks and Talks of an American Farmer in England,* 2 vols. in 1 (New York: Dix, Edwards and Co., 1852), I, 86–87.

57. Olmsted to Henry Sargent Codman, from Chislehurst, July 30, 1892, OP.

58. Olmsted to partners from Yattendon Court, Newbury, England, July 17, 1892, OP.

59. Roper, *FLO,* 444–454.

60. Olmsted to partners, from Biltmore, Oct. 28, 1893, OP.

61. Olmsted to partners, from Biltmore, Nov. 1, 1893, OP. The emphasis is Olmsted's.

Epilogue   Olmsted: The Second Century

1. Albert Fein, "The Olmsted Renaissance: A Search for National Purpose," in *Art of the Olmsted Landscape,* ed. Bruce Kelly, Gail Travis Guillet, and Mary Ellen W. Hern (New York: New York City Landmarks Preservation Commission, 1981), 99–109.

2. August Heckscher, *Open Spaces: The Life of American Cities* (New York: Harper and Row, 1977), 74–81, 232–233.

3. Norman T. Newton, *Design on the Land: The Development of Landscape Architecture* (Cambridge, Mass.: Harvard University Press, 1971), 517–537.

4. Newton, *Design on the Land,* 620–627. Galen Cranz, in "Changing Roles of Urban Parks: From Pleasure Garden to Open Space," *Landscape* 22, no. 3 (Summer 1978), 12–15, has labeled playgrounds and small neighborhood parks "reform parks."

5. Newton, *Design on the Land,* 628–637; Cranz, "Changing Roles of Urban Parks," 15–16.

6. Fein, in "Olmsted Renaissance," 100–101, discusses the effect of the automobile on Prospect Park.

7. A particularly flagrant example is Delaware Park in Buffalo, which was divided by an expressway in the early 1960s. See Heckscher, *Open Spaces,* 179–182.

8. Fein, "The Olmsted Renaissance," 107.

9. Newton, *Design on the Land,* 637–639; Heckscher, *Open Spaces,* 243–349; Cranz, "Changing Roles of Urban Parks," 16–18.

10. *Charles-to-Charles: A Conservation and Recreation Corridor for Boston, Brookline and Newton* (Boston: Boston Conservation Commission and Brookline Conservation Commission, 1972); Gary Bloss et al., *Charles to Charles Open Space Corridor: Middle Segment* (Cambridge, Mass.: Community Assistance Program, Harvard Graduate School of Design, prepared for the Brookline Conservation Commission, 1975). Easements have been obtained on two sites in the middle segment; otherwise there has been little action on this project.

11. Metropolitan Area Planning Council, *Boston Harbor Islands Comprehensive Plan* (Boston, 1972).

12. U.S. Department of Transportation, Urban Mass Transportation Administration, *Final Environmental Impact Statement: Orange Line Relocation and Arterial Street Construction (Southwest Corridor Project), South Cove to Forest Hills, Boston, Massachusetts* (Boston, March 1978) I, 7-31–7-32 ("Regional Path and Open Space System"); II, Fig. A-14.

13. New York has several projects for Central Park recently completed or in progress, approximately a third of which are privately funded. A master plan for Central Park has also been announced. See Central Park Administrator's Office, "Central Park Capital Projects Status Report" (Sept. 1981); New York City Department of Parks and Recreation and Central Park Conservancy, *Rebuilding Central Park for the 1980s and Beyond: An Outline for a Restoration Plan* (New York, 1981); and *New York Times,* Oct. 14, 1981.

14. Max Robertson, ed., *The Encyclopedia of Tennis* (New York: Viking Press, 1974), 14–30. Court tennis, the ancestor of lawn tennis, goes back to at least medieval times. It is rarely played today except in England, where it is called "real tennis." Today's tennis is the lawn tennis game that developed in England in the 1870s, although it is now played on clay and other surfaces as well as on grass courts.

List of Illustrations

———

Index